JUDGES

THE ANCHOR BIBLE is a fresh approach to the world's greatest classic. Its object is to make the Bible accessible to the modern reader; its method is to arrive at the meaning of biblical literature through exact translation and extended exposition, and to reconstruct the ancient setting of the biblical story, as well as the circumstances of its transcription and the characteristics of its transcribers.

THE ANCHOR BIBLE is a project of international and interfaith scope: Protestant, Catholic, and Jewish scholars from many countries contribute individual volumes. The project is not sponsored by any ecclesiastical organization and is not intended to reflect any particular theological doctrine. Prepared under our joint supervision, THE ANCHOR BIBLE is an effort to make available all the significant historical and linguistic knowledge which bears on the interpretation of the biblical record.

THE ANCHOR BIBLE is aimed at the general reader with no special formal training in biblical studies; yet it is written with the most exacting standards of scholarship, reflecting the highest technical accomplishment.

This project marks the beginning of a new era of co-operation among scholars in biblical research, thus forming a common body of knowledge to be shared by all.

William Foxwell Albright
David Noel Freedman
GENERAL EDITORS

Following the death of senior editor W. F. Albright, The Anchor Bible Editorial Board was established to advise and assist David Noel Freedman in his continuing capacity as general editor. The three members of the Editorial Board are among the contributors to The Anchor Bible. They have been associated with the series for a number of years and are familiar with its methods and objectives. Each is a distinguished authority in his area of specialization, and in concert with the others, will provide counsel and judgment as the series continues.

EDITORIAL BOARD

Frank M. Cross	Old Testament
Raymond E. Brown	New Testament
Jonas C. Greenfield	Apocrypha

THE ANCHOR BIBLE

JUDGES

Introduction, Translation,
and Commentary by

ROBERT G. BOLING

DOUBLEDAY & COMPANY, INC.

GARDEN CITY, NEW YORK

ISBN: 0-385-01029-X
Library of Congress Catalog Card Number 72–96229
Copyright © 1975 by Doubleday & Company, Inc.
All Rights Reserved
Printed in the United States of America
First Edition

PREFACE

This book is written for layman and scholar alike, in the understanding that there is no legitimate difference either in how each learns from ancient writings or in the substance, ultimately, of what each can learn by studying them. The Book of Judges stems from an exciting period in history which is now undergoing a radical reevaluation; there are no large areas of scholarly consensus. Hence the NOTES on the translation must often be quite technical. At such points my recommendation to the general reader is unabashed: skim. Scholars, on the other hand, are likely to object that I have not in fact given sufficient space to other views. But I have not been unmindful or indifferent. It is indeed a problem of space and so I hope that there are sufficient indicators along the way to lead interested readers into an immense literature on many a point large or small.

My family, former teachers and current colleagues, and especially students have helped in a myriad of ways to write this book. Here especially I must acknowledge the General Editor David Noel Freedman whose name appears in a multitude of NOTES, thanks to the care with which he read the manuscript, making many pages of arguments and helpful suggestions.

RGB

CONTENTS

LIST OF ILLUSTRATIONS

195, 1969. Courtesy Nancy L. Lapp. Reprinted by permission

c. Reconstruction of a typical Old Testament house. Illustration by Marjorie Quennel from *Everyday Life in Old Testament Times,* by E. W. Heaton, is used by permission of Charles Scribner's Sons. Copyright 1956 Charles Scribner's Sons

9. Samson staged there a party for seven days (14:10)

a. A Philistine beer jug from Tell Aitun. From *Christian News from Israel* 20, 1969. By courtesy of the Israel Department of Antiquities and Museums

b. Philistine beer jugs from tombs at Tell Fara. From *Archaeology in the Holy Land,* by Kathleen Kenyon. New York: Praeger, 1960. By permission of Ernest Benn Limited, Tonbridge

10. The Philistines dominate us (15:11)

Battle between a Sea Peoples ship and a ship of Rameses III. Illustration by C. F. Stevens. From *Biblical Archaeology,* by G. Ernest Wright. First published 1957 in the U.S.A. by The Westminster Press, and Gerald Duckworth & Co., Ltd., London. New & Revised edition, 1962. Used by permission

MAPS

Maps by Rafael Palacios

PRINCIPAL ABBREVIATIONS

1. PUBLICATIONS

ALUOS[D]	Annual of the Leeds University Oriental Society, Godfrey Rolles Driver, vol. 4, 1962–63
ANET[3]	*Ancient Near Eastern Texts Relating to the Old Testament,* ed. J. B. Pritchard, 3d ed., Princeton University Press, 1969
BA	The Biblical Archaeologist
BASOR	Bulletin of the American Schools of Oriental Research
Burney	C. F. Burney, *The Book of Judges,* 2d ed., London: Rivingtons, 1930; reprinted with Prolegomenon by W. F. Albright, New York: Ktav, 1970
BWANT	Beiträge zur Wissenschaft vom Alten und Neuen Testament
CBQ	Catholic Biblical Quarterly
IDB	*The Interpreter's Dictionary of the Bible,* eds. George Arthur Buttrick et al., New York and Nashville: Abingdon Press, 1962
IEJ	Israel Exploration Journal
JAOS	Journal of the American Oriental Society
JBL	Journal of Biblical Literature and Exegesis
JNES	Journal of Near Eastern Studies
LOB	*Land of the Bible,* by Yohanan Aharoni, Philadelphia: Westminster, 1967
MLC	*Myth, Legend, and Custom in the Old Testament,* by Theodor H. Gaster, New York: Harper, 1969
Moore	George F. Moore, *Judges,* The International Critical Commentary, New York: Scribners, 1901
RA	*Revue d'Assyriologie et d'Archéologie orientale,* spec. F. Thureau-Dangin, "Nouvelles lettres d'el-Amarna," vol. xix, 1921
Retterbuches	*Die Bearbeitungen des "Retterbuches" in der deuteronomischen Epoche,* by Wolfgang Richter, Bonner Biblische Beiträge, 210, Bonn: Peter Hanstein, 1964
Shechem	*Shechem: The Biography of a Biblical City,* by G. Ernest Wright, New York: McGraw-Hill, 1965
TenGen	*The Tenth Generation: The Origins of the Biblical Tradition,* by George E. Mendenhall, Johns Hopkins University Press, 1973

VT	Vetus Testamentum
YGC	*Yahweh and the Gods of Canaan,* by William F. Albright, Garden City, New York: Doubleday, 1968
ZAW	Zeitschrift für die alttestamentliche Wissenschaft

2. VERSIONS

EVV	English versions in general
LXX	The Septuagint
LXX^A	Codex Alexandrinus
LXX^B	Codex Vaticanus
LXX^{AL}	LXX^A and LXX^L (yet another manuscript) have the same reading
MT	Masoretic Text
NEB	The New English Bible
OL	The Old Latin
RSV	The Revised Standard Version
Syr.	Syriac version, the Peshitta
Syr.^{h}	The Syriac version of Origen's Hexapla
Targ.	Aramaic translations or paraphrases, the Targum
Vulg.	The Vulgate
AB	The Anchor Bible
J	Ancient Israel's national epic, the main Yahwist narrative stratum in the books of Genesis through Numbers, with at least two substrata: J_1, the more secular, and J_2, the more religious
L	The "lay" source in Genesis through Numbers, following the analysis by Otto Eissfeldt, *The Old Testament: An Introduction,* tr. Peter R. Ackroyd, New York: Harper and Row, 1965. This corresponds generally to J_1 in the earlier studies
E	The northern or Ephraimite version of the national epic, preserved only in part in the books of Genesis through Numbers; also known as the Elohistic epic, since it uses the generic noun for "God" (*ᵉlohim*), prior to the call of Moses in Exod 3
D	The bulk of Deut 4:44 – 28:68

3. OTHER ABBREVIATIONS

Heb.	Hebrew
Akk.	Akkadian
4Q Judges^a and 4Q Judges^b	Unpublished manuscripts from Qumran Cave 4
NT	The New Testament

OT	The Old Testament
C.E.	Common Era; corresponds to A.D.
B.C.E.	Before the Common Era; corresponds to B.C.
lit.	literally
	especially

GLOSSARY OF TERMS

ben, the Hebrew word for "son," often part of a personal name, as in Joshua ben Nun. It is also used with a variety of secondary senses (similarly Heb. *'āḥ,* "brother") to express membership in a class or group, chiefly sociopolitical in Judges. To reflect such usage the translation places "son(s)" or "brother(s)" within quotation marks.

chiasm or *chiasmus* (adj., *chiastic*), the arrangement of words (or lines) in an "X" pattern.

construct, the shortened form that a noun in Hebrew assumes before another noun or verb in the genitive case, e.g. absolute *dābār,* "word," but in construct *dᵉbar 'ᵉlōhīm,* "word of God."

dittography, accidental repetition by a scribe of a letter, word, or section of material; see *haplography.*

hapax legomenon, a word or form that occurs only once.

haplography, accidental omission by a scribe of a letter, word, or section of material; see *dittography.*

hendiadys, a rhetorical figure using two words to express one idea.

hiphil, the causative verb form in Hebrew, also used with elative force to heighten the root idea.

homoioarkton, words beginning with the same consonant or consonant cluster.

homoioteleuton, words ending with the same consonant or consonant cluster.

kethib, "what is written," a term used by the Masoretes to indicate that what is written in the received text is at variance with their vocalization; see *qere.*

*kaph, the eleventh letter of the Hebrew alphabet (our "k").

*lamedh, the twelfth letter of the Hebrew alphabet (our "l").

*mem, the thirteenth letter of the Hebrew alphabet (our "m").

merismus (adj., *meristic*), a rhetorical figure in which totality is expressed by mentioning the two extremes of a class, e.g. "heaven and earth" as an ancient way of saying "the universe."

niphal, the passive or reflexive form of the simple stem in the Hebrew verbal system.

nota accusativi, the particle *'ēt* (or *-'et*), introduces the definite direct object in a sentence.

* Through the survival of archaic linguistic features, these letters have a greater variety of prepositional and adverbial uses (vocative, emphatic, enclitic; see Index of Subjects) than is commonly recognized in the Hebrew grammars. Such usage will be indicated in NOTES.

piel, the third Hebrew verbal conjugation which often intensifies the root idea, but which can also convey other nuances.

pointing, the addition of vowels and punctuation to the consonantal Hebrew text.

qal, the light form, that is the simplest form, of the Hebrew verb.

qere, a term employed by the Masoretes to indicate that their pointing is at variance with the consonants of the received text.

TRANSCRIPTION EQUIVALENTS

'=aleph	q=qoph
'=ayin	s=samek
h=heth	$ṣ$=tsade
$ṭ$=teth	$ś$=sin
t=taw	$š$=shin
k=kaph	y=yod

In the translation we have not revised traditional spellings except to level throughout the k/q distinction in many words. Traditional spellings unfortunately blur that distinction and even compound the problem by using *ch* for spirant kaph (Taanach) and *c* for initial kaph (Canaan) and thus *k* for initial qoph (Kenite), among others! A number of these spellings are so familiar, of course, that they ought to be retained in translation.

Use of *y* as a vowel letter requires special comment. The Hebrew verb "to judge," for example, may be transcribed either *dīn* (actual pronunciation) or *dyn* (indicating verbal root). We use the latter wherever possible, giving the vocalized spelling only where it helps to avoid ambiguity.

Dagesh forte is not represented in the unvoweled transcriptions.

LIST OF ANCIENT NEAR EASTERN TEXTS

Amarna Correspondence, a corpus of cuneiform letters discovered in 1887 at Tell el-Amarna in central Egypt. Written around 1350 B.C.E. from kings and administrators in Palestine and Syria to the Pharaoh in Egypt, they are of special interest because of their language (the scribes were mostly Canaanites trying to write Akkadian) and evidence of social organization in Canaan in the last century of Egyptian domination.

Mari texts, more than twenty thousand cuneiform tablets discovered at Tell Hariri (ancient Mari) in northern Mesopotamia. These tablets date to the general period and illustrate the social milieu of the Hebrew patriarchs, esp. Abraham and Jacob.

Mesha Inscription, also called the Moabite Stone, found at Diban in Transjordan. It was set up by Mesha, king of Moab, in the ninth century B.C.E., to recount his victories.

Ugaritic texts, hundreds of cuneiform tablets from the fourteenth century B.C.E., excavated at the Syrian coastal site of Ras Shamra.

CHRONOLOGY OF

THE GREAT POWERS

Sumerian Age in Mesopotamia, c. 2800–2400
Pyramid Age in Egypt, c. 2700–2200
Akkad: first semitic dynasty in Mesopotamia, c. 2400–2200
Sumerian Revival in Mesopotamia, c. 2100–2000
Amorite dynasties: Babylonia to the Mediterranean, c. 2000–1700

Hyksos domination: Egypt and Canaan, c. 1710–1550

Asia Minor: Hittite Empire, c. 1600–1200
Egypt: New Kingdom, c. 1500–1200
Decline of Pharaonic power, c. 1400–1200
Crete: Golden Age of Minoan culture, fall of Crete, c. 1400

Greece: Dorian invasion, end of Mycenaean culture, c. 1200

Sea Peoples' invasion of Egypt and coast of Canaan, c. 1200–1125
End of Hittite Empire, c. 1200

Assyria quiescent, c. 1197–1125
Thessalian Federation in northern Greece, c. 1100

Neo-Assyrian supremacy, 727–633
Neo-Babylonian supremacy, 626–539

Persian supremacy, 539–334
Alexander's conquest of Egypt and Asia, 334–323

THE BOOK OF JUDGES

ERAS

ERA OF THE PATRIARCHS
(Genesis 12–50)
Canaan effectively or nominally controlled from Egypt

2100	Middle Bronze I	
1900	Middle Bronze II A	
1700	Middle Bronze II B	
1600	Middle Bronze II C	
1500	Late Bronze I	
1400	Late Bronze II A.	Amarna Age: Labayu at Shechem
1300	Late Bronze II B.	The Exodus, c. 1297
		Conquest of Canaan, c. 1225
		Shechem Confederation, c. 1200

ERA OF THE JUDGES

1200	Iron Age I.	Othniel, c. 1190 (?)
		Gideon, Abimelech: sack of Shechem, c. 1150
		Shamgar, Deborah, Baraq: defeat of the northwest coalition of kings, c. 1125
		Danite migration north, c. 1100

ERA OF THE KINGS

Saul, c. 1020–1000
David, c. 1000–961
Solomon, c. 961–922
Yahwist epic (*J*), c. 950
Elohist epic (*E*), c. 800
Destruction of Samaria, end of the northern kingdom of Israel, 721
Josiah, c. 640–609
Deuteronomic Historical Work, c. 615
Destruction of Jerusalem, end of the southern kingdom of Judah, 587

ERA OF THE BOOK

Deuteronomistic Historical Work, c. 550

INTRODUCTION

INTRODUCTION

Illustrious Men and Women

The judges too, each when he was called,
    all men whose hearts were never disloyal,
who never turned their backs on the Lord—
    may their memory be blessed!
May their bones flower again from the tomb,
    and may the names of those illustrious men
live again in their sons.
Ecclesiasticus 46:11–12 (The Jerusalem Bible)

The stories of the judges were nearly a thousand years old when the poetry of Ecclesiasticus was assembled, in about the second century B.C.E., by Jesus Ben Sira. Ben Sira's account of old Israel's legacy of Law (Heb. *tōrāh*), Prophets (Heb. *nᵉbī'īm*), and Writings (Heb. *kᵉtūbīm*) reads like an Old Testament Who's Who, especially in the last seven chapters: "Let us now praise famous men" (44:1, Authorized Version). His poetry also presents a capsule illustration of the problem of historical memory which in all its ramifications will confront us throughout this book. For curiously, Ben Sira makes no specific mention of any of the great characters in the Book of Judges, with the single exception of Caleb, an associate of both Moses and Joshua in biblical traditions. Rather, Ben Sira speaks for those who in his day held positions of responsibility for the religious education of his people. He thinks that the best thing to be said about the judges is that they "never turned their backs on the Lord. . . ."

Such a blanket statement of praise would have been impossible for Israel's earliest traditionists who gathered and preserved the judges stories, for they lived too close to the period to glorify the judges. Rather, they portray the judges realistically, with fears as well as courage, faults as well as faith. Their attitudes toward Yahweh, the God of Israel, are not consistently praiseworthy either. Actually, as we shall see, the stories describe an ancient international community in miniature struggling to realize a way of life that affords an equal range of opportunities for all its citizens. To many moderns it will be their candor in reporting the struggle—and not Ben Sira's rhetoric—that will sustain Ben Sira's own high hope: "May their bones flower again."

The writer of the epistle To the Hebrews also composed a section on ancient worthies. He included "Gideon, Baraq, Samson, Jephthah," in that order, together with "David, Samuel, and the prophets" (Heb 11:32, AB, vol. 36, 1972) after devoting the bulk of the chapter to examples of faith extending all the way from Abel to Rahab the harlot (Heb 11:1–31). In his list of the achievements by which the ancient heroes earned their fame, the writer of the letter To the Hebrews confined himself to historical hardships: they "extinguished power of fire, fled [the] mouths of [the] sword, became strong in war. . . . They were stoned, tested, sawed in two . . ." (Heb 11:34–37). The bulk of this description is clearly drawn from the careers of prophets. But it is surely significant for the edifying impact of judges tradition that the list begins with the statement that "through faith" they "struggled against kingdoms" and "achieved righteousness," having "obtained promises" (Heb 11:33). The verse involves a rhetorical appeal to the elements of election and service on the part of old Israel's public officials; see for example Jephthah, who is portrayed as the last *great* judge in the Book of Judges. The recital of Jephthah's career attains its first climax with his own recital of promissory "words" at the Transjordan Mizpah sanctuary (Judg 11:11). Then follows Jephthah's law enforcement in both foreign affairs (11:12–28) and domestic matters (11:34 – 12:4), presented as impeccably correct, and resorting to force only when diplomacy has failed, but then conquering a kingdom (11:29–33).

We may conclude that the writer of Heb 11 did indeed know his Jephthah tradition, because his list is organized to center in Jephthah. Jephthah is preceded by Gideon, Baraq, and Samson (in that uncanonical order) and followed by David, Samuel, and the prophets (equally uncanonical, but Samuel is here regarded as prophet, not judge). The reason, perhaps, that the Hebrews list centers in Jephthah is that nowhere else in the Book of Judges is there depicted such a clear relationship between the "swearing in" of the judge and his activity in both foreign and domestic affairs. Compare Othniel at the beginning of the period (3:7–11), and Samuel at the end of it (I Sam 7:5–9); each won a battle over the opposition subsequent to leading the straying Israelites in repentance before Yahweh.

Yet the writer of the Hebrews letter fails to mention such matters as Gideon's penchant for divination, Baraq's reluctance to do any fighting without Deborah on the scene, Samson's preference for conducting the siege in a Philistine boudoir, and Jephthah's tragic literalism which leads to the sacrifice of his daughter in fulfillment of a hastily worded vow. In short, Ben Sira generalized on the loyalty of good judges, and the Hebrews writer celebrated the faithfulness implicit in exemplary administration.

It is possible to say more than this. Modern critical research has opened the world of ancient Israel to an extent that was unimagined and in fact impossible in the days of our intertestamental and New Testament (NT) forebears. There is no doubt that some of our renderings and interpretations in the Book of Judges would have startled Ben Sira, until he could have studied them with all the appropriate aids. Similarly there is nothing here to undermine the Hebrews letter's concept of faith on its way to the realization of a city of God. For the Book of Judges is an ancient exploration of a people's claim to have been ruled by Yahweh in a period that was, for them, one of revolutionary social change.

WHY "JUDGES"?

The English titles of the Old Testament (OT) books are derived from the Latin. Originally such titles were descriptive labels based upon a book's internal characteristics or opening words (e.g. Genesis is called *bᵉrēšīt,* which is simply the first word in the Hebrew Bible). Judges (Heb. *šōpᵉtīm*) is derived from the fact that nine or ten of the book's protagonists are said to have "judged" (Heb. *šāpaṭ*) Israel. The verb clearly has a wider semantic range than that of the strictly judicial function in the modern western world. Thus it was explained, in tenth-century prose, that Absalom's rebellion had failed because Yahweh had "judged" (*šāpaṭ*) for David and against his enemies (II Sam 18:19, 31). Absalom had made the mistake of setting himself up as a self-seeking "judge" in Israel (II Sam 15:1–6). Similarly the verb šāpaṭ can be traced in both pre-Israelite and postexilic extrabiblical sources, and shown to connote "to rule." The verb šāpaṭ "does not designate a unique act of deliverance or of condemnation, but a series of acts of government."[1] This definition will be sustained by detailed exegesis of the texts.

Within the book, apart from the introduction (2:16–18), the noun "judge" appears only once, as a title of Yahweh, in Jephthah's diplomatic communique to the king of Ammon (11:27). As universal judge, Yahweh retained a prerogative that had been here and there attributed to various deities in Israel's pagan background and among her contemporaries.

Is it merely historical accident that none of the famous protagonists in the judges book is identified by the noun "judge"? We shall have to return to this query. In the meantime we shall perpetuate traditional usage and continue to refer to the protagonists as "judges" for lack of a better word. And here it must be noted that the period in question was remembered with a certain critical nostalgia far antedating the days of Ben Sira and the writer of Heb 11. The story of Ruth, which is built around a clear ex-

[1] Henri S. Cazelles, "Shiloh, the Customary Laws and the Return of the Ancient Kings," in *Proclamation and Presence,* eds. J. I. Durham and J. R. Porter (Richmond: John Knox, 1970), p. 241.

ample of "justice in the city gate," has its setting "in the days when the judges judged" (Ruth 1:1). The story of Ruth depicts local legal machinery at work, surely implying a contrast with the immediately preceding book, Judges. In the Book of Judges the matter of justice is explored in cosmic perspective.

Equally striking as the absence of the noun "judge" from the narratives of the Book of Judges is the presence of the noun "savior" (Heb. $mōšī^{a'}$), or its related verb ($yš'$), in referring to three of the protagonists: Othniel, Ehud, and Tola. In the case of a fourth, Samson, it was specified only that he should begin the process of "saving" Israel from the Philistines; someone else would have to finish the task. "A sudden and more or less supernatural intervention is what is meant"[2] by the use of the salvation word group, $hōšī^{a'}$, and its derivatives. This definition too is sustained by close exegesis. Certain of the judges were lauded as saviors, perhaps indicating that the story of Moses had some influence on the stories about the judges. Numerous similarities between the judges stories and the accounts of the birth, enlistment, and diplomatic functioning of Moses in Exod 1–13 (see esp. NOTES and COMMENTS on Gideon in ch. 6) support this hypothesis.

"The historicity of Moses in the role of the first of the 'major Judges' of course cannot be proved—but also it cannot be disproved. . . ."[3] Scholars have often sought in these "Moses-like" careers of a handful of heroes a clue to the growth of the Book of Judges out of a core collection of savior stories.

It is indeed clear that the judges stories have had a long editorial history. The NOTES and COMMENTS will abound with observations and queries about the "traditionists," those men who first told the stories for public edification and delight, and the "redactors," those who compiled the preformed narrative units into a continuous historical presentation and put it through several expanding editions.

The most serious objection to the theory that a nuclear "savior book" was transformed by theological revision or traditionary merger to become a "judges book" is the uniform absence of the salvation language precisely in those cases where the popular lore was most prolific: Deborah and Baraq, Gideon, Jephthah (Samson, as noted above, is a special case). Indeed, in the case of Gideon neither the "judicial" language nor the "salvation" language occurs! *What did Gideon do?* Perhaps that is precisely the question. That is to say, mere lexical collocation will not suffice; the pattern of lexical distribution must be studied with an eye to the integrity of both the narrative structure and the larger history-writing enterprise that went on for centuries in ancient Israel.

---

2 Ibid. Cazelles notes how precisely the combination—deliverance followed by judgment—characterizes Ezekiel's eschatological hope (Ezek 34:20–22).

3 Rudolf Smend, *Yahweh War and Tribal Confederation,* tr. Max G. Rogers (New York and Nashville: Abingdon, 1970), p. 128.

MINOR JUDGES

The following list collocates the affirmations made directly or by clear implication about each of the great protagonists, from Othniel who was remembered as the first to Samuel who was reckoned as the last of the judges. For example, that Deborah and Jephthah each "saved" Israel—kept it from going out of existence—is clearly conveyed by the narrator, though not said directly. Neither activity (as judge or as savior) is unambiguously imputed to Gideon in the Gideon materials, though Jotham, Gideon's son, makes the salvation claim for his father in 9:17.

After the lengthy portrayal of Gideon's exploits and Abimelech's aspirations the idea that Tola "saved" Israel by virtue of his activity in "judging" (clear from the Hebrew syntax) is of pivotal importance.

Othniel	saved and judged	3:7–11
Ehud	saved Israel and judged Moab	3:12–30
Shamgar	saved	3:31
Deborah	"saved" and "judged"	4:1 – 5:31
Gideon		6:1 – 8:32
Abimelech		8:33 – 9:57
Tola	saved as he judged	10:1–2
Jair	judged	10:3–5
Jephthah	"saved" and judged	10:6 – 12:7
Ibzan	judged	12:8–10
Elon	judged	12:11
Abdon	judged	12:13–15
Samson	judged	13:1 – 16:31
Eli	judged	I Sam 4:18
Samuel	"saved"(?) and judged	I Sam 7:2–17

Little information survives regarding Tola, Jair, Ibzan, Elon, and Abdon; regarding Shamgar we are told even less. These five or six names are conveniently grouped together—Samson is often included too—as minor judges. We retain the designation as a convenient umbrella, but exclude Shamgar and Samson (see NOTES on 3:31 and ch. 13) from its shade.

Scholars have generally sought to relate these minor judges to one or the other of the two main types of biblical law (to be discussed below, pp. 9–11) and have generally recognized a difference between them and the early saviors. (These theories are addressed in NOTES and COMMENTS on the minor judges.) On the whole we may assume that the minor judges represent a combination of relatively peaceful interludes and effective administration that was rare enough in Israel's existence prior to the tenth-century statecraft of the great King David.

The most telling evidence against the notion of a sharp distinction be-

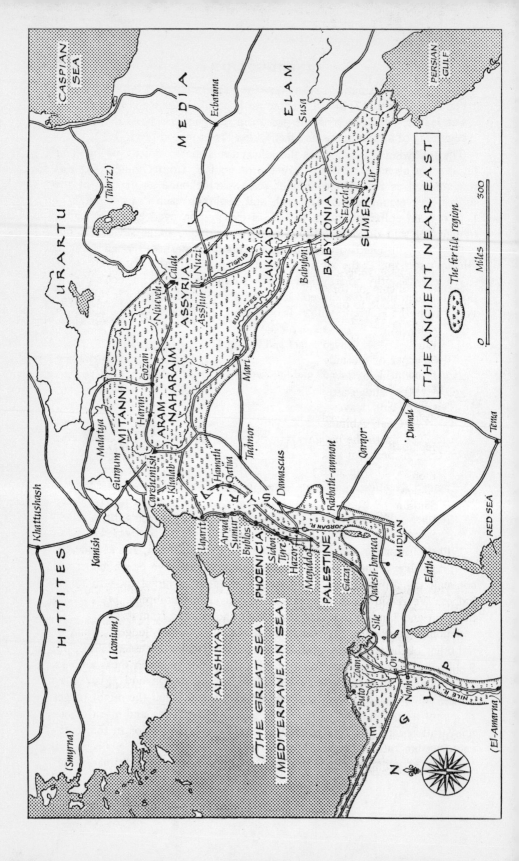

THE ANCIENT NEAR EAST

The fertile region

0   Miles   300

tween the "charismatic" saviors and the "institutional" minor judges is the pericope of Josh 17:14–18.[4] There an intertribal dispute is brought to the war leader, whose later death without a designated successor marked the beginning of a tumultuous and nearly disastrous period (Judg 1:1).

ON THE TRAIL OF ANCIENT ISRAEL

They shall beat their swords into plowshares
and their spears into pruning hooks.
Isaiah 2:4b || Micah 4:3b (RSV)

The Book of Judges has never been regarded as one of the more eloquent exponents of the prophets' grand theme. Critical study of Judges has, in fact, gone to one or another of two extremes. Sir Flinders Petrie, a great pioneer of scientific archaeology, could write near the beginning of the twentieth century:

The period of the judges was a terribly barbaric age; its fragmentary records speak of savage retaliations, and fierce struggles of disorganized tribes. Judge after judge rises out of a mist of warfare, only to disappear and leave a confusion as black as before. Ehud, Baraq, Gideon, Gaal, Abimelech, Jephthah, Samson, with their bloody record, lead up to the hideous tragedy of the slaughter of Benjamin. Not a trace of peaceful arts do we find; not even the arts of civilized warfare. . . . The invasion of the nomad horde of Israelites on the high civilization of the Amorite kings . . . must have seemed a crushing blow to all culture and advance in the arts; it was much like the terrible breaking up of the Roman Empire by the northern races, it swept away nearly all the good along with the evil; centuries were needed to regain what was lost, along with the further gain of a better moral order than that which had been destroyed.[5]

This lengthy quote from the pioneering excavator presents a capsule illustration of the problem that is compounded of scholarly method and private values in historical description. The trouble was the critical concept of "the invasion of the nomad horde of Israelites on the high civilization of the Amorite kings." While the warfare of the twentieth century has complicated enormously the task of distinguishing between "high" and "low" civilizations, the twentieth-century experience has also introduced greater sociological precision into historical description.

4 Albrecht Alt, *Kleine Schriften zur Geschichte des Volkes Israel,* I (Munich: Beck, 1953), 190–91. Alt, however, resists the logic of his own observation. So also, most recently, did Smend in *Yahweh War,* ch. 3. The best reason for the lack of the minor judge rubrics in the case of Joshua is that he was a major one, that is, field commander par excellence.
5 Sir Flinders Petrie, *Tell El Hesy* (London: A. P. Watt, 1891), pp. 16–17.

The theory of "the nomad horde" was one of the seemingly assured results of nineteenth-century scholarship. It persists today, in highly attenuated form, in theories about Israel's taking possession of Canaan by gradual infiltration over a span of centuries. But the valuation of the nomadic life is different today.

At the same time that the great archaeologist was unearthing data that would upset his own inherited opinion, analysis of Israel's literature was being highly refined by comparison with the traditions and records of Israel's neighbors and forebears. The ruling idea was that the distinctiveness of Israel's achievement would emerge clearly from careful descriptive attention to it as part of antiquity's literature, not from any theological dictum. The idea is here to stay.

Moreover the literary question is today divided in two parts. The form-critic asks what the standard forms were, as determined inductively from the international survey of ancient literature. What was the life setting of each form, the specific occasion which called for its use, or which provides an interpretive clue from some correspondence between form and social context? The life settings of many literary forms have turned out to be extremely elusive, so the interpreter must give rigorous attention to all data available for historical understanding, especially the contributions of archaeological exploration and discovery.

Meanwhile the gains made in "form criticism" for the understanding of Judges are immense. Here it will suffice to mention the classification of OT legal materials according to form. On the one hand there is the vast bulk of laws in Exod 21–23 (the "Covenant Code"), Leviticus, and Deuteronomy. These laws are conditional, built up with qualifying clauses which limit precisely the appropriateness of the stipulation to particular cases (hence "casuistic" laws). Parallels with extrabiblical legal codes abound. Here Israel drew deeply from a vast reservoir of local and international legal experience in providing for the order of her life in Canaan.

Scattered here and there throughout the three great collections are stipulations of another sort altogether, expressed in direct, unqualified, positive or negative generalities. The Ten Commandments are the prime example of sustained listing in this apodictic (absolute) formulation. Compare also the form of the covenantal curses in Deut 27:15–26. Yet another striking example of apodictic legal form is found in the series of three curt directives with which Deuteronomy sets the standard for an elaborate judicature: "You shall not pervert justice. You shall not show partiality. You shall not take a bribe" (Deut 16:19a). Deuteronomy in this passage is apparently addressed to Israel under the monarchy, inasmuch as it envisages judges and officers "in each of the towns" (vs. 18). Since the "officers" are nowhere mentioned explicitly in the Book of Judges, it is impossible to say to what extent the Deuteronomic legislation represents the later elaboration of the older tribal provisions for judicial review (cf. Deut 1:16; 17:8–9; 19:16–18). The apodictic law remained, in any case, persistently unrevisable to any significant extent.

Scholars have often viewed the minor judges in biblical tradition as propounders and expositors of one or the other of these types of law. Especially valuable sociological comparison in this connection has been made with the "law speakers" (lögsögunder) of Nordic tradition.[6] It is no longer possible, however, to discuss biblical law apart from the tradition of the Sinai covenant (see below, pp. 24–25). Here it will suffice to say that, with the antiquity of the covenant form and of the legal substance being equal, the basis for all moralizing devaluations of the judges literature simply evaporates.

Moreover, the quest for clarity on the origins of ancient Israel has been carried into the preliterary stages of the formation of the books. While the great literary critical enterprise of the modern era has sought to date the production of literary sources in material such as the Book of Judges, it is now clear that the writing down of such material belongs to the end of a transmitting process, not the beginning. The fixation of ancient Israelite tradition in written form, from roughly the ninth to the seventh centuries B.C.E. (by which time, as we shall see, the Book of Judges was virtually complete), means that certain oral narrative tradition was itself considered inviolable, whether for artistic considerations, or theological, or both. New connectives between stories might be added. Certain stylistic adjustments and lexical substitutions might take place. But wholesale literary revisions were out of the question. Indeed, the Book of Judges gives the impression of being built up piecemeal, out of a large store of preformed narrative units, each complete (or once so) in itself. Hence the frequent repetitions and apparent contradictions within the book.

A continuation of the Israelite epic was generated in the period of the Book of Judges, that is, the two centuries preceding the tenth-century establishment of monarchy in the empire-building reigns of Saul, David, and Solomon. "The days when the judges judged," however, make up one of the dark ages in Palestinian history, and one of the most poorly documented periods for the wider world as well. Egypt and Mesopotamia, the two great sources of documentation outside Israel, were in decline. (See Chronology.) A situation which was conducive to the success of the little Israelite experiment in Canaan also helps to account for Israel's minor significance in the fragmentary Egyptian records. Israel is mentioned only

6 Originally proposed by August Klostermann, Der Pentateuch, Leipzig: A. Deichert, 1893, the idea was taken up by Max Weber in Ancient Judaism, trs. Hans H. Gerth and Don Martindale, New York: The Free Press, 1952, and has often been emphasized.

in the famous Merneptah stele, a hymn recording Pharaoh's version of the solution to the Palestine question c. 1230 B.C.E.:

> The princes are prostrate, saying: "Mercy!"
>   Not one raises his head among the Nine Bows.
> Desolation is for Tehenu; Hatti is pacified;
>   Plundered is the Canaan with every evil;
> Carried off is Ashkelon; seized upon is Gezer;
>   Yanoam is made as that which does not exist;
> Israel is laid waste, his seed is not;
>   Hurru is become a widow for Egypt!
> All lands together, they are pacified. . . .[7]

That the pacification of Canaan which Merneptah claimed was neither complete nor enduring is proved by a whole series of excavated towns, mostly concentrated in the Judaean hills but ranging to Bethel in the near north and including mighty Hazor in northern Galilee. The destruction of these places in the late thirteenth and early twelfth centuries, together with the silence of archaeology and tradition regarding military activity in the north central hill country (the area centering in Shechem) calls for a theoretical model of Israel's establishment in Canaan that will do historical justice both to the highly stylized claims of the Book of Joshua and to an alleged rival tradition in Judg 1 (see below, pp. 63–64).

Such a model has recently been erected; its influence will become apparent and its implications explored in NOTES and COMMENTS. In capsule form the theory is that the rapid establishment of Israel on the soil of Canaan in the thirteenth and twelfth centuries is explained neither by the oversimplified Joshua account nor by the protracted unrelated migrations of tribes posited by many modern scholars. Rather, historical Israel was able to establish itself in Canaan because of a peasant revolt up and down the land. The catalyst was the arrival in Canaan of the Yahweh-covenanters, many of whom traced their ancestry through a group of state-slaves in Egypt to an earlier sojourn in Canaan and, ultimately, to Mesopotamian origins.[8] Their distinctive social and political organization they attributed to the convergence of the careers of Moses and Jethro.

The archaeological basis for this approach to Israel's conflict traditions[9]

---

[7] Tr. John A. Wilson, ANET[3], p. 378.

[8] The theory was proposed by George E. Mendenhall, BA 25 (1962), 66–87. It has been carefully developed in connection with the Judges era in an excellent little introduction to the period by John L. McKenzie, *The World of the Judges*, Englewood Cliffs, N.J.: Prentice-Hall, 1966. See also Albert E. Glock, "Early Israel as the Kingdom of Yahweh," *Concordia Theological Monthly* 41 (1970), 558–608.

[9] We speak of "conflict" rather than "conquest" traditions because of the involvement of the participants in socioreligious covenants. See Norman C. Habel, *Yahweh Versus Baal*, New York: Twayne, 1964.

is complemented, first of all, by the situation that is known to have prevailed in Egypt's Canaan in the fourteenth century, the period of the famous Amarna letters (see Map 1). Those letters comprise the diplomatic correspondence to Pharaoh from lesser kings, his vassals ruling the many Canaanite city-states. The letters have proved to be an incredibly rich mine of data on social and economic life, on political institutions which here and there continued in vogue (e.g. the kingship of Abimelech in ch. 9), as well as political and diplomatic structures and usage that a century or so after the Amarna Age acquired high theological significance in Israel. In general the picture of fourteenth-century Canaan is one of a dysfunctional network of hypothetically interlocking city-states, redounding neither to the credit of the princes nor to the well-being of the Canaanite masses.

For example, Shuwardata writes, regarding the dead opportunist lord of Shechem (Labayu) that his independent administrative style was now being emulated by 'Abdu-Heba, king of Jerusalem:

> Labayu is dead, who seized our towns; but behold, 'Abdu-Heba is another Labayu, and he (also) seizes our towns! So let the king take thought for his servant because of this deed! And I will not do anything until the king sends back a message to his servant.[10]

Compare Samson, who alone bears or claims the title "servant" of Yahweh in the judges era (like Joshua at the close of the preceding era, Judg 2:8) and in the next breath demands of God to know whether he is going to be allowed to die (15:18)! See also the treatment of Zebul, Abimelech's "recruiter" at Shechem, in 9:28.

Forced labor for the king (corvée) was repugnant policy in later Israel, as it had been in the Amarna period in the plain of Esdraelon:

> To the king, my lord, and my Sun-god say: Thus Biridiya, the true servant of the king. At the feet of the king, my lord, and my Sun-god, seven times and seven times I fall. Let the king be informed concerning his servant and concerning his city. Behold, I am working in the town of Shunama, and I bring men of the corvée, but behold, the governors who are with me do not as I (do): they do not work in the town of Shunama, and they do not bring men for the corvée, but I alone bring men for the corvée from the town of Yapu. . . . So let the king be informed concerning his city![11]

One more citation is in order, for the light that it sheds on Hebrews in Bronze Age Canaan. Shuwardata writes:

---

10 J. A. Knudson, ed., *Die El-Amarna Tafeln* (Leipzig: Vorderasiatische Bibliothek, 1915), Letter 280. Tr. William Foxwell Albright, ANET[3], p. 487.
11 RA, p. 97. Tr. Albright, ANET[3], p. 485.

. . . Let the king, my lord, learn that the chief of the 'Apiru has risen (in arms) against the lands which the god of the king, my lord, gave me; but I have smitten him. Also let the king, my lord, know that all my brethren have abandoned me, and it is I and 'Abdu-Heba (who) fight against the chief of the 'Apiru. And Zurata, prince of Accho, and Indurata, prince of Achshaph, it was they (who) hastened with fifty chariots—for I had been robbed (by the 'Apiru)—to my help; but behold they are fighting against me, so let it be agreeable to the king my lord, and let him send Yanhamu, and let us make war in earnest, and let the lands of the king, my lord, be restored to their (former) limits![12]

Note that in this letter 'Abdu-Heba is now allied with Shuwardata and is not a hesitating menace as above. Notice also the kinship language ("my brethren") used to express politicomilitary affiliation, a usage which appears repeatedly in Judges. Note also that in principle the prince's land is claimed as a gift of the overlord's god, though in hard fact the prince's land belongs to the overlord.

These examples might be multiplied many times over from the Amarna corpus. Especially interesting for our period are the numerous references to the *'Apiru* (Akk. *Habiru*), which may be taken as a cognate of Biblical "Hebrew." The identification is, however, only linguistic. Careful comparison of social context is necessary before any social equation can be proposed. The 'Apiru appear in Hittite and Mesopotamian sources far antedating the Amarna period, and references are particularly numerous in the Mari archives (eighteenth century B.C.E.), to be discussed in the following paragraphs. Here the problem is the semantic range of 'Apiru/Habiru. The only plausible etymology for the word in West Semitic is "dusty." While warning against the exploitation of predictive models in this area, W. F. Albright succeeded in comprehending the bulk of references to the "dusty ones" in terms of the fluctuating fortunes of the donkey caravaneers of the second millennium B.C.E.[13] Early Israelite traditions, from Abraham to Moses, can now be related at point after point to a vast network of donkey caravan routes which connected Mesopotamia, Canaan, and Egypt from earliest historical times and which are known to have extended to South Arabia by the fifteenth century B.C.E.[14] In the time of Moses and Jethro, Midian (see Map 1) sat firmly astride the gateway to South Arabia and extended its suzerainty as far north as the

---

12 RA, p. 106. Tr. Albright, ANET[3], p. 487.

13 YGC, pp. 73–91.

14 Albright, "Midianite Donkey Caravans," in *Translating and Understanding the Old Testament,* eds. H. T. Frank and William L. Reed (New York and Nashville: Abingdon, 1970), pp. 197–205.

emerging kingdoms of Edom and Moab.[15] Through the priest Jethro, father-in-law of Moses, the Midianite recommendation for judicial practice made a major contribution to the rapidly expanding Yahwist organization in the Middle East (Exod 18:13–27).

The effective domestication of the camel, which did not take place until the close of the Late Bronze Age, brought revolutionary changes, which indeed posed one of the most serious threats to early Israel (the Midianite crisis in ch. 6). Prior to that, commerce between states depended of necessity on donkey caravans, and in periods of widespread insecurity the caravaneers might resort to freebooting brigandage, service as mercenaries, or, indeed, find themselves subject to the corvée. In the time of Joshua they must have constituted the courier service of rapidly expanding resistance to the operation of the Canaanite minimonarchies (cf. the Song of Deborah, ch. 5, esp. vss. 10–11).

Of two tribes in the extreme northwest of Mesopotamia in the eighteenth century B.C.E. (the Mari corpus), the northernmost, called "Sons of the Left," is clearly identified with the 'Apiru. Many parallels have been noted between the other tribe, the "Sons of the Right" ("Benjaminites"), and the biblical Hebrews of the patriarchal period.

The Mari archives are a nearly inexhaustible mine of data pertinent to ancient tribal organization, especially important here in the modern west, where popular preconceptions of tribes and tribesmen are formed by the American experience with its "Wild West" and the European experience with colonies. It is quite clear that the ancient tribe was a political structure, for which genealogy and kinship terminology provided a sort of narrative glue.[16]

Thus in the Old Testament, differences in genealogies and kinship groupings (e.g. fluctuations in the names of the twelve tribes) represent not so much competing traditions as shifting political reality. Compilers of the judges narratives, accordingly, often had no idea how many tribes were involved in this or that crisis; all they knew was that Israelites were involved. "All Israel" enters the picture explicitly at only three points: the angel's indictment (2:4), Gideon's ephod (8:27), and the Gibeah outrage (20:1). The Book of Judges clearly presents the period as one of fluctuating solidarity. It does leave "all Israel" united at last, after the tragedy. The implication is that no political structure can be as binding as the already ancient covenantal ideal represented by the name "Israel."

The Mari sources also enable Israel's kinship terminology to evoke diplomatic nuances. At Mari (see Map 1) a treaty expressed legal "brotherhood" between equals, as it did later between Ahab and Ben-

15 Otto Eissfeldt, "Protektorat der Midianiter über ihre Nachbarn im letzten Viertel des 2 Jahrtausends v. Chr.," JBL 87 (1968), 383–93.

16 Abraham Malamat, JAOS 82 (1962), 143–50.

Hadad (I Kings 20:32). Between unequals the King of kings, for example Zimri-Lim at Mari, is "father" and the vassal is "son."[17]

The same sources shed a flood of light on land tenure and military organization and practice.[18] In the former category it will suffice here to mention the Amorite *naḥalum* (Heb. *naḥᵃlā,* inadequately rendered "inheritance"). At Mari it stood for the king's grant of a plot of ground in return for a man's pledge of future military service.

> The sequence is land grant — warfare — land use. In a society where warfare is not a specialized occupation it is no accident that Joshua, the war leader par excellence, is the administrator of land allotment (Josh 13–22).[19]

It is not accidental that "the promised land" attained such theological importance. With the tenth-century reversion to what was already "old-fashioned" monarchy, the kings found their precedents in the same ancient customs; cf. Saul's recruitment of personal soldiers (I Sam 14:52) and their endowment with crown lands (22:7).

Equally important is the Amorite expression "to eat the *asakkum*" of a god or king. At Mari it had to do with the violation of a decree that marks certain spoils of war for the treasury of the royal house or for sacrificial offering to the deity. The biblical equivalent is *ḥerem* ("ban," see NOTE on 1:17), which must originally have pertained to the building up of the central treasury in the rapidly expanding Yahwist league. In the judges period the *ḥerem* is already passé, mentioned only in the introduction (1:17) and conclusion (21:11). The latter is clearly related to the story of Gideon's ephod (8:22–27), where the institution seems also to be in view.

Still a third cluster of institutions belonging to Mari warfare that is relevant to the background of Judges comprises those provisions for the muster of the feudal army: periodic ceremonies involving census, land distribution, sign-seeking, and oath-taking on the part of those being enrolled for future service to their sovereign. Somehow integral to the tribal muster was the ceremony of ritual purification known as the *tebibtum*. It "had to take place where the water was plentiful for use in the ritual purification"[20]; cf. Judg 5:11, 7:7, and the climactic significance of water at

[17] A. E. Glock, "Warfare in Mari and Early Israel." Unpublished Ph.D. dissertation, University of Michigan (1968), p. 46. The writer is especially indebted to Professor Glock for providing access to this important study. See now F. Charles Fensham, in *Near Eastern Studies,* ed. Hans Goedicke (Johns Hopkins University Press, 1971), pp. 121–35.

[18] See now Jack M. Sasson, *The Military Establishment at Mari,* Rome: Pontifical Biblical Institute, 1969. This work is restricted to description of the Mari institutions and thus needs to be supplemented by such works as those of Glock (see fn. 17 above) and Miller (see fn. 20 below).

[19] Glock, "Warfare," p. 46.

[20] Patrick D. Miller, Jr., "Holy War and Cosmic War in Early Israel." Unpublished doctoral thesis, Harvard University (1963), pp. 32–34.

the enlistment of Samson in 15:18–19. The same configuration occurs with the narrative theme of wilderness-wandering as divine discipline in the famous Massah-Meribah incident as recounted in Exod 17:1–7.

Within Israel the cultic appropriation of the idea of Yahweh's cessation of warfare with Canaan (cf. 2:1–5) seems to have cleared the way for the development of *tebibtum* language in connection with the sabbatical year. However this may be, the military significance of ritual washings enjoyed a new heyday and its fullest elaboration in the thinking of apocalyptic sectarians of the intertestamental period (the Manual of Discipline and War Scroll found in Qumran Cave 1). That discipline climaxed a long history.

At Mari there are indications that the muster and its attendant ceremonies had been more than a little distasteful to those being thus enrolled. By contrast, early Israel seems to have tried to rely on much less sophisticated arrangements for fielding a fighting force. But with appropriate restraints, the Mari muster provides a jagged "life setting" for materials such as Deborah's Song (ch. 5) and the reduction of Gideon's outsized army (7:2–7).

Many other entries in old Israel's military lexicon find clarification in Mari usage and will be appropriately noted. One especially significant semantic development involves the word *'alāpīm,* not always "thousands" but very often "contingents" (seldom of more than a dozen men each!)[21]; see NOTE on 1:4. Needless to say, the element of exaggeration in OT accounts of warfare will be sizably diminished, and many stories will be brought into quite credible perspective, together with the assertion that victory with the odds against Israel meant that Yahweh fought for Israel!

Yet a third treasure-trove of data pertinent to the translation and interpretation of Israel's earliest traditionary materials is the tablets from Late Bronze Age Ugarit (Ras Shamra on the Syrian coast), steadily ac-

---

21 Mendenhall, JBL 77 (1958), 52–66. Referring to the situation in the Amarna period, cf. Campbell:

City-states often joined forces in repelling an enemy, in a way comparable to many biblical instances (Gen xiv, Josh x, etc.). It is interesting to note that many of the threats to established princes call forth letters to the court requesting forces to help in repelling the enemy. Often such a request is for less than 100 men . . . and only on one occasion (132:56 where the reading is uncertain and the intent perhaps one of exaggeration) does the number exceed 400. It is true that the major efficacy of such a troop movement would be to show that the king supported a certain vassal, but still these numbers hint at the nature of the warfare which was going on. The size of the punitive forces wanted also hints at the population density. Only at Byblos do the numbers exceed 200; the point is that the population in Palestine, and especially in the hill country, must have been very small. One estimate suggests 200,000 for all of Palestine, about 20,000 to 25,000 for the wooded central hill country.

Edward F. Campbell, Jr., BA 23 (1960), 21, reprinted in *The Biblical Archaeologist Reader 3* (Garden City, N.Y.: Doubleday, 1970), p. 74.

cumulating since the first spectacular discoveries in 1929 (Map 1). These materials have yielded a flood of information for social and economic structures—an added bonus to the contribution of three great Canaanite religious epics. Especially significant for elucidation of the Book of Judges is the access now gained to the pre-Yahwist history of poetic idiom, mythological imagery, and rhetoric in Canaan itself. See especially the beginning of the Song of Deborah (5:4–5), which harks back to the original arrival of the Yahweh-army in Canaan. What is presupposed there is that Yahweh has already defeated the hosts of Egypt and thus legitimated his claim to kingship in Israel. Moreover, Israelites have already built his movable palace, the venerable Tabernacle. These are the two great organizing themes — mighty victory and splendid new abode — in the mythological recounting of Baal's victory in Canaan. The difference is that Yahweh's victories are historical; they are the kind of victories that liberate and order the well-being of his people.

RELIGION AND LIFE

What about religion in the period of the judges?

In the Book of Judges the most frequent and sustained interest in what might be considered the specifically religious lessons of Israel's life under the judges is found in the connectives between stories, the "pragmatic formula," to be discussed below (p. 35). Here, however, we are concerned with the contents of the stories themselves, where we have the most direct witness to life in the period of the judges. The "religious" data are meager: two prophets (one of them a woman), three angels, two Levites, numerous examples of oracular inquiry, three cases of divination (two by Gideon, the other by the God of Gideon), a handful of references to religious assemblies at one or another of many sanctuaries (about evenly distributed between "legitimate" and "questionable" in the opinion of the ancient narrators). In general, the picture is one of old Canaanite religious structures and usage in continued tension with the Yahweh monotheism, as the new settlers and converts found themselves alternately repelled by certain aspects of Canaanite culture and enticed by others.

Following directly upon the creative period in Israel's life, that is, the career of Moses and the consolidation of rapidly expanding tribal relationships under Joshua, the judges stories belong to the early phase of the adaptive period in the nation's life, the climax of which was the transition to centralized monarchies: ultimately "Israel" in the north and "Judah" in the south.[22] See Map 2.

---

[22] The period of the divided monarchy (c. 921–721), together with Judah's independent survival until 587, is the traditional period during which such material as the Book of

As will be clear to readers who study the judges stories, the historian's task is enormously complicated in the Book of Judges by the sense of humor in the very narratives which witness to religious organization in the period. Yet there can be no doubt that the organization of Israel was, in this period, essentially religious. Striking parallels have been noted between the twelve-tribe structure and other religiously related tribal groups, known best from the classical world. There the indigenous label was the Greek word *amphictyony*, "those who dwell around"; the term was first used in biblical studies as a cautious sociological analogy.[23]

There is evidence that twelve tribes formed an amphictyonic unit in many semitic cultures. Twelve Aramaean tribes arose from the twelve sons born to Abraham's brother Nahor (Gen 22:20–24), and twelve Ishmaelite tribes from Abraham's outcast son Ishmael (Gen 25:13–16). The five Edomite tribes from the sons of Esau (Gen 36:9–14) joined the seven Horite tribes in the land of Seir (Gen 36:20–28) where Esau settled away from his brother Jacob in Canaan. The twelve tribes of Israel are descendants of Jacob's twelve sons (Gen 35:22–26). See the indicated chapters, with NOTES and COMMENTS, in Speiser, AB, vol. 1, 1964.

The appeal to the ancient amphictyonies to provide a theoretical base for the historical reconstruction of this obscure period has gained wide acceptance through the brilliant analysis of Israel's twelve-tribe organization by Martin Noth.[24] Noth argued that the twelve-tribe organization was held together by an essentially religious bond and that the separate tribes were largely unrelated and had, for the most part, separate histories prior to the great covenantal assembly described in Josh 24. The result, for historical understanding, was a diffusion of traditionary claims which made it quite impossible to comprehend Israel's claims and memories about Moses and the still earlier period of the ancestors, that is, the traditions taken up in Gen 12–50.[25] While the "religious league" as a theoretical construct has been of enormous heuristic value to scholars, the word "amphictyony" has attained such currency in its new setting that it must be clearly delimited by the biblical commentator.[26] The term is explained by the institution of

---

Judges received its definitive form. For the necessity of some such periodization, and for the terminology adopted here, see Mendenhall, "Biblical History in Transition," in *The Bible and the Ancient Near East*, ed. G. Ernest Wright (Garden City, N.Y.: Doubleday, 1961), pp. 42–45.

23 See Weber, *Ancient Judaism*, p. 90.

24 Martin Noth, *Das System der zwölf Stämme Israels*, Stuttgart: W. Kohlhammer, 1930. This pivotal work, which remains untranslated, is the basis for Noth's later work, *The History of Israel*, tr. Peter R. Ackroyd, New York: Harper, 1960.

25 John Bright, *Early Israel in Recent History Writing*, London: SCM Press, 1956, provides a vigorous critique of the methods employed by Noth. Bright's subsequent work, *A History of Israel*, 2d ed., Philadelphia: Westminster, 1972, has become the standard reference in English.

26 See now George W. Anderson, "Israel: Amphictyony: *'AM; ḴĀHĀL; 'ĒDĀH,*" in *Translating and Understanding the Old Testament*, pp. 135–51.

one central religious sanctuary, the prime focus of religious loyalties of each of the member tribes, who assume rotating responsibility for the up-keep of the sanctuary one month in the year. The central sanctuary does not, of course, preclude the use of other, local, shrines; it properly pre-supposes them.

Historians find a variety of factors leading to the emergence of the Greek amphictyonies. The Calaurian League, a sacral union of maritime states on the eastern Greek coast, met at the temple of Poseidon at Calauria on the Argive coast. "But in historic times the commerce which gave rise to this league was nothing but a memory."[27]

The best known amphictyony originally had its religious center at Anthela, a border town. Only secondarily did Anthela come to share its prestige and role with the great Apollo sanctuary at Delphi, from the mid-sixth century on. The nucleus of this great amphictyony — which endured as a wide-ranging religious organization for centuries after new political configurations developed — was the older Thessalian League of northern Greece. The Thessalian League was fully operative by the beginning of the seventh century. It began roughly around the time of the Dorian inva-sion, therefore overlapping with the last judges of Israel. Scholars are ex-tremely hard put, however, to find a specifically religious binder for the early Thessalian League; it was comprised of newcomers to northern Greece who resisted cultural assimilation and attained political and eco-nomic domination as far south as the Demeter temple at Anthela.

One effect of the Thessalian League was the formation—under the military pressure of Thebes—of the rival Boeotian League, in full devel-opment by the mid-sixth century. Unlike the Thessalian, it had been pre-ceded by a sacral union for which delegates from all over Boeotia at-tended annually the festival of Pamboeotia at the temple of Athena Itonia near Corona.

It is the early Thessalian League, rather than its successor, the great Delphi amphictyony, that is more nearly contemporary with and more closely comparable to premonarchical Israel. The cities of Thessaly were grouped in four *tetrades,* "cantons," each of which had a tetrarch holding office, probably, for life. While Israel shows no functionary comparable to the tetrarch, the founder of the Thessalian League, Scopus, had, according to the tradition, organized the recruitment of the federal army: a quota of soldiers from each large estate. Compare the Song of Deborah and the en-listment problem in stories about Gideon, Jephthah, and Samson.

The chief official of the Thessalian League was the *tagus,* who ap-parently functioned only in emergencies, probably for the duration of the

[27] Max Cary, "Northern and Central Greece," in *The Cambridge Ancient History,* III, eds. J. B. Bury, S. A. Cook, F. E. Adcock (New York: Macmillan, 1925), 610.

crisis which singled him out.[28] There is evidence of a federal assembly for the election of the tagus.

These federal institutions in northern Greece originated as a check against city rivalries and as a facility for commerce as well as warfare. The early Thessalian League originated and endured for primarily military purposes. With this background Thessaly came to dominate the later Delphi Amphictyonic League from the sixth century on, when the amphictyonic structure was becoming more and more restricted in its influence to the care of festivals and the traditions of the liberated sanctuaries.

This sketch of the emergence of the Thessalian League and its successor, the great amphictyony will make it clear that to speak of an "Israelite amphictyony" in the twelfth to eleventh centuries is not at all far-fetched, but too often imprecise.[29]

In Canaan and Transjordan, archaeology now requires some explanation for a striking series of outlying but elaborate cultic places belonging to the Middle Bronze and early Late Bronze periods.[30] They are plausibly interpreted as pre-Yahwist league-centers.

A full thousand years before the establishment of Israel in Canaan or the emergence of the Thessalian League in northern Greece, the Ur III empire encompassed a twelve-part religious association of cities owing political allegiance to Ur and religious loyalty (out of a long prior commitment) to the temples at Nippur.[31]

Whether or not all these configurations deserve the label "amphictyony" is perhaps merely academic. The significant fact is that they represent similar responses to fluctuating political realities, most often connected with population movements, first discernible in one of the great cradles of civilization and then here and there to the west in later centuries.[32] Such

[28] Cary, pp. 601–2.

[29] Smend's study, *Yahweh War and Tribal Confederation*, has brought a certain corrective, arguing for an early polarity with "Rachel-tribes" as carriers of a Yahweh War tradition and "Leah-tribes" as contributors of the amphictyonic element. Of the latter, however, he can speak only provisionally, as his own amphictyonic concept is almost totally dependent upon usage among biblical scholars. It needs, in turn, a corrective that can only be supplied from the Thessalian forerunner of the Greek amphictyony.

[30] E. F. Campbell, Jr., and G. Ernest Wright, BA 32 (1969), 104–16. They discuss mainly Shechem and Amman. We should probably add Nahariya and Deir 'Alla. See now Wright's "The Significance of Ai in the Third Millennium B.C.," in *Archäologie und altes Testament, Festschrift für Kurt Galling*, eds. Arnulf Kuschke and Ernst Kutsch (Tübingen: J. C. B. Mohr, 1970), esp. pp. 313–19.

[31] William W. Hallo, *Journal of Cuneiform Studies* 14 (1960), 88–114.

[32] Harry Meyer Orlinsky has rightly objected to oversimplifications in comparison of Israel and the amphictyonies, in an essay in *Studies in Honor of Abraham A. Neuman*, ed. Meir Ben-Horin et al. (Leiden: Brill, 1962), pp. 375–87. But he has not demonstrated the analogical inadequacy of the Delphi amphictyony, especially its original Thessalian phase. The latter also goes unrecognized in the excellent study by Anderson in *Translating and Understanding the Old Testament*, pp. 135–51. With specific reference to the evidence

patterns enable the student of ancient history to better comprehend the well nigh complete disappearance of Early Bronze Age traditions from Canaan.[33] Israelite history begins with the patriarchs, originally at home in Middle Bronze Age Mesopotamia.

Attention to the Thessalian predecessor of the Delphi amphictyony, with its predominantly secular interest in control of the Anthela sanctuary, allows for more precision in the search for early Israel's central sanctuary. Thus it is possible to account, roughly to be sure, for the shifting focus of early Israelite traditions: from Gilgal in the first half of the Book of Joshua to the Shechem assembly in Josh 24. The Yahweh sanctuary at Shechem (Map 2, C-3) "was visited and used in common by the whole federation of Israelite tribes, and may perhaps have been their only sanctuary in Palestine."[34] Within the Book of Judges, however, the only likely candidates for the role of central sanctuary are Bethel and Shiloh. For the latter, see 18:31 and 21:12, 15–21. Bethel is clearly being devalued in 2:1–5 and only momentarily legitimated in ch. 20 at the expense of Mizpah. The legitimation is made explicit by the comment that, when the Israelites at last sought oracular guidance at Bethel, "the Ark of God's Covenant was there, at that time" (Judg 20:27). In other words, Israel's earliest central sanctuary was wherever the portable Ark was. The Ark had for years moved back and forth from the field to the throne room of the Tabernacle, Yahweh's less portable palace.

Elsewhere the Ark of the Covenant is regularly associated with Shiloh (Map 2), where a tent sheltered it and from which it goes forth at the head of Israel's forces late in the premonarchical period (I Sam 4–6). By that time it was also traditional for the judge (Samuel) to make an annual circuit of key Yahwist sanctuaries "Bethel, Gilgal, and Mizpah," according to I Sam 7:16, RSV. It is safe to assume that the holy Ark (from the earliest period the place of highest legitimacy for Yahwist oracular inquiry and amphictyonic assembly) accompanied the judge, successor to Moses, whose decision making was supposed to be articulated before the box that contained the constitution.

Here it is worth noting that both of the concluding segments of Judges (Micah and the migration of Dan in chs. 17–18, and the Gibeah outrage and its sequel in chs. 19–21) focus on the problem of reliable sanctuar-

---

of the Book of Judges, Anderson writes: "The indications are not so much of centralization and unity as of the fragments of a lost unity surviving as an ideal. . . . It seems natural, therefore, to look for the establishment of this unity, not in the emergence of an amphictyony on Canaanite soil in the wake of invasion, but rather, where so much of ancient Israelite tradition would lead us to expect to find it, in the period before the settlement, and, more specifically, in the establishment of the Sinai covenant between Yahweh and the Israelite tribes" (p. 149).

[33] See Mendenhall, in *The Bible and the Ancient Near East*, pp. 38 ff.

[34] M. Noth, *Das System*, p. 65 f.

ies and legitimate oracular inquiry. Neither set of narratives mentions a judge. The reason for this failure to say anything about judges is that by the mid-eleventh century they were probably quite ineffective and increasingly corrupt (see Eli and sons at the outset of Samuel's story).

If the comparison drawn between the establishment of Israel and the emergence of the Thessalian League is a valid one, then the essential difference between the two must be underscored: while the Thessalians celebrated no common cultic tradition to hold them together and tell them who they were, the Israelites celebrated the kingship of Yahweh and attempted to make that a political fact.

THE CHRONOLOGICAL PROBLEM

Thus far it has been assumed that no one would challenge the relegation of most of the judges to the twelfth and eleventh centuries, the era preceding Saul's rise to leadership about 1020 B.C.E. But that period is far too brief to accommodate all the chronological data of the Book of Judges, particularly if it is somehow to harmonize with I Kings 6:1, where Solomon in the fourth year of his reign (c. 957) began the construction of the Temple. That was "in the four hundred and eightieth year" (I Kings 6:1) after the Exodus. It should be obvious from the frequency of round numbers, especially "twenty" and "forty," that the problem of harmonization is more an ancient one than a modern one. That is, the available archives were incomplete when the redactor worked the round numbers into the Book of Judges.

Of the numerous solutions proposed, the most plausible is one which simply adds together the first 4 years of Solomon's rule, the 42 regnal years of Saul and David, the 136 years from Tola to Eli, the 200 years of peace under the saviors, the 53 years of oppression, and the 45 years implied in Josh 14:1. The total is 480.[35] The recognition that the fully developed chronological scheme involves the emergency use of round numbers supports the attribution of this scheme to the first full Deuteronomic edition[36] (see below, pp 34–35).

The correct historical sequence of the judges (see Chronology) is a more elusive problem. We have tried to do justice to the archaeological data, chiefly from Shechem and Taanach (Map 4), looking for Gideon in the first half of the twelfth century (see COMMENT on Sec. XX) and Deborah in the third quarter of that century (see COMMENT on Sec. IX).

[35] W. Richter, *Retterbuches*, pp. 132–40.
[36] *Retterbuches*. See further our discussion of "The Growth of the Book of Judges," in the Introduction.

HEAVEN AND EARTH: YAHWEH'S KINGDOM

It is easier to say what early Israel was not than to say what it was. That it was not merely another amphictyony has become certain from the discovery of an extremely close analogical relationship between international legal forms (and practice) and the patterns of Israel's own earliest organization. Over the past twenty years the intense critical pursuit of the relationship between the treaty forms (especially those of the great Hittite kings in the Late Bronze Age) and Israel's early narrative forms[37] has shown that the Sinai covenant (and the Shechem sequel at the conclusion of the "conquest" in Josh 24) casts Yahweh in the role of Suzerain, Great King, King of kings, so that every man confessing faith in Yahweh becomes thereby a citizen of Israel and one of Yahweh's freed kings. In other words, Israel is the nucleus of the earthly half of the kingdom of Yahweh. The apodictic law, such as the Ten Commandments, provided legal policy for the realm, while the elements of casuistic law were brought together from all over the Near East and given Israelite formulation as descriptive of legal practice within the realm where Yahweh was confessed as King. Note the tenacious conservatism of the apodictic generalities, whereas the case law was periodically updated in lagging adjustment to social change.

One regularly recurring element in the Suzerain's treaty was a section listing blessings to be attendant upon the faithful vassal, and curses (usually considerably longer) which the gods as witnesses to the treaty are to put into effect in the event of rebellion. How the biblical curses were to be administered, given Israel's monotheistic commitment, is not entirely clear. Jotham's fable, however, maintains that the traitors will destroy each other (9:15–20).

For the most part the covenant form lies in the background of the Book of Judges. On the other hand, treaty terminology is very much in the foreground. The Heb. *ṭōb,* generally "good," is often precisely the "amity" that belongs to the faithful relationship that obtains between Suzerain and vassal, or between fellow vassals.[38] The Heb. *yāda',* lit. "he knew," in

---

[37] *Covenant: The History of a Biblical Idea,* Johns Hopkins University Press, 1969. This pulls together the impact of a mass of studies which followed from George E. Mendenhall's epoch-making essays, "Ancient Oriental and Biblical Law," and "Covenant Forms in Israelite Tradition," BA 17 (1954), 26–46 and 50–76; reprinted together as *Law and Covenant in Israel and the Ancient Near East,* Pittsburgh: The Biblical Colloquium, 1955, and again, separately, with original titles in *The Biblical Archaeologist Reader 3.* See also Albert E. Glock, "Early Israel as the Kingdom of Yahweh," *Concordia Theological Monthly* 41 (1970), 558–605, and esp. the introductory chapter of *TenGen.*

[38] Hillers, BASOR 176 (December 1964), 46–47.

covenantal contexts denotes the fact of political recognition, "to acknowledge another" as Suzerain or as vassal.[39] Treaty peers are "brothers."
Even the Heb. *'āhab,* "he loved," has its frequent equivalent in the
treaties, describing the relation that exists between treaty partners.[40] This
language is especially important in the material relating to Deborah early
in the book and Samson toward the close of it. The verb *nāqam,* in the
Hebrew Bible as in the Amarna letters, stands for the Suzerain's exercise
of his executive prerogatives in the world—vindication, not "vengeance."[41]
The result of such vindication, in Israel as at Amarna, was deliverance. All
this casts an entirely new light upon the tragic end of Samson's life, where
the Philistines have unwittingly submitted themselves to Yahweh's judge,
and Samson prays to Yahweh for deliverance. From that point on to the
end of the book, stories are assembled in which there is no judge in Israel,
thus driving home the point that Israel had no properly acknowledged king.

There is, in short, a particular judicial provision which is assumed from
start to finish in the stories of the Book of Judges, including by implication
the minor judges. According to tradition the system had its roots in the organizational recommendation of Jethro, Moses' Midianite father-in-law
(Exod 18:13–27). When Joshua died leaving no designated successor to
the highest administrative office in the Yahweh Kingdom, resort was made
to popular election, which had somehow to be "ratified" by successful performance, often military in character and, when military, always defensive throughout the judges period. For example, Gideon is represented as
going far beyond his orders in ch. 8, and for strictly personal reasons.
Gideon neither truly "judged" nor "saved," except unwittingly, in the view
of the ancient traditionists.

The prime symbol of Yahweh's participation in the raising up of the
judge is "the Yahweh spirit." This spirit "comes upon" Othniel (3:10)
and Jephthah (11:29), begins "to prod" Samson (13:25) and regularly
strengthens him in the nick of time (14:6, 19; 15:14), thus saving him for
the office of judge (15:20). On one occasion, it was recalled, this spirit so
completely took charge of Gideon that the latter mobilized far more fighting men than were really needed (6:34), a rare achievement in the period. In all these contexts, as repeatedly outside the Book of Judges, the
Yahweh spirit is an abstraction referring to a quality or force which can
infiltrate or be absorbed into human beings and exert great power. It is, in
other words, the "Yahwistic spirit" (see NOTE on 3:10). The same narrative contexts make it clear that the presence of the Yahweh spirit does

39 Herbert B. Huffmon, BASOR 181 (February 1966), 31–37; H. B. Huffmon and
Simon B. Parker, BASOR 184 (December 1966), 36–38.
40 William L. Moran, CBQ 25 (1963), 77–87.
41 Mendenhall, *The Wittenberg Bulletin* 45 (1948), 37–42; *TenGen,* pp. 69–104.

not make the man an automaton; the Yahweh spirit is one of many components in the personality.

None of these considerations provides much support for the idea, widely popularized in recent years, that the savior judges were charismatic men and therefore do not reflect a publicly recognized office, in contrast to the minor judges listed in 10:1–5 and 12:7–15. The term "charisma" has entered upon a crisis so far as its use in sociological description is concerned, thanks mainly to its appropriation by the modern communications industry. It is now urged by prominent scholars that "we cannot separate the charismatic and the merely institutional functions in the amphictyony all too sharply from one another."[42] From the sociological perspective one should now say that the heroes of the Book of Judges were remembered for having a variety of distinctive qualities and abilities, so that the influence of the Yahweh spirit in stories about them is strictly subordinate to the idea of Yahweh's will for the salvation of Israel. They illustrate various aspects of a certain "office charisma"[43] in sociological usage.

While the Yahweh spirit is not personified in the Book of Judges, angels are present, though their appearances are few. As functionaries of the heavenly court (2:1–5), they participate on earth in the enlistment or promise of a judge (Gideon in ch. 6 and Samson in ch. 13).[44] For it is Yahweh who raises up the judge, even when the social machinery for the process breaks down.

Appropriate social machinery for the election of a judge existed in the form of popular tribal assemblies or their gathered representatives. Neither the judge nor the assembly had the authority to declare war; that remained the divine Sovereign's prerogative. Yahweh's will in the matter was to be sought by the judge in some divinatory manner.

With the passing of time and the rapid expansion of territory to be administered as Israelite land, a crisis developed which was compounded by institutional inertia on the one hand, and rising popular longing for the amenities of a culture once repudiated on the other. The federation's leaders were immobilized, to judge from the kinds of narratives in chs. 17–21. As a result the Philistines moved into the breach, nearly putting an end to the Israel experiment. Tragedy was averted only by the media-

---

42 Rolf Rendtorff, *Journal for Theology and the Church* 4 (1967), 31.

43 The term is Weber's. See *Ancient Judaism*, p. 284, where, commenting on the state of affairs between Jeremiah and contemporary priests, Weber writes: "the bearer of personal charisma refused to recognize office charisma if the priestly teacher is unworthy." Weber used many modifiers — "hereditary charisma," "liberal charismatic artisans," "mere charismatic war leaders," "charismatic rulers" — in an effort at precision, which is often obscured by an artificial distinction between the charismatic and the institutional.

44 The *mal'ak yhwh* who is mentioned in 4:8–9 (LXX) and 5:23 probably belongs to another category altogether; see NOTES on those chapters. For the explanation of *mal'ak* as related, in the earliest period, to Yahweh's self-manifestation for executive action, see *TenGen*, pp. 60–61.

tion of Samuel who, as judge, gave his personal sanction and immense prestige to the movement for inauguration of life-term monarchy. There would now, however, be a division of the old administrative responsibility, with the king exercising judicial and military power, and the prophet in charge of oracular duties, probably by Samuel's design after he saw the corruption of the high judicial office when it became briefly hereditary in the hands of his own sons. Thereafter the kings of Israel and Judah would not be able to wage war without at least going through the motions of consulting Yahweh for authorization.

Prophecy at last came to flourish politically in Israel and Judah, as indeed it had a millennium earlier at Mari, with the significant difference that it was now subordinate to the heritage of Yahweh's kingship, deeply rooted in the two centuries "when the judges judged." This is the reason that prophecy became such a hard way to make an honest living in Israel and Judah. Amos, for example, remembers the period immediately following Moses as a time when Yahweh made "some of your sons prophets and some of your young men Nazirites" (Amos 2:11). For the military discipline accepted by the Nazarite, see Samson (chs. 13–16).

According to Deut 32:8–9—one of the archaic poems of the Pentateuch —responsibility for the nations had been delegated to various members of the heavenly court; Yahweh had as his own possession the Israelites whom he long ago found all unassisted in the howling wilderness.[45] There can no longer be any doubt that early Israel made a sharp and deliberate, revolutionary break with the political and religious past. "Israel" was a unique and novel religious entity, a bold political experiment, and was evaluated as such by those who compiled her history. For they evaluated the history of the covenant people in the light of the Suzerain's lawsuit.

The Suzerain's lawsuit is most familiar from the prophetic books of the eighth century and later, when the covenant was something of a hallowed memory but apparently not much more than that. The roots of the lawsuit (Heb. *rīb*) have been traced into the same great second-millennium chancelleries that used the suzerainty treaty form. In the absence of international courts the *rīb* was a declaration that a state of war exists, un-

---

45 In this passage, the deity who assigns the nations to the various "sons of God" (*benē 'El*) is called Elyon. In a private communication, D. N. Freedman has followed up the view of Eissfeldt (*Journal of Semitic Studies* 1 [1956], 25–37), understanding Elyon here as the epithet of El rather than Yahweh (cf. Gen 14:19, 20, 22). He suggests that "the passage reflects the original suzerainty of El stemming from patriarchal times, with Yahweh's original role as guardian of Israel emerging from relative obscurity as one of El's subordinates." See Frank Moore Cross, Jr., *Harvard Theological Review* 55 (1962), 255–59. Freedman continues: "Deut 32:8 may reflect a non-Mosaic attempt to reconcile the conflicting claims of El and Yahweh followers (reflected in the bloody episode of the Golden Calf where the Calf surely reflects El worship as against the Yahweh faith introduced by Moses). I would agree in any case that Deut 32:8–9 is very archaic, perhaps one of the most archaic pieces of theology in the post-Patriarchal period."

less the charge is refuted. There is no reason why, a priori, the covenant, and lawsuit may not be of equal antiquity, that is, Mosaic (cf. the Massah-Meribah incident in Exod 17 and the entire depiction of Moses as the bearer of Yahweh's indictment against Pharaoh). The *rīb* language is played upon in the Gideon narratives, where we meet some of the most archaic vocabulary in the Book of Judges; the story of Gideon's call swarms with allusions to Exod 3–4. Jotham in ch. 9 wields the Suzerain's lawsuit in something more than "domestic" matters. Jephthah dispatches the Great King's justification with admirable restraint and unassailable Yahweh-kingdom logic, and only then does he take to the field. His story stands in the middle of the minor judges list among the highly successful if otherwise little known covenant administrators.

Thus we have come full circle to the question initially posed by the conclusions of an earlier generation: What is the character and sacral significance of warfare in Israel's earliest traditions? It goes without saying that the obligation to bear arms, at the call of the Suzerain, was a vassal's standing duty. Yet the pioneering efforts to delineate old Israel's ideology of Holy War have generally localized that ideology in the period of the judges and interpreted the Holy War as primarily or purely a defensive war.[46] Such conclusions are based, however, on a partial reading of the evidence. The defensive war theory is a corollary of the critical devaluation of the Book of Joshua in favor of Judg 1, and it begs the question of the formal integrity of the biblical books in their final edition.[47]

The holy war par excellence was the one at the Reed Sea in which Yahweh and his heavenly army defeated the hosts of Egypt (Israelites did no fighting) and thus laid the basis (Exod 1–15) for Israel's acknowledgment of his total sovereignty (Exod 18–24). So holy was that one "war" that it provided the organizing principle for the first half of Gideon's story (6:11 – 7:22), where Yahweh did it again. Note that Israelites did no fighting until Gideon took matters into his own hands and went far beyond his orders (7:23 – 8:21). In other words, times had changed radically since the days when "Israel" marched away from Sinai[48] organized as the Yahweh army and bent on reclaiming Yahweh's ancient Canaanite patrimony.[49] Throughout the second millennium the Sinai

---

[46] See esp. Gerhard von Rad, *Der Heilige Krieg*, Zurich: Zwingli Verlag, 1951, and the refinement of the concept by Norbert Lohfink, *Biblica* 41 (1960), 105–34.

[47] See now Smend, *Yahweh War*, which traces the tradition of the Yahweh War through the agency of the "Rachel-tribes" to the figure of Moses.

[48] Yahweh "created Sinai as his sanctuary," according to Ps 68:18, one of the most ancient and archaic songs of the Yahweh wars. For the translation, see Mitchell Dahood, *Psalms II, 51–100*, AB, vol. 17 (1968), and third NOTE, ad loc.

[49] On the linguistic evidence for the pre-Sinaitic origins of the divine name, and a prior cultic unity, "Israel," definitively reconstituted during the career of Moses, see Cross, *Harvard Theological Review* 55 (1962), 255–59.

Peninsula had remained a cultural backwater, where the differentiation of Yahweh worship out of a parent El religion could develop untouched by the inroads in Canaan of the Amorite Baal-Hadad, the vigorous young fertility god and the warrior in the Ugaritic texts.[50]

Thus tradition regarded the wars of Joshua's days as the holiest of all the ones that Israelites actually fought, and it devoted one whole chapter to a trifling violation of the *herem* (the sin of Achan in Josh 7) so that we would not miss the point. The results were at last, however, so ambiguous that an angel arrived at the beginning of Judg 2 to announce that Yahweh will no longer participate in expansionist battles against the Canaanites. The wars of the judges are indeed defensive, but they are not primarily holy.

With the tenth-century burgeoning of the Jerusalem administration the transition becomes nearly complete. The anonymous Court Historian who compiled II Sam 9–20, had to use the language of indirection, but he clearly depicts David as regularly going through the holy motions, in preparation for war. David, however, failed to reckon with the proper piety of his soldiers, among them Uriah the Hittite. All of which was to say that David's wars were the most successful ones to date, but the most secular, and therefore the least holy. They provided the Chronicler with a plausible rationale for David's lack of success in building the great Yahweh Temple (I Chron 22:8). Somewhere in the middle, between the stylized depiction of Joshua's success and the candid portrayal of David's success, we are to apprehend the judges stories as stemming from the daily reality of ancient Israel's struggle for survival in Canaan—a struggle for survival as Yahweh's very real historical kingdom.

THE GROWTH OF THE BOOK OF JUDGES

The structure of the Book of Judges is primitive by modern literary standards; blocks of successive editorial remodeling are piled around the edges of the nuclear stories. The result is that old Israel's narrative art survives in its purest form in the Book of Judges, where theological updating across the centuries was confined almost exclusively to the connectives between units; rarely did it invade their essential contents. This means that the stories stemming from the early days were fixed in all their essentials before they were ever employed in telling the authoritative story of Israel's life in Canaan. The growth of the Book of Judges may be compactly summarized in the following Schematic Outline.

[50] This is the thesis of Ulf Oldenburg, *The Conflict Between El and Ba'al in Canaanite Religion*, Leiden: Brill, 1969, as adapted by Richard L. Strait in an unpublished seminar paper, McCormick Theological Seminary, 1970.

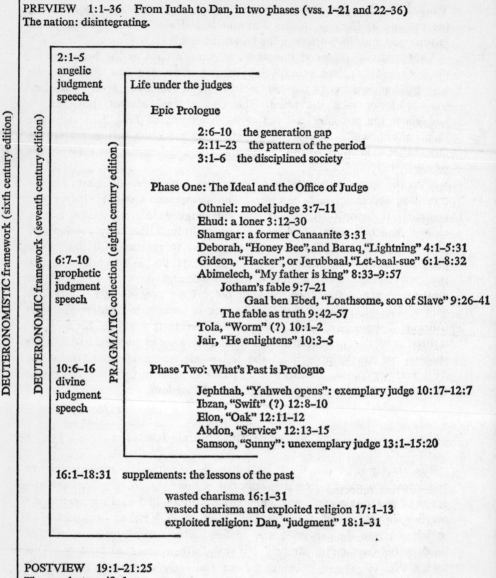

PREVIEW   1:1–36   From Judah to Dan, in two phases (vss. 1–21 and 22–36)
The nation: disintegrating.

2:1–5
angelic
judgment
speech

DEUTERONOMISTIC framework (sixth century edition)

DEUTERONOMIC framework (seventh century edition)

PRAGMATIC collection (eighth century edition)

Life under the judges

Epic Prologue

2:6–10   the generation gap
2:11–23   the pattern of the period
3:1–6   the disciplined society

Phase One: The Ideal and the Office of Judge

Othniel: model judge 3:7–11
Ehud: a loner 3:12–30
Shamgar: a former Canaanite 3:31
Deborah, "Honey Bee", and Baraq,"Lightning" 4:1–5:31
Gideon, "Hacker", or Jerubbaal,"Let-baal-sue" 6:1–8:32
Abimelech, "My father is king" 8:33–9:57
   Jotham's fable 9:7–21
      Gaal ben Ebed, "Loathsome, son of Slave" 9:26–41
   The fable as truth 9:42–57
Tola, "Worm" (?) 10:1–2
Jair, "He enlightens" 10:3–5

6:7–10
prophetic
judgment
speech

Phase Two: What's Past is Prologue

Jephthah, "Yahweh opens": exemplary judge 10:17–12:7
Ibzan, "Swift" (?) 12:8–10
Elon, "Oak" 12:11–12
Abdon, "Service" 12:13–15
Samson, "Sunny": unexemplary judge 13:1–15:20

10:6–16
divine
judgment
speech

16:1–18:31   supplements: the lessons of the past

wasted charisma 16:1–31
wasted charisma and exploited religion 17:1–13
exploited religion: Dan, "judgment" 18:1–31

POSTVIEW   19:1–21:25
The people: reunified

In other words, we recognize four main stages: (1) composition of individual narrative units and the formation of early Israelite epic, (2) a didactic collection of such stories (the pragmatic edition) completed by the eighth century, (3) incorporation of the collection in a seventh-century Deuteronomic historical work (the bulk of Deuteronomy through II Kings), (4) a sixth century updating to produce the final or Deuteronomistic edition of the same books.

Let us consider first the unredacted stories. To what category shall such stories be assigned? Perhaps the most appropriate label, if applied with due caution, is "historical romance." Such stories are much better known from the classical world, where they fall regularly into one of two categories: ideal or comic.[51] The ideal genre presents the story of an exemplary figure in popular language for popular edification and delight. By contrast the comic genre was always a much more sophisticated one intended for more discriminating attention.

The Book of Job presents a clear canonical illustration of the same two types. The prose story of Job (chs. 1–2 and 42:7–17, AB, vol. 15, 3d ed., 1973) is in the ideal genre — a popular story of one who was the ideal patriarchal image. But the poet in the author of Job has broken the old story open and turned his book into an example of the comic genre,[52] for in the poetry Job is anything but the model of endurance who by his faithfulness enables Yahweh to win a wager. Rather, in the poetry Job is a most self-righteous man who talks himself into a theological stalemate. He successfully defends the abstraction "God" ($^{e}l\bar{o}^{a}h$) against all opposition, and in the process persuades himself that Yahweh (as he momentarily blurts out in 12:7–10) is wrong about his servant Job. Job goes on, however, to be so successful against the false defenders of God that he becomes a false accuser, until at last the voice from the whirlwind silences him, using the same "argument from nature" as did Job in 12:7–10. Job at last gets the message, intercedes for his comforters, and all of them are given life. In other words, the poet has exegeted the venerable story of Job, no doubt for the benefit of hard-pressed wise men, while at the same time protecting the old story from a gross misunderstanding. He successfully counters any superficial interpretation of the story as meaning that "piety pays."

The process reflected in the growth of the Book of Job is similar to that of the Book of Judges. Editors of both these stories were confronted by narrative tradition that was already fixed and inviolable in all essentials. A significant difference from Job is that none of the judges (with the possible exception of Othniel in 3:7–11) is presented as an ideal figure. They are clearly presented as historical leaders whose varying Yahwistic effectiveness is evaluated in their stories.

Who produced these stories? The question has received little systematic attention by critical scholars, due to the sheer paucity of evidence which

[51] See Ben Edwin Perry, *The Ancient Romances,* University of California Press, 1967.

[52] Christopher Fry has described Job as "the great reservoir of comedy." See "Comedy," in *The New Orpheus,* ed. Nathan A. Scott, Jr. (New York: Sheed and Ward, 1964), p. 288.

might relate to one or another of the three great literary circles in ancient Israel: the priesthood, the prophetic guilds, and the teachers (that is, the "wise men," who comprised a sort of civil service including the training of young administrative personnel). These circles, their range of interests, prerogatives, and perspectives, are known well enough to be noted for their lack of influence in the formation of nuclear narratives in Judges, for these narratives are folkloric in nature rather than scholarly. On the other hand the judges stories exhibit a competence of their own; they are definitely not unsophisticated yarns.[53] Indeed, the evidences for skillful structure, together with an abiding interest in edification and entertainment, point to a guild of professional storytellers in premonarchical Israel as the most likely source of the judges stories and comparable material. Compare especially the story of Ruth and, as noted above, the prose framework of the Book of Job. Another canonical example, from a much later era, is the Book of Esther.

The modus vivendi of the man whose charisma was to become a disciplined teller of tales must have been comparable to that of oral poets in modern times whose life and work have been open to close field study.[54] Allowing for enormous differences in historical context and corporate memory, it was the festival occasions—large and small—which enabled the professional storyteller to earn his milk and honey. Are the contents of the stories historical? Definitely so. But it will be the business of NOTES and COMMENTS to ferret out those elements of common historical memory and the structures of the common life which were essential to grasping punch lines.

Meanwhile the question persists: Who were the professional storytellers in early Israel? The Levites?[55] The "legislative" sections of the books of Leviticus and especially Deuteronomy are characterized by a certain paraenetic or hortatory concern, which makes those books quite different from legal codes. They preserve "preached law," to which Deuteronomy is apparently an even earlier witness than the Holiness Code (Lev 17–26) to judge from the mixture of forms in the latter. Recent studies have

[53] See the studies of J. Blenkinsopp: *Scripture* 11 (1959), 81–89; *Biblica* 42 (1961), 61–76; JBL 82 (1963), 65–76. Also A. D. Crown, *Abr-Nahrain* 3 (1961–62), 90–98. See esp. Luis Alonzo-Schökel, *Biblica* 42 (1961), 143–72, and *Estudios de poética hebréa*, Barcelona, 1963. See also James Muilenberg on rhetorical structure, in *Congress Volume: Copenhagen, 1953*, Vetus Testamentum Supplement, I (Leiden: Brill, 1953), 97–111.

[54] See A. B. Lord, *The Singer of Tales*, Harvard University Press, 1954, for description of studies and massive documentation. The lead of Lord and others has been followed in a search for comparable phenomena in the Psalter, by R. C. Culley, *Oral Formulaic Language in the Biblical Psalms*, University of Toronto Press, 1967. On the larger question of the generic distinctiveness of the biblical narrative style, see Erich Auerbach, *Mimesis*, tr. W. R. Trask (Princeton University Press, 1953), chs. 1–3.

[55] This is the interesting and very sensible suggestion of E. F. Campbell, Jr. (oral communication). See his forthcoming *Ruth*, AB, vol. 7, 1975. See also Wright, VT 4 (1954), 325–30.

increasingly recognized the rural life setting of the homiletical traditions preserved in the Book of Deuteronomy, and which account for the whole tone of that book:

> Behind it, as its representatives, stands a body of Levites, perhaps turned proletarian, which had long outgrown the cultic sphere proper and was busying itself with the scholarly preservation and transmission of the old traditions.[56]

Putting to one side the curious concept of the outgrown cultic sphere, we may promptly underscore the common ground between the paraenetic treatment of amphictyonic law in Deuteronomy (and later the Holiness Code) and the moralistic structure of the judges stories. Again, to develop this point will be the business of NOTES and COMMENTS.

The first products of an Israelite historiography do not appear until the tenth century, when historiography answered a new need for a nation's self-understanding in the wake of David's amazing successes at empire building. Two great works emanate from the Solomonic era and its immediate sequel. One is the "Court History of David" (also called "Succession Document") that fills the last half of II Samuel. To the same period is traced the definitive literary edition of old epic materials that form the core of the books of Genesis through Numbers. This material is commonly identified by the symbol J in critical discussion, since it represents that version of the old national epic which attained favored status in the southern kingdom of Judah, and, in dealing with periods prior to Moses, is notable for its use of the divine name Yahweh.

Many other lexical and stylistic differences, as well as consistently theological ones, distinguish this J material from its northern (Ephraimite) counterpart, which was committed to writing perhaps a century later than the J. The northern or E version is distinguished by the use of the generic noun for deity (Elohim) prior to the call of Moses in Exod 3. See Map 2.

In general, the J materials display a simpler, earthier, livelier account of the old days than does E, which shows its own theological view of the events it describes. This is clear from E's concentration upon prophets, miracles, and related concerns, in such a way as to elicit from Israel a new decision to enter into the covenant again in the ninth century.

The distinction between these two great blocks of traditionary material, originally thought of as written documents which might be analyzed as a sort of literary collage compressed into a single plane, has been further refined to disclose greater compositeness: at least two strands apiece (J_1 and J_2; E_1 and E_2). But such fine distinctions are generally rejected today

56 G. von Rad, *Studies in Deuteronomy*, tr. David Stalker (London, 1953), p. 68.

because of what we know about the nature of oral transmission (see above, and fn. 54).

The theory is generally accepted that *J* and *E* were brought together following the collapse of the northern kingdom and the destruction of Samaria in 721 B.C.E., when *E* documents were carried into the south and used to supplement the version that was already established there; hence the siglum *JE*. Finally, these traditions of Israel's prehistory and early years were re-edited in the sixth century by priests who had been forced into exile in Babylonia (siglum *PJE*).

Literary analysis along earlier lines has continued well into the twentieth century, with various revisions and alternative symbols now and then proposed. Especially significant for discussion of Judges has been the recommendation to substitute *L* for what is essentially J_1, as a decidedly less spiritual, more profane, lay source.[57] How far did the old epic tell the story? It is clear that after a long interruption by the bulk of Deuteronomy, the *JE* material surfaces again in Deut 34. Attempts have been made to trace these sources on into the books of Joshua and Judges and to connect them with related sources in Samuel and Kings.[58] Two great English commentaries will be cited frequently in this book; both of them make convenient use of the *J* and *E* classifications.[59] On the whole, however, it will become apparent in the NOTES and COMMENTS that the old distinctions drawn between *J* and *E* in Judges are vastly oversimplified, especially where they cannot account for the alternation of divine names.

By far the clearest literary connections in the Book of Judges are to the material that precedes and follows in the books of Deuteronomy through II Kings. These books are the result of a full-scale history writing project, mainly completed in the period of Judahite revival under King Josiah (c. 640–609); see II Kings 22–23. An old Book of Deuteronomy, which had taken shape around the reforms of King Hezekiah roughly a century earlier (II Chron 29–35) was given a new introduction (Deut 1:1 – 4:43) and altogether served as a sort of theological preface to the material of Joshua through II Kings, where the entire history of Israel's life in her land now reads like one long covenant lawsuit. That is, the nuclear Deuteronomy lays the basis for one of the two themes that reverberate throughout the whole historical work of Joshua through II Kings (labeled

---

[57] Eissfeldt, *The Old Testament: An Introduction*, tr. Peter R. Ackroyd (New York: Harper, 1965), pp. 191–99. For a response to Eissfeldt's earlier work on the Judges material, and an alternative approach that apprehends much larger narrative unity, a very valuable work is that of Kurt Weise, "Zur Literarkritik des Buches der Richter," BWANT, III, 4, 1926.

[58] For the most recent attempt to delineate the Judges sources (with hyper-precision, in this writer's view), see Cuthbert Aikman Simpson, *Composition of the Book of Judges*, Oxford University Press, 1958.

[59] Burney; Moore.

"Deuteronomic History"): the reality of ancient covenantal curses as accounting for the recent demise of the old northern kingdom.

The disaster of 721 only heightened one of Deuteronomy's enduring concerns—to find provision for jobless rural Levites at the central Yahweh sanctuary (Deut 18:1–8). Provision for the Levites presents, in fact, the most notable discrepancy between the Deuteronomic platform of the reform and its implementation as reported in Kings and Chronicles. That discrepancy became a source of controversy that now provides an important key to the redactional history of the Book of Judges; compare the contrasting characterizations of two Levites in chs. 17 and 19.

The second recurring theme of the Deuteronomic History—God's promises to David—was based on Judah's own experience: nearly four hundred years with a single dynastic house. As noted above, this Deuteronomic History was essentially complete in the time of King Josiah, c. 640–609.

Later, in the wake of the disaster of 587, the great historical work went through a last major edition, updating the story to include destruction and deportation, and ending on a hopeful note—the release of the Davidic King Jehoiachin from a Babylonian prison. For this final edition we use the label "Deuteronomistic." In this final edition, as has recently been shown, the demise of Judah is attributed to King Manasseh's long, paganizing reign in the first half of the seventh century.[60]

Evidence for the evolution of the Book of Judges corresponds, in general, to the foregoing description of the main lines of the historical work in its two main editions: Deuteronomic (late preexilic) and Deuteronomistic (exilic). Traditions taken up in Judges are neither very clearly promonarchical nor antimonarchical.[61] They must be essentially premonarchical, and they are employed in an evaluative presentation of Israel's historical life in that period.

It used to be thought that the clearest evidence for the presence of Deuteronomic influence in Judges was to be found in the "pragmatic formula" within which many narrative units (rather, mostly clusters of stories) are contained. With modifications here and there, the formula introduces a period of oppression with the statement that "the Israelites did what was evil in the sight of Yahweh" (3:7, 12a; 4:1; 6:1a; 10:6; 13:1a). Then follows the identification of Israel's historical adversary (3:8, 12b; 4:2; 6:16; 10:7; 13:1b). When the people appeal to Yahweh, he raises up a deliverer. Then follows the widely varying contents of the hero's stories. Finally, the formula most often reappears in the statement at the end of the unit that "the land was calm" (with or without a chronological note), and

---

60 F. M. Cross, Jr., "The Structure of the Deuteronomic History," *Perspectives in Jewish Learning*, 3 (1967), 9–24.

61 Against Martin Buber, whose main thesis concerning early Israel's striving for direct theocracy is not affected by the mistaken locus of divine kingship language in "nomadic" religion. See his *Kingship of God*, tr. Richard Scheimann, New York: Harper, 1967.

often concludes with a notice on the death of the deliverer (3:11, 30; 5:31b; 8:28–32; 12:7; cf. 15:20 and 16:31).

Actually the only clear lexical or stylistic parallel with Deuteronomy in this formula is the statement "they did evil" (cf. Deut 17:2)—exceedingly slim support for the notion that the book of Deuteronomy guided the bulk of the internal organization of Judges. It is much more likely that in describing the premonarchical period, the Deuteronomic historian was able to incorporate segments of an older cycle of Joshua-Judges stories, which probably had its literary roots in the same tenth-century milieu which produced J and the Court History, and which had already passed through the hands of the pragmatic compiler.

How extensive was the Judges segment of the pre-Deuteronomic work? We can only conjecture that it went on to include something of Eli and Samuel. It is reasonable to suspect that the climactic assertion of judicial function in 15:20 marks the end of the pre-Deuteronomic stratum within the Book of Judges itself. Chapter 16, which is widely recognized as having a separate source from the bulk of the Samson stories, belongs to the Deuteronomic edition, with the assertion of judicial function repeated by the Deuteronomic editor in appropriately revised form (16:31).

In updating the old epic, however, the first act of the Deuteronomic historian, was to segment it so it could serve his own theological and political purposes. Joshua's death was the end of one era and the beginning of another. The report of the death and burial of Joshua was left intact at the end of Joshua but revised by mere transposition of sentences to be more appropriate as introduction in Judg 2:6–10, which he then expanded. To the enlarged book was prefixed the scene with the Yahweh angel in 2:1–5, probably in direct sequence to some such question as that of 1:1. The content and import of the messenger's speech are strikingly similar to the speeches of the anonymous prophet in 6:7–10 and the divine organizer of Israel in 10:11–14. All three are characteristically Deuteronomic.

There is reason to believe that the Deuteronomic edition included both the narrative nucleus and the archival additions (minor judges), which comprise the bulk of the extant book up to the climactic reference to Shiloh (Map 2) in 18:31 the verse which caps off the stories about the easy exploitation and corruption of a promising young Levite at secondary shrines (chs. 17–18).

To the exilic (Deuteronomistic) redactor is left the addition of the bulk of ch. 1 (in itself a configuration of some of the oldest material in the book), exegeting by anticipation the angel's speech in 2:1–5. The new introduction was balanced by the concluding account of the Gibeah outrage, which was touched off by a failure of Yahwist "hospitality" toward another Levite (chs. 19–20), and the abduction of the Shiloh maidens (ch. 21). In its finished form, the book begins with Israel disintegrating in ch. 1 and concludes with Israel united at last, for most unexpected reasons. This hypothesis of the redactional expansion of the old Israelite epic in three main phases ("pragmatic," "Deuteronomic," and "Deuteronomistic") will be examined and supported in detail in NOTES and COMMENTS (see esp. ch. 9). Here it should be noted that such a view of the growth of the book correlates well with the otherwise baffling conclusion of the Book of Joshua, which also seems to end twice. Josh 24 recapitulates the great tribal convocation at Shechem, where Joshua presides in a covenantal affirmation by all the tribes that have thus far participated in the Yahwist revolution in Canaan. The documentary basis of Josh 24 is a very old one, and many scholars see in it a reflection of the definitive emergence of the specifically Israelite amphictyony. It leaves the matter of the success or failure of the new experiment an open question: Will the Israelites maintain the covenantal constitution or not?

What is affirmed through the lively narrative depiction of covenantal negotiation and ratification in Josh 24 now has eloquent hortatory preparation in Josh 23. But as "Joshua's Farewell Address," ch. 23, is complete in itself, a preformed unit which has been inserted in such a way that the last two chapters are most inefficiently redundant. The most striking thing about the farewell speech, however, is its largely negative expectation for the survival of the federation, spiraling downwards to a devastatingly negative conclusion. "If you break the covenant . . . you will quickly vanish from the good land he has given you" (Josh 23:16). Josh 23 clearly reflects Deuteronomic eloquence. But from the standpoint of the question about redaction it fits best the period of the final "Deuteronomistic" updating of the great historical work, and it correlates well with our understanding of Judg 1 and 19–21 as part of the post-587 edition.

Even more striking is the correlation between the latest "frame" of the judges period in these chapters and the latest work on Deut 1–2, where the rebellion at Qadesh and the abortive attempt to invade Canaan from the south unfold with inverted use of the sacral warfare language: Yahweh versus Israel.[62]

In other words, while the exilic work ("Deuteronomistic" edition) involved only minor modifications, they were skillful ones. In the Book of Judges the main "Deuteronomistic" contribution was to revive during the exile some previously neglected traditionary units, which now provide the entire book with a tragicomic framework: chs. 1 and 19–22. In its finished form the Book of Judges begins with Israel scattered and ineffective by the close of ch. 1. It ends with a very delicate, persistent

---

[62] Moran, "The End of the Unholy War and the Anti-Exodus," *Biblica* 44 (1963), 333–42.

ideal—*Israel*, reunited at last in the wake of a tragic civil war—in an account that swarms with incongruities (chs. 19–21). Any exilic updating of a work previously organized so as to climax and conclude with a celebration of King Josiah's program (II Kings 22–23) would of necessity sound very different from the original if it were to be relevant to the new context. We suspect that it is a subtle matter indeed, and that the exilic editor is profoundly concerned with such questions as the one raised poignantly in Ps 137—how to sing the Lord's song in a pagan country. The Deuteronomistic answer is a positive one. The final editor counters the disillusionment of exile, for "comedy is an escape, not from truth but from despair: a narrow escape into faith."[63]

The Text

Developments since the initial Dead Sea scroll discoveries of 1947 have brought a glimmer of light to what one scholar calls "the miasmal precincts" of textual criticism.[64] The systematic effort to unravel the history of the formation, transmission, and translation of the text is based upon the fact that ancient manuscripts may be classified by common characteristics. Considerations of style and internal organization give evidence of classes for which the technical term is "recensions." Scholars try to reconstruct the best text by comparing the recensions known. The terminology of recensional classes in biblical studies has always been based upon Jerome's description of the three principal Greek (Septuagint [LXX]) recensions known to him at the end of the fourth century: the Hesychian, the Lucianic, and the Origenic.[65] They all developed from the Old Greek translation of the OT (from the Hebrew) produced during the third and second centuries B.C.E. The first is probably to be connected with a martyred Alexandrian bishop of the third century C.E.; it is most obscure. The second is associated with Antioch where Lucian was martyred c. 311. The Origenic will be treated at some length below.

Greek manuscripts written exclusively in capital letters are known as uncials, and each one is assigned an identifying letter (A, B, etc.). Those written in small letters are called minuscules (identified as *a, b,* etc.). A

---

63 Fry, "Comedy," in *The New Orpheus*, p. 286.

64 The phrase belongs to Cross, whose brilliant new synthesis of the data that has become available over the past twenty-five years, furnishes improved guidelines for much of the following discussion. See fn. 70.

65 Henry Barclay Swete, *An Introduction to the Old Testament in Greek*, rev. Richard R. Ottley (Cambridge University Press, 1902), Part I, chs. 1–4. Reprinted New York: Ktav, 1968. This standard introduction should now be read alongside Sidney Jellicoe, *The Septuagint and Modern Study*, Oxford: Clarendon Press, 1968, which is not intended to replace it.

palimpsest is a reused manuscript, with a new text written over an erased original.

A full-scale attempt to reconstruct the Lucianic Greek text was initiated by Lagarde in the nineteenth century; principal carriers of Lucianic readings, it is now generally agreed, are the minuscules boc_2e_2 and the Old Latin (OL) version. Subsequent refinements have called into question the precision with which Lagarde grouped his manuscripts while, in the main, validating his general approach.

Origen (185–253), head of the catechetical school of Alexandria, set himself the enormous task of producing a single work in which the principal Greek texts extant in his day were set out in parallel columns, with another column for his critically reconstructed LXX text, and a diacritical system to indicate how it was related to the content and organization of his main sources. The work went through several editions, with sometimes fewer, and in certain books more, columns. The most persistent lineup was: (a) the Hebrew text, (b) the Hebrew text transliterated in Greek characters, (c) Aquila, (d) Symmachus, (e) Origen's LXX, and (f) Theodotion. Of the sources used by Origen, the scholars Aquila and Theodotion were both probably Jews, while Symmachus was an Ebionite Christian. Each in his own way had endeavored to bring the Greek text of his day into closer conformity with a developing Hebrew text.

Manuscripts of Origen's Hexapla (so named for its six columns) have not survived, except for a palimpsest which contains roughly a hundred and fifty verses of the Psalms. Apart from quotations in other works, the principal witness to Origen's LXX survives in a very good Syriac translation of the Hexapla (siglum Syr.[h]), from the first quarter of the seventh century. Origen's critical "apparatus" persists in the uncial G and a group of minuscules; all, however, exhibit texts of various mixtures.

Qumran Cave 1 produced some valuable first-century Judges fragments, one group attesting to the text of 6:20–22; 8:1; 9:1–4 (another to 9:4–6); 9:28–31, 40–42 (another to 9:40–43), 48–49. None of these pieces includes whole lines, and the height of the column is unknown, so that complete reconstruction of lines is impossible. The publication of Cave 1 material assigns yet another thirty pieces to the Judges manuscript, each containing one to three words or portions of words, most often on more than one line![66]

These fragments are extremely interesting because of the relationship displayed between them and the ancient versions in ch. 9, which by a happy accident in otherwise massive deterioration is where the larger fragments cluster. Cave 1 Judges sides once with the Vulgate (Vulg.) against the Masoretic Text (MT), and once with Vulg. and Arabic against

---

[66] Jean-Dominique Barthélemy and Jozef T. Milik, *Qumran Cave 1*, Discoveries in the Judaean Desert of Jordan, I (Oxford University Press, 1955), pp. 62–64.

MT. Once clearly it agrees with LXX against MT, and partially so in another two passages with additional support of Vulg. At two points it goes its own way.[67]

The unpublished material from Qumran Cave 4 is similarly intriguing but likewise difficult to characterize as to text type. In a communication to the writer Frank M. Cross, Jr., reports:

> There are two manuscripts, one represented by a single fragment (4Q Judges[a]) and a short group of badly preserved fragments (4Q Judges[b]). 4Q Judges[a] preserves 6:3–13 in part; it does reflect the type of text in the better Septuagint tradition. The second manuscript preserves 21:12–25 plus a very small fragment of 16:5–7. There are no remarkable readings in 4Q Judges[b]. In 4Q Judges[a] in verse 3 note the omission of w'lw 'lyw. Verse 7a is omitted. However, 4Q has a much larger omission extending apparently from the beginning of verse 7 down to verse 10. In vs. 13 the text reads 'lhym instead of yhwh. In vs. 13 we have the strange reading šsprw.

This is the total data on variations in the 4Q Judges manuscripts. Cross thinks it would not be surprising to find that it followed pretty much the pattern of Joshua and the books of Samuel, but he urges that we cannot extrapolate very much from these few fragments.

The Qumran Judges fragments serve only to compound our curiosity about the textual history of the book, especially in the Hebrew that lies behind the LXX and related versions. What is "the better Septuagint tradition"? In the case of Judges the two great Greek uncials (LXX[A] and LXX[B]) differ so consistently that they have often been assigned to separate translation enterprises. The tools are now at hand for a reexamination of that question, for the handful of published Qumran Judges fragments is complemented by much more extensive remains in the historical books, especially I Samuel.

The emergence of the major Greek recensions was a process of development, from an Old Greek translation of the third century B.C.E. progressively adapting it to one or another of the existing Hebrew texts. A partial breakthrough, prior to the Qumran discoveries, into the era when the LXX was still developing, was based precisely upon the books of Samuel and Kings. In large sections of LXX[B] and most major manuscripts it was observed that we have a Greek text which in points of style and translation technique is a marked departure from the standards that prevailed in producing the bulk of the extant LXX text.[68]

---

[67] These differences are all very clearly footnoted in *Qumran Cave 1*, pp. 62–63.

[68] Henry St. John Thackeray, *The Septuagint and Jewish Worship*, Schweich Lectures, 1920, London: H. Milford, 1921. The criteria for distinguishing the sections of II Sam 11:2 – I Kings 2:11 and I Kings 22:1 – II Kings 25:30, which he assigned to a "later translator," are tabulated in Appendix I, pp. 114–15.

One of the biggest bonuses of the cave explorations that have continued over twenty years since the initial Qumran finds is the recovery of fragments of a Minor Prophets scroll in Greek, with a text that certainly stems from the same enterprise as the later stratum of the Greek Samuel and Kings.[69] This text type has been given the designation "Kaige" from the Greek word *kaige* (roughly, "and indeed"), due to the ubiquity in these materials of the compound particle where, in the Old Greek, *kai* (simply "and") normally suffices. Further comparison of these materials has disclosed additional criteria for tracking the Kaige text in other books. The upshot of the surprising variety of textual types being saved and studied in Palestine at the turn of the era has been the beginning of a revolution in textual criticism.[70] See Appendix A.

In brief, the new directions in textual criticism allow increasingly for the early development of local Hebrew texts, each one the property of one of the three great centers of ancient world Jewry: Egypt, Palestine, and Babylonia. Early in the second century C.E. rabbis selected as authoritative a Hebrew text type which had more of its roots in the Babylonian textual tradition than in either of the other two. The emergence of the pointed text (MT), was, therefore, a process which stands in sharp contrast to the development of the LXX text. The latter was a process of successive revisions bringing the Greek into closer harmony with interacting Hebrew texts that were still developing. Origen was following an already well established precedent in the production of his Hexapla, the last great revision of the Greek text.

So now the quest continues for signs of Origen's unnamed predecessors. There was a "Proto-Lucianic" recension (surviving as a distinct substratum in the Lucianic manuscripts boc_2e_2 for Samuel), which emanated probably from Palestine in the first century B.C.E. In Judges it has left its marks chiefly in the uncial κ and in minuscules *gn dpt*.[71]

The second major Greek recension was that of the Kaige. This recension is marked by a pronounced tendency to level throughout its text uniform translation equivalents. Stemming probably from the last third of the first century C.E. (thus also appropriately nicknamed "Proto-Theodotion"), it stands as close to a developed Hebrew text as did Proto-Lucian to the Old Greek.

The problem of the Kaige recension (or "Proto-Theodotion") in Judges has been obscured by the competition of the two great uncials, A and B, for critical attention and scholarly loyalty on the assumption of a unilinear

69 Jean-Dominique Barthélemy, *Les devanciers d'Aquila: Premiere publication integrale du texte des fragments du Dodecapropheton*, Leiden: Brill, 1963.

70 J. D. Shenkel, *Chronology and Recensional Development in the Greek Text of Kings*, Harvard University Press, 1968. See also Cross, *Harvard Theological Review* 57 (1964), 281–99; IEJ 16 (1966), 81–95.

71 Cross, IEJ 16 (1966), 84.

textual development. In Appendix A is summarized the evidence for Kaige in the Judges of A and B.

Patterns there described demonstrate conclusively that a higher percentage of first-rate readings will survive in A than scholars have generally allowed. It will, accordingly, be taken very seriously in NOTES on the translation, where each set of witnesses in problematic texts has to be considered on its own merits. This reverses a dominant trend in textual reconstruction, for scholars have generally followed MT wherever it made sense and could be translated; recourse to the versions was had only when MT refused to yield any sense at all. Such a method is unsound, since the versions must have superior readings in other situations as well. It might indeed be argued that since MT has received most attention in the past, there should be compensatory emphasis on alternate texts now, especially the *Vorlage* of the LXX. In this respect, a number of text-critical judgments in this volume may be considered too conservative.

In brief, the principles of textual criticism have not changed significantly; what has changed is the picture of the relationship between Hebrew texts and the versions. This is the understanding that will be operative in the translation and NOTES, wherever we have recognized the possibility of improving on MT.

SELECTED BIBLIOGRAPHY

See also Principal Abbreviations; titles there are not repeated here.

Albright, William F. "The Earliest Forms of Hebrew Verse," JPOS 2 (1922), 69–86.

———"A Catalogue of Early Hebrew Lyric Poems (Psalm lxviii)," HUCA 23 (1950–51), 1–39.

———"Midianite Donkey Caravans," in *Translating and Understanding the Old Testament,* eds. Harry Thomas Frank and William L. Reed (New York and Nashville: Abingdon, 1970), pp. 197–205.

Alonzo-Schökel, Luis. "Erzahlkunst im Buche der Richter," *Biblica* 42 (1961), 143–72.

Alt, Albrecht. *Kleine Schriften zur Geschichte des Volkes Israel,* I, Munich: Beck, 1953.

Anderson, Bernhard W., and Harrelson, Walter, eds. *Israel's Prophetic Heritage,* New York: Harper, 1962.

Anderson, George W. "Israel: Amphictyony: *'Am; Ḳāhāl; 'Ēdāh,*" in *Translating and Understanding the Old Testament,* eds. Harry Thomas Frank and William L. Reed (New York and Nashville: Abingdon, 1970), pp. 135–51.

Barnett, R. D. "The Sea Peoples," *The Cambridge Ancient History,* rev. ed., vols. I–II, fasc. 68, Cambridge University Press, 1969.

Barthélemy, Jean-Dominique. *Les devanciers d'Aquila: Premiere publication integrale du texte des fragments du Dodecapropheton,* Leiden: Brill, 1963.

Blenkinsopp, J. "Ballad Style and Psalm Style in the Song of Deborah: A Discussion," *Biblica* 42 (1961), 61–76.

———"Structure and Style in Judges 13–16," JBL 82 (1963), 65–76.

Bright, John. *Early Israel in Recent History Writing,* London: SCM Press, 1956.

———*A History of Israel,* 2d ed., Philadelphia: Westminster, 1972.

Buber, Martin. *Kingship of God,* tr. Richard Scheimann, New York: Harper, 1967.

Burney, C. F. *The Book of Judges,* 2d ed., London: Rivingtons, 1930; reprinted with "Prolegomenon" by William F. Albright, New York: Ktav, 1970.

Campbell, Edward F., Jr. "The Amarna Letters and the Amarna Period," BA 23 (1960), 2–22, reprinted in *The Biblical Archaeologist Reader 3,* eds. Edward F. Campbell, Jr., and David N. Freedman (Garden City, N.Y.: Doubleday, 1970), 54–75.

Cary, Max. "Northern and Central Greece," in *The Cambridge Ancient History,* III, eds. J. B. Bury, S. A. Cook, F. E. Adcock (New York: Macmillan, 1925), 598–630.

Cazelles, Henri S. "Shiloh, the Customary Laws and the Return of the Ancient Kings," in *Proclamation and Presence,* eds. J. I. Durham and J. R. Porter (Richmond: John Knox Press, 1970), pp. 239–51.

Cross, Frank M., Jr., and Freedman, David Noel. "Studies in Ancient Yahwistic Poetry," an unpublished Ph.D. dissertation available in Baltimore, 1950; microfilm Xerox reprint, Ann Arbor, 1963.

——"The Contribution of the Qumran Discoveries to the Study of the Biblical Text," IEJ 16 (1966), 81–95.

——"The Structure of the Deuteronomic History," *Perspectives in Jewish Learning,* 3 (1967), 9–24.

Dahood, Mitchell. *Psalms I, 1–50,* AB, vol. 16, 1966; *II, 51–100,* AB, vol. 17, 1968; *Psalms III, 101–150,* AB, vol. 17A, 1970.

Eissfeldt, Otto. *The Old Testament: An Introduction,* tr. Peter R. Ackroyd, New York: Harper, 1965.

——"Protektorat der Midianiter über ihre Nachbarn im letzten Viertel des 2 Jahrtausends v. Chr.," JBL 87 (1968), 383–93.

Freedman, David N., and Greenfield, Jonas C., eds. *New Directions in Biblical Archaeology,* Garden City, N.Y.: Doubleday, 1969.

Goedicke, Hans, ed. *Near Eastern Studies in Honor of William Foxwell Albright,* Johns Hopkins Press, 1971.

Gray, John. *Joshua, Judges and Ruth,* London: Nelson, 1967.

Habel, Norman C. *Yahweh Versus Baal,* New York: Twayne, 1964.

Hillers, Delbert R. *Covenant: The History of a Biblical Idea,* Johns Hopkins Press, 1969.

Jellicoe, Sidney. *The Septuagint and Modern Study,* Oxford: Clarendon Press, 1968.

Knudson, J. A., ed. *Die El-Amarna Tafeln,* Leipzig: Vorderasiatische Bibliothek, 1915.

Malamat, Abraham. "Aspects of Tribal Societies in Mari and Israel," in *XVe Rencontre Assyriologique Internationale: La Civilisation de Mari. Les Congrès et Colloques de l'Université de Liège,* vol. 42 (1967), 129–38.

——ed. *Eretz-Israel,* 9, W. F. Albright Volume. Jerusalem: Israel Exploration Society, 1969.

McKenzie, John L. *The World of the Judges,* Englewood Cliffs, N.J.: Prentice-Hall, 1966.

Mendenhall, George E. "The Census Lists of Numbers 1 and 26," JBL 77 (1958), 52–66.

——"The Hebrew Conquest of Palestine," BA 25 (1962), 66–87, reprinted in *The Biblical Archaeologist Reader 3,* eds. Edward F. Campbell, Jr. and David Noel Freedman (Garden City, N.Y.: Doubleday, 1970), pp. 100–20.

Moore, George F. *A Critical and Exegetical Commentary on Judges.* International Critical Commentary, New York: Scribner's, 1901.

Myers, Jacob M. "Judges: Introduction and Exegesis," *The Interpreter's Bible,* II (New York and Nashville: Abingdon, 1953), 677–826.

Noth, Martin. *Das System der zwölf Stämme Israels,* Stuttgart: W. Kohlhammer, 1930.

————*The History of Israel,* tr. Peter R. Ackroyd, New York: Harper, 1960.

Oldenburg, Ulf. *The Conflict Between El and Ba'al in Canaanite Religion,* Leiden: Brill, 1969.

Rad, Gerhard von. *Der Heilige Krieg,* Zurich: Zwingli Verlag, 1951.

Richter, Wolfgang. *Die Bearbeitungen des "Retterbuches" in der deuteronomischen Epoche,* Bonn: Peter Hanstein, 1964.

Sasson, Jack M. *The Military Establishment at Mari,* Rome: Pontifical Biblical Institute, 1969.

Shenkel, J. D. *Chronology and Recensional Development in the Greek Text of Kings,* Harvard University Press, 1968.

Smend, Rudolf. *Yahweh War and Tribal Confederation,* tr. Max G. Rogers, New York and Nashville: Abingdon, 1970.

Speiser, Ephraim A. *Genesis,* AB, vol. 1, Garden City: Doubleday, 1964.

Swete, Henry Barclay. *An Introduction to the Old Testament in Greek,* revised by Richard R. Ottley, Cambridge University Press, 1902. Reprinted New York: Ktav, 1968.

Thackeray, Henry St. John. *The Septuagint and Jewish Worship,* London: H. Milford, 1921.

Vaux, Roland de. *Ancient Israel,* tr. John McHugh, New York: McGraw-Hill, 1961.

Weber, Max. *Ancient Judaism,* trs. Hans H. Gerth and Don Martindale, New York: The Free Press, 1952.

Wright, G. Ernest. "The Literary and Historical Problem of Joshua 10 and Judges 1," JNES 5 (1946), 105–14.

————, ed. *The Bible and the Ancient Near East: Essays in Honor of William Foxwell Albright,* Garden City, N.Y.: Doubleday, 1961.

————*Shechem: Biography of a Biblical City,* New York: McGraw-Hill, 1965.

Yadin, Yigael. *The Art of Warfare in Bible Lands,* I, New York: McGraw-Hill, 1963.

THE BOOK OF JUDGES

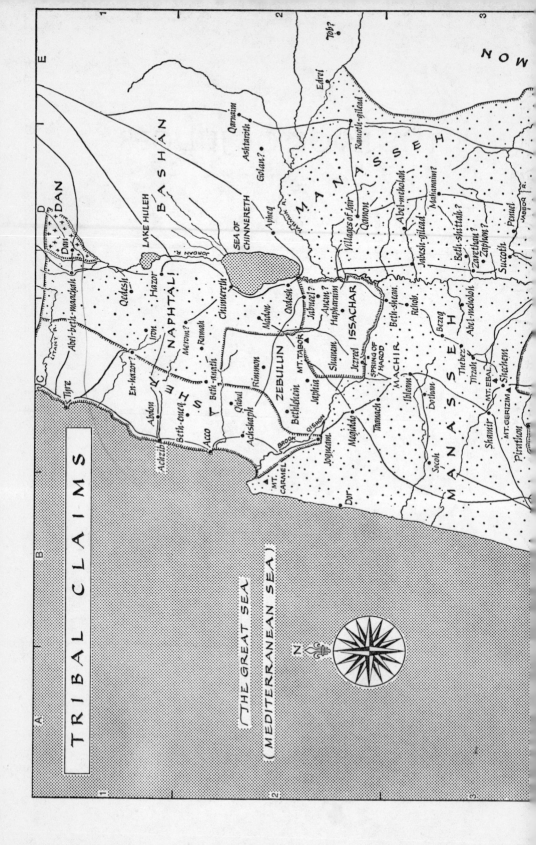

TRIBAL CLAIMS

THE GREAT SEA
(MEDITERRANEAN SEA)

N

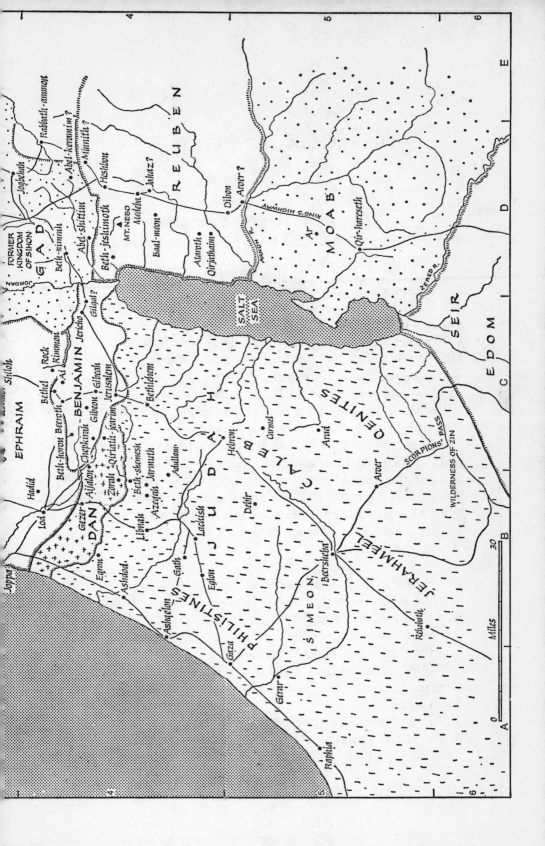

THE PRELUDE AND THE BEGINNING

I. The Indecisive Settlement
(1:1 – 2:5)

Judah First

1 ¹ There was a time, after Joshua's death, when the Israelites had asked Yahweh, "Who will be first to go up for us against the Canaanites to fight them?"

² Yahweh had said, "Judah shall go. I have granted the land to him." ³ And Judah had said to his brother Simeon, "Come with me into my allotment and we will fight the Canaanites! Then I will go with you into your allotment." So Simeon went along with him.

⁴ When Judah went up, Yahweh subjected the Canaanites and Perizzites to them. They defeated them at Bezeq — ten contingents! ⁵ At Bezeq they caught up with the prince of Bezeq; they fought him and defeated the Canaanites and Perizzites. ⁶ The prince of Bezeq fled but they chased after him. They captured him and cut off his thumbs and big toes. ⁷ Said the prince of Bezeq: "Seventy kings with amputated thumbs and toes used to scavenge under my table! Exactly as I did, so God has requited me!" They brought him to Jerusalem and he died there.

Jerusalem and the South

⁸ The Judahites fought against Jerusalem and captured it; they put it to the sword and sent the city up in flames. ⁹ After that the Judahites went down to fight the Canaanites who were living in the hill country, the Negeb, and the foothills.

¹⁰ Judah attacked the Canaanites who were living in Hebron (Hebron used to be called Qiriath-arba) and defeated Sheshai, Ahiman, and Talmai.

¹¹ From there they attacked the inhabitants of Debir. Debir used to be called Qiriath-sepher.

¹² Caleb had said, "Whoever devastates Qiriath-sepher and cap-

tures it, to him I'll give my daughter Achsah as wife." 13 Othniel ben
Qenaz, Caleb's "brother"—who was younger than he—captured it;
and so he gave him his daughter Achsah as wife.

> 14 When she arrived, he nagged her
>   To ask tilled land from her father.
> But when she alighted from the donkey
>   And Caleb said to her: "What's wrong?"
> 15 She said to him: "Give me a blessing!
>   The Negeb-land you have given me
>   And you shall give me basins of water!"
> So Caleb gave her her heart's desire,
>   The upper basins
>   and the lower basins.

Qenites for Contrast
16 The people of Hobab the Qenite, Moses' son-in-law, had gone
up from Palm City with the Judahites to the plain south of Judah,
going down from Arad (. . .) And they went and lived among the
Amaleqites!

Judah Reciprocates
17 Judah went with his "brother" Simeon. They defeated the Canaanites living in Zephath, and put it under the ban. The city came
to be known as Ban-town.
18 Judah captured Gaza with its territory, Ashqelon with its territory, Eqron with its territory, and Ashdod with its territory.

Summary
19 Yahweh was indeed with Judah. He took over the hill country;
but he could not evict the inhabitants of the plain, for they had iron
chariots.

Postscripts
20 They gave Hebron to Caleb, exactly as Moses had ordered. He
took possession of the three towns and evicted from there the three
"sons" of Anaq.
21 But the Benjaminites did not evict the Jebusites living in Jerusalem. The Jebusites live in Jerusalem, with the Benjaminites, to this
day.

Meanwhile: Manasseh and Ephraim

22 Likewise the house of Joseph had moved against Bethel; and Judah was with them. 23 The house of Joseph reconnoitered Bethel carefully; the town used to be called Deception. 24 When the sentries saw a man coming out from the city, they said to him, "Just show us an entrance to the city and we will deal justly with you." 25 So he showed them a way into the city, and they put the city to the sword. But the man and his entire family they released. 26 The man went to the Hittite country, built a city, and called it Deception. That is its name until the present day.

Elsewhere

27 Manasseh did not dispossess Beth-shean and its dependencies, Taanach and its dependencies, the inhabitants of Dor and its dependencies, the inhabitants of Ibleam and its dependencies, or the inhabitants of Megiddo and its dependencies; the Canaanites were determined to dwell in this land. 28 When Israel became strong, they subjected them to forced labor; they did not completely dispossess them.

29 As for Ephraim, they did not dispossess the Canaanites who were living in Gezer; rather, the Canaanites lived right in their midst at Gezer.

30 As for Zebulun, they did not dispossess the inhabitants of Qitron or the inhabitants of Nahalal; rather, the Canaanites lived in their midst and were subjected to forced labor.

31 As for Asher, they did not dispossess the inhabitants of Acco or the inhabitants of Sidon, or Ahlab, Achzib, Helbah, Aphiq, or Rehob. 32 Rather, the Asherites settled down in the midst of the Canaanites, the inhabitants of the land; they did not dispossess them.

33 As for Naphtali, they did not dispossess the inhabitants of Beth-shemesh or the inhabitants of Beth-anath; rather, they settled down in the midst of the Canaanites, the land's inhabitants. And the inhabitants of Beth-shemesh and Beth-anath were subjected to forced labor for them.

A Stand-off

34 The Westerners crowded the Danites into the hills, since they did not allow them to come down to the plain. 35 The Westerners were determined to live in Har-heres, in Aijalon, and in Shaalbim.

When the house of Joseph gained control over them, they were put to forced labor.

Note
36 The Amorite border was from Scorpions' Pass, from Sela and upward. . . .

Do Not Go

2 ¹ Yahweh's envoy went up from The Circle to The Weepers and said:

"Lord Yahweh brought you up from Egypt! And he brought you to the land that he promised on oath to your fathers. He said:

I won't break my covenant with you—ever! ² and you shall not make any covenant with the inhabitants of this land. You shall tear down their altars. But you have not obeyed my voice! How could you do this? ³ Furthermore, I said: I will not drive them out before you. They will lie in wait for you! Their gods shall be a bait for you!"

⁴ When Yahweh's envoy had proclaimed these words to all the Israelites, the people cried aloud and wept. ⁵ The name of that place they called Weepers. There they sacrificed to Yahweh.

NOTES

1:1. *There was a time.* Heb. *wayhī,* lit. "and it happened," signals the resumption or continuation of narrative.

after Joshua's death. The phrase presupposes an awareness of Joshua's achievement.

asked. That is, sought oracular guidance at an amphictyonic sanctuary, as in the next to last vignette of the book, where the response is the same, "Judah first" (20:18). These passages form a redactor's inclusio, "a rhetorical device also called 'cyclic composition' in which the author returns to the point from which he began." Dahood, *Psalms I, 1–50,* AB, vol. 16 (1966), NOTE on 1:6. Here the inclusio functions to express both the primacy of Judah and the unified nature of the enterprise. As at last becomes clear in 2:1–5, the question in 1:1 was the wrong question (see NOTE on 2:1–5 and COMMENT); the question in 20:18 was posed at the wrong sanctuary (the ark was not there). From first to last, the problem of legitimate and proper inquiry plays a pivotal role in the Judges stories. Taking our lead from the progressively negative results in this chapter, we may suspect that the question ought to have been similar to the one in 20:28 (where the response is at last reliable): "Shall we again resume the march to battle?" Yahweh is commander-in-chief (II Sam 2:1; 5:19; I Kings 22:6, 15; cf. I Kings 12:24). Presumably a variety of simple means could be used for determining the lot; a striking archaeological example from the period is a collection of arrowheads inscribed with the owners' names, to be shot or shaken from a quiver in such a way as to answer the question posed. Samuel Iwry, JAOS 81 (1961), 27–34.

2. *Yahweh had said*. The tense must be inferred from context. The older critical notion that an Israelite traditionist had relocated the entire conquest period by merely prefixing the first four Hebrew words to an older but not normative account (the bulk of ch. 1), without tampering with the report of Joshua's death and burial in 2:6–10, is no longer tenable. Attention to redaction history suggests that the past perfect tense (had said) may be implicit here, with the entirety of ch. 1 intended as a flashback on the generation that survived Joshua. See COMMENT.

I have granted the land. It presupposes a long familiarity with the contents of Israel's historical credo and the language of the early Yahweh wars. The Akkadian equivalent, *ina qati nadānu*, "give into the hand," is used with reference to a god granting victory over enemies, as early as the Old Akkadian period. W. L. Moran, *Biblica* 44 (1963), 337, n. 1.

3. *Judah . . . Simeon*. A prime narrative motivation in vss. 1–20 is to show how Simeon, originally at home in the north central hill country (Gen 34:25, 30–31) is subsequently situated in the south where it is virtually swallowed up by the mighty tribe of Judah. The conjecture that the mention of "Simeon and Levi" is secondary in Gen 34 has produced no convincing rationale for the insertion of the names there, as noted by Roland de Vaux, in *Translating and Understanding the Old Testament*, p. 117, n. 33, who nevertheless removes the references, in favor of the notion that Simeon entered independently from the south. See Map 2, B-5.

allotment. Heb. *gōrāl*, reminiscent of the account of partitioning of the land in Josh 15 ff. Cf. the equivalent term *naḥᵃlā* in 2:6. On the allotment to Simeon, specifically placed within Judah, see Josh 19:1–9. Cf. Josh 15:26–32, 42; I Chron 4:28–33.

Canaanites. The term is used generically to comprehend the dominant element among all non-Israelite occupants of the land, as indicated by the review of mixed success in vss. 27–33.

4. *Perizzites*. Precise sense uncertain, for the term may either be ethnic (Hurrian) or appellative (cf. *pᵉrāzōt*, "unwalled villages," Esther 9:19, Ezek 38:11, Zech 2:8). Stylistic considerations favor the latter, in a meristic combination heightening the boast: thus approximately, "city slickers and country bumpkins." In the early traditions Perizzites appear in the hill country of Ephraim (Josh 17:15) and in the vicinity of Shechem (Gen 34:30). See Map 2, C-3.

defeated. Heb. *way-yakkūm*, a general verb for fighting victoriously, variously nuanced by context. See vs. 17; 3:29–31; 6:16; 8:11; 9:43, 44; 11:21, 33; 14:19; 15:8, 15, 16; 20:31, 37, 39, 45, 48; 21:10.

contingents. Heb. *'ᵃlāpīm*, often "thousands," but reflecting a complex semantic history. The word is etymologically connected with "head of cattle,"

like the letter aleph, implying that the term was originally applied to the village
or population unit in a pastoral-agricultural society. From that it came to
mean the quota supplied by one village or "clan" (Heb. *mišpāḥā*) for the
military muster. Abraham Malamat, "Aspects of Tribal Societies in Mari and
Israel," in *XVᵉ Rencontre Assyriologique Internationale: La Civilisation de
Mari. Les Congrès et Colloques de l'Université de Liège*, vol. 42 (1967), p. 135.
Originally the contingent was quite small (see 20:35), five to fourteen men in
the quota lists of Num 1 and 26, as shown conclusively by Mendenhall, JBL
77 (1958), 52–66. Finally the word became a technical term for a military
unit of considerable size, which together with the use of the same word for the
number "1,000" has tended to obscure its broader semantic range.

5. *the prince of Bezeq*. Heb. *'ᵃdoni-bezeq*, which standard translations have
treated as a personal name, under the influence of "Adoni-zedeq, king of
Jerusalem" in Josh 10:1, 3. But it is not clear that bezeq is a divine appellative,
which is needed to make the name conform to a known pattern. More likely
it is a title, not a name. Bezeq is perhaps to be identified with Khirbet Bezqa,
a site near Gezer. But cf. I Sam 11:8 which knows of a "Bezeq" northeast of
Shechem. See Map 2, C-3.

6. *cut off his thumbs and big toes*. To prevent his ever taking up arms
again, and in anticipation of his dispatch to Jerusalem for the purpose of in-
stilling fear at Jerusalem. Similar practices involving decapitated bodies are
mentioned in the Mari texts and in classical sources and are widespread
among preliterate and semiliterate cultures. See Gaster, MLC, pp. 416–17, 528.

7. *Seventy*. Probably more than shorthand for "a great many." It seems
to be a political number, referring to some sort of ruling council in Exod 24
and Num 11. It is used for the heirs of Gideon (9:2, 5) and the "family" of
the judge Abdon (12:14). Later, King Ahab had a council of "seventy sons"
in Samaria. In our passage the prince has apparently "confused his military
prowess with a standard or ideal council involved in the government of city-
states or nations," as David Noel Freedman once wrote to me.

under my table. Gaster calls attention to an interesting parallel to the
practice of feeding the captives on scraps, in *Ugaritica* V (Paris: P. Geuthner,
1967), i 6–8, where "the supreme god El invites the other gods to a banquet.
Those who acknowledge him and are therefore regarded as his friends are
offered viands, whereas those who do not, and are therefore regarded as 'gate-
crashers', are ordered to be 'beaten with a stick (till they sink) under the
table.'" See MLC, pp. 417–18, 529.

8. *Jerusalem*. Perhaps only the unfortified southwest hill. See Hubbard,
Palestine Exploration Quarterly, 98 (1966), esp. 136–37. Kenyon's rejection of
the possibility is too heavily influenced by the absence of archaeological data
where centuries of intense cultivation must be taken as a weighty variable.
Kathleen M. Kenyon, *Jerusalem* (New York: McGraw-Hill, 1967), ch. II.
On the breakup of the realm of Jerusalem in the post-Amarna period, see
Zechariah Kallai and Hayim Tadmor, *Eretz Israel* 9 (1969), 138–47 (Hebrew
with English summary).

sent the city up in flames. Cf. 9:49, 52; Josh 6:24, 8:8, 11:11. On the imagery
of holy war, according to which Yahweh goes before, "as a devouring

fire" (Deut 9:3), see P. Miller, CBQ 26 (1964), 256–61. This claim for
Judah's victory at Jerusalem is difficult to interpret, for in vs. 21 it is claimed
that the Benjaminites could not evict the Jebusites, while in Josh 15:63 the
latter assertion is made about Judah! We suspect that the key to all these
differences is the frustration of a unified revolutionary plan for the reorganization of the country under Yahwist control. Thus the redactor who
finally allowed all these texts to stand understood them somewhat as follows:
while the great southern tribe of Judah managed to sack "Jerusalem," meaning
by that the unfortified southwest hill, the Benjaminites, who shared a border
with the stronger Jebusite city on the eastern hill, faced a more formidable
opponent. Thus, despite initial success (1:8), Josh 15:63 asserts that Judah
failed to clear out the Jebusites, and Judg 1:21 adds a reminder that
Benjamin was no more successful.

10. The discordant character of the text has long been recognized. The
victory at Hebron, credited to Caleb in vs. 20, is here credited to the larger
tribe to which Caleb was assimilated at a very early period.

Qiriath-arba. "Town of Arba." The latter element was originally a divine
name with Babylonian relations. Burney, pp. 43 f. "Arba" is the father of
"Anaq," the latter being the ancestor of certain famous giants: Josh 15:13,
21:11.

Sheshai, Ahiman, and Talmai. They were among the "sons of Anaq" defeated by Caleb (not Joshua or Judah) according to Josh 15:14.

11–15. The verses are nearly identical to Josh 15:15–19.

11. *Debir.* "Governor's Town," a translation of *debīr* which reflects
D/Tapara, "lord, governor," as suggested by Mendenhall in *TenGen,* p. 163.
The most likely location of Debir (Qiriath-sepher) remains Tell Beit-Mirsim
(Map 2, B-5), inasmuch as the recently proposed alternative, Tell Rubad,
belongs to the wrong administrative district of Judah (Albright, oral communi-
cation). Qiriath-sepher, the old name, means "Town of the treaty-stele."

12. *Caleb.* Lit. "dog."

Achsah. Etymology uncertain, perhaps "Bangles" or the like. See the
corresponding verb in Isa 3:16. Freedman in a private communication calls
attention to the sequence of verbs in vss. 8 (*lkd* and *nkh*) and 12 (*nkh* and
lkd), an example of a favorite literary device in poetry and popular narrative:
chiasm or inversion.

13. *Othniel.* The first savior judge in Israel. See 3:7–11.

ben Qenaz. EVV "Kenizzite," a member of a southern clan established at an
early period in southern Judah and the northern Negeb. See Map 2, Gen 36:11,
I Chron 1:36.

"brother." That is, military confederate, as in well-known Mari usage of
aḫu. In the course of traditional differentiation, Othniel was regarded as
either Caleb's brother (LXX^A) or nephew (LXX^B). Intricate Calebite genealogies in I Chron 2 and 4 imply complex tribal histories. See in general Malamat,
JAOS 88 (1968), 163–73.

14–15. This translation is adapted from that of Albright, who first recognized
the text's "scarcely disguised metrical form" (YGC, p. 48).

14. *he nagged her.* With LXX, Vulg., against MT which reads "she nagged

him." The latter does less damage to the image of the first "savior judge" (3:7–10) and may be taken as a tendentious development. The proposal to relate ṣnḥ, "dismount," to Akk. ṣanāḥu and render "she broke wind" as in NEB (Godfrey Rolles Driver, "Problems of Interpretation in the Hexateuch," *Mélanges biblique rediges en l'honneur de André Robert* [Paris: Bloud and Gay, 1966], pp. 75–76) has not found wide acceptance. It founders on scanty Akkadian evidence and semantic confusion in such a paraphrastic translation as the NEB in our verse. In any case the revival of this pericope by the final redactor suggests a reason why the earlier compiler of the body of the book confined himself to rubrics in reporting the career of Othniel as the first and ideal judge.

15. *The Negeb-land . . . basins of water*. Freedman has called the writer's attention to this strictly chiastic structure.

her heart's desire. With LXX, where kᵉlibbāh has dropped out of MT by haplography, thus spoiling the play on the name kālēb. Wilhelm Rudolph, "Textkritische Anmerkungen Zum Richterbuch," in *Festscrift O. Eissfeldt*, ed. Johann Füch (Halle: Max Niemeyer, 1947), p. 199. On the true function of the heart in early Israelite psychology as seat of mind and will, see 5:9 and NOTE.

The upper basins and the lower basins. Albright suggests subterranean pockets and basins underlying wadi beds and compares the deep shaft of the well el-Baiyārah, south of Tell Beit Mirsim, *The Excavation of Tell Beit Mirsim*, vol. 2 (New Haven: American Schools of Oriental Research, 1938), p. 4. They are to be a "blessing" to Achsah, a physical gift or bestowal.

16. *The Hebrew is corrupt*. The translation follows Albright's partial reconstruction on the basis of LXX plusses and glaring haplography in MT. Albright, YGC, pp. 40–41.

people. Heb. bᵉnē in its common usage to designate members of a class or group.

Hobab the Qenite, Moses' son-in-law. The full name of the clan-ancestor, who was probably ḥātān, "son-in-law," (not ḥōtēn, "father-in-law"), survived only in LXX. On the background of Heb. qēnī as "smith," "metal worker," see Albright, *Archaeology and the Religion of Israel* (Johns Hopkins Press, 1953), p. 98 f. The Qenites (Map 2, C-5) were, in all probability, also "Midianites" by political affiliation. De Vaux, "Sur l'Origine Kenite ou Madianite du Yahvisme" in *Eretz Israel* 9 (1969), 29.

Palm City. Probably Jericho and its oasis, which was in ruins at the time, or at most sparsely occupied. With contemporary Israelite headquarters at nearby Gilgal (2:1 and NOTE), the undeveloped oasis was a place from which friendly nomadic groups would first go up into the hill country before proceeding very far south. An alternative identification with 'Ain Hosb (the "Tamar" of I Kings 9:18 and Ezek 47:19), in the Arabah sixteen and a half miles southeast of the Dead Sea, has been proposed in connection with a theory of Simeon's entry into the land from the south. But this text is concerned with a Qenite group.

the plain . . . Arad. See illustration 1.

Arad. See Map 2, C-5. The site is known from excavations to have been only lightly occupied between the early third millennium and the tenth century, perhaps only as a seasonal (Qenite?) high place; it was regarded by the later traditionist as jumping-off point for the desert, as it is today. Yohanan Aharoni, BA 31 (1968), 31, locates the old Canaanite (Middle to Late Bronze Age) Arad at Tell el-Milḥ, some seven miles southwest of Tell Arab. See illustration 1a.

Amaleqites. The restoration of *'m[lqy]* follows Moore, p. 34, and others.

17. *Zephath . . . Ban-town.* The site is probably Tell Meshash, as proposed by Aharoni (see NOTE on *Arad*), just four miles west of Tell el-Milḥ. The new name (Heb. *ḥormā*) also encompasses a cluster of towns in Num 21:3. Here the name *ḥormā* is explained with reference to a key religio-economic institution in Israel — the ban (Heb. *ḥerem*).

put it under the ban. Heb. *way-yaḥrīmū.* The unilateral action of Judah and Simeon is irregular. See the story of Achan in Josh 7. The ban, or *ḥerem*, frequent in Joshua but uncharacteristic of the judges period, was originally the result of an ad hoc decree, as was the one at Mari (see p. 16). See 21:5 and 11 (cf. 8:24–27), the only other instances of *ḥerem* in the Book of Judges. It was at the outset, presumably, a way of building up the treasury in the emerging covenant league, the accumulation of booty marked for the king, Yahweh. See Abraham Malamat, *Biblical Essays: Proceedings of the Ninth Meeting of Die Ou-Testamentiese Werkgemeenskap in Suid-Afrika* (1966), pp. 40–49. The ad hoc character of the ban is clear in Num 21:1–3, which our passage parallels in part.

18. *Judah captured.* The claim is not readily harmonized with the verse following. It is often taken to mean that, despite initial successes there, Judah was unable to extend its sway effectively into the coastal plain. Moshe Dothan and D. N. Freedman, *Ashdod I. 'Atiqot,* English Series, VII (Jerusalem: Igra Press, 1967), 9. We suggest that the verb "captured" (*lkd*) is used with reference to the strategic ideal for the pacification of the plain; that is, Judah took these places mostly in the planning. LXX in this verse explicitly states that Judah did not "dispossess" the people of the plain, using the same verb as in the following verse (*yrš*). There is no way of explaining this divergence except to posit genuine traditions reflecting somewhat different concerns.

Ashdod with its territory. Dropped out of the Hebrew through haplography, but is retained in LXX. It was the arrival of the Philistines, presumably, that prevented the consolidation of Judahite claims. See Map 2, B-4. See now Moshe Dothan, "Ashdod of the Philistines," in *New Directions in Biblical Archaeology,* eds. Freedman and Greenfield (Garden City, N.Y.: Doubleday, 1969), pp. 15–24.

19. *Yahweh was indeed with Judah.* Introductory *wayhī;* see NOTE on vs. 1. Emphasis upon the subject here.

could not evict. The situation is also reflected in 3:1–3 and Josh 13:2–3. The translation reads *lō'yākōl lᵉhōrīš* in agreement with Josh 15:63 and 17:12. The ungrammatical and unparalleled *kī lō' lehōrīš* of MT is the result of haplography, in an early text. Two manuscripts retain the full reading.

iron. Probably used figuratively—a part for the whole—as chariots made entirely of iron would have been impractical. The Sea Peoples (among them the Philistines) are credited with the introduction of iron to the region, and it was used in the assemblage and fittings of the war chariots, for which the chief raw materials were wood and leather. Yigael Yadin, *The Art of Warfare in Bible Lands,* I (New York: McGraw-Hill, 1963), pp. 86–90.

he could not evict . . . iron chariots. See illustration 2.

20. *took possession of the three towns.* With LXX[A], missing in MT and LXX[B] through a haplography (*wyrš . . .*) *wygrš*. This verse is presumably an early annotation, by a scribe who did not want Caleb's role to be obscured. See NOTE on vs. 10.

21. *Jebusites.* They remained in Jerusalem. See NOTE on vs. 8.

to this day. This appears to be a redactional use of the formula, which addresses the tradition to a time when Judah and Benjamin are all that is left of Israel, i.e. late seventh to early sixth century. The secondary use of the formula here should be distinguished from the etiological character of vss. 22–26, which end on the same note. See the important study by Brevard Springs Childs, JBL 82 (1963), 279–92. See NOTE on 6:24b.

22. *house of Joseph.* Ephraim and Manasseh's pivotal achievement is here considered to be the reduction of Canaanite Bethel, "Temple of God" (Map 2, C-4); it was an ancient cult center reorganized as one of Jeroboam's two royal-temple cities but which continued to be a source of syncretism offensive to prophets throughout the biblical period. With no account of a Bethel battle in Joshua, we must reckon with the strong possibility of traditionary displacement, the appellative *Hā - 'Ai,* "The Ruin," crowding out "Bethel" in Josh 7–8. Evaluation of Joseph A. Callaway's proposal that it worked the other way around must await the publication of Et-Tell (*'Ai*) pottery and clarification of his adjusted Late Bronze–Iron I classification. See JBL 87 (1968), 312–20.

and Judah was with them. Despite the lack of details about Judah's role in the near north, this is the better text, surviving in LXX[AL] and OL. MT and other witness read "Yahweh" instead of "Judah," a difference of one letter and most probably the result of contamination from vs. 19.

23. *reconnoitered Bethel carefully.* Heb. *wayyātīrū* is here taken as an example of the hiphil elative. D. N. Freedman, private communication.

Deception. Heb. *lūz,* which means "to turn aside," "to depart," with devious or crafty connotations. The equation of Luz and Bethel occurs also in Josh 18:13, and the change of name is uniformly credited to Jacob (Gen 28:19; 35:6; 48:3).

24. *show us . . . the city.* See illustration 3.

an entrance. Not "the Gate." Nothing as massive and obvious as the excavated Late Bronze–Iron I structures can be in mind. A. F. Rainey compares the underground postern gate of the citadel at the Jerusalem suburb Ramat Raḥel, just wide enough for one person to enter at a time. *The Biblical World,* ed. C.F. Pfeiffer (Grand Rapids: Baker, 1966), p. 473.

deal justly with you. Lit. "do *ḥesed* (covenant loyalty) with you." Cf. the spies and Rahab (Josh 2:12) and the treaty with the Gibeonites (Josh 9). See also 8:35 and NOTE.

26. *the Hittite country.* See Map 1. Apparently his ancestral home. Thus the story which begins on an ominous note ends as a clear example of keeping treaty-faith.

built. With MT, where LXX adds "there" (Heb. *šm*). The latter, however, may be explained as contamination from "its name" (*šmh*) three words later. "New Luz" has not been located.

the present day. See second NOTE on vs. 21.

27–33. Anecdotes have set the tone of the introduction; review of the "transition" is now completed with brief listing of fortresses not reduced in Joseph and four other tribes. Transjordan is not in view, presumably on the basis of uniform tradition considering it the earliest and most satisfactorily settled, although it was the first to be lost by the monarchy. On the origin of the Judg 1 list in a prototype which also yielded the scattered notices of unconquered territory within the acount of the Joshua allotment, see Yohanan Aharoni, LOB, pp. 212–17.

27. *Beth-shean . . . Taanach . . . Dor . . . Ibleam . . . Megiddo*. Map 2, B-2–C-3. Did these five cities form a pentapolis? Freedman, private communication. Cf. Josh 17:11–13 (where En-dor may be a variant for Dor) and I Chron 7:29 (minus Ibleam).

dependencies. Lit. "daughter (town)s." The places mentioned by name were all strategically located centers of small city-states controlling important commercial and military traffic. Archaeology largely validates the traditional claims: such centers did not become Israelite until the rise of a strong monarchy.

27 and 29. Note the inversion of word order: in 27 the pattern in Hebrew is verb plus name (Manasseh), and in 29 it is name (Ephraim) plus verb, with the latter pattern then maintained to the end of the unit, vs. 33.

30. *Zebulun*. Cf. Josh 19:10–16. Ancient Qitron and Nahalal continue to evade modern identification.

31. *Acco . . . Rehob*. Cf. Josh 19:24–31. All of the towns in the Judges version have been identified—Acco and the coast north of Mount Carmel—with the exception of Rehob which must lie to the southeast of Acco (Map 2, B-2). Freedman has called the writer's attention to the interesting fact that this list of seven towns is divided grammatically into 2 + 5. These arrangements may reflect political organizations, that is, a strong pentapolis on the northern coast, with another pentapolis near the coast just south of Mount Carmel (vs. 27), like the famous Philistine pentapolis in the south.

LXX is longer: "they were subjected to forced labor," including "the inhabitants of Dor" in the list.

33. *Beth-shemesh and Beth-anath*. The extensive list in Josh 19:32–39 (nineteen towns) is, unfortunately, not reflected in the two towns mentioned here, both of which continue to resist location. Aharoni reviews the possibilities, LOB, p. 214. Old style religion is reflected in both names, "Temple of Sun" and "Temple of Anath," which perhaps explains why only they survive in this partial overview of nonconquest. See the "message" in 2:2.

to forced labor. The statement in Judg 1 is generally taken to be anachronistic, since it is not until the tenth century, with David and Solomon, that the corvée is considered to be oppressive. It is in fact remembered as a decisive ground for the secession of the northern tribes (I Kings 12); the exigencies were then at hand to make it oppressive. But the kings in the tenth century must have had some precedent; and it would be remarkable if Israelites, many of whom had been recruited from the ranks of forced laborers, did not make use of the same system when faced with the problems of geographical expansion. On the other hand, confronted by the alternatives to fight or to flee, many Canaanites had offered to serve.

34–35. Least successful of all was Dan's attempt to revolutionize the foothills between the coastal plain and the Judean high country (Map 2, B-4), leading ultimately to Dan's migration to the far north, chs. 17–18.

34. *Westerners.* "Amorite" in its original sense (as in 6:10), in this case denoting peoples indigenous to the west of old Dan's geographical center.

allow them. With LXX which reflects a plural suffix where MT reads singular, "him."

35. *Har-heres . . . Shaalbim.* The first is "mountain of the sun." Of the three towns listed, only this remains to be located, unless, as generally supposed, it is to be identified with the southern Beth-shemesh, "house of the sun," which is also called Ir-shemesh, "city of the sun." Map 2, B-4. Archaeology requires an early date for the attempt at Danite settlement there. Elihu Grant and Wright, *Ain Shemesh Excavations,* V (Haverford College, 1939), 11 f.

gained control over them. MT omits the prepositional phrase, which is here adapted from the parallel passage in Josh 19:47. LXX reads "over the Amorites."

they were put to forced labor. Some time after Dan had retreated, the Joseph tribes were able to organize the area, and this statement forms an inclusio with vs. 22, comprising "Nonconquest, Part II."

36. *The Amorite border.* The verse is obviously a fragment. The translation follows MT, although there is strong LXX support for reading "Edomite."

Scorpions' Pass. Most likely Neqb es-Safa, which descends from Beersheba to the Wadi Murra (Map 2, B-5).

Sela. Presumably one of the Edomite (Map 2, C-6) strongholds of that name.

Thus both readings, Amorite and Edomite, may be correct. It is the same border that is being commented upon, but two ways of registering perplexity over the use of Amorite in its original sense (Westerner) in the preceding unit. This verse is a gloss which stands outside a carefully organized chapter.

2:1–5. These verses return to the original and larger question of 1:1, where the specific question was premature. Other contexts indicate that orderly oracular inquiry requires first a general question: "Shall we go?" or the like (II Sam 2:1; 5:19, 23; I Kings 12:24; 22:6, 15). Such decisions were Yahweh's prerogative alone. On the pivotal significance of individual judges as oracle seekers, see H. C. Thomson, *Transactions of the Glasgow University Oriental Society,* 19 (1961–62), 74–85. Here the supposedly etiological story serves a much more profound historical purpose. Cf. the use of the etiology of Lehi in NOTES on 15:9 and 14.

1. *Yahweh's envoy.* An angelic being who functions in early narrative as courier and representative of the heavenly court, appearing in human form. With the rise of classical prophecy under the monarchy references to such

heavenly functionaries are few and far between until the "postprophetic" period. Claus Westermann, *Basic Forms of Prophetic Speech* (Philadelphia: Westminster, 1967), pp. 98–100. It should be emphasized that the function of the *mal'ak Yhwh*, before and after the classical prophecy, is diplomatic. In view of the angel's performance elsewhere in the judges period (6:11–24 and 13:2–22), there seems to be no reason for not taking this vignette as a statement of exasperation, which implements previously formulated policy (Exod 23:20–33; *E*); an old story of one incident involving Yahweh's heavenly envoy has here absorbed something of the character of the prophetic covenant lawsuit. Cf. the speech of the sole prophet to appear in the book (6:7–10) and the speech of the divine "judge" (10:11–14).

The Circle. Heb. *hag-gilgal.* An important sanctuary town of the old amphictyony (still flourishing in the eighth century: Amos 4:4, 5:5, Hosea 4:15, 9:15, 12:11), where cultic celebration gave particular emphasis to conquest motifs. Gilgal is treated as an Israelite base-camp in conquest narratives: Josh 4:19–20; 5:10; 9:6; 10:6–9, 15, 43; 14:6. Exact location uncertain; see Map 2, C-4.

The Weepers. Heb. *hab-bōkīm.* Omission of the definite article with the place name in vs. 5 yields a transparent wordplay which requires something like 1:1 for its presupposition. LXX specifies "to Bochim and Bethel and the house of Israel," i.e. Weepers and Bethel may be identical. Cf. "Oak of Weeping" near Bethel in Gen 35:8, AB, vol. 1, 1964.

Lord Yahweh brought you. With LXX^A, where MT reads "I brought . . ." (*'a'alē*), which seems to be a fragment of the tradition behind LXX^B. The latter treats the entire speech as Yahweh's direct address and introduces it with "Thus Yahweh has said." In other words, the entire speech in the LXX^B MT tradition has been assimilated to the prophetic indictment speech form. For the older narrative usage involving direct address to Lord Yahweh, see 6:22.

the land that he promised on oath. The language of the envoy of the old epic sources is here thoroughly Deuteronomic: see Deut 1:8, 35; 6:10, 18, 23; 7:13; 8:1; 11:9, 21; 19:8; 26:3, 15; 28:11; 30:20; 31:23.

your fathers. Generations of the wilderness and conquest periods, 3:4. Background material: Exod 23:23–33, 34:11–16, which are variously echoed in the earliest introduction to the judges period, 2:20 – 3:6. Covenants with indigenous Canaanite people would necessarily involve their deities. The prohibition of secondary alliances and the command to wreck such altars is preserved in Exod 34:12–13.

2. LXX^A is longer; it adds "I will no longer drive out the people whom I said I would dispossess." Cf. Num 33:50–56.

How could you do this? The thrust of the question becomes clear from LXX, which renders Heb. *mh* as though it were *ky*, "because you did these things." I owe this observation to D. N. Freedman.

4. *and wept.* As they did on the eve of solution to the problem of wives for Benjamin, with which the book concludes (21:2) and in the crisis that was countered by the administrative genius of Samuel, last judge in early Israel (I Sam 11:4).

5. *place*. The common noun is *māqōm*, but here it is used in the specific sense of "sacred place," "sacred precinct" (as in Gen 12:6, 13:3). See below on the Shechem Temple (ch. 9), and the usage in 20:22.

There they sacrificed. Cf. the climax to preparations for Gideon's rout of the Midianites, where at last he "fell prone" (7:15a), and the immediate sequel to Hannah's good news that she would have a son (I Sam 1:28b): "there they fell prone, before Yahweh!"

COMMENT

The death of Joshua, leaving no designated successor, posed an un-paralleled crisis of leadership for the federated tribes. The reader should compare this introduction to the judges era with the elaborate divine commission of Joshua at the beginning of the preceding one (Josh 1:1–9). Judges begins on quite another note, with a question which was originally a question about leadership: who is now to take the lead in the military operations? The answer, however, designates a tribe, not a leader. That this is something out of the ordinary is confirmed by the nearly identical answer to the same question in 20:18, "Judah first." The context of the latter is a somewhat stylized picture of a tragic civil war, in which the entire might of the federation is mobilized against the small tribe of Benjamin, for one man's claim. Except for these chapters, used to frame the traditions of the judges, there is nowhere any indication that oracular means were used to assign individual tribal responsibilities in the military operations.

We conclude that the relation of question and answer in 1:1–2, like that of the question and answer of the narrative context in 20:18, is an artificial one. This means that the editor of ch. 1 is presenting his people's historical traditions about the early period as the word of Yahweh. As noted in the Introduction (pp. 26–32), the final editor was probably living in exile. He recognizes no possibility for a military future but succeeds in bringing the book to a positive and hopeful conclusion (ch. 21).

His sources for the long and composite answer to the question of 1:1 were already ancient in his day. This chapter is unlike anything else in the book. It is certainly not a unified literary composition, but is built up of preformed narrative units together with archival details and notices of various sorts. The materials have, however, been carefully arranged to report tribal activities roughly on a line from south to north, beginning with Judah eager for the offensive, and ending with Dan and native westerners at a stalemate (see Map 2, B-4). There are duplications of Joshua material and some discordant details. See G. Ernest Wright, "The Literary and Historical Problem of Joshua 10 and Judges 1," JNES 5 (1946), 105–14.

The bulk of the chapter is generally assigned by scholars to *J* (Eissfeldt to *L*), as stemming from a great tradition-gathering enterprise of the tenth to ninth centuries. In later centuries *J* came to the surface in Judg 1 because the northern recension of the conquest tradition (*E*) had already become the normative version, filling the first half of the Book of Joshua. But the purpose of the revival of the old traditions was not to bring in a minority report about the overall claims for Israel's entry into Canaan. It prepares instead for a largely negative evaluation of the entire period of the judges, showing why the question of 1:1 was finally answered by 2:1–5, the speech of a heavenly envoy. The final (exilic) redactor of the introduction was thus supplementing the critical perspective of the seventh century Deuteronomic Historian when he built into the interim between Joshua's death and Othniel's rescue of the nation (3:7–11) this prelude to the era, a little-known period which he indicated unfolded from an eagerly united beginning to a scattered and indecisive conclusion. Compare the movement within the body of the book, from Othniel in the south (3:7–11) to the Danite traditions in chs. 13–18.

In the events of chs. 19–21, on the other hand, the admission of defeat is the prelude to victory and peace at last in Israel (20:27). Moreover, this last and latest "frame" to the judges period can be correlated with the final (exilic) editorial work on the introduction to Deuteronomy, which also shows inverted use of the warfare terminology to present the rebellion at Qadesh: only with the demise of that whole generation of warriors was Israel prepared for the conquest! See Moran, *Biblica* 44 (1963), 333–42.

The improved understanding of the rapid expansion and consolidation of Israel in Canaan along the lines of a peasant revolt touched off by arrival of the Yahweh-covenanters helps to explain how Judges 1 could so crudely caricature the role of Judah, while the normative conquest book mirrors the predominant role of northern tribes. That is, throughout the twelfth and eleventh centuries Israel was repeatedly being reconstituted and reactivated by covenant renewal at one important sanctuary or another. The later historians merely added together the exploits and achievements of individuals and tribes in various combinations to document their statement of Yahweh's case against Israel.

The precise historical role of Judah in the emergence of Israel is notoriously difficult to assess. Archaeology in the southern hill country has documented a widespread upheaval in the late thirteenth and early twelfth centuries in the area where Judah later lived. On the special problem raised by Jerusalem and "Adoni-bezeq," see NOTES on vss. 4–8 and 21. The tradition remembered, on the other hand, that except for the notice in vs. 22 and the contribution of Judge Othniel, the south did not again assume a history making role until the time of David.

With the rapid expansion of territorial claims by member tribes, Yahweh's government of Israel would now embrace variables that Moses had never dreamed of. Caleb's daughter Achsah (vss. 12–15) ignores the request of her husband, who will be judge in 3:7, and substitutes her own desire (surely the editor implies a contrast with the Shiloh maidens in ch. 21, and the quick-thinking elders who there attend to the future of all Israel). Such a reading of this introductory story helps to understand why the "pragmatic compiler," whose own southern hero (Othniel) stood at the head of the list, had confined himself to essential rubrics in reporting the career of the first great judge (3:7–11). The pragmatic compiler was the first (whose work has survived) to excerpt stories from the epic sources and bring them together for practical instruction about the meaning of the period in question.

While the notice about the Qenites ("Smiths") is only fragmentary (vs. 16), it seems to have been placed so as to point a contrast. The Qenites constituted an element in the Yahwist confederation which was originally at home in the deserts to the north and northeast of Sinai. In Canaan they acquired a reputation for unilateral action (cf. 4:11–12 NOTES and COMMENT), and here they represent the polar opposite of Judah in this review of "conquering" Israelites. It is possible that the recently discovered Israelite temple at Arad occupies a site considered holy by this early Qenite settlement. Benjamin Mazar, JNES 24 (1965), 297–303. See illustration 1.

Amaleqites were arch-antagonists of the confederation from the early days of the Exodus generation (Exod 17:8–13) to Saul (I Sam 15). The long enmity provided a pivotal theme of the Book of Esther ("Haman the Agagite" belongs to an Amaleqite clan and his death puts an end to that ancient feud). In the second crisis of the book, Amaleqites are in league with Moabites and Ammonites against Israel (3:12–13); later they are aligned with Midian (6:3).

Verses 17 and 18 pick up the theme of vs. 3 (Judah's big brother policy), showing how Judah helped Simeon to make a conquest and then turned immediately to the raiding of prime coastal towns for Judah. The towns in question were very soon in Philistine control; and it may be that the text indicates little more than Judah's claim, based on strictly formal partitioning of land yet to be pacified.

Verse 19 caps off the "preview of the period, part I" with the assurance, "Yahweh was indeed with Judah."

Verses 20 and 21 are individual and unrelated contributions made perhaps by scribal annotators over the years who did not want this or that element of tradition to be lost.

The northern half of the chapter (vss. 22–36) begins, like the southern half, with an anecdote, recounting the capture of Bethel (formerly Luz) as part of a cooperative maneuver involving the tribes of Joseph and Judah. This old story of negotiation with a prominent citizen resulting in the capture of Luz, while in itself a story of the commendable keeping of treaty faith by all parties concerned (an editorial inversion with Rahab and the spies in Josh 2?), seems to have served the final editor as an example of the convenant-making that had been outlawed by Yahweh according to the indictment of Israel in 2:2.

The remainder of the chapter drives home the lesson of the anecdote. One after another the west Jordan tribes failed to follow through on the reforms that were assigned, perhaps by the federation's assembly, to introduce an equalization of wealth and to avoid the reassertion of the old feudal structure. Here is another witness to the origin of such legislation as that regarding the Sabbatical year (Exod 23:11; Lev 25:4; Deut 15:9) and the jubilee year (Lev 25:8–22) in the revolutionary amphictyonic period. These laws all dealt with the periodic cancellation of debts, restoration of lands, and release of Israelite debtor-slaves. The heinous aspect of the corvée was precisely the lack of legal protections. To resort to the corvée, the late redactor implies, was to take the easy way out.

Against the repeated assertion here that they "did not dispossess," the text of Joshua asserts twice that they "could not": Josh 15:63 (Judah versus Jebusites in Jerusalem) and 17:12 (Manasseh versus "cities" of which the referent is obscure). In our chapter the only occasion upon which they "could not" is immediately explained; the opposition had "iron chariots" (vs. 19).

The review of the performance of individual tribes concludes with a notice about Dan extracted from still another source. Here the attempts at Yahwist pacification of the area were so unsuccessful that Dan would eventually pull up stakes and migrate to the far north (ch. 18) in the early eleventh century, as is known from excavations at Tell Dan (Abraham Biran, IEJ 19 [1969], 123). Thus the review of the tribes in ch. 1 is structured by the fixed organization of the earlier (Deuteronomic) book (from Judah to Dan, in two parts).

Verse 36 is not integral to the chapter but appears to be a marginal "correction" by a scribe who missed the etymological sense of "Amorite" (*Westerner*) in the preceding verse. Here, on the contrary, Amorite seems to be a proper noun.

In summary, Judg 1 is intended neither as a rival account of the conquest period nor as a corrective to the normative statement. Rather, it is a review of the performance of the generation that outlived Joshua, when Othniel was one of the few remembered links. It is compiled from various sources, some superior to the Joshua account (e.g. vss. 22–25), others much more problematical (e.g. vss. 5–8). The purpose is to indicate the contrast between the situation under Joshua, the great war leader, and the subsequent deterioration of federation structure and the concomitant erosion of Yahwist loyalties. It is neither specifically pro- nor anti-monarchical. It affirms Yahweh's gracious preservation of the realm in a hectic period.

In ch. 2 the scene involving the Yahweh angel (vss. 1–5) is loose at both ends. The first chapter was prefixed to the book to explain why the Israelites were weeping at the outset of ch. 2. The connection between 2:1–5 and what follows is still more difficult.

The story of the advent of the heavenly envoy arriving to communicate a change of heaven's strategy has the marks of popular celebration only in its introduction and conclusion. The content of the speech, on the contrary, bears many marks of the Deuteronomic school, e.g. the explicit concern with entangling "covenants" and the specific reference to "their altars," where such covenants were established and remembered. Each of these elements has its roots in the old epic tradition (see esp. Exod 23:20–33). Their configuration here is strikingly similar to the Deuteronomic portrayal of developments in Josiah's reign (II Kings 22–23), once the lost lawbook was rediscovered. The result of the confrontation at the outset of the judges period was a new act of allegiance: "There they sacrificed to Yahweh."

Thus the Deuteronomic edition is the covenant renewal version of Judges, presenting a state of affairs so drastic as to require God's judicial intervention in order to reconstitute Israel.

The beginning of ch. 2 presupposes for its setting an occasion of public lamentation. Such occasions regularly involved oracular inquiry, posing questions that are familiar from the psalms: "How long?" "Why?" Perhaps the abrupt appearance of the angel in 2:1 had its narrative motivation in the need to head off an oracular response to some such question, a question now displaced by 1:1 and the lengthy historical implementation as background for the envoy's proclamation. Thus the angel appeared to the inquiring Weepers and announced a change of policy of such moment that they renamed that holy place Weepers. Such reversals are an invariable constituent of the most clearly Deuteronomic sections of the book, e.g. the speech of the unnamed prophet in 6:7–10 and the work of the divine organizer of Israel in 10:10–16.

In thus introducing the judges as part of a history that climaxed in his day with the great Josiah, the Deuteronomic Historian was elaborating upon a perspective that was already inherent in the early saga materials. See below, on vss. 20–23 and 3:1–4. The pre-Deuteronomic (or "pragmatic," see p. 65) version of Judges was a still livelier account, as becomes clear in the study of the hero stories.

THE HISTORY OF ISRAEL
WITH THE JUDGES

II. A GENERATION GAP
(2:6–10)

2 ⁶Joshua had discharged the troops and each one of the Israelites had gone to his own plot to take possession of the land. ⁷The troops had served Yahweh throughout Joshua's days and the days of the elders who outlived Joshua, who had witnessed the whole of Yahweh's great work, which he did on behalf of Israel.

⁸But Joshua ben Nun, Yahweh's Servant, had died, at the age of one hundred and ten. ⁹They buried him in his inherited territory at Timnath-heres in the Ephraimite hill country, north of Mount Gaash. ¹⁰Finally, all of that generation were gathered to their fathers, and after them there arose another generation that knew neither Yahweh nor the work that he had done on behalf of Israel!

NOTES

2:6. *the troops*. Heb. *hā-ʿām*, lit. "the people," originally designated merely kinsfolk but later connoted "people" in the widest sense. In conquest traditions *hā-ʿām* alternates with *ʿam ham-milḥāmā*, "the people-at-war." Cf. Josh 8:1, 3 and 8:5, 9, 10, 13. Boling, VT 16 (1966), 298, n. 2.

7. *great work*. For example 2:1, the exodus from Egyptian slavery and the gift of a land, two standing themes of the historical credo in its earliest formulations. See G. von Rad, *The Problem of the Hexateuch and Other Essays*, tr. E. W. Trueman Dicken (Edinburgh: Oliver and Boyd, 1966), pp. 1–78.

8. *ben*. Lit. "son," but actually part of the name.

Yahweh's Servant. As administrative title borne first by Moses (Josh 1:1) and then Joshua, who left no designated successor. Elsewhere, among the figures of the judges era, only Caleb is designated "servant," and that in a confidential communication to Moses (Num 14:24). Within the Book of Judges, Samson takes the title (15:18). Later on, "servant" is used in reference to three members of the Davidic house (David, Hezekiah, Zerubbabel) and applied honorifically to the three great patriarchs (Abraham, Isaac, Jacob) but is especially frequent in contemporary references to prophets. The title would have a distinctive history, climaxing in the songs of the Second Isaiah (Isa 40–55, AB, vol. 20, 1968). There Yahweh's suffering "servant" is the diplomat and Cyrus is "the anointed," in a poetic drama of international reconciliation that leads from exile (Isa 40) to an eschatological feast (Isa 55).

9. *Timnath-heres.* "Portion of the sun," located some fifteen miles south-west of Shechem. See *The Westminster Historical Atlas to the Bible*, ed. G. E. Wright, *et al.* (Philadelphia: Westminster, 1955), Plate VI, C-4. This is prob-ably the original name. By mere transposition of first and last letters, the name reads *timnath-serah* "left-over portion," as in Josh 19:50 (the story of the as-signment of Joshua's allotment from land that was "left over") and Josh 24:30. The latter spelling thus reflects a popular etymology.

10. *gathered to their fathers.* Israel's expression for entry upon the afterlife, not merely a euphemism for death. Eric M. Meyers, BA 33 (1970), esp. 15–17.

knew neither Yahweh nor the work that he had done. The verb "to know" is here used as in Exod 1:8 (a king who knew not Joseph). The statement marks the turn of an era, not merely the passage of time but also a basic change in situation and relationships, as will become clear in the following verse. On the semantics of *yd'* "to know" in covenantal formulations, clarified from their treaty background, see Huffmon, BASOR 181 (February, 1966), 31–37. The knowing expressed is the action of acknowledgment, entrance into a formulated relationship. Cf. the description of Joshua's generation, which "served Yahweh . . . and knew all the work he did" (Josh 24:31). Those who outlived Joshua "served Yahweh" although it was only the elders who had "seen" great things (vs.7), thus fulfilling the requirements of the context of Deut 11:7.

COMMENT

Here begins the early epic segment of the introduction, as is clear from the shift to an expansive narrative style that is in abrupt contrast to the preceding material. A striking fact is the identity of vss. 6–9 (but in another sequence) to Josh 24:28–31. It appears that an old Joshua-Judges narrative has been broken open, in order to be updated in terms of a theological review of historical epochs (see Introduction, "The Growth of the Book of Judges"). The transitional sentences were repeated, but their sequence revised, yielding a structure more appropriate to the beginning of a story. The new period begins with an indictment. The "lawsuit" that is pressed by the Deuteronomic Yahweh envoy (2:1–5) exegetes the older narrative's climactic comment in vs. 10. Thus the statement of the generation gap is a corporate accusation, not an excuse. See NOTES.

The logical narrative sequel to Israel's alienation from Yahweh in vs. 10 is the eruption of the divine wrath in vs. 20 (i.e. the old epic's counterpart to the Yahweh envoy scene). It thus appears that the old book has been broken open once again for the insertion of heterogeneous material, chiefly Deutero-nomic, in the second half of the chapter.

III. The Pattern of the Period
(2:11–23)

2 11 Israelites did what was evil in Yahweh's sight and served Baal.
12 They deserted Yahweh, their fathers' God, who led them out of
the land of Egypt, and followed other gods from among the gods of
the peoples all around them. They fell prone before them! They
vexed Yahweh! 13 They deserted Yahweh and served Baal and
Astarte! 14 Yahweh's wrath blazed against Israel, and he delivered
them into the hand of plunderers who plundered them. He sold them
into the hand of enemies on all sides; they could no longer withstand
their enemies. 15 Whenever they ventured forth, Yahweh's hand was
with them—for evil!—exactly as Yahweh had said, exactly as he had
assured them on oath. They were besieged!

16 On the other hand Yahweh raised up judges, and the latter
saved them from the hand of their plunderers. 17 Still they did not
listen to their judges; indeed, they prostituted themselves to other
gods and bowed themselves before them. They promptly turned aside
from the path that their fathers had followed—obedience to Yahweh's
commands! That is exactly what they did not do!

18 So long as Yahweh was elevating judges for them, Yahweh was
with the judge. He would rescue them from their enemies' power
throughout the days of a given judge, for Yahweh was moved to sorrow by their moaning, because of those who oppressed them (and
those who harried them). 19 And when the judge died, they turned
and behaved more corruptly than their fathers, following other gods,
serving them, falling prone before them! They did not discard any of
their practices. They did not turn aside from their obstinacy.

20 Yahweh's wrath blazed against Israel. He said, "Because this
people have violated my covenant, which I commanded their fathers,
and have not obeyed my voice, 21 I will not continue to evict anyone

for their sake from the communities which Joshua left when he died, 22 so as to test Israel with them."

Would they be careful about the ways of Yahweh, walking in them as carefully as had their fathers, or not? 23 Yahweh let those communities remain without evicting them at once, since he had not surrendered them to Joshua's hand.

NOTES

2:11–23. This segment of the introduction describes a pattern of apostasy, hardship, moaning, and rescue, a pattern to be illustrated for various segments of Israel in the stories which follow, where Yahweh is represented as the great saving administrator of the realm.

11. *did what was evil.* "Evil" is here considered a religious offense with sociopolitical consequences (note the same word in vs. 15) as in the framework of the various judges pericopes (3:7, 12; 4:1; 6:1; 10:6; 13:1) and in Deut 4:25; 9:18; 17:2; 22:19.

Baal. This name in vss. 11 and 13 forms an inclusio to a vivid narrative scene. The alternation in the Hebrew between *'t b'lym* in 11 and *lb'l* in 13 (the same verb in both, *'bd*) reflects the survival of two linguistic features well known from Ugarit. The ending of *b'lym* may be explained as enclitic; the prefix of *lb'l* may be taken as emphatic use of the particle *lamed*, frequent in Hebrew as in Ugaritic. Dahood, *Psalms III, 101–150*, AB, vol. 17A (1970), p. 406. The vignette first announces the theme: indictment of Israelites for treason, desertion to Baal (11). It then recounts a period of frenzied pursuit of other gods (12) before fastening, as first asserted, on Baal and his consort Astarte (13). The latter appears as a plural in Hebrew, not to be taken numerically as she is the one who in herself sums up the variations of her identity in numerous forms and places. The mention of Baal and his consort here, in 3:7 (where she is named Asherah), and in 10:6 (where she is again named Astarte; the redactors did not harmonize) together with thematic and other stylistic continuities in all three sections, will yield a segmented or two-cycle presentation of the judges era. The fluctuation in the name of the consort indicates redactional use of preformed units. See the Schematic Outline, p. 30.

14. *into the hand.* See NOTE on 1:2.

on all sides. The earliest judges have to deal with threats posed by neighbors in the immediate vicinity: the southern hills (3:7–11), Moab (3:12–30), Philistia (3:31), and the Canaanite coalition (4:1 – 5:31). Thereafter the enemy base is either farther afield (Midianites, Ammonites) or a problem within Israel itself (Abimelech). See Moran, *Biblica* 46 (1965), 227, who, however, retains the reference to Aram in 3:7–11.

15. *besieged.* With LXX and OL, reading *way-yāṣor* (root *ṣwr/ṣrr*) where the MT form is peculiar (*way-yēṣer*, as though from the root *yṣr* "to form, fashion").

16. *Yahweh raised up judges.* Johannes Pedersen concluded that "judging" is acting so as to uphold the covenant. *Israel* I, 3d reprinting (Oxford University Press, 1959), 348 ff.

saved. Heb. *yš'.* See Introduction, p. 6.

17. *prostituted themselves.* An apt theological metaphor for religious defection, arising from the early clash of Yahwism with the commonly assumed fertility rites of sub-Mosaic religion.

18–23. Awareness of both Yahweh's "sorrow" and his "wrath" were necessary to a theological understanding of Israel's entry into a new historical phase.

19. *They did not turn aside.* With LXX^A where MT and other witnesses reflect a haplography in the Heb. *mm'llyhm (wl' ysr)w mdrkm.*

20. *violated.* Heb. *'āb^erū,* lit. "passed by," but with stealth. See how Ehud "escaped" in 3:26, how Gideon "went on the prowl" in 8:4, how Gaal also "went on the prowl" in 9:26, and how Jephthah "stalked" the Ammonites in 11:29. Alternative idiom involves the verb *'āz^ebū,* "they forsook," "abandoned," as in I Kings 19:10, 14, and the LXX *Vorlage* of this verse. Both idioms seem to refer to the larger covenant relationship rather than to specific terms of it.

21. *I will not continue to evict.* Not a rash decision, but one which followed upon long deliberation and repeated frustration. Yahweh is here represented as concluding a session of the heavenly court, rendering his just decision regarding Israel.

communities. On this rendering see NOTE on 3:1.

22. *ways of Yahweh.* Freedman suggests (private communication) that the initial *yōd* of "Yahweh" may be taken as serving double duty at the end of *drk(y),* thereby yielding grammatical agreement with the plural *bām.*

Would they . . . or not? A literary device of the double (and triple) rhetorical question, common to both Ugaritic and Hebrew. Held, *Eretz Israel* 9 (1969), 71–79, cites also 6:31, 9:2, 11:25, and 20:28. We should add 18:3. This rhetorical conclusion is scarcely an alternative to the reason given in vs. 20; rather it is the didactic climax of the whole unit.

23. The divine decision is supported by reference to historical precedent.

COMMENT

Critical scholars are generally agreed that these verses comprise a "pragmatic introduction" that is related to the framework passages enclosing the careers of individual hero judges. It is necessary, however, to distinguish at least three hands at work in ch. 2, none of them tampering with the work of a predecessor, but each supplying a paragraph or two for the sake of a fuller picture.

Proceeding on the assumption that the earliest audiences for the judges stories would have needed no description of the office (it was still alive in their memory), we can confidently isolate vss. 20–23 as the earliest strand of the section, harking back to the climactic statement on nonalignment with Yahweh in vs. 10. Significantly it is this segment which uses the word "covenant" (vs. 20).

The convenantal sense of the verb "to know" (vs. 10), on the other hand, was widely obscured in later years, remaining alive, so far as anyone can tell, only in Deuteronomic and prophetic circles. Thus the "pragmatic introduction" is in essence an exegesis of what is involved in a failure to know Yahweh. That is, to "do evil" was to commit a sociopolitical offense, where God was previously acknowledged as chief executive of the state. The invariable concomitant of not knowing Yahweh was to fall into the clutches of the only alternatives (vs. 11), the great storm god and his consorts, as they were served at a multitude of local establishments. Each new threat in the period was subsequently interpreted as Yahweh's very real provision for the restoration of his realm. It is important to note that this is an introduction to the period as a whole; it does not imply a cyclical view of historical process. The one element in the framework formula that might support such a view, the statement that in hard times Israelites appealed to Yahweh, is conspicuously absent here. The right of appeal could also be exploited (e.g. Amarna Letters), as the Deuteronomic redactors later made explicit (2:1–5, 6:7–10, 10:6–16). Here nothing is permitted to divert attention from Yahweh's even-handed administration of the realm, in the period after Joshua.

Verses 18 and 19 are often assigned also to the "pragmatic" stratum. (Richter, *Retterbuches,* p. 87). However, the section is repetitive and adds little (the reminder of Yahweh's compassion in 18b is here for the first time explicit). That each generation "behaved more corruptly" (Heb. *hišḥītū*) states the problem in a way that does not occur again in the books of Judges through II Kings (Moran, *Biblica* 46 [1965], 227). We may therefore suspect that this most severe statement of the case against Israel belongs, with chs. 1 and 19–21, to the exilic updating of the Deuteronomic work.

One common denominator of all three strata in this chapter is the explicit contrast between the generations under the judges and that of the fathers (vss. 12, 19, 20). This is not a reference to the patriarchs. There is no hint of double entendre in any of these verses; the "good" generation of the fathers was that of Joshua and Moses, covenanters par excellence. But after Joshua's death, Israel's activity was such as to arouse the wrath of Yahweh and stimulate his sorrowing compassion.

IV. Israel: A Disciplined Society
(3:1–6)

3 ¹ These are the communities Yahweh let remain in order to test Israel with them, all, that is, who had no experience of any Canaanite wars ² (only for the education of the Israelite generations, to teach them about war; only for those who had not formerly experienced them): ³ the five Philistine Tyrants, and all the Canaanites, Sidonians, and Hivites living on Mount Lebanon, from Mount Baalhermon to the approach to Hamath. ⁴ They were there to test Israel, to learn whether Israel would obey Yahweh's commands, which he had enjoined upon their fathers through Moses.

⁵ But the Israelites settled down amidst the Canaanites, Hittites, Amorites, Perizzites, Hivites, and Jebusites; ⁶ they took their daughters for themselves as wives and their own daughters they gave to their sons. And they served their gods!

Notes

3:1–6. This section is compounded of two lists of peoples in the midst of whom Israel was to be tested. The first list is introduced by the hair-raising explanation that Israel had yet to acquire adequate experience of war. Verse 4 echoes the note on which the preceding section ends (2:23) and gives the question an explicitly covenantal setting in terms of commands. Verse 5 summarizes results. How is this "devoid of any strictly religious purpose" (Burney, p. 54)? The point is not merely that the new generation will learn about war the hard way, that is, by experience. For vs. 5 summarizes results. To the redactors of the stories, the presence of the communities made possible the alternation of times of crisis and peace, depending upon Israel's behavior.

1. *These are the communities.* Cf. Josh 23:4, 7, 12. Policy was being updated.

communities. Heb. *gōyīm,* usually rendered "nations." The Mari cognate is "gang," "group of workmen." *The Assyrian Dictionary,* Oriental Institute of the University of Chicago, (1956–   ), vol. V, p. 59. For sociological description see

Malamat, *Les Congrès et Colloques de l'Université de Liège* 42 (1967), 133–35.
The nonterritorial sense clarifies to some extent the odd juxtapositions in our
lists: e.g. both "Canaanites" and "Sidonians" in the first list, but both "Canaanites" and "Amorites" in vs. 5. Cf. also the ethnic-gentilic origins of many modern youth gang names.

2. . . . *education . . . experienced.* . . . A parenthetical play on the verbal
root *yd'*, connoting "to know from experience" (cf. 8:16 and NOTE). With
Yahweh as subject it is rendered "to learn" in vs. 4. The effect of the parenthesis is to shift the emphasis and obscure the narrative movement from ex-
periential prospect in vs. 1 to covenantal contingency in vs. 4, which had set
the stage for the negative conclusion in vs. 5.

to teach them about war. The piel theme of stative verbs is often factitive.
"To learn them a lesson" is a good colloquial equivalent. Thus the statement is
not to be classified with the psalmist's praise after the fact, "Who trained my
hands for battle . . . ," Ps 18:35. See Dahood, *Psalms I, 1–50,* AB, vol. 16
(1966), 18:35 and NOTE.

3. *five Philistine Tyrants.* A reference to the new political organization
introduced to their part of the country. This phrase at the head of the list is
further evidence that *gōyīm* in this context does not have territorial denotation.
That is, five "Tyrants" make up one gang.

Hivites. Newcomers, like the Philistines, probably from southeastern Asia
Minor. *TenGen,* pp. 154–63.

4. *to learn.* The subject of this verb, by implication, is Yahweh.

5–6. The second list includes not only near neighbors (from the geographical
perspective of the later nation) but enclaves in the heart of contested territory.

5. Seven "nations" are mentioned in Deut 7:1, to which this list is related. We
suspect that "Girgashites" has been omitted by accident in our text.

Hittites. See Map 1. Descended from small kingdoms left behind by the once
mighty Anatolian empire. By the time of our literary sources they are "fully
assimilated to the surrounding Semitic population." I. J. Gelb, IDB II, p. 613.

Amorites. See NOTES on 1:34–36.

Perizzites. Probably "rustics." See NOTE on 1:4.

Jebusites. See 1:21 and NOTE on 1:8.

took their daughters . . . and their own daughters they gave. Regarded as
undesirable not because it threatened genealogical purity but because of the
problem that it posed for league security. The problem of "wives for Benjamin"
in ch. 21 is a particular one; here it is generalized: "they served their gods!"

COMMENT

These verses bring to a close the long composite introduction. Form criticism has ably demonstrated that it was the beginning and end of major segments
that experienced the most vicissitudes, as the tradition was taken up in successive editions in order to keep the record theologically relevant.

Presumably the same redactional strata detected elsewhere in the introduction to the stories are represented here. Verses 5–6 clearly relate to the list in Deut 7:1 and may be assigned to the work of the Deuteronomic Historian, the age of Josiah's reform. These verses offer a negative example out of the past in order to underscore the enormous import of the present.

To the Deuteronomistic enterprise of the exilic period we may probably assign the parenthetical remarks of vs. 2. They emphasize explicitly what is implicitly a major theme of ch. 20 (a chapter which also stems from that enterprise), the theme of divine discipline through the experience of warfare.

V. Othniel: The Idea of the Office
(3:7–11)

3 7 The Israelites did what was evil in Yahweh's sight. They forgot Yahweh their God and served Baal and Asherah! 8 Yahweh's wrath blazed against Israel. He sold them into the hand of Cushan-rishathaim, king of Armon-harim, and the Israelites served Cushan-rishathaim for eight years. 9 But the Israelites cried out to Yahweh; and Yahweh raised up a savior for the Israelites who rescued them, Othniel ben Qenaz, Caleb's "brother" (who was younger than he). 10 Yahweh's spirit came upon him; and he judged Israel. He went forth to war, and Yahweh subjected to his power Cushan-rishathaim, king of Armon-harim; his hand clamped down on Cushan-rishathaim.

11 The land was calm for forty years; then Othniel ben Qenaz died.

Notes

3:7. *forgot.* Far stronger than mere absent-mindedness, as indicated by the specification immediately following.

served Baal and Asherah. Cf. 2:11 and 10:6.

8. *sold them.* A conclusion quite consistent with the source of the imagery in Israel's freed slave relationship to Yahweh, and one that would have been especially meaningful in a society which continued, however liberally, to institutionalize slavery. The imagery of the divine slave trader had a checkered history, but reached its peak in prose commentary on nascent apocalyptic writing; e.g. Joel 3:6–8.

into the hand. See second NOTE on 1:2.

Cushan-rishathaim. The Masoretic scholars associated the second element of the name with *ršʻ* "wicked," and pointed the ending so that it meant "two," hence "Cushan Double-Wickedness" or the like. That the early narrator was also interested in the name is suggested by the envelope construction in which the name occurs four times: twice in vs. 8, twice in vs. 10. I owe this recognition to Susan Seuling.

king of Armon-harim. MT reads "king of Aram-naharaim," apparently taking the text to refer to northern Mesopotamia and eastern Syria. But the period of the judges was not one in which threats to Israel came from so far afield. Scholars often emend this phrase, therefore, by reading "Edom" (*'dm* instead of *'rm*) and understanding *nhrym* as a secondary addition in vs. 8. It also occurs in vs. 10 of LXX[B]. A more likely explanation is that the reading *'rm nhrym* is a result of misdivision in an unpointed text (originally *'rmn hrym,* "Fortress of the Mountains") which subsequently suffered a haplography due to homoioteleuton in the *Vorlage* of LXX[A]. This king remains embedded in the Othniel tradition. Albright, "Prolegomenon" to Burney, p. 13.

9. *the Israelites cried out to Yahweh.* Probably in a public assembly. The introduction to Deborah's story may be taken as the reflection of the process without using the verb (4:4–5). We might, in fact, render "the Israelites rallied." The general introduction in 2:11–22, on the other hand, makes no mention of "crying out" as pivotal to the rise of a judge. Rather Yahweh is there said to be moved to pity by their suffering, their "moaning" (2:18).

Othniel . . . Caleb's "brother." See NOTES on 1:12–15. The parenthesis may be secondary here, whereas in 1:13 the explanation serves to avert misunderstanding of the relative ages of Othniel and Achsah his prize.

LXX[A] adds "and they obeyed him."

10. *Yahweh's spirit.* The expression should elicit neither the sense of "Holy Spirit" in later Christian formulations, nor the overtones of amorphous "wind," which is the etymological origin of Heb. *rūᵃḥ.* Nor, apparently, is the "spirit" here conceived as an individual functionary of the sovereign's heavenly court, for then the verbs would be masculine, as in I Kings 22:21. In the latter passage, as Freedman has reminded me, the heavenly functionary, when he does his task on earth, loses his masculine identity and becomes a lying spirit in the mouths of the opposing prophets. In the Book of Judges the expression stands for an impersonal power or force which can be absorbed or can so envelop a man that he becomes capable of extraordinary deeds. This spirit is distinguishable from other spirits in that it is a Yahwistic one and thus lends itself to correlation with the administrative freedom of Israel's Sovereign.

came upon. The exemplary character intended by this representation of Othniel's judgeship is clear from the sequence of (a) election (b) judging (c) victory and peace in Israel. Cf. the effect of the Yahweh spirit in the activity of Gideon (6:34). In 11:29 the activation of Jephthah by "Yahweh's spirit" is presented as gracious confirmation of Israel's own elevation of a judge. In the Samson stories which deal with the tragic thwarting of potential and the gracious vindication of election, the Yahweh spirit is prominent (13:25; 14:6, 19; 15:14).

judged. That is, "mobilized" Israel for a Yahwist war, a primary sense of the verb *špṭ* (Richter ZAW 77 [1965], esp. 61–68). Its frequent poetic synonym *dyn* has a similar semantic range. See 5:10 with NOTE and COMMENT. The "charismatic" deliverers were "actually leaders of prominent rank, originating in the tribal order." Malamat, *Les Congrès . . . ,* p. 133. Othniel's story is carefully constructed. What could the narrator assume that his audience would bring to the story? Perhaps the oracular lot was used to provide the judge with a basis for deciding in each new crisis whether Yahweh's complaint was against Israel or the opponent. It was a very simple approach, adopted, we may be sure, by bands of confederate tribes moving about the wilderness of Sinai. It remained in use throughout the rapidly complicating judges period and on into the monarchy. David and his successors will regularly go through the motions (see I Kings 22, where prophets have replaced the divinatory approach and the problem of knowing whether or not to declare war has become still more complex). The frequency with which the oracle (and therefore the covenant lawsuit) went against Israel in the period (2:1–5; 6:7–10; 10:11–14), according to the Deuteronomic Historian, only reinforces the literal sense in which Yahweh was regarded as King in ancient Israel.

COMMENT

Othniel's career notice is a compact unit, which employs the framework rubrics and parades the outlook that is variously evidenced in the stories of other judges, while information about Othniel himself is minimal. His story is offered as an "example," as argued convincingly by Richter in *Retterbuches,* esp. pp. 90–91. However, Richter regards the compact formulation of the Othniel notice as secondary to the work which produced the "pragmatic formula." In view of the close relationships often noted by critics, it is much more likely that the story of Othniel and Israel is presented as exemplary; it is told at the outset in such a way as to expose the problems with which Israel had to wrestle in remembering the rest of the era. There is, accordingly, good reason to conclude that this little pericope is a carefully researched composition by the pre-Deuteronomic redactor, beginning the "Pragmatic Collection" of judges stories. See the Schematic Outline, p. 30. The problem with such meager narrative pieces about Othniel as have survived is that they focus on his private life, not his public responsibilities (1:12–15).

The identity of Cushan-rishathaim is not clear. Malamat proposes to connect him with one Irsu, a Syrian usurper in Egypt during the period of anarchy which concluded the Nineteenth Dynasty. JNES 13 (1954), 231–42. After the reign of Seti II (c. 1210–1205), Egyptian influence in Palestine collapsed completely, providing a plausible context for this subjugation of Israel. Yet Irsu remains obscure in Egyptian records, while Cushan remains embedded in the Othniel tradition, which is a distinctly southern tradition (see De Vaux, "The Settlement of the Israelites in Southern Palestine and the Origins of the Tribe of Judah," in *Translating and Understanding the Bible,* pp. 120–21). Apparently Cushan's mountain fortress had been successful in holding its own amidst the local power struggles reflected in the movements of groups such as Calebites, Qenazites, Qenites, and Jerahmeelites; and he now emerged as master of the southern hills.

Verse 9 presents the closest possible correlation between the rallying of the people and the emergence of their leader. The mechanics of the process were lost in an early period; but the question persisted, and vs. 10 provided evidence for its original viability. The success of the judge was traced to his display of the Yahweh spirit by mobilizing Israel in face of the crisis. His role was charismatic in the sense that he was Yahweh's gracious provision for the well-being of the people. What the narrator meant by the statement "he judged Israel" is much debated. Perhaps he presided over a confessional reaffirmation of ultimate loyalties much in the manner of Samuel at the end of the period, when the latter "judged" the people before proceeding to a victory over Philistia (I Sam 7:5–6). Compare the nucleus of the Song of Deborah (5:8–11). The judge, in this view, was both cultic president and, when necessary, field commander ex officio.

This notice will be followed by the career of a wild and woolly Benjaminite (Ehud), who will indeed be a savior of Israel. With "honorary judge" Deborah the balance will be more or less restored. But with Gideon there will be a pronounced combination of military ability and excessive divinatory curiosity. In the case of Jephthah the "pragmatic" edition will build to a climax, first with the captains' assumption of heaven's prerogatives in designating their own savior, and then Jephthah's near-perfect performance as Yahwist diplomat (exactly the opposite of Ehud). The "pragmatic" edition then trails off, depicting Samson as the polar opposite of Othniel.

To summarize: by stripping Othniel's story to its bare essentials, the "pragmatic" historian gave us his understanding of how the constitution of the Moses-Joshua federation was supposed to work. The remainder of the period was filled (from his perspective) with major and minor malfunctions, deviations from the Othniel standard.

It is also important to note that success in warfare is here regarded as the consequence of election by Yahweh. The fact that success in warfare is emphasized only for the major judges may mean simply that they lived in especially violent periods.

VI. Eglon versus Ehud, the Benjaminite
(3:12–30)

The Eastern Coalition

3 12 When Israelites continued doing what was evil in Yahweh's sight, Yahweh strengthened Eglon, king of Moab, against Israel, because they did what was evil in Yahweh's sight. 13 He enlisted as allies the Ammonites and Amaleqites; they went out and defeated Israel, and gained control of Palm City. 14 Israelites served Eglon, king of Moab, for eighteen years.

Ehud, the Benjaminite

15 But the Israelites appealed to Yahweh, and Yahweh raised up a savior for them, Ehud ben Gera, the Benjaminite, a man restricted in his right hand. The Israelites sent tribute to Eglon, king of Moab, by his hand. 16 Ehud made himself a short sword (it was double-edged) a foot and a half long and fastened it under his clothes on his right thigh. 17 He presented the tribute to Eglon, king of Moab. Now Eglon was an exceptionally fat man.

18 When he had finished presenting the tribute, he escorted the troops who carried the tribute. 19 He, however, returned from the images, which were near Gilgal, and said, "I have a confidential message for you, O King." He said, "Depart!" And all those who were attending him went out. 20 Ehud approached him—he was sitting in his cool upper room all by himself—and Ehud said, "I have God's message for you." When he got up from the seat, Eglon was close at hand. 21 And as he rose up, Ehud reached with his left hand, took the dagger from his right thigh, and plunged it into his belly. 22 Even the hilt went in after the blade, and the fat closed over the blade, as he did not withdraw the dagger from his belly. 23 Ehud departed by way of the porch. He had closed the doors to the roof garden and locked them.

24 He had already gone when his servants went in. They looked, and, to their surprise, the doors to the upper room were locked. They said, "He's no doubt relieving himself in the palace restroom." 25 They waited till they were at their wits' end. No one was opening the doors of the upper room. When they took the key and unlocked them, to their surprise, their lord had fallen to the floor, dead!

26 Ehud had escped while they were arguing among themselves; he slipped past the images and escaped to Seirah. 27 When he arrived, he sounded the trumpet in Mount Ephraim, and the Israelites went down with him from the hill country; he was at their head! 28 He said to them, "Follow mc, for Yahweh has subjected your enemies (Moab) to your power!" They went down after him and captured the Jordan crossings to Moab; they would not let anyone cross. 29 They struck down at that time about ten contingents of Moabites, all of them plump but burly warriors; not a one escaped! 30 Moab was subdued on that day under Israelite power. And the land was calm, for eighty years. And Ehud judged them until he died.

NOTES

3:12–30. Ehud's story is rhythmical in large parts. But it is neither poetry nor simple prose. It is narrative art (*Kunstprosa*). Alonzo-Schökel, *Biblica* 42 (1961), 143–72.

12–14. The statement of crisis. See COMMENT.

12. *Israelites . . . Israel*. The latter is the official name of the alliance; the former specifies membership. Whether or not either designation is all-inclusive is left to be determined by context, thanks to the syntactic ambiguity of the Hebrew construct state.

continued doing. Heb. *way-yōsīpū*, as in 4:1; 10:6; and 13:1. Only with the addition of the particle *'ōd* does the verb mean "to do again" (e.g. 11:14, the second round of negotiations).

Eglon. "Young bull," "fat calf."

13. *Palm City*. Jericho, as in 1:16. Map 2, C-4.

15. *appealed . . . savior*. See first NOTE on 3:9.

Ehud. Introduced as devious prophet-diplomat (cf. Jephthah, ch. 11). Note the vivid stylistic contrast between the Othniel unit and this one with its wealth of detail and obvious narrative humor. The Ehud story is drawn directly from the corpus of Israelite saga. See Klaus Koch, *The Growth of the Biblical Tradition*, tr. S. M. Cupitt (New York: Scribners, 1969), pp. 138–39, for a succinct description of saga or epic as a vehicle for historical memory. The story was simply incorporated without revision, so as to point the contrast between Ehud and the administration of Othniel at the outset of the period. Ehud is a "loner."

Gera. Ehud's clan. For another "son" of Gera, see Shimei in II Sam 16:5; 19:16, 18.

the Benjaminite. Use of the definite article in the Hebrew text suggests that he is presented as typical—the Benjaminite par excellence. The name means, etymologically, "son of the right hand," and it came to be used as a geographic designation (son of the south) at Mari and in Israel. The narrator here is playing upon the ambiguity of the word by emphasizing that Eglon was singlehandedly defeated by this famous left-handed Benjaminite, as the Israelites chose to send tribute "by his hand."

restricted in his right hand. This roundabout way of saying "left-handed" is an indication that left-handedness was considered peculiar and unnatural. In the final vignette of the period, the civil war following upon the Gibeah outrage, Benjamin will be said to field seven hundred crack left-handed slingers (20:16).

16. *a foot and a half*. If the rare word *gōmed* means "cubit" (it occurs only here in MT), this is the length. As near as can be determined, the cubit was 17.49 inches according to the common measure, 20.405 inches according to the standard known to Ezekiel. Ovid Rogers Sellers, IDB IV, p. 838.

18–19. The rapid pace of developments seems to be a reflection of the vicissitudes of oral style, not the imperfect blending of sources. Emil G. H. Kraeling, JBL 54 (1935), 205–7.

18. *escorted*. The verb is *šlḥ* used in the same sense in Gen 12:20, as pointed out to the author by Freedman. The text appears to assert that Ehud accompanied his tribute bearers from the temporary court of Eglon to the sanctuary (at Gilgal?), for the safe deposit of the tribute.

19. *the images, which were near Gilgal*. Reference to "the images" again in vs. 26 forms an inclusio and indicates that the referent is of pivotal importance. This is a device by which the narrator builds and relieves suspense. Ehud will be safe in vs. 26 once he has put behind him the site of the sanctuary whose gods behold the treaty documents, evidence of his earlier negotiations.

near Gilgal. The preposition *'et* used as in 4:11 (beside Qedesh). See Map 2, D-4. The location of Gilgal remains uncertain. It was apparently an Israelite foundation as "no trace of an LB (Late Bronze) sanctuary site" has been discovered in the area of Tell es-Sultan (Jericho) and its environs. H. J. Franken, *Oudtestamentische Studien* 14 (1965), esp. 199–200.

O King. With LXX, dropped from MT through homoioteleuton, the definite article here (*ham-melek*) parses as vocative.

Depart. Freedman (private communication) proposes this translation for the interjection *has* and compares Amos 6:10 and Hab 2:20.

20. *cool upper room*. The implication of vss. 28–30 is that the massacre occurred as Moabites tried to beat a retreat across the river, suggesting that Eglon's field headquarters had been at or near Jericho, where most of the year the only "cool place" (Heb. *meqērā*) is on the roof.

20–21. *Eglon was close at hand. And as he rose up*. With LXX, where MT reflects a haplography due to homoioarkton.

22. With LXX, omitting *wyṣ' hpršdnh*, "and he came out through the

parš^edōnā," where MT appears to be conflate, preserving two ways of describing the hero's exit. There is perhaps an Akkadian cognate, *parašdinu*, "hole," which may well refer to some architectural feature. In any case there is no warrant for taking the word as referring to the vent of the human body and reading the feminine noun, *ḥereb*, as subject of the masculine verb, *way-yēṣē*. So NEB, following ALUOS^D, 7; VT 4 (1954), 240–45. The "sword" is regularly construed as a feminine noun in this story (vs. 16) as regularly in the Hebrew Bible.

23. *by way of the porch.* Lit. "in the direction of the porch." On the plausibility of *misd^erōn* as porch, see Kraeling, JBL 54 (1935), 208: "correct as it stands, and must mean a platform with pillars." That is, instead of exiting the way he came in, Ehud went over the side, after using Eglon's own key to bolt the door from the inside.

locked them. The verb *n'l* should probably be read as infinitive absolute, rather than the anomalous perfect of MT; hence the object "them" is implied. Freedman, private communication. He compares the same form, which must be similarly repointed, in II Sam 13:18.

25. *at their wits' end.* With Burney, p. 74, who compares II Kings 2:17, 8:11 for the sense of Heb. *bōs,* "be ashamed."

26–30. His Samson-like exploits in the past, Ehud now performs like Deborah in ch. 4, except that he does not consult the oracle (against Alonzo-Schökel, *Biblica* 42 [1961], 148).

26. *while they argued among themselves.* Heb. *htmhmhm,* "they (said) to one another: What? What?" This explanation of the peculiar verb form as a doubling of the interrogative *mh,* "What?" was offered by Professor Frank R. Blake in his Johns Hopkins University classes. The word expresses consternation and confusion as well as delay. Cf. 19:8.

slipped past. Heb. *'ābar.* See NOTE on 2:20.

Seirah. Location unknown.

27. *Mount Ephraim.* Either a reference to the early tribal allotment claimed by Ephraim (see Map 2, C-4) or a narrator's use of the label for a later administrative district. *Shechem,* pp. 141–43.

sounded the trumpet. On the trumpet as simultaneously military and liturgical equipment, see Num 10:9, 31:6. When Saul sounded it, the accompanying shout was "Let the Hebrews (i.e. the Israelite resistance) hear" (I Sam 13:3, RSV).

28. *(Moab).* This word is probably either a variant for "your enemies" or an explanatory gloss.

29. *burly warriors.* The colloquial rendering is intended to reproduce popular respect for military prowess. Heb. *'īš ḥayl,* which alternates with *b^enē ḥayl* (18:2, 21:10), *gibbōr ḥayl* (6:12, 11:1), and *'anšē ḥayl* (20:46), is apparently a technical military classification; but detailed definition eludes us.

30. *And Ehud judged them until he died.* This concluding statement survived in LXX, where MT displays a haplography due to homoioarkton. Without this sentence, the beginning of vs. 31 has no antecedent in the neighboring context, so "after him" must refer to Ehud. In vs. 30 the antecedent of "them" is apparently Moab.

COMMENT

The centripetal effects of geographical expansion on the part of the Israelite tribes, constituted by covenant as the Yahweh Kingdom, left them exposed to the higher military efficiency of slightly older Trans-Jordanian kingdoms, chiefly Moab and Ammon. On the late thirteenth and early twelfth century emergence of these kingdoms, as clarified by archaeological and literary sources, see George M. Landes, BA 24 (1961), 68–86, reprinted in *The Biblical Archaeologist Reader II* (Garden City, N.Y.: Doubleday, 1964), pp. 69–88.

The nomadic Amaleqites (see 1:16; 6:3 and NOTES) provided any non-Yahwist state with a highly effective communications network inside Israel, posing such a continual threat that Saul's failure to stamp out the Amaleqites was remembered as the last straw in his relations with Samuel (I Sam 15).

Except for problems stemming from the character of oral transmission (see vss. 18–19 and NOTES), the unit shows few signs of editorial activity and cannot be assigned with confidence to any of the main Hexateuch sources (Kurt Weise, *Zur Literarkritik* . . . , BWANT III, 4 [1926], 11–12). There are clear affinities with the Court History of David in II Samuel. Verses 12, 14–15 are the pre-Deuteronomic or "pragmatic" formula, now bound inextricably to the body of the story by 15b. Additional details (from an archival source?) which are not resumed or echoed in the remainder of the unit are supplied in vs. 13. Verse 30 is the concluding counterpart of the introductory formula. The round number "eighty" (two generations?) may be the contribution of the Deuteronomic Historian who systematically leveled throughout a chronological note at the end of narrative units, taking his cue, we may suppose, from such texts as vs. 11, where "forty years" is integral to the transition with which that example concludes. See Introduction, "The Chronological Problem."

Ehud was a savior who subdued Moab. The narrator is mainly interested in the piece of single-handed diplomatic treachery which won for Ehud his following and, to be sure, seemed to settle matters for eighty years (two generations?). Only with the story of Deborah and Baraq will the delicate balance between corporate renewal and military defense be witnessed again.

That Ehud is called a "savior" of Israel and one who "judged" Moab reflects precisely the problem with which the early narrator and his hearers were wrestling: What had it meant to be "Israel" in that early period? In this regard it is worth noting that there is no mention of the Yahweh spirit in connection with Ehud.

3　31 After him came Shamgar, the Anathite. He struck down a Philistine brigade single-handedly, using an oxgoad. He too rescued Israel.

NOTES

3:31. This one verse has occasioned some of the longest Judges articles. There is a complete absence of any familiar rubrics, whether of the salvific or administrative forms. Certain LXX recensions have the Shamgar notice following the Samson conclusion in 16:31 and include for Shamgar the characteristic formula. MT preserves the more difficult tradition and is thus considered to be the older one.

Shamgar. The name is apparently Hurrian, occurring in Nuzi texts. Benjamin Maisler, *Palestine Exploration Quarterly,* 66 (1934), 192–94.

the Anathite. Lit. "son of Anath." It has long been thought that the identification is intended to relate Shamgar to the town of Beth-anath in Galilee (Map 2, C-2). Albright, *Journal of the Palestine Oriental Society,* 1 (1921), 55–62. Yet the label *bn-'nt* may be merely a military designation involving the name of the famous goddess who was consort of Baal and warrior goddess in her own right. Analogical evidence connecting Anath with the seminomads known as Haneans in Mari texts, who on several occasions provide the king of Mari with sizable military contingents, lends support to the identification of Shamgar as a mercenary. P. C. Craigie, JBL 91 (1972), 239–40.

a Philistine brigade. Lit. "Philistines, six hundred men." The figure is not to be taken literally. "Six hundred" is a unit of military organization, an optimum figure rarely reached in practice (cf. 18:11; 20:47), and, we may suppose, often deliberately kept below strength (like the six thousand that constituted the Roman legion).

single-handedly. With LXX^A and OL, where *mlbd* has dropped out of MT and the LXX^B *Vorlage,* immediately before the similar cluster *bmlmd.* The latter was lost in LXX^A, so that attention to all three traditions yields a text that is better than any one of them.

oxgoad. Heb. *malmad,* formed on the causative stem of *lmd,* "to learn." Cf. the now obsolete wooden paddle for discipline in the classroom which was often ruefully known as "the board of education."

He too rescued. The verb is *yš',* in the same sense that Ehud was a savior raised up by Yahweh (vs. 15).

COMMENT

Shamgar was one who was almost forgotten. His story, brief as it is, is an example of traditionary erosion, perhaps spurred on by confusion regarding the Anathite background. Stylistic discontinuity with the brief formulations about the "minor judges" (10:1–5, 12:8–15) suggests that his memory at this point in the narrative is another contribution of the Deuteronomic Historian, drawn from an independent source.

Shamgar's victory is probably to be connected with the Sea Peoples' migration down the coast from bases as far away as Ugarit. See Richard David Barnett, "The Sea Peoples," in *The Cambridge Ancient History,* rev. ed., I–II (Cambridge University Press, 1969), 10. The pre-Philistine Sea Peoples controlled much of the coastal plain, and in the period reflected by the Song of Deborah (ch. 5) had moved inland, via the Esdraelon plain, as far as Deir 'Alla in the southern Jordan valley, as known from excavations there. Thus the label Philistine may be a bit anachronistic; but otherwise there is nothing in his notice that is out of harmony with the poetic statement that "his days" marked the beginning of better days in early Israel.

In brief, Shamgar engineered a significant victory for the federation. It is within the realm of possibility that he rose to the office of judge; but the redactor's source was meager, and he had no authority to decide on such matters.

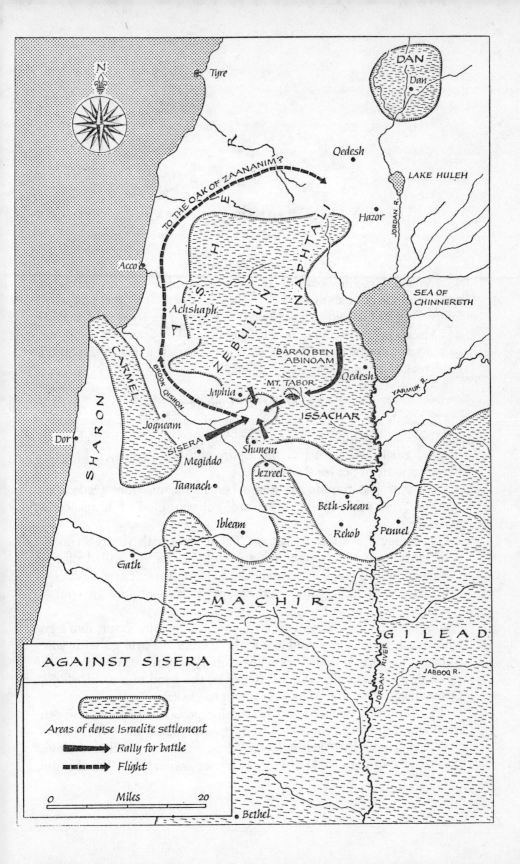

N

• Tyre

DAN
• Dan

• Qedesh

LAKE HULEH

• Hazor

TO THE OAK OF ZAANANIM?

A S H E R

Acco •

ZEBULUN

NAPHTALI

JORDAN R.

SEA OF
CHINNERETH

Achshaph •

BARAQ BEN
ABINOAM

BROOK QISHON

MT. TABOR

• Qedesh

Japhia •

ISSACHAR

YARMUK R.

CARMEL

Joqneam •

SISERA

• Shunem

Dor •

• Megiddo

• Jezreel

SHARON

• Taanach

• Beth-shean

• Ibleam

• Rehob

• Penuel

• Gath

M A C H I R

G I L E A D

JORDAN RIVER

JABBOQ R.

AGAINST SISERA

Areas of dense Israelite settlement

Rally for battle

Flight

0   Miles   20

• Bethel

VIII. Deborah and Baraq
(4:1–24)

The Northwest Coalition

4 ¹ When Israelites continued doing what was evil in Yahweh's sight, and Ehud was dead, ² Yahweh sold them into the power of Jabin, king of Canaan, who reigned in Hazor. His army commander was Sisera; he lived at Harosheth-hagoiim. ³ The Israelites *cried out* to Yahweh. For he had nine hundred iron chariots and had oppressed the Israelites severely for twenty years.

Deborah the Prophetess

⁴ Deborah was a prophetess, the wife of Lappidoth. She was judging Israel at that time. ⁵ She was presiding under Deborah's Palm, between Ramah and Bethel in the Ephraimite hill country, when the Israelites went to her for the judgment.

⁶ She sent and summoned Baraq ben Abinoam, from Qedesh in Naphtali, and said to him, "Has not Yahweh, God of Israel, commanded:

Go, deploy the troops at Mount Tabor; take with you ten contingents from the Naphtalites and Zebulunites. ⁷ I will deploy Sisera, Jabin's army commander, against you at the Wadi Qishon, with his chariots and troops; I will put him in your hand!"

⁸ Baraq said to her, "If you go with me, I'll go. But if you don't go with me, I won't go!" ⁹ And she said, "Certainly I will go with you. But you must know that there will be no diadem for you on the path you follow, for Yahweh will sell Sisera by the hand of a woman!" So Deborah got ready and went with Baraq to Qedesh.

¹⁰ Baraq called Zebulun and Naphtali together at Qedesh, and ten contingents under his command went up. Deborah went up with him.

¹¹ Now Heber the Qenite, having departed from Smithland, from the environs of the people of Hobab, Moses' son-in-law, pitched camp

near the "Oak in Zaananim" which is beside Qedesh. 12 And they
made it known to Sisera that Baraq ben Abinoam had gone up to
Mount Tabor. 13 So Sisera called out all his chariots—nine hundred
iron chariots—and all the force who were with him, from Harosheth-
hagoiim, to the river Qishon.

14 Deborah said to Baraq, "Up! This is the day in which Yahweh
has put Sisera in your power! Does not Yahweh advance before you?"
And Baraq descended from Mount Tabor, with ten units following
him.

15 Yahweh confounded Sisera, all the chariotry and fighting force,
before Baraq. Sisera jumped down from his chariot and fled on foot!
16 And Baraq chased the chariotry and fighting force all the way to
Harosheth-hagoiim. Sisera's entire force fell to the sword; not one
was left.

17 Sisera fled on foot to one Jael, wife of Heber the Qenite, as
there was a peace treaty between Jabin, King of Hazor, and the house
of Heber the Qenite. 18 Jael came out to meet Sisera and said to him,
"Turn here, sir. Turn here to me. Do not be afraid." So he turned to
her, toward the tent. She covered him with a (. . .). 19 He said to
her, "Please give me a little drink of water. I am thirsty!" And she
opened the milk-skin, gave him a drink, and covered him. 20 He said
to her, "Stand at the entrance to the tent. If anyone should come and
ask you, 'Is there anyone here?' you will say, 'There is no one.'"
21 Jael the wife of Heber took a tent peg, and put the mallet in her
hand. She tiptoed in to him. She pounded the peg into his neck and
it went on into the ground. He had been sound asleep. He twitched
convulsively and died.

22 Just then Baraq arrived in pursuit of Sisera. Jael went out to
meet him and said to him, "Come, I will show you the man whom
you seek." He went in to her, and, to his surprise, Sisera was lying
dead, with the peg in his neck.

23 On that day God subdued Jabin, king of Canaan, before the
Israelites. 24 Israelite power bore continually harder on Jabin, king of
Canaan, until they had destroyed Jabin, king of Canaan.

NOTES

4:1–3. These verses introduce the new crisis, under rubrics comparable to
3:12–14.

1. *continued doing*. See NOTE on 3:12.

and Ehud was dead. This statement is missing in a number of LXX manuscripts, which may be explained as another example of haplography due to homoioarkton. On the other hand, scholars have often considered this statement to be out of place in MT, and have suggested that it belongs to the gap at the end of 3:30. There, however, LXX has its own tradition, as adopted above. Moreover, there is no way to explain this as an addition in 4:1. We conclude that it is original. It contributes to the initial building of suspense by the narrator, concerning Yahweh's administrative strategy. The reason that Shamgar is skipped over, we may suspect, is that his story did not speak directly to the need for wide-ranging organizational ability, as did the story of Ehud.

2. *Yahweh sold them.* See NOTE on 3:8.

Jabin, king of Canaan. An example of traditionary assimilation. Jabin is called "king of Hazor" in Josh 11, but in Joshua's day Hazor's king was probably known as "king of Canaan," a title as old as the Mari period, when already one of them is known to have borne the name "Jabin." Malamat, JBL 79 (1960), 12–19. Moreover, the opposition to Baraq is provided by "the kings (plural!) of Canaan" in 5:19, headed by Sisera.

Sisera. The name is neither Hebrew nor its ancestral Canaanite, but it might well have arrived in Canaan with one of the Sea Peoples. On the linguistic problem, see Albright, *Journal of the Palestine Oriental Society*, 2 (1922), 60 f. For the two-wave onslaught of Sea Peoples in the thirteenth and twelfth centuries, among whom were the famous Philistines, see Barnett, *The Cambridge Ancient History*, vol. II, ch. 28.

Harosheth-hagoiim. Lit. "Harosheth of the Gentiles"; it is perhaps to be identified with *Muḥrashti* of the Amarna Letters (*Die El-Amarna Tafeln*, 335:17), which is to be sought somewhere in the plain of Sharon (Map 3). Gus W. van Beek, IDB II, p. 526.

3. *cried out to Yahweh.* See NOTE on 3:9.

iron chariots. Like "the inhabitants of the plain" in 1:19. The iron age in Canaan began with the arrival of the Philistines, who controlled their secrets of ironworking under monopolistic conditions that were not finally broken by Israel until after the time of Saul. See illustration 2.

4–24. These verses recount the exploits of Deborah and Baraq.

4–5. Note the abrupt shift from narrative tense to nominal and participial sentences.

4. *Deborah.* The popular etymology would have been "Honey Bee." On the significance of implicit popular etymologies in the stories of the judges see Alonzo-Schökel, *Biblica* 42 (1961), esp. 160–61. The Israelites consulted Deborah. In ch. 14 toward the end of the book in its earlier "Pragmatic" version is the story of Samson discovering a "congregation" of bees and a small store of honey but missing a sign (see NOTES and COMMENT on that chapter). There is in fact a number of indicators, to be noted below, which point to a narrative relationship between this story of the honorable honorary judge Deborah early in the book and dishonorable divinely appointed judge Samson late in the book.

Deborah was a prophetess. Offered as both a statement of fact and the narrator's own value judgment, the latter being indicated by the exclamatory syntax. A variety of female prophets having political involvements at Mari is well known. Huffmon, BA 31 (1968), 101–24.

wife of Lappidoth. Heb. *'ēšet lappidōt.* The second element is possibly her husband's nickname (cf. the kenning relationship between "Jerubbaal" and "Gideon," the latter meaning approximately "hacker"); it does not occur again. The name appears to be related to the common masculine noun for "torch" (see the Gideon story of 7:16–20; and the Samson story in 15:4–5) with an abstract (not feminine plural) ending. It thus means roughly "Flasher." We suggest that this explains why the name Lappidoth does not occur again in the story; tradition knew him chiefly as Baraq (lit. "Lightning"). We may assume that those for whom the story was first composed were already familiar with the main events of their recent history. The narrator's expertise was thus exercised in the way he took up the themes of public tradition and recomposed the stories for the entertainment and edification of his audience. Thus the force of this opening play upon the name of a great military hero will only emerge from a careful scrutiny of the story's characterization of Baraq who is away on a campaign as the story begins.

She. Not any one else. The emphasis is clear from the Hebrew word order, independent pronoun preceding the verb for emphasis.

judging. That is, functioning with reference to a recognized office.

5. *presiding.* Lit. "sitting," cf. Isa 28:5–6. Cf. the arrival of the Yahweh envoy in the Gideon cycle (6:11) and the relative value of various sources of "shade" in Jotham's Fable (9:7–15). That is, how to "sit," or "dwell," was a continuing preoccupation of those who compiled the Book of Judges.

Deborah's Palm. That she had a tree named after her suggests a setting in which she was responsible for Yahwist oracular inquiry. Cf. the figure of Samuel as "man of God" in I Sam 9. The freedom of the diviner, and later the prophet, is a major theme of Yahwist traditions, e.g. I Kings 22, concerned precisely with oracular inquiry before battle, where the moral of the story is not easily distinguished from that of Judg 1.

the judgment. Heb. *ham-mišpāṭ;* here it stands for her decision in response to a particular inquiry. For comparable use of *mišpāṭ* in Judges, see 13:12 and NOTE. H. C. Thomson, *Transactions of the Glasgow University Oriental Society,* 19 (1961–62), 74–85.

6. *Baraq.* Lit. "Lightning." Heb 11:32 preserves a tradition which regarded Baraq as the judge, and makes no mention of Deborah.

Qedesh in Naphtali. The site is possibly Khirbet Qedish in southeastern Galilee (LOB, p. 204). See Map 2, D-2.

Has not Yahweh . . . commanded. The question assumes that the audience is already generally aware of Baraq's reluctance, to be detailed later.

6b–7. In the Hebrew text the entirety of vss. 6b–7 is presented as that which was commanded by Yahweh, not by Deborah. LXX, on the other hand, rendered as though Deborah were the subject of the first verb, in vs. 7.

6b. *Go, deploy the troops.* The verb is *mšk*, as in 20:37 (see NOTE). Only a fragment of Baraq's orders survives in the narrative. For a full form-critical treatment on the subject of "Orders for Retreat and Attack," see Robert Bach, *Die Aufforderungen zur Flucht und zum Kampf in Altest-*

amentlichen Prophetenspruch (Neukirchen Kreis: Neukirchener Verlag, 1962),
with special attention to early Yahwist warfare and later classical prophecy.

Mount Tabor, at the northern edge of the plain of Esdraelon (see Map 2,
C-2), was some ten miles away from the beginning of the Wadi Qishon
(see Map 3), and it was ideally suited for the muster of troops from the
Galilean hills. The poetic tradition, however, locates the decisive battle much
farther to the southwest "At Taanach by Megiddo's stream" (5:19). In this
way, by putting the divine command into the form of a promise, the narrator
illustrated his opening line: Deborah was a prophetess! This command is
promptly followed (vss. 8–9) by another example of her prophetic competence.

contingents. See NOTE on 1:4.

7. *I will deploy . . . at the Wadi Qishon.* The problems were geographical,
and the differences are probably to be explained in terms of the time lag
between the early poetic account (ch. 5) and its reduction to the prose form.

Wadi Qishon. The battle occurred where the pass between Megiddo and
Taanach opens into the Plain of Esdraelon, presumably near the confluence of
streams which flow together to form the Qishon (see Map 3). A cloudburst
and flash flood (5:20–21) won the battle.

8–9. These verses deal with the theme of camaraderie in the administration.
There is irony in Baraq's casuistic acceptance of the apodictic command.
Alonzo-Schökel, *Biblica* 42 (1961), 160–61. Baraq's hesitancy is further spelled
out in LXX: "for I never know what day the Yahweh angel will give me
success," suggesting perhaps that he had been going out and coming in from
battle without benefit of adequate or proper inquiry.

9. *know.* With LXX, where a verb is needed, reading Heb. *da'* (root *yd'*),
lit. *know,* that is, "realize," "acknowledge." See NOTES on 2:10 and 3:2.

diadem. Cf. Isa 28:5–6.

by the hand of a woman. A double meaning? The normal interpretation
would be that she thinks of herself as the woman by whom Sisera's defeat
would be accomplished (vs. 7). But the narrator and his audience know that it
will be accomplished by another woman, Jael. Deborah is thus represented
as speaking better than she knows, an example of unconscious prediction,
which adds poignancy to the outcome.

10. *under his command.* Lit. "at his feet." Cf. 5:27.

11. The verse begins a new unit, as indicated by the disjunctive clause which
interrupts the consecutive-imperfect narrative sequence.

Heber the Qenite. Lit. "Heber the smith"; *heber* (originally "enclave") is a
personal name that in this context is still very close to its appellative original,
now clarified from Mari. *The Assyrian Dictionary,* VI, p. 181. Malamat,
Les Congrès . . . (1967), esp. pp. 137–38.

Smithland. Heb. *qayn.* See NOTE on 1:16.

Moses' son-in-law. See NOTE on 1:16.

near. Heb. *'ad.* On this sense of the preposition see Harold Louis Ginzberg,
BASOR 124 (December 1951), 29 f.; most recently Dahood, *Psalms I, 1–50,*
AB, vol. 16, 1966, fourth NOTE on 42:5.

the "Oak in Zaananim." Probably a place name, but clearly being played
off against *Deborah's Palm* (vs. 5). See Map 3. Elon-bezaananim was perhaps a Galilean cult place under control of the northern Qenite splinter group.

Yohanan Aharoni, in *New Directions in Biblical Archaeology* (Garden City, N.Y.: Doubleday, 1969), p. 36. However, the site of Qedesh in this verse is to be sought near the northern end of the border between Asher and Naphtali (Josh 19:33), a town taken by Joshua (Josh 12:22) and turned into a city of refuge (Josh 20:7). Apparently mention of the Oak of Zaananim was sufficient to distinguish this Qedesh from the place of Israelite muster in vs. 10. The only alternative to the recognition of two towns with the same name in our chapter would be the picture of Sisera "retreating" directly to the center of Israelite strength.

12. *And they made it known to Sisera.* Most of them had defected.

14. *This is the day.* To prod Baraq at last to victory she proclaimed it "the day" of the Lord. On the general background of later cultic conceptions of the day of Yahweh in early Israelite battlefield practice, see G. von Rad, *Old Testament Theology* II, tr. D. M. G. Stalker (New York: Harper and Row, 1965), pp. 119–25.

15. *Yahweh confounded.* A pivotal conviction of the early Israelite warriors. Cf. Josh 10:10; II Sam 5:24; and esp. Exod 14:24. Freedman (private communication) observes that the Exodus victory at the Reed Sea is so strikingly similar to the one at the Qishon (chariots mired in mud, panic) that the accounts must be attributed to the same author or editor. See also NOTE on vs. 16.

and fighting force. MT continues at this point: "to the sword's edge." The phrase is grammatically isolated and was probably introduced in accidental anticipation of the same phrase in 16b.

16. *not one was left.* Almost verbatim agreement in Hebrew with the conclusion of Exod 14:28.

17. *Sisera.* He fled in a different direction from his routed army, toward the confirmation of Deborah's taunt to Baraq.

Jael, wife of Heber the Qenite. See NOTES on vs. 11 and 1:16. Here it is explained that an entire clan migrated and changed sides in the time of Jabin, so that in Deborah's day it would be recognized as providential that a Galilean Qenite chieftain had a loyal Yahwist wife. Although the gutturals are not distinct in cuneiform, what is probably the Amorite equivalent of her name appears, together with the cognate of *ḥeber*, as a town related administratively to Mari. *Archives royales de Mari*, I, eds. A. Parrot, G. Dossin, et al., (Paris: P. Geuthner, 1940), 119:10. The tradition of a treaty bond between Jabin and Qenites in the earlier period accounts for the secondary introduction of Jabin's name into the framework of this narrative. For the prior treaty, between Israel and Qenites, see Fensham, BASOR 175 (September 1964), 51–54.

18. *Do not be afraid.* Heb. *'l tyr'*, as in the divine command to Joshua before the earlier battle at Hazor (Josh 11:6); a standing exhortation to the warriors in Deuteronomy is *l' tyr'*, "do not ever be afraid!" (Deut 1:29; 7:18; 20:1).

She covered him. With a *sᵉmīkā*. Used only here, the word remains unclear. A "rug" would scarcely have been welcome after the long, hot flight. Burney's proposal (on p. 92) to render "fly-net" is plausible, although the verse as a whole suggests that he was asking for concealment.

19. Burney's reminder (p. 93) that certain goat milk products have a strongly

soporific effect suggests that at this point the prose has not misconstrued the parallelism of 5:25. In both accounts, that is, she duped him and doped him. Against the idea that the poetry represents him standing at the door of the tent when she attacked, see NOTES on 5:27.

20. *Stand.* The incongruity of addressing her with a masculine imperative (MT *'ᵃmōd*) is best resolved by repointing to read infinitive absolute (*'āmōd*) with strong imperative force as in the Decalogue (Exod 20:8; Deut 5:12). Freedman, private communication.

21. *a tent peg . . . the mallet.* Here it appears that the prose account has taken literally the poetic parallelism of 5:26.

tiptoed. Lit. "went in secrecy to him."

neck. Precise referent of the rare word *rqh* is obscure, although it certainly refers to some portion of the head visible from the outside (Song of Songs 4:3; 6:7). Thus it cannot be "brains," as proposed by Driver, *Mélanges Bibliques—Robert* (1957), p. 73. The NEB translation in Judg 4:21, "skull," is unlikely. As the location of the *rqh* is behind the veil in the Song of Songs passages, we are led to look for some vulnerable spot such as the upper neck, behind the lower jaw (Freedman, private communication). Sisera's death prefigures the near demise of Samson early in ch. 16.

it went. Heb. *tṣnḥ,* another rare word, occurring elsewhere only in 1:14, where Achsah "alighted" (went down) from the donkey. We have treated the feminine noun *ytd* as subject; it is also possible to interpret Jael as subject, in which case she collapsed after dealing the fatal blow.

twitched convulsively. The Hebrew root is either *'wp* (Driver, *Mélanges Bibliques,* 74) or *'pp* (cf. Isa 14:29; 30:6; Ezek 32:10), not *y'p* "to be tired" as in MT.

23–24. These verses are the redactional wrap-up. "Jabin, king of Canaan" remains obscure.

COMMENT

As is clear in the NOTES, it is impossible to discuss this prose account of the Sisera crisis, without frequent reference to the Song of Deborah, an older poetic celebration of the same cluster of events in ch. 5. In general we can say that the prose presents Deborah as Yahweh's prophetess and "honorary" judge. Thus it becomes possible to comprehend the following essentials of the prose story: (a) the next thing to be said after the announcement that the prophetess was judging Israel is that she was basking in the shade of her own tree; (b) the camaraderie within the administration, depicted as Deborah's taunting of Baraq, at last gives no great credit to either one of them; (c) vss. 4–14 in finished form tell the story so as to make the point that Deborah, the diviner, was a first rate military leader, the ideal judge, who trusted the outcome to be decided in the field by the God of Israel (vss. 15–23; cf. the account of Jephthah's exemplary diplomacy in 11:12–28).

Deborah's Palm is often identified with the burial place of the earlier Deborah (Gen 35:8), which was thereafter called Allon-bakuth, "Oak of Tears" (cf. "Bochim," probably Bethel, in 2:1–5). With that possible identification our story begins by asserting that the latter day Deborah had turned a venerable place of lamentation into a little oracular oasis; the palm tree at that altitude may be growing metaphorically. The divinatory oasis par excellence was the southern Qadesh (Qadesh-barnea), known anciently as Spring of Judgment, 'ēn mišpāṭ, in Gen 14:7. The narrator's obvious interest in names perhaps explains why the notice about the northern Qenite splinter group (vs. 11) specifically locates the Oak of Zaananim near a northern Qedesh, that is, the wrong Qedesh for Yahweh-deserters! The northern Qedesh was also a city of refuge, dedicated to the curbing of blood feuds, in the revolutionary Yahwist law (Josh 20:7).

In view of the political involvements of female prophets as far back as eighteenth century Mari the title "prophetess" can no longer be assumed to be anachronistic in reference to Deborah. The introductory statement represents a narrator's value judgment, to be sure, shifting focus momentarily from the office of judge to the particular qualities of Deborah. That value judgment was most likely made in the premonarchical period when the simple relationship between the functions of diviner and field commander was a living social reality, but increasingly subject to the mounting pressures for which the arrangement was at last inadequate.

The premonarchical integrity of the narrative (vss. 4–22) also provides a plausible explanation for the alleged clash with Josh 11, regarding the historical role of Jabin, king of Hazor (see NOTES on vss. 2 and 23); there were not yet available the kind of archives created by the great tenth-century reorganization under David and Solomon, to which a professional chronicler might resort for "recorded memory." "Jabin, king of Canaan" belongs to the framework (vss. 1–3, 23), while "Jabin, king of Hazor" is mentioned but once in the narrative (vs. 17). The latter is quite intelligible as a digression reminding the narrator's audience of the background of Hazor's treaty with the Qenite splinter group, established, we may assume, in Jabin's pre-Joshua days. Striking archaeological clarity on the situation has resulted from the discovery at Hazor of a thoroughly non-Israelite temple belonging to the post-Joshua period. That means the amazing Israelite victory there (Josh 11:10–13), a traditional claim that appears to be supported by the late thirteenth-century destruction level, was not followed by enduring pacification of the area under Yahwist auspices.

Apart from the puzzle that Jabin's title posed for the pragmatic redactor, who no longer understood the digressional character of vss. 11–12, his introduction confines itself to exegesis-by-emphasis. Neither Deborah nor Baraq is said to have saved Israel; the pragmatist read the old story as telling how Yahweh had done the saving. For the Israelites make their appeal through Deborah, who is herself surprised by the response to her own inquiry. In her activity as prophetess, Deborah is represented as going about the business routinely, until that day when the Israelites, by-passing judge Baraq, took matters into their own hands. It is in connection with her success in apprehending the correct oracular response that she is honored as "a mother" (see 5:7).

Consultation with Yahweh before battle (however obscure the mechanics) was the judge's responsibility. Note the thematic treatment of divination in the stories of Gideon (esp. 6:17–40; 7:1–7; 8:22–27) and Micah (chs. 17–18) and Samson's birth (ch. 13). Divination before battle was an invariable aspect of warfare in the ancient world, amply documented from Mari to I Kings 22. The same custom provided the organizing rubric for the final redaction of the Book of Judges (chs. 1 and 19–21; see NOTES and COMMENT).

Thus the point of the narrative is that neither Deborah nor Baraq subdued Sisera on that day—but God did! This accounts for the meager information about individual tribal participation, for so long a puzzling contrast with the Song. The only tribes mentioned here (Naphtali and Zebulun) are those under Baraq's immediate sphere of influence, while he is away in the north.

Contrary to superficial criticism, the figures are entirely plausible. To Baraq's ten units must be added those of other tribes responding to the summons. From the figure of nine hundred chariots on Sisera's side must be subtracted those left behind as a rearguard (vs. 16). Note the dramatic reversal at the point where Yahweh "confounded" Sisera, that is, became too much for his military brain. In contrast to Shamgar, the mercenary, who was remembered for saving Israel from Philistines, Sisera was a Sea Peoples deserter outdistancing his own routed forces in retreat. Baraq gave energetic chase, but the flight was cut short by one woman's exception to a whole clan's desertion. Jael was a covenant loyalist, which explains why she is "most blessed" in 5:24.

While archaeological work at Hazor and elsewhere has provided a vividly detailed backdrop to the traditions taken up in Josh 11, there is no clear indication that the later victory against Sisera was followed by reprisals against Hazor. Indeed, it appears that Hazor's prominence in the early days of the Joshua generation had been eclipsed, and the site was not a town of any significance in Deborah's day.

Accordingly, Sisera was not fleeing to Hazor; nor would he be safe at home. His flight to the vicinity of the Qenites suggests that he was headed for the northern Qedesh. Perhaps the latter was already renowned as a city of refuge (Josh 20:7). In Israel there was "one law for you and the resident alien"! The denouement came by the hand of Jael, only a short distance from Qedesh. See Map 3.

The alternation between use of the divine name "Yahweh" in narrative description (vss. 2 and 15) and the generic noun for deity (Heb. 'elōhīm) in the redactor's concluding comment, reflects a distinction that occurs elsewhere in the book. The word "God" is used confessionally. See NOTES on 6:36–40. This brings into sharper focus the fact that "Yahweh, God of Israel" occurs only at climactic points in the early narrative units; at this point (vs. 6) the narrator expresses his agreement with Deborah. That the phrase in question is remembered as a prime constitutional element in Israel's religious language is clear from its still more ancient use in the following song of victory (5:3, 5) and its pivotal occurrence in subsequent editions of the book. See, e.g. 6:8, a prophetic indictment; 11:21–23, the pragmatic formulation of Jephthah's diplomacy; and 21:3, where the confessional formula has become a cliche, in the view of that narrator. In the last of these passages the practice of appealing to Yahweh the God of Israel is reduced to mere habit—as almost happened very early, in the time of Deborah.

IX. The Song of Deborah and Baraq
(5:1–31)

5 ¹ Deborah and Baraq ben Abinoam sang on that day!

(Part I)	(Hebrew syllable count)
² When they cast off restraint in Israel	10
When the troops present themselves—bless Yahweh!	10
³ Hear, O kings	5
Listen, O princes	7
I to Yahweh	6
I, I will sing	6
I will chant to Yahweh	6
God of Israel!	6
⁴ O Yahweh, when you came out from Seir	9
When you marched here from Edom's land	9
Earth quaked	4
With thunder the skies rained	7
With thunder the clouds rained water!	8
⁵ Mountains shook	5
Before Yahweh, The One of Sinai	8
Before Yahweh, God of Israel!	11
⁶ In the days of Shamgar the Anathite	7
In the days of Jael, they ceased	7

The caravans and the wayfaring men   10
Who travel the winding roads.   10
7 The warriors grew plump   6
In Israel they grew plump again   8
Because you arose, O Deborah   6
Because you arose, a mother in Israel!   8

8 One chose new gods   8
Then they fought in the gates.   7
Neither shield nor spear was to be seen   9
Among the forty contingents in Israel.   9

9 My heart is with the commanders of Israel   9
Those presenting themselves with the troops—bless Yahweh!   12

(Part II)
10 O riders of tawny she-donkeys   9
O you who sit on the judgment seat   6
O wayfarers on the road   6

11 Attend to the sound of cymbals   6
Between watering troughs   4

There let them retell Yahweh's victories   8
Victories by his own prowess in Israel!   8

Then Yahweh's troops went down to the gates   11
12 Awake. Awake, Deborah   7
Awake. Awake. Sing a song!   8

Arise, Baraq   3
Take your prisoners   6
O ben Abinoam!   5

13 Then the survivor went down to the nobles   10
Yahweh's troops went down against the knights for me!   10

(Part III)
14 Those of Ephraim have taken root in Amaleq   11
Behind you, Benjamin, with your troops.   12

    From Machir commanders came down   11
    From Zebulun, bearers of the ruler's scepter.   12

15 Issachar's captains were with Deborah   11
    Issachar was Baraq's support   7
    Dispatched to the plain, under his command.   7

In Reuben's divisions are command-minded chieftains. 12
   16 Why then did you squat between hearths   11
       Harking to pastoral pipings?   8
To Reuben's divisions belong fainthearted chieftains! 12

(Part IV)
17 Gilead bivouacked beyond Jordan   9
    Why did Dan take service on ships?   9
Asher squatted at the seashore   8
    He bivouacked by his harbors!   7

18 Zebulun is a troop   4
    That scorned death   6
Naphtali too   4
    On the heights of the plain!   6

19 The kings came and fought   8
Then fought the kings of Canaan   9
    At Taanach by Megiddo's stream   9
    Silver booty they did not take.   7
20 From the heavens fought the stars   11
From their courses they fought against Sisera! 11

(Part V)
21 The Wadi Qishon swept them away   6
The Wadi overwhelmed them—the Wadi Qishon 7
(You shall trample the throat of the mighty).   6

   22 Then the horses' hoofs pounded   9
     His stallions racing, racing!   9

(Part VI)
23 "Oh, curse Meroz!" says the divine adviser 10
  "Utterly curse its inhabitants!" 8

    For they did not come to Yahweh's aid 9
    To Yahweh's aid, with knights. 9

(Part VII)
24 Most blessed among women is Jael 8
  The wife of Heber the Qenite 5
  Among women in tents she's most blessed! 8

    25 Water he asked 4
    Milk she gave 5

    In a lordly bowl 5
    She brought cream. 5

26 With her left hand she reached for a tent peg 8
  With her right hand for the workman's mallet 9

    She pounded Sisera 7
    She broke his head 5
    She struck and pierced his neck! 11

27 At her feet he slumped. He fell. He sprawled. 10
  At her feet he slumped. He fell. 8
  At the place where he slumped, there he fell. Slain! 10

(Part VIII)
28 From the window she looked down and wailed 12
  Sisera's mother, that is, from the lattice: 9

    Why tarries 4
    His chariot's arrival? 4

    Why so late 5
    The sound of his chariotry? 6

29 The wisest of her captains' ladies answers her   10
   Indeed, she returns her own words to her: 9

   30 Are they not looting   5
      Dividing the spoil?   6

      One or two girls   7
      For each man   3

      Spoil of dyed cloth for Sisera   8
      Spoil of dyed cloth, embroidered   7

      Two pieces of dyed embroidery   5
      For the neck of the spoiler!   6

(Part IX)
31 Thus may they perish   4
   All enemies of Yahweh!   7

   Let his lovers be   4
   Like the sunburst in full strength!   8

And the land was calm, for forty years.

NOTES

5:1–31. Verse 1 is the early narrator's link which, prior to the insertion of the Song, perhaps was followed directly by the exclamation of vs. 31. In the latter, meter is less obvious and the curt parallelism of the Song is lacking.

A catalogue of full-dress studies of the Song of Deborah would read like a Who's Who in biblical research. However, a pioneering study by Albright in 1922, regularly updated in his later writings, sets the pace for all recent work on the Song. See esp. *Journal of the Palestine Oriental Society*, 2 (1922), 69–86 and 284–85; BASOR 62 (1936), 26–31; 163 (1961), 42–43. The dissertation by Frank M. Cross, Jr. and David Noel Freedman, "Studies in Ancient Yahwistic Poetry," Baltimore, 1950; microfilm Xerox reprint, Ann Arbor, 1963, offers an improvement over Albright's earlier treatment and also incorporates some of his unpublished materials. Blenkinsopp has more recently published an excellent literary analysis of the Song, reflecting the influence of

Ugaritic studies, in *Biblica* 42 (1961), 61–76. He treats it as an early war ballad secondarily adapted to the situation of the Yahweh cultus. The excellent study by Weiser in ZAW 81 (1959), 67–97, is unnecessarily bounded by a particular view of the cultic setting, and consequently sacrifices close attention to philological problems. Our NOTES will deal primarily with the latter.

Special attention must be given to the life setting of the oral poet in the ancient near east, whose work was neither that of a strict memorizer nor that of the uninhibited literary artist of the modern western world. Rather, the poet was a person momentarily in the spotlight, recreating poetry under the scrutiny of a public which had assembled to be entertained and edified by the performance. See now Culley, *Oral Formulaic Language in the Biblical Psalms* (1967), esp. the Appendix; and Julian Obermann's essay, "Early Islam," in *The Idea of History in the Ancient Near East*, ed. Robert C. Dentan (Yale University Press, 1955), pp. 237–310.

Certain built-in controls for analysis of the Song are the regularity (not absolute consistency) of metrical patterns and strophic arrangements, both of which were prime elements in Albright's fresh approach to the Song. The meter of Hebrew poetry is based upon the two-segment line (bicolon) and the three-segment line (tricolon). The individual segment (colon) has either two or three beats, and the pattern may be mixed, with two-beat and three-beat cola appearing in the same line. Thus vs. 2 may be scanned as 3:3 meter, vs. 3 as 2:2/2:2/2:2, vss. 4b–5 as 2:3:3/2:3:3, etc. These same verses display patterns of repetitive parallelism that are closely comparable to Ugaritic epic forms and mark the Song as archaic. On the subject of metrical variety and repetitive parallelism in archaic poetry, see Albright's studies of Ps 68 in *Hebrew Union College Annual*, 23 (1950–51), 1–39, and Hab 3 in "The Psalm of Habakkuk," in *Studies in Old Testament Prophecy*, ed. H. H. Rowley (Edinburgh: T. & T. Clark, 1946, repr. 1957), pp. 1–18.

The metrical variety in the Song complicates the analysis of strophes or stanzas considerably. For strophic structure in Hebrew lyric poetry in general, see the studies of Charles Franklin Kraft, esp. his essay, "Some Further Observations Concerning Strophic Structure in Hebrew Poetry," in *A Stubborn Faith*, ed. Edward C. Nobbs (Southern Methodist University Press, 1956), pp. 62–89. It is now clear that the strophes need not be of uniform length. A line by line count of syllables in a poem will often disclose that it was the overall length of line or strophe, and not the recurring accent pattern, that was most important to the poet. See Freedman, ZAW 72 (1960), 101–7, and his essay in *Near Eastern Studies in Honor of William Foxwell Albright*, ed. Hans Goedicke (Johns Hopkins University Press, 1971), pp. 188–205. Our division of the Song into nine parts of considerably varying length is based largely upon his syllable-counting system, together with the observation that the contents of the Song are readily correlated to the patterns which emerge. This is clear in the outline of the Song according to length of lines. Verse 2 is a bicolon of ten syllables per segment ($10+10=20$) echoed in the concluding verse of Part I by the bicolon of vs. 9 ($9+12=21$). The three short bicola of vs. 3 total 36 syllables, balanced by two longer bicola totaling 33 syllables in vs. 8. Verses 4–5 have a bicolon and two tricola for a total of 61 syllables, whereas vss. 6–7 use four bicola with a total of 62 syllables. Such a clearly chiastic arrangement in balanced subunits of nearly identical length was deliberate on the part of the poet who produced the written version of the Song. See Appendix B.

Also belonging to the category of poetic style shared by Israelite poets and their Canaanite contemporaries and forebears, special mention should be made of the inclusio. The inclusio is ubiquitous in the Psalms, and its frequency in the Song of Deborah (vss. 2 and 9 offer a prime example) affords another key to understanding the form.

2. *When they cast off restraint in Israel.* For this translation, see Gaster, MLC, p. 529. Our rendering is far less poetic than EVV, and we part reluctantly with the familiar "When locks were long." There is a lively tradition about the hairy fighters in ancient Israel, despite the disclaimer of Chaim Rabin who, on the other hand, presents the best explication of "present themselves," Heb. *hitnaddēb*, "to go to war in answer to a call," *Journal of Jewish Studies* 6 (1953), 125–34. In the first colon, the root *pr‘* is best connected with Ar. *faraga*[1], as in "I will apply myself exclusively to thee," likewise used in the sense of volunteering for war. Craigie, VT 18 (1968), 399. The divergent versional evidence related to *pr‘* in vs. 2 may be understood as a reflection of textual confusion (generally acknowledged) in vs. 8, which obscured the poetic imagery. However, a relationship is clearly recognizable between vss. 2–9 and Deut 32:34–42 (see NOTES on vs. 8) which supports this interpretation.

troops. Heb. *‘ām.* See NOTE on 2:6.

bless Yahweh! In early Israelite usage, "blessing" was comprehensive wellbeing understood as the gift of God. The command to bless Yahweh, in a military context, would have meant roughly, "Give it all you've got!" In both verses the exclamation lies firmly within the poetic construction, not in rubrics. The divine name occurs exactly seven times in the first unit of the poem, as does the name "Israel." This, as Freedman has reminded me, can hardly be accidental; and it cautions against any emendations which violate stylistic pointers to the craftsmanship of the final written version.

3. *Hear . . . Listen.* The pairing of synonyms and especially the relative positioning of words in parallelism was fixed by long usage and perpetuated by the conditions of oral composition. The poet necessarily relied heavily upon a stock of familiar formulaic phrases. The same pair of imperatives and in the same sequence are standard in the Psalms (e.g. 49:2; 54:4; 143:1); see the writer's study in *Journal of Semitic Studies,* 5 (1960), 241.

kings . . . princes. They are told to consider the relationship between Yahweh and the singer!

I to Yahweh/I. An excellent example of early repetitive parallelism.

sing . . . chant. Heb. roots *šyr* and *zmr* in the familiar Psalm sequence (e.g. 68:5; 101:1; 104:33; 105:2, *et passim*). Boling, *Journal of Semitic Studies,* 5 (1960), 239.

The precision with which vss. 2–3 conform to prevailing metrical structures,

together with smooth transitions from vss. 2 to 3 and 3 to 4, make it impossible
to subtract vs. 3 from the cultic song to get back to the original war ballad,
with Blenkinsopp, *Biblica* 42 (1961). Rather it appears that elements of
cultic origin have been used to applaud an element of the amphictyonic constitution: Yahweh is King in Israel. The occasion for such a song would seem to be
either the eve of an amphictyonic war, or a post-victory celebration.

4–5. The second unit sustains the imagery of the first, with Yahweh taking
the field (a flashback), marching into Canaan at the head of his vassals. The
first two units end with the same words: "Yahweh, God of Israel!"

4. *Seir . . . Edom's land.* Not a contradiction in tradition regarding the
location of Sinai (vs. 5) but an affirmation that Yahweh and Israel conquered
a large extent of Canaan together, coming by way of Edom in southern
Transjordan (Map 2, C-6). Nelson Glueck's archaeological surveys convinced
him that the territory of the early kingdom of Edom never extended west of
the Arabah; the handful of scattered references placing Edom in the south of
Palestine he traces to the later Nabataean displacement of the Edomites. JAOS
56 (1936), esp. 464 f. On the "theophany" here as Yahweh's entrance into
the land of Canaan, see esp. Blenkinsopp, *Biblica* 42 (1961).

For a treatment of vss. 4 and 5 as the clearest representative of Israel's
category of "theophany," see Jörg Jeremias, *Theophanie: Die Geschichte einer
alttestamentlichen Gattung,* Neuenkirch: Neuenkirchener Verlag, 1965.

With thunder. Interpreting *gm* as "sound, voice, thunder," following Dahood's
analysis of the Ugaritic cognate. *Biblica* 45 (1964), 399; *Psalms I, 1–50,*
AB, vol. 16 (1966), NOTE on 25:3; *Psalms II, 51–100,* AB, vol. 17 (1968),
NOTE on 52:7; *Psalms III, 101–150,* AB, vol. 17A (1970), fourth NOTE on
137:1. The imagery reflects the theophany described in Exod 20, with its
thunder and lightning as well as smoke.

5. *shook.* Reading *nāzōllū* (root *zll*), as in Isa 63:19 (Heb.), 64:2, instead
of the unintelligible *nāzᵉlū* in MT.

Poetic participation by natural elements has deep roots in the mythology of
Canaan. On the rapid demotion and effective depersonalizing of the elements,
see Wright's discussion of the role of "heaven" and "earth" in OT covenant
lawsuits. "The Lawsuit of God: A Form-Critical Study of Deuteronomy 32,"
Israel's Prophetic Heritage, ed. by Bernhard W. Anderson and Walter Harrelson
(New York: Harper, 1962), esp. pp. 41–49. It is within the realm of possibility
that "earth" and "mountains" here "quaked" and "shook" at the arrival of the
Universal Judge. It is more likely that they are represented as having been used
at the conquest (e.g. Josh 3:11–17, 10:11), as in the recent victory (vss. 20–
21).

The One of Sinai. For the persuasive argument that an archaic pronoun
du lies behind both the element *zē* in our verse and the later relative *'ᵃšer*
in the formulaic names of Yahweh in Exod 3, see Cross, *Harvard Theological
Review,* 55 (1962), esp. 239, n. 61, and 255 f. "Yon Sinai" (RSV) is impossible
and truly diverts the attention from the current scene of Yahweh's historical
activity.

6–7. The verses present recent history as being of comparable significance
to the first arrival of Yahweh and Israel in Canaan (vss. 4–5).

6. *Shamgar the Anathite.* See NOTES and COMMENT on 3:31.

days . . . days. This repetition, an archaic poetic pattern, also evokes comparison with the social setting of pre-Islamic poetry and prose, where oral tradition organizes the memory of outstanding occurrences in the feuding history of clans as "Day of Kulab," "Day of Shi'b Jahala," etc. Like Deborah and Baraq, "the pagan poet is not only a spokesman but as a rule also a chieftain and warrior of his clan and even of his tribe, so that he often describes raids he himself has instigated, days in which he has taken a leading part." Obermann, *The Idea of History,* esp. pp. 255–57.

Jael. Anticipating her role in vss. 24–27. There is no longer any difficulty in understanding Shamgar, Jael, Deborah, and Baraq as contemporaries in one period of success and achievement.

wayfaring men. The Hebrew caravaneers who formed the core of the Yahwist revolution in Canaan.

winding roads. Presumably not the main trade routes of the coastal plain, which had never been in their control, but those from the hill country to Arabia and other remote regions.

7. *warriors.* Heb. *perāzōn,* not "villagers." Albright YGC, p. 49, cites Papyrus Anastasi 1, 23, line 4.

grew plump. A word play involving homonyms, *ḥdl* I, "to cease" and *ḥdl* II, as suggested by Marvin Chaney in an unpublished study. See COMMENT, p. 118. For the discovery of *ḥdl* II, which in I Sam 2:5 (with double *lamedh* as in our verse), is the opposite of to starve, be hungry, see Philip J. Calderone, CBQ 23 (1961), 451–60; 24 (1962), 412–19; Dahood, *Psalms I, 1–50,* AB, vol. 16 (1966), NOTE on 36:4. *Ḥdl* II means not only "fat" or "plump," but also "obtuse, complacent," which prepares for a plausible transition to the next verse of the Song. Cf. Deut 32:15–17 which similarly describes a situation of rebellious complacency as the setting in which Israel chooses "new gods."

again. Relating *'d* to the preceding use of the verb *ḥdl* precisely as in I Sam 2:5.

Because. Heb *'ad ša-,* lit. "until pertaining to," an archaic use of the particle *ša.* See also 6:17 and NOTE and compare the compound *še-'al* in 7:12, "(which is) on" and 8:26 "that were on."

a mother. Deborah is lauded for providing the prophetic answer to the concern of inquiring leaders of Israel. This verse anticipates the concluding scene where "Sisera's mother" propounds the question and the "wise" women provide the incorrect answer (vss. 28–30).

8. *One chose new gods.* This entire verse is notoriously difficult to translate. After repeated attempts to explain it in terms of a mutilated text, I have been forced, especially by the persuasiveness of Chaney's proposal on *ḥdl* II in vs. 7, to recognize a text which is mispointed in one word, but otherwise entirely consistent, using vocabulary that is common to the Song. Deities were regularly listed as witnesses and guarantors of treaty. The choice of "new gods" may therefore derive its context from the collapse of trade route agreements and general security that brought on the warfare. See *TenGen,* p. 133, n. 56.

There are numerous points of affinity between this poem and the "lawsuit"

Song of Moses in Deut 32. On the latter, see Wright, *Israel's Prophetic Heritage,* pp. 26–27. The Song of Moses goes on to assert that when Israel is utterly defenseless, and when Yahweh sees that their "power is gone," then Yahweh will act to "judge" (Heb. *dyn,* poetic equivalent of *špṭ*) his people (Deut 32:36). Other solutions have appropriated Deut 32:17 in relation to the Song of Deborah and emended the latter to read a direct reference to demonolatry. Thus, ALUOS[D], 8; independently, and on other grounds, Hillers, CBQ 27 (1965), 124–26. The result, however, is to leave the poetic line isolated from its context, as Hillers readily admits.

Then they fought in the gates. MT "Then was bread (*leḥem*) of the gates" becomes intelligible by vocalizing as a qal perfect (*lāḥᵃmū*). Cf. Ps 35:1, where the verb form is also qal. The sequence *'āz*+perfect is a recurring pattern in the Song (vss. 11d, 13, 19b, 22).

Neither shield nor spear. The larger context of the oath of allegiance (vss. 2 and 9) indicates that the particle *'im* is here the emphatic negative. The Israelites were not armed with aristocratic weapons; shields and spears belonged to professional military men. The paucity of weapons is also alluded to in connection with Saul and Jonathan (I Sam 13:22).

Forty contingents. More in keeping with the description of the times in vss. 6–7 than the later, literal, "forty thousand." So also *'ām* in vs. 9 is "troops," not "people." See NOTE on 2:6.

contingents. See NOTE on 1:4.

9. *heart.* Heb. *lēb* often has the meaning of "will," supported here by the usage in vss. 15 and 16.

presenting themselves . . . bless Yahweh! The verse forms a powerful inclusio with vs. 2. Note the shift from temporal construction at the outset to the participle here: "Those presenting themselves" now.

10–11. These verses celebrate how the force was mustered, thanks to Deborah. An assembly of tribal representatives such as that described in 4:5–6 seems to be the setting. For another example of direct address, but in the "victory assembly," see vs. 14.

10. *O riders . . . O wayfarers.* The latter, lit. "walkers." Gaster recognizes a merismus here—the entire population is included by mentioning two extremes, the wealthy (riders) and the lowly (walkers). MLC, pp. 418–19, 529–30. More precisely the former are the caravan owners and chief clients; the latter are the groomsmen.

on the judgment seat. For the clarification of the middle term in this tricolon, I am indebted to Freedman, who compares Prov 20:8, which addresses itself to the king "sitting on the throne of judgment" (*ks' dyn*). He proposes to recognize the problematical *mdyn* in our verse as a noun with the typical *mem* preformative derived from the verb *dyn,* "to judge." As noted above, this root is another point of affinity between this Song and the "lawsuit" Song of Moses in Deut 32.

11. *Attend to the sound of cymbals.* Redividing MT, and reading the initial *mem* in vs. 11 as the enclitic accidentally separated from its verb, the line becomes perfectly clear: *syḥw-m qwl-mḥṣṣym.* Freedman, private communication.

let them retell. The verb is piel, with iterative or durative force, "tell again," "tell continually," cf. 11:40. Its Ugaritic usage verifies the meaning "to recite antiphonally," according to Weiser. ZAW 71 (1959), 79. Deborah tells them to take their celebration to the water holes.

11e–13. Three of the five words in 11e occur again in vs. 13, forming an inclusio or envelope construction, enclosing the climactic appeal of vs. 12. The frame (11e and 13) represent the action inspired by the exclamation in vs. 12.

Yahweh's victories. Heb. *ṣidqōt,* lit. "his righteous acts," by which he vindicates his own saving prerogatives. The equivalent in early Priestly sources is *(mi)špāṭîm,* "judgments": Exod 6:6, 7:4, 12:12; Num 33:4; and repeatedly in Ezekiel.

12–13. These verses transport the celebrant to town and village wells and describe the enthusiastic public response to those who had earlier sought out Deborah for the judgment.

12. *Awake . . . Sing a song!* We might paraphrase: "Begin! Begin! Sing a Song!" as the words are in parallelism. "The reference is not to the present song but to that customarily chanted by the womenfolk when the warriors return with the loot." Gaster, MLC, p. 419, citing I Sam 18:7–8 and Ps 68:12 (Heb. vss. 13–14a). The latter is especially illuminating:

> O mighty host, will you linger among the sheepfolds
> while the women in your tents divide the spoil—
> (NEB)

We would compare also the story of Jephthah's daughter greeting her victorious father in Judg 11:34.

13. *Yahweh's troops.* On the semantics of *'ām* "troops," see vss. 2 and 9 and NOTE on 2:6.

went down . . . went down. Reading both verbs as qal perfect, in conformity with usage after *'āz* at other points in the Song. In MT the first occurrence is mispointed (*yᵉrad*), the result of contamination from the second occurrence, where *yārad*>*yᵉrad* with emphasis on the enclitic *-lî* (*for me*).

knights. Those adult males prosperous enough to equip themselves for warfare. There were so few of them in Israel as to elicit special comment when they appear (or fail to!): 5:23, 6:12, 11:1 (cf. 18:2 and 20:46).

14–18. The scene is the victory celebration. These verses review the performance of various tribal contingents.

14. *Those of Ephraim.* Reading the introductory *mny* as partitive.

have taken root. The verb is *šrš* which in the third verbal conjugation means "to take root, be firmly fixed"; cf. Isa 40:24; Jer 12:2. The line is highly pejorative; the Ephraimites decided to sit this one out. Cf. the perspective on Ephraim in 8:1–2, 12:1–6, and 17–21.

in Amaleq. Cf. 12:15, "in the land of Ephraim, in the Amaleqite hill country." Amaleqites put in their appearance in stories ranging all over the country. It is therefore reasonable to assume that some of them had settled in a certain section which bore their name.

Behind you, Benjamin, with your troops. It is extremely difficult to know what to make of this line. Hosea 5:8–9 uses the expression "Behind you,

Benjamin" sarcastically and follows it with an announcement of bad news for Ephraim. It may have something to do with an obscure technical military term for "bringing up the rear" (cf. Josh 6:9, 13; I Sam 29:2; Ps 68:26).

Machir. This is poetic usage singling out western Manasseh. Burney, p. 135. The Transjordanian tribes of Reuben and Gilead are later censured for staying at home.

scepter. Connecting Heb. *sōpēr* with Akk. *šapāru* "to rule." Matitiahu Tsevat, *Hebrew Union College Annual* 24 (1952–53), 107.

15. *Issachar's captains.* Reading with Targ., where MT has "My captains in Issachar." The latter is a mispointed construct chain, with intervening preposition (see also vs. 31), pointed out to me by Freedman, who compares *hry bglb'*, "mountains of Giboa," in II Sam 1:21.

Issachar. Repetitive parallelism, perhaps prompted by the meaning of the tribal name, "hired man."

support. Heb. *kēn.* For this sense, see ALUOS^D, 11.

the plain. Esdraelon; considerable knowledge of its extent and character is presupposed (e.g. vs. 18). See Map 2, C-2. An Amarna letter speaks of forced labor (Heb. *mas,* as applied to Issachar in Gen 49:15) for the prince of Megiddo and mentions several Esdraelon towns and villages. ANET[3], p. 485 and n. 7.

under his command. Lit. "at his feet." Cf. 4:10.

15d–16. The structure of this unit follows the pattern of vss. 2 and 9, which is repeated again in vss. 11e and 13. Once again we have an inclusio, with a subtle variation from the initial statement (vss. 2, 11e, 15d) to the restatement in which the poet speaks for himself (vss. 9, 13, and 16).

15d. *command-minded . . . fainthearted.* A play on the word for "heart" (*lēb*) as the seat of mind and will: *hqqy-lb,* lit. "resolutions of heart," and *hqry-lb,* lit. "searchings of heart," that is, second thoughts. Such wordplay abounds in the prophetic books (cf. Isa 5:7).

16. *hearths.* Heb. *mišpᵉtayim* is clarified from Ugaritic. Albright, *Hebrew Union College Annual,* 23 (1950–51), 22. The same word is used in Gen 49: 14–15 to characterize the expedient servitude of Issachar. YGC, p. 265 f.

Reuben's divisions . . . fainthearted chieftains. In Gen 49:4a Reuben is denounced with the same root (*phz*) used to characterize the fellows hired by Abimelech in 9:4.

17. *bivouacked.* Heb. *šākēn,* lit. "tented," and used derisively in another inclusio. Cf. 19:9, where the word is *'ōhel.* On the alternation of finite verb forms in biblical poetry (here *škn/yškn*), see Dahood, *Psalms III, 101–150,* AB, vol. 17A (1970), pp. 420–23.

Why did Dan. The tradition behind this line clearly reflects Dan's early attempt at settlement bordering the Sharon and Philistine plains (Map 2, B-4), where no doubt many individual Israelites found their chief livelihood as crewmen aboard the Sea Peoples' merchant vessels (see illustration 10). Dan's later location in the far north (chs. 17–18) was some twenty miles from the coast and, except for one winding river bed, effectively barred from ships by the Lebanon mountains. See Map 3.

Asher. Another negative report, but with poetic effect heightened by the

shift from 2+2 to 3+3 meter, introducing a new unit but reusing the derogatory action verbs in parallel: he "squatted . . . bivouacked."

18. *death*. Heb. *napšō lāmūt*, lit. "his soul to die." The force of the statement
becomes clearer by comparison with Jonah 4:8, where the reluctant prophet
at last "petitions" *napšō lāmūt*.

heights of the plain. The Heb. *mrwmy śdh* has a semantic equivalent in II
Sam 1:21, *śdy trwmt* (unnecessarily emended to read "upsurging of the deep"
in RSV), and refers to the fact that the Esdraelon plain is characterized by
undulations and hillocks which provided positions of relative advantage for
the opposing forces. Precisely where these particular heights were in relation
to the Qishon is not clear.

19–22. These verses recapitulate the battle and Israel's victory thanks to a
maneuver by the heavenly host (cloudburst and flash flood).

19–20. *fought . . . fought*. Repetition of the main verb forms an envelope
construction in characteristic patterns. Verse 19 is in the chiastic pattern
A B C / C B[1] (with the ballast variant); vs. 20 is A B C/ D B E.

19. *Taanach . . . Megiddo's stream*. See Map 3. On the problem of
historical locus, see COMMENTS. Lit. "waters," "stream" is a poetic anticipation of the outcome in vs. 20. The name "Megiddo" is connected with Heb.
g^edūd, "troops," and means "place of troops," "garrison." Paul Haupt,
JAOS 34 (1914), 415.

Silver booty. This introduces the theme which will be poignantly developed
in the final unit of the Song.

20. *the stars*. They are considered the source of rain in Canaanite mythology.
Blenkinsopp, *Biblica* 42 (1961), 73, citing 'Anat II, 41.

21–22. The fighting involved Canaanites and Israelites, but the victory was
attained by force beyond any human control. "Israel" is where they retell
"Yahweh's victories," as in vss. 4 and 11.

21. *The Wadi Qishon*. Repeated at the end of the parallel line in characteristic chiastic arrangement.

overwhelmed them. Repointing the obscure *q^edūmīm* to read *qidd^emām*,
as proposed by Cross and Freedman, *Studies in Ancient Yahwistic Poetry*,
pp. 29 and 35.

You shall trample the throat of the mighty. It is possible that a parallel to
this line has been lost, but aside from the proposal to read *npšy* as reflecting
the genitive case ending, "throat of" (Freedman, private communication),
there is no reason to challenge the text. The sudden shift to second person
echoes and fills out the two earlier occurrences (vss. 7 and 12). Together the
three laud the role of Deborah as initiator, leader, and victor. The final image
is that of the conquering warrior with his foot on the neck of the vanquished
(see Josh 10:24).

22. *horses' hoofs*. The anomolous *mdhrwt* may be understood as a misdivision and readily improved by detaching the *mem* and reading the preceding
noun as plural *sws-m*.

racing. Heb. root *dhr*, elsewhere only Nahum 3:2. For the meaning "to
race chariots," see Albright, BASOR 62 (1936), 30.

23–24. The transitions are abrupt. Parataxis or the coordinative ranging of propositions one after another, without expression of syntactic connection, is characteristic of oral epic. Lord, *The Singer of Tales*, p. 65.

23. This verse alone, with abrupt introduction of the theme of treason, indicates that widely held notions of "Holy War" as something involving Israel's calm and confidently faithful participation are vastly oversimplified.

Oh, curse Meroz. Cf. Shamshi-Adad's decree: "The king is going on a campaign. All (men) down to the youngest (soldiers) are to be used. The administrator whose troops have not all been used, who exempts (even) a single man, shall be cursed." *Archives royales de Mari,* I (tr. by Glock, *op. cit.* p. 68). The curse follows upon a failure, thus removing vs. 23 from the description of the battle itself.

Meroz. Otherwise unknown. The root meaning "calamity, doom," occurs in Isa 24:16, *rozī-lī,* "woe is me!" which enables Gaster (MLC, p. 419) to recognize a pun in our passage: "Cry doom on Doomsville." On the larger subject of OT cursing in general, and convenantal curses in particular, see Herbert C. Berichto, *The Problem of "Curse" in the Hebrew Bible,* JBL Monograph 13, 1963, and esp. Hillers, *Treaty-Curses and the Old Testament Prophets,* Johns Hopkins University Press, 1964.

the divine adviser. Heb. *mal'ak yhwh,* lit. "messenger of Yahweh." Inasmuch as the prose account and the remainder of the poetry present the victory as a matter of sheer providence, it is likely that Gaster is correct in recognizing here a reference to the professional diviner, invariably consulted in ancient warfare. See MLC, pp. 419, 530, which compares the role and poetry of Balaam in Num 22–24. Note also that in the Greek of Judg 4:8 Baraq complains that he never knows when "the divine adviser" will give him success. But Deborah was adviser par excellence. Here an adviser's recommendation to curse, developed only in a short strophe, seems to be interrupted by the poet's present enthusiasm for blessing.

24. *The wife of Heber the Qenite.* This appositional phrase is often regarded by critics as secondary, originally a marginal comment based on 4:17, and that is entirely plausible. We have retained it, however, in view of the sizable number of tricola in the Song (this one balances another tricolon in vs. 27) and our sketchy knowledge of early Hebrew prosody. The curse and the blessing seem to form a quotation from the earliest traditions of the battle, allowing, say, a century for the crystallization of the Song in its present form. Ackroyd, VT 2 (1952), 160–62.

25. *Water . . . Milk.* There is no evidence that these are traditionally fixed pairs in poetic parallelism. Rather the effect is to focus attention upon Jael's cunning, giving him a "mild sedative" before proceeding to the bloody deed. Burney, p. 93, and Powell, *Biblica* 9 (1928), 47.

26. *her left hand . . . her right hand.* For this meaning of the traditional pair *yād/yāmīn* in Psalm parallelism and Ugaritic, see Dahood, *Psalms III, 101–150* (AB, 1970), p. 449.

she reached. Repointing MT *tišlaḥnā* (plural!) to read the archaic energic form *tišlaḥannā.* Freedman, ZAW 72 (1960), 102. For the high incidence of energic forms in Hebrew poetry as in Ugaritic, see Dahood, *Psalms I, 1–50,* AB, vol. 16 (1966), NOTE on 8:2.

pounded. Heb. *hāleʿmā.* The same verb first appears in vs. 22, where "horses' hoofs" is the subject. Jael's deed is presented as a part of Yahweh's victory, in a play on the word *halmūt,* "mallet."

neck. For this meaning of *rqh,* see NOTE on 4:21.

27. *At her feet.* Heb. *bēn raglēhā,* lit. "between her feet," but reminiscent of the military usage of *beʿraglō,* "under his command," in 4:10 and 5:15. Jael had taken orders ("water . . . milk"), but Sisera had obeyed. That this is not reading too much into the phrase is clear from the repetition of verbs (he slumped, he fell) in the two bicola of the verse. Only the last word is different (sprawled . . . slain). Thus, 27b recapitulates his arrival at the tent and his collapse in exhaustion, while 27c makes that the point of his undoing.

At the place. Reading *b'šr* as noun and preposition, mistakenly pointed in MT as the relative pronoun, which does not occur elsewhere in the Song; the Song uses instead the archaic equivalent *š* (vs. 7). Here the climax of the Song displays an elaborate repetitive pattern: ABCD/ABC/EBFCG (cf. vss. 19–20 and NOTE). The repetition of the two verbs binds the three units together, while other terms are used to vary the imagery.

28–30. These verses are the older conclusion of the Song. Following upon the vivid image of Jael hovering above the corpse of Sisera, the final unit began with another woman (Sisera's mother), and a poetically inverted vantage point.

28. The metrical scheme here appears to be 4:4//2:2/2:2, with the first pair of lines arranged chiastically and both sets of parallel lines showing repetitive style. The syllable count cautions against any rearrangement of the text: 12+9=21//8+11=19.

29. *The wisest.* Heb. *ḥokmōt* may be taken as a Canaanite/Phoenician spelling of the feminine singular. Dahood, *Psalms I, 1–50,* AB, vol. 16 (1966), NOTES on 45:15.

30. *Dividing the spoil?* For another double-duty interrogative, see vs. 16.

One or two girls. The verse attributes to the Canaanite warrior a special license with captive women that was strictly proscribed by the rules of Yahwist warfare (Deut 21:10–14).

the neck of the spoiler. MT *ṣawweʿrē* is plural construct with singular meaning; cf. Gen 27:16. I am indebted to Freedman for the proposal to repoint the final word, where *šālāl* is unintelligible in context, but *šōlēl,* "the spoiler" (Sisera), makes excellent sense.

31. This conclusion to the Song probably belonged to the early narrative tradition. The couplet is in the form of a two-edged wish; on the larger category, see Ernst Sellin, *Introduction to the Old Testament,* revised and rewritten by Georg Fohrer, tr. David E. Green (New York and Nashville: Abingdon, 1968), pp. 74–76. Prior to the incorporation of the larger Song, which had circulated independently, this is what the narrative said that "Deborah and Baraq . . . sang that day" (5:1). The verse is itself archaic, as witnessed by the contrast between *'wybyk* and *'hbyw,* "enemies" and "lovers." The final *kaph* of the former is probably not a pronoun suffix, but the enclitic *kaph* in the middle of a constant chain. A good example is Ps 24:6 *pny-k y'qb* "the Presence of

Jacob," Dahood, *Psalms I, 1–50,* AB, vol. 16 (1966), 24:6 and NOTE; *Psalms II, 51–100,* AB, vol. 17 (1968), Introduction, "Grammar."

his lovers. Heb. *'hbyw.* It is important to note that the opposite of Yahweh's enemies are those who love him. For the international treaty background of *'hb* in this covenantal sense, see Moran, CBQ 25 (1963), 77–87.

Like the sunburst in full strength! Lit. "when the sun comes out at its strongest." The figure, originally of sunrise and freighted with mythic significance, calls to mind that the sun had been hidden by storm clouds on the day of the battle. As it now stands, the verse forms a fitting inclusio with the outset of the Song in vs. 4a, "Yahweh, when you came out. . . ."

COMMENT

An up-to-date reading of the Song of Deborah departs significantly from its predecessors, thanks mainly to the recovery of a plausible social setting for the Song. What is new is our access to early Israel's provisions for civil defense, that is, the Yahwist variation upon institutions of the military muster, as known from Mari, together with its related conceptions of land tenure (inheritance) and regulations for distribution or restriction of booty (ḥerem).

Ancient Israel was justifiably proud of the restraints imposed upon her fighting men, although later generations (in *E* and *D*) obscured the administrative significance of the ḥerem. Thus one ḥerem story was used to highlight the faithfulness of Joshua's generation. Achan is an "example" in Josh 7; it did not happen twice, not while Joshua was in command!

Thanks to continued archaeological work, a historical context consistent with the small numbers and makeshift military procedure in Israel is coming into focus. There is a gap in occupation levels (archaeological strata) at Megiddo. The site was either abandoned or lightly occupied from 1125 (end of Stratum VII) to the beginning of the first Israelite town there about 1100–1050 (Stratum VI). Taanach in the twelfth century was, like Hazor, not extensively occupied; and Taanach was destroyed about 1125, according to the recent excavations (Lapp, BASOR 195 [September, 1969], esp. 33–49). The excavator was inclined to associate the destruction of twelfth century Taanach with the events celebrated in the Song of Deborah.

Archaeological evidence thus provides entree to the poetic mention of Megiddo (stronghold). Nothing of opposing significance then stood on the mound; what interested the poet was the role played by "Stronghold's Stream" (vss. 19–21). Modern archaeological campaigns supply a striking parallel:

> . . . It is interesting to note Sellin's report that spring rains made travel for his supply wagons difficult in the muddy plain. In fact, three of his horses drowned in that same swollen Qishon in 1903.
> Carl Graesser, in *The Biblical World,* ed. by Charles Pfeiffer, p. 561.

As indicated above in NOTES, the participation of the stars was probably understood in terms of their responsibility for the unexpected cloudburst which forced the Qishon and its tributaries out of their banks, miring Sisera's heavy chariots in the muck and giving the advantage to Israel's footmen standing high and dry on "the heights of the plain" (vs. 18).

This is a cultic song in the sense that for early Israel common life is best understood in terms of the covenant with Yahweh. In its finished form the Song is a carefully structured unity, showing few traces of early or late liturgical adaptation (see NOTES on vss. 2, 9, and 23). Its qualities are rooted in the necessities of an oral poet laboring to perform satisfactorily for an audience that had assembled to be entertained and edified on that occasion. Note

> the frequent dramatic juxtapositions, so effective for holding attention and directing it to the essentials in the story, the vivid dialogue with dramatic repetitions, the use of poetical words and the constant hammering on proper names, the names of dramatis personae, the catch phrases, puns, and strong sonic patterns, all calculated to spin out the story and hold the attention of the hearer to what is being told—the age-old art of the story teller, in short.
> Blenkinsopp, *Biblica* 42 (1961), 64.

In such poetry the clues to formal structure must be deduced from content. We may assume that they sang Judg 5 in premonarchical Israel whenever the amphictyony assembled (vss. 2 and 9) to do the sort of thing that Deborah did (vss. 10–11), that is, to put an army into the field or celebrate its victorious return.

The genre of the victory hymn is well known in examples from fifteenth to twelfth century Egypt and Assyria. Especially instructive are the "Hymn of Victory of Thutmose III" (ANET³, pp. 373–75); the one deriving from Ramses III at the temple of Medinet Habu (William F. Edgerton and John A. Wilson, *Historical Records of Ramses III* [University of Chicago Press, 1936], pp. 111–12); and the "Hymn of Victory of Merneptah" with its earliest extrabiblical mention of "Israel" (Wilson, ANET³, pp. 376–78). From Assyria there are extensive portions of a triumphal poem of Tukulti-Ninurta I, c. 1234–1197 (Ebeling, *Mitteilungen der Altorientalischen Gesellschaft,* 12 [1938], 3 and 37 f.).

In these extrabiblical examples the mixture of new (historical) and old (poetical) material is much more readily discernible than in the more compact Song of Deborah. Still one notes a wealth of thematic and formulaic continuities: god works a wonder for his son (Thutmose), and the enemy force is left in mutinous disarray as its commander flees by night, only to find those awaiting his return "too aggrieved to receive him," whereas the whole debacle of Pharaoh's enemies had been foretold by the stars (Merneptah stele). The climax of Merneptah's hymn is precisely parallel to the outset of Deborah's: "One walks with unhindered stride on the way, for there is no fear at all in the heart of the people" (Wilson, ANET³, p. 378). Yet here is the surprising contrast. Pharaoh and god never tire of telling what each has done for the other, for the pacification of the empire is to their mutual personal advantage.

In vss. 2–3 the Hebrew poet adopts a stance toward the new Israelite officers comparable to that of Deborah in the manpower shortage of her day. The "troops" (the people, Yahweh's army) are invited to put their vows to music, as the poet will now do, turning in direct address to Yahweh.

Verses 4–5 turn briefly to historical retrospect, making use of the *Gattung* of theophany in perhaps its clearest OT exemplar (so Jeremias, *Theophanie . . . ,* 1965, pp. 7–16). Yahweh is represented as striding into Canaan at the head of the Sinai covenanters and winning a mighty victory, thanks to the terrestrial and cosmic elements in the service of "Yahweh, God of Israel!" (vs. 5c). The climactic significance of this basic confession in vss. 3f and 5c is often stressed. But note is seldom taken of its absence in the remainder of the Song. That is, vss. 6–30 are concerned with Yahweh's reestablishment in Deborah's day of his claim to be Israel's God.

After the flashback in vss. 4 and 5 to the brilliant initial successes of Yahweh and Israel, the poet turns in vss. 6 and 7 to his nuclear theme, the events surrounding the career of Deborah. The Israelites concentrated in the hill country were responsible for the cessation of caravans traveling to and from the remoter regions to the south and east, the caravans that followed "the winding roads," not the level main roads of Esdraelon and the coastal plain. This circumstance profited Israel since usually caravans were the monopoly of kings and other wealthy nobility who bled the country.

One is reminded of the oppressive fiscal policies of Solomon, which led at his death to the secession of the northern tribes. Compare also the conditions that had prevailed in the earlier Amarna period (Introduction, pp. 13–14). The turning point in Deborah's day was collaboration between Israelites concentrated in the hill country and certain Hebrew caravaneers, as celebrated in vs. 10. In this new situation a rally of the tribes by Deborah and Baraq turned a prosperous and complacent Israel into a Yahweh army once again in order to take control of Esdraelon and other territories belonging to the promised land. It thus appears that the cutting off of the caravan routes represents the expanding power of the Israelites under Deborah's leadership and their successful challenge to those engaged in that sort of trade. In other words, Deborah had organized the battle in which Israel for the first time was able to defeat the Canaanites on their own preferred ground, where the Canaanites could use their chariots. All this suggests a time far into the Philistine period, a suggestion further supported by the non-Semitic sound of Sisera's name (whereas that name could well be found among the Sea Peoples or Philistines) and the late twelfth-century destruction level at Taanach. At the climax of this section Deborah is lauded as "a mother." As there are absolutely no hints elsewhere in the poem to support a literal interpretation of this choice of words, in a poem where key words and key images are carefully repeated, we are forced to look for other connections. The title "mother" in vs. 7 appears to be honorific, bestowed by the poet for the entertainment of folk who customarily associated oracular technique with the priestly title of "father" (see 17:10 and NOTE, and 18:19).

Verse 8 is another flashback, this time to the more recent period of warfare in which Jael, Shamgar, Deborah, and Baraq had taken part. The time reference appears, more specifically, to be the beginning of that period, when the initial successes against the caravans had led to a sense of satisfaction with the status quo. Here is an Israel that was prosperous and complacent and turning to other gods (Baal and his consort Astarte or Asherah, as specified in 2:13, 3:7, and 10:6), fighting with each other, with many unwilling to take up Yahweh's cause, to take control of Esdraelon and other crucial territories belonging to the promised land, especially in face of superior Canaanite arms and Philistine military leadership. In this situation Deborah had roused an army for Baraq and spurred both on to action. It was a paradigmatic example which the singer posed for the new recruits, and he says so explicitly in vs. 9, where he affirms his presence in a strong inclusio with 2b and the repetition of first person pronouns in 3.

Verses 10–11d urge the use of Deborah's enlistment technique for all such occasions in Israel: sing the old Yahweh victory songs! In actual practice the responsibility for fielding a requisite number of units resided with local elders, and we may assume that it is they who have consulted Yahweh through Deborah in 4:5. Thus while the prose proceeds at once to the summons of Baraq, the poetry develops the theme of the consultation and its outcome: "Awake, Deborah . . . Arise, Baraq" (vs. 12). That is, be as active militarily as the God of the venerable Ark of the Covenant—portable safe deposit box for the constitution. See the archaic "Song of the Ark" in Num 10:35.

Verses 12–13 celebrate the success of the muster and the battle which followed. In vs. 13b the poet affirms his presence once again.

A partial review of those who responded to the call (or failed to respond) is presented in vss. 14–18. Not all of the tribes are mentioned. References to Reuben and Gilead in Transjordan reflect an instability east of the river that is obscured by the later organizational assumptions. Especially conspicuous by its absence is Judah, which has apparently gone its own way so completely, since the revolution's early days (1:8–20; cf. 3:7–11), that it comes in for neither praise nor blame, but is mentioned only fleetingly (10:9) until at last it is involved in the extradition of Samson to Philistia (ch. 15).

But those who were there have great memories (vss. 19–22)—Yahweh's victory against a whole coalition of kings. To Deborah is here attributed the poet's own perspective, as the description of the battle is interrupted by a much more legalistic adviser (see NOTES on vs. 23), who does not want the town (clan?) of Meroz to go uncensured for its failure to send a contingent to battle (vs. 23). The poet, however, will accentuate the positive, and instead of cursing Meroz blesses Jael.

The scene with Sisera's mother (vs. 28), who could get only the wrong answer from the "wisest of her captain's ladies" (vs. 29), forms a strong inclusio with the initial climax of the Song where Deborah is honorary "mother in Israel" (vs. 7), the one who gave the right answer.

If by this time the poet has not succeeded in making hearers identify with the story, it is doubtful that any poet can do so. After all the mustering and fighting was over and done, it was Yahweh who felled Sisera by the hand of one loyal Qenite woman who had perhaps remained Israelite by preference.

The poet concludes with a notable contrast to the predatory plushness of a Canaanite court. Thanks to the restrictions which the amphictyony imposed upon its fighters (see NOTE on vs. 30), their women were not supposed to have the kind of mixed emotions that plagued Sisera's mother and the officers' wives. On this note the poem concludes. Transition to the narrative is made via the couplet in vs. 31, which perhaps was already in place as the "song of Deborah and Baraq," until a redactor exegeted it by inserting this priceless poem.

It is surely significant that in chs. 4 and 5 the words for "judgment" are used in reference to both the act of assembly (*mdyn* in 5:10), and the result of a particular inquiry (*mišpaṭ* in 4:5).

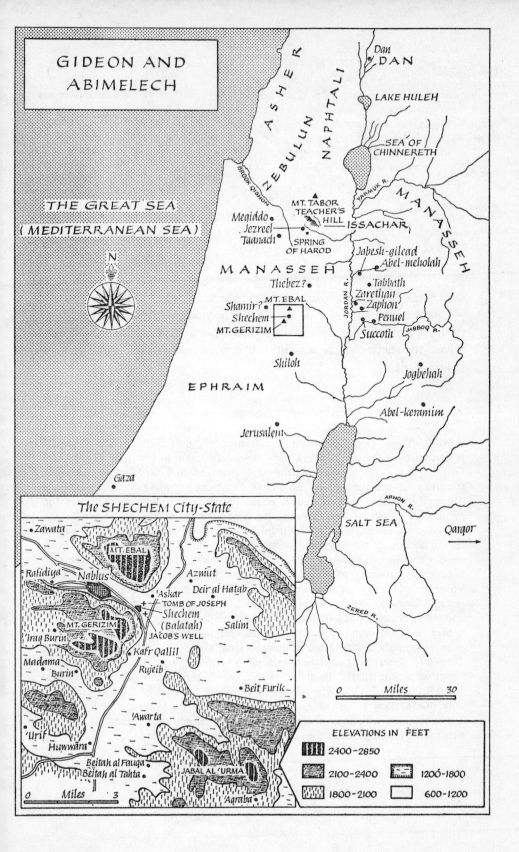

GIDEON AND ABIMELECH

THE GREAT SEA
(MEDITERRANEAN SEA)

N.

ASHER

ZEBULUN

NAPHTALI

Dan
DAN

LAKE HULEH

SEA OF
CHINNERETH

BROOK QISHON

MT. TABOR
TEACHER'S
HILL

ISSACHAR

MANASSEH

YARMUK R.

Megiddo
Jezreel
Taanach

SPRING
OF HAROD

Jabesh-gilead
Abel-meholah

MANASSEH

Thebez?

Tabbath
Zarethan
Zaphon
Penuel

Shamir?
Shechem
MT. GERIZIM

MT. EBAL

JORDAN R.

Succoth

JABBOQ R.

Shiloh

Jogbehah

EPHRAIM

Abel-keramim

Jerusalem

Gaza

ARNON R.

SALT SEA

Qarqor

ZERED R.

0   Miles   30

The SHECHEM City-State

Zawata

MT. EBAL

Rafidiya   Nablus

Azmut

Deir al Hatab

'Askar
TOMB OF JOSEPH
Shechem
(Balatah)
JACOB'S WELL

Salim

MT. GERIZIM

'Iraq Burin

Kafr Qallil

Madama
Burin

Rujeib

Beit Furik

Urif

'Awarta

Huwwara

Beitah al Fauqa
Beitah al Tahta

JABAL AL 'URMA

0   Miles   3

Aqraba

ELEVATIONS IN FEET

▦	2400-2850		
▦	2100-2400	▤	1200-1800
▦	1800-2100	☐	600-1200

X. The Evil
(6:1–2)

6 ¹ Israelists did what was evil in Yahweh's sight, and Yahweh subjected them to Midian's power for seven years. ² Midian's power prevailed against Israel; because of Midian the Israelites made for themselves the dens which are in the mountains, and the caves and strongholds.

Notes

6:1–2. These verses belong to the framework, now well developed by the presentation of Othniel (3:7–11) and the introduction to Ehud (3:12–14) and Deborah (4:1–3). See the Schematic Outline in the Introduction. The one obscurity in the passage is the hapax legomenon, *minhārōt*. The root *nhr* suggests a ravine, or river valley; hence the *dens* are clefts or defiles in the mountains caused by river erosion, which make excellent hiding places. Repetition of some details from this unit in the one which follows should be viewed as a reflection of the older narrative units. The fixed forms of the old stories were virtually canonical but seldom explicitly satisfactory to the redactor in posing the enormity of Israel's offense and the quality of Yahweh's mercy. Thus the old story remains unaltered and receives a new introduction. The general thrust of the following narrative is to show how Gideon was enlisted and went through "basic training" or "boot camp."

Midian is the name of a desert confederation with a long history that had been intermeshed with Israelite history ever since Sinai (Exod 2:15 – 4:31; 18:1–27). Subsequent warfare with Midian (Num 25 and 31) was long remembered as a particularly disastrous development, and was variously interpreted (Hos 9:10; Ps 106:28). The revival of Midian in the days of Gideon was probably due to new waves of immigration from eastern Anatolia and northern Syria, bringing with them the domesticated camel and thus presenting a whole new military configuration. See now *TenGen*, pp. 105–21, 161–73.

COMMENT

In the case of Gideon, the pragmatic introduction is confined to the formulaic statement correlating Israelite evil and Midianite oppression. Attention focuses upon the gravity of the crisis for Israelite well-being. No mention is made of Yahweh's gracious provision of a savior once again. The old Gideon stories were apparently seen to cover that point adequately. Similarly no mention is here made of Israelites presenting their appeal to Yahweh; that particular point is mentioned in the older narrative itself (vs. 6), where it was most surprisingly answered according to both the old story (vs. 11) and later the Deuteronomic Historian (vss. 7–10). In order to comprehend the significance of the pragmatic restraint at this point, the reader should turn at once to the "example" of Othniel in 3:7–11 and ask himself: how is Gideon going to be different?

XI. The Menace
(6:3–10)

6 3 Whenever Israel sowed seed,

> Midian would come up, along with Amaleq
> Even the Easterners would come up against him.

4 They would encamp against them and destroy the land's produce all the way to the neighborhood of Gaza; they would leave no means of livelihood—sheep, ox, or donkey. 5 They and their cattle would come up, and their tents they would bring—as numerous as locusts. They and their camels were too many to count! They would enter the land to devastate it. 6 So Israel became utterly destitute because of Midian. And the Israelites appealed to Yahweh.

7 On one occasion the Israelites appealed to Yahweh on account of Midian, 8 and Yahweh sent a prophet to the Israelites! He said to them, "Here is what Yahweh, God of Israel, has said:

> I brought you up from Egypt
> I brought you out of slave-barracks
> 9 I rescued you from Egypt's power
> and from the power of all your oppressors
> I drove them out for your sake
> and gave to you their land.

10 And I said to you, 'I am Yahweh your God. Do not ever be afraid of the gods of the Westerners, in whose land you are living!' But you have not obeyed my voice!"

NOTES

6:3–10. These verses pose a larger problem concerning "all Israel" (see 8:27) which the redactor considered should be dealt with prior to the call of Gideon which begins in vs. 11. It appears that the old Gideon cycle had represented Israel (at least Gideon and associates) as acquiescing so completely to the Midianite oppression that it required exceptional effort for God to get in touch with Gideon. A redactor has thus plugged a gap in the cycle of the period and maintained the view expressed in 2:1–5 and 10:11–14 that Yahweh remained free and saving sovereign in Israel.

3. *Amaleq*. A nomadic people here represented as carrying on an enmity as old as the pre-Sinai period. See COMMENT on 1:16.

The recognition of the archaic couplet embedded in vs. 3 I owe to Freedman. For the emphatic *waw* before the perfect form of the verb (*wa-'ᵃlū*) in the final position (or following the subject), see Dahood, *Psalms III, 101–150*, AB, vol. 17A (1970), pp. 400–1.

the Easterners. Heb. *bᵉnē qedem*, lit. "sons of the east," which is used as a summarizing appositive after "Midian" and "Amaleq" and which sets the stage for a totally unexpected statement about "Westerners" in vs. 10. For the later role of "people of the east" in eschatological prophecy, see Isa 11:14; for their place in the concurrent prophetic critique of international affairs, see Jer 49:28 and Ezek 25:1–10, the latter especially reminiscent of the Gideon narrative.

come up against him. The referent of "him" is Israel. This phrase is missing in 4Q Judges*ᵃ*, which may be explained as due to haplography, where six out of twelve words in sequence begin with the letter *waw*.

6. *appealed to Yahweh*. Lit. "cried out." See NOTE on 3:9.

7–10. These verses are generally attributed to an ultimate *E* source. Through skillful redaction of older material they now appear as part of a larger and highly unified Deuteronomic vignette. These verses are missing in 4Q Judges*ᵃ*, which may therefore be witness to an early, preexilic, textual tradition. See Introduction, p. 40.

7. *On one occasion*. On the introductory *wayhī* see NOTE on 1:1.

8. *a prophet*. Lit. "a prophet-man"; cf. the designation of Deborah as prophetess, lit. "a prophet-woman" in 4:4. Prophets in the Book of Judges are otherwise unknown, though one should compare the traditions about Samuel (I Sam 7:1–11) and the work of the divine organizer of Israel in Judg 10:11–14. All of them make speeches comparable to that of the Yahweh envoy in 2:1–5 and reflect a common traditionary source, concerned with the problem of how to maneuver Israel or the potential Israelite leader into confrontation with Yahweh. The old Gideon narrative had concentrated on how to confront Gideon. Here, moreover, the prophet is represented as functioning in a manner quite consistent with the pattern of prophets-in-politics that is becoming increasingly clear at Mari, the major difference being that in Israel there had been a redistribution of power. A prophet in the book is thus no anachronism,

although his speech here carries the later imprint of traditional Yahwist covenant usage.

8–9. *up from Egypt . . . their land.* The bulk of the speech is clearly poetic, making use of two great nuclear themes of Israel's credo and having the Sinai covenant as the presupposition of the current indictment. The speech is a bit more detailed than the angel's indictment in 2:1–5.

slave-barracks. Lit. "slaves' house," an accurate Yahwist designation for Egypt.

10. *I am Yahweh your God.* First article in Israel's version of the international suzerainty treaty form. Exod 20:2, cf. vss. 3 and 5.

The conclusion of the speech is based upon a prime commandment: Do not ever be afraid. In Deuteronomic usage, as has recently been demonstrated, to fear God is the basic treaty stipulation. Kamol Aryaprateep, "A Study of the Deuteronomic Conception of the Fear of God." Unpublished Th.M. thesis in the Library of McCormick Theological Seminary (1970). The usual explanation of *yr'*, "to fear," as having to do with reverence or worship improperly restricts the word to the formal cultic setting. In the present context the Deuteronomic redactor is making up for the pragmatist's failure to say anything about foreign gods in the preceding section. The pragmatist had concentrated on the threat from the "Easterners." The Deuteronomic redactor now explains that threat in terms of Israel's relations with "Westerners" and their "gods."

Westerners. The Hebrew is generally transliterated (Amorites), but here retains its etymological meaning (as in 1:34–36), in an abrupt inclusion with "the Easterners" in vs. 3. It is thus explained that Israel's inability to meet the menace of Midian and Amaleq from the east was a reflection of its own failure really to be Yahwist west of the Jordan in Canaan. But that was not the end of the matter, and this rigidly reflective redacting of the book was probably also designed to avoid possible misunderstanding of the folksy exchanges between Gideon and heavenly representatives in the older material, which comes next.

COMMENT

The earliest cycle of Gideon stories made explicit mention of Israel's collective offense against Yahweh only in its conclusion (8:22–27), not at the outset. That is, Gideon and Israel were credited with making more than God intended out of Gideon's great achievement. At the outset of the old story, on the other hand, nothing is permitted to detract from the severity of the threat to Israelite life posed by the military superiority of the camel corps. The invaders were not nomads; they were ruled by kings. (On the ecology of nomadism see now D. L. Johnson, *The Nature of Nomadism,* University of Chicago, 1969). The domesticated camel was probably introduced from the north, as part of the same movement that brought new Midianite emigrants from their Anatolian homelands into Transjordan (*TenGen,* pp. 163–73). It appears that the former donkey caravaneers and Canaanite society's outcasts (Israel) had no sooner begun their social revolution in Canaan than the whole structure threatened to disintegrate under the impact of an external revolution in transportation and the resulting Midianite bid for supremacy (see especially Albright, BASOR 163 [September 1961], 38, n. 9; *History, Archaeology, and Christian Humanism* [New York: McGraw-Hill, 1964], p. 158, n. 2; YGC, pp. 58–90; see also Eissfeldt, JBL 87 [1968], 391). Ultimately David and Solomon were able to turn the rapidly developing caravan trade to Israel's economic advantage, but in Gideon's day the camel riders were a plague and a bother.

That the opponents were "as numerous as locusts" (vs. 5) is reminiscent of a pre-Exodus plague, while the subsequent account of Gideon's enlistment will abound with allusions and quotations from the call of Moses (Exod 3) and the Song of Moses (Deut 32). It appears, however, that the Deuteronomic Historian has broken the story open to insert something from his own file, a prophetic indictment of Israel. Instead of an answer to their appeal for relief from the Easterners they are reminded how they have accommodated themselves to the gods of the Westerners. Again, the insertion was exegetical, based upon the old narrative's concentration upon the initial subservience of Gideon and his contemporaries.

6 ¹¹ Yahweh's envoy came and sat down beneath the oak at Ophrah, which belonged to Joash the Abiezrite, while his son Gideon was beating out wheat in the wine press, to whisk it away because of the Midianites. ¹² Yahweh's envoy appeared to him and said to him, "Yahweh is with you, aristocrat!"

¹³ Gideon said to him, "Pardon me, sir, but if Yahweh is with us, why has all this happened to us? Where, pray tell, are all his wonderful acts which our fathers told us about when they used to say, 'Did not Yahweh bring us up from Egypt?' Right now Yahweh has abandoned us! He has surrendered us into the hand of Midian!"

¹⁴ Yahweh turned to him and said, "Go in the strength of this one, and you will rescue Israel from Midian's hand! Have I not sent you?"

¹⁵ He said to him, "Pardon me, sir, but by what means can I rescue Israel? Look here, my contingent is the weakest in Manasseh, and I am the most insignificant of my company."

¹⁶ Yahweh's envoy said to him, "Because Ehyeh is with you! You shall defeat Midian as one man."

¹⁷ He said to him, "Please, if I have found favor in your sight, produce for me a sign pertaining to what you are telling me! ¹⁸ Do not go away from here, please, until I come to you and bring my gift and set it before you!" And he said, "I will wait till you come back."

¹⁹ Gideon went in and prepared a kid and unleavened cakes, using an ephah of flour! The meat he put in a basket, and the broth he put in a pot. He went out to him, as far as the shade of the oak, and he divined. ²⁰ God's envoy said to him, "Take the meat and unleavened cakes, put them on that rock, and pour the broth." And he did so. ²¹ Yahweh's envoy extended the tip of the stick that was in his hand and touched the meat and the unleavened cakes, and the fire came up

from that Rock and consumed the meat and the unleavened cakes, while Yahweh's envoy walked away from his eyes. Gideon realized then that he was Yahweh's envoy. 22 Gideon said "Oh no! Lord Yahweh! I have seen Yahweh's envoy face to face!" 23 But Yahweh said to him, "You are safe. Do not panic. You will not die."

24 Gideon built there an altar for Yahweh and called it, "He creates peace!"

(To this day it endures as Ophrah, which belongs to the Abiezrites.)

25 That night something happened! Yahweh said to him, "Take the bull which belongs to your father—that's right, the second one, seven years old—and dismantle your father's altar to Baal and chop down the Asherah alongside it. 26 You will build an altar for Yahweh your God on the highest point of this stronghold (. . .); you will take the number two bull and present it as a burnt offering, using the wood of the Asherah which you will chop down."

27 So Gideon took ten men from among his servants and did exactly as Yahweh had told him. But he was too afraid of his father's household and the townsmen to do it in the daytime. He did it at night.

28 The townsmen got up early in the morning and, to their surprise, Baal's altar had been torn down and the Asherah alongside it chopped down, and the number two bull was being consumed on the altar which had been built. 29 They said to one another, "Who did this deed?" They searched and made inquiry. And they said, "Gideon ben Joash did this deed."

30 The townsmen said to Joash, "Bring out your son; let him die! For he tore down Baal's altar and chopped down the Asherah alongside it!" 31 Joash said to all who stood around him, "Will you prosecute for Baal? Are you going to rescue him? Whoever prosecutes for him will be put to death by morning! If he is a god, let him make his own case, because he tore down his altar!"

32 He named him on that day—Jerubbaal!—saying, "Let Baal prosecute him, for he tore down his altar!"

NOTES

6:11–32. The only early narrative in the book where Yahweh speaks directly to a protagonist or to Israel. All other places have an intermediary or imply one. Here, the clear implication is that Gideon was very slow to recognize the speech of Yahweh, a foreshadowing of Israel's problem in ch. 10.

One of the most problematical conclusions of the older source criticism and its current refinement is that of a sharp disjunction between vss. 11–24 (*J*—an account of Gideon's call linked with a legitimation of the Ophrah altar) and vss. 25–32 (*E*—concerned with local introduction of Yahweh worship, and an etiological note about the name Jerubbaal). So Sellin and Fohrer, *Introduction to the Old Testament,* pp. 209–10, where, however, the *JE* sigla are not employed later than 2:5. Most of the criteria for such analysis vanish, however, with the observation that Yahweh is depicted in the alleged *E* sequel with much the same administrative singlemindedness as the Yahweh envoy in the first scene, to whom Yahweh himself lends a hand. The two supposed "pericopes" are a unity; Yahweh ambushes Gideon into a direct confrontation, through his envoy (getting a new altar), and then turns directly to dream media (destroying the old altar). Slowly but surely Gideon is spurred to action. Verses 36–40, the most clearly *E* pericope in the entire book, makes precisely the same point about Gideon. See below.

11. *Yahweh's envoy.* For early Israel's administrative understanding of angels, see Introduction, p. 26 and NOTES on 2:1–5. This story presupposes an awareness of another sort of possible response to the arrival of "Yahweh's army commander" (Josh 5:13–15).

sat down beneath the oak at Ophrah. Location uncertain, perhaps 'Affuleh in the center of the Jezreel Valley, which seems to correspond to the place name *'pr,* No. 53 in the list of Thutmose III. Jans Jozef Simons, *Handbook for the Study of Egyptian Topographical Lists Relating to Western Asia* (Leiden: Brill, 1937), p. 117. This identification is proposed by Aharoni, LOB, p. 241.

Specification of "the oak" suggests that Joash was proprietor of a place of oracular inquiry, like "Deborah's Palm" in 4:5. This cult place, however, is Baalist not Yahwist; for an elaborate story had to be told in order to give Yahwist legitimacy to the baal-name bestowed by the father, Joash. To anyone familiar with the prose story of Deborah the introduction to Gideon would immediately suggest that in this new crisis raising up a deliverer is going to take even more extended effort.

This pattern of alternating good examples (Othniel, Deborah, Jephthah) and problematic leadership (Ehud, Gideon, Abimelech, Samson) perhaps explains why the received tradition is out of phase with archaeological evidence from Shechem and Taanach. The latter indicates that Gideon and Abimelech are to be dated a half century earlier than Deborah and Baraq (see Chronology and COMMENT on Sec. IX). If the earliest compiler produced a book which centered on a crisis of kingship (the story of Abimelech in ch. 9), subsequent editors have retained that sequence, so that the book now centers and ends (21: 25) on the same note. See Introduction, "The Growth of the Book of Judges."

Gideon. The name means "hewer" or "hacker," a kenning of his original name Jerubbaal (vs. 32), "Let-Baal-sue." Albright, YGC (1968), 199, n. 101.

to whisk it away. Heb. *lᵉhānīs,* not "to hide it," but "to cause it to flee," that is, to move it quickly. ALUOSᴰ, 12.

12. *you.* The singular form is used, but Gideon misses the point and replies about the current plight of "us" in vs. 13. The assertion, "Yahweh is with

you," is itself ambiguous; it can either be a statement of fact or a wish. Sellin and Fohrer, *Introduction to the Old Testament*, p. 75.

aristocrat. Heb. *gibbōr ḥayl.* See NOTE on 5:13. In contrast to the situation behind the Song of Deborah, the feudal order has here reasserted itself inside Israel. "Instead of tribal divisions an aristocratic regime is presented to us; and it is only to be expected that the religious organization fluctuated *pari passu* with the political." Stanley Arthur Cook, *Journal of Theological Studies*, 28 (1927), 378.

13. *Pardon me, sir.* Strictly polite address, as in vs. 15, and 13:8 (Manoah's prayer to Yahweh).

pray tell. On the idiomatic use of the *waw* conjunction here, see Burney, p. 317. It occurs again in 11:26. See NOTE.

which our fathers told us. 4Q Judges*ᵃ* preserves the archaic particle *šā* (cf. MT vs. 17) which collates with a number of other surviving archaisms in MT of ch. 6. This one, however, gave way to the standard prose *'ašer.*

up from Egypt. An unshakable element of Israel's historical credo, it could also become a cultic cliche.

Yahweh. 4Q Judges*ᵃ* has *'lhym* "God" instead of the divine name in this verse. See Introduction, p. 40.

14. *Yahweh turned . . . and said.* The statement is generally, but imprecisely, taken to indicate the identity of Yahweh and the Yahweh envoy. In the prophetic book entitled "My Envoy" (Malachi), however, it is specified that the envoy goes in advance to prepare the way for Yahweh (Mal 3:1–2); Yahweh himself remains invisible and will be hard at work "till they present right offerings to the Lord." In the present context Yahweh has caught up with his envoy, and Gideon is in a three-way conversation without realizing it.

in the strength of this one. Spoken by Yahweh to Gideon, the referent of "this one" is the Yahweh envoy, presumably in his capacity as commander of Yahweh's army (Josh 5:13–15). The translator has adopted a proposal of Freedman (private communication) to recognize enclitic *kaph* in the expression *b-kḥ-k zh.* The traditional rendering "in this strength of yours" might have been *b-kḥk h-zh,* but even that would not be smooth. For another example of enclitic *kaph* within a construct chain, see 5:31 and NOTES, with reference to the works of Dahood.

Hearers of the story would assume the relationship of the visible messenger to his own invisible commander and respond accordingly. It is in fact characteristic of other narrative contexts, once the emissary from the divine court is introduced, not to distinguish between the speech and actions of the emissary and those of his heavenly sovereign: Gen 21:17–19; 22:11–14, 15–18; 31:11–13; Exod 3:2–16. In the last of these passages Cassuto proposed a comparable solution to the vexing question of alternate names for the deity: "wherever the Lord is spoken of objectively, the name Yahweh occurs; but when the reference is to what Moses saw or felt subjectively, the name Elohim is used." Umberto Cassuto, *Exodus*, tr. Israel Abrahams (Jerusalem: Magnes Press, 1967), p. 32. The distinction cannot be sought with a slavish consistency. But compare the use of divine names in Job, where the situation is exactly the reverse; only *'elōᵃh* is used in the dialogue, except where Job himself lapses, forgetting his grand subject matter, and actually blurts out a testimony to "Yahweh" (Job 12:9), using the same argument from nature as the voice from the whirlwind (chs. 38–41). See esp. the presentation of the communication problem at the outset of Samson's story (13:2–23) and its solution (16:28).

15. *contingent.* See NOTE on 1:4.

company. A remnant of poetic parallelism? That *bet-'āb,* a "father's house," can denote the smaller military unit in Israel as at Mari is now clear. The definition of the military *bet-'āb* will obviously not be by genealogy in a social structure which establishes citizenship by confession of faith. Gideon's modesty in this context is apparently normal operating procedure. Saul uses similar self-deprecating language in speaking to Samuel (I Sam 9:21; cf. I Sam 15:17). Compare esp. the account of the call and commissioning of Moses (Exod 3:1 – 4:23) where, as here, a vastly disproportionate space is given to the eliciting of the dutiful response. That this account is, in fact, deliberately reminiscent of the enlistment of Moses becomes clear in vs. 16.

16. *Yahweh's envoy.* With LXX, where MT represents Yahweh as the speaker (as in vs. 14). LXX reflects the opposite solution to the problem of the three-way conversation and has "Yahweh's envoy" speaking in both verses.

Because Ehyeh is with you. A direct quotation, Exod 3:12. Gideon is represented as slow to respond until the envoy uses a variant of Yahweh's own proper name: "Ehyeh," as disclosed to Moses in Exod 3:14. Mere translation of the form (EVV) provides no clue to the transformation in Gideon's behavior to which this detail leads. Even when the interview is finished, Gideon thinks that he has been commanded by the Yahweh envoy, not by God himself (vs. 22). Rather the divine name "Ehyeh" is used here much as in the climax to the child-naming pericope of Hosea 1:9: "For you are not my people! And I am not *Ehyeh* to you!" Buber, *The Prophetic Faith,* Carlyle Witton-Davies, Harper Torchbook (New York: Harper, 1960), p. 116. On the background of the parallel first and third person forms of the name of the God of Moses, see Freedman, JBL 79 (1960), 151–56; Cross, *Harvard Theological Review,* 55 (1962), esp. 250–55.

as one man. That is, as though Midian were a single man.

17–18. The use of the rare name of the God of Moses has turned the trick. Now Gideon is in command. He is represented as giving the orders, apparently over his shoulder as he hastens to prepare an offering, so that with his back turned he is still unaware that the voice which persuades him is the voice of Yahweh, not a mere messenger who can be required to authenticate his communique.

17. *a sign pertaining to what you are telling me.* That is the only way Gideon will really be enlisted. For the translation of the archaic particle *ša* (pertaining to) see Theophile James Meek, JBL 79 (1960), 334. See also 5:7 and fourth NOTE, 7:12. Demand for a sign is the narrator's calculated reminiscence of initial negotiations with Moses in Exod 3:1 – 4:23.

18. *Do not go away.* The divine response is wryly acquiescent: *I will wait.*

19–23. The climax of Gideon's enlistment. The Hittite "Soldier's Oath" (tr. Albrecht Goetze, ANET[3], pp. 353–54) involves an array of such visual aids as a bowl of fermenting yeast, crackling sinews, and mutton fat dissolving on a hot pan. The angel here turns Gideon's religiosity into an enlistment opportunity.

19. *an ephah of flour*. Moore suggests that the quantity (more than a bushel) is altogether disproportionate; he compares I Sam 1:24 where an ephah of flour makes enough unleavened bread to go with a three year old bullock, Moore, p. 187. Gideon never does anything in proper proportion. Dafydd Rhys Ap-Thomas compares Lot's hospitality in Gen 19:3, but his emendation to secure a perfect bicolon is forced. *Journal of Theological Studies*, 41 (1940), 175–77.

he divined. Repointing the anomalous *way-yaggaš* as hiphil, with LXX[B]. For the argument that hiphil forms of *ngš*, "to bring near," here and there retained an older, independent meaning, "to divine, to make contact with the deity," see Iwry, JAOS 81 (1961), 33–34. That this is the meaning in our passage seems clear from LXX[A] which reads instead "he worshipped"; here the *Vorlage* would be *wyšth*, to judge by the standard equivalents elsewhere, in 2:12 (fell prone), 2:17 (bowed themselves), 2:19 (falling prone), and 7:15 (fell prone). There is no way of explaining this divergence except in terms of authentic variants stemming from the oral period.

20. *God's envoy*. But "Yahweh's envoy" in LXX[AL] and some Syr. manuscripts as in the following verse. The reversion to *'elōhīm* at this point, together with the two words for "rock" in vss. 20 and 21, indicate something of the manner of transmission, but can scarcely be taken as source critical keys when *'elōhīm* thus abruptly intrudes into the hypothetical *J* story (vss. 11–24) while the divine name "Yahweh" is the only one to be found in the alleged *E* story (vss. 25–32). It is in fact essential to the climax in vs. 22 that there be a clear distinction between God and his envoy at the outset of this climactic scene.

that rock. The use of the archaic demonstrative with a generic noun, *has-selaʿ hal-lāz*, prepares the audience for the narrator's use of an archaic divine name in the next verse.

21. *that Rock*. Heb. *haṣ-ṣūr*. For the God of Israel as "The Rock," i.e. "the Mountain One," see esp. the archaic Song of Moses, Deut 32:37. For another play upon the same name in allusion to Sinai, where these structures were adopted, see the climax of the story of Samson's birth, 13:19. On the pre-Israelite use of *ṣur* in divine appellatives, see now Albright, YGC, p. 188 f.

walked away from his eyes. That is, disappeared. Cf. 13:20–21 where Manoah only recognized the Yahweh angel from the fact that "he did not come anymore." His wife had been much quicker to get the message. Here, on the other hand, the "sign" serves to precipitate a direct confrontation between God and Gideon. From this point on they can deal directly with one another.

22. *Oh no*. Heb. *'ahā*, for which the older English equivalent "alas!" has lost currency. See 11:35.

I have seen Yahweh's envoy face to face. Cf. Deuteronomy's formulation of relations between Yahweh and Moses, "whom Yahweh knew (that is, acknowledged as leader of the vassals) face to face" (Deut 34:10). Behind the latter lie such old narrative traditions as Exod 33:20–23, where Yahweh promises that his glory will precede him when he passes by "the rock" (*haṣ-ṣūr*) where

Moses has been directed to take refuge. We note that once past that spot, Yahweh will withdraw his protective hand, so that Moses may indeed see him, but only from the rear, as he walks away. For deep-seated popular beliefs that deity is too pure, holy, and dangerous to be seen directly by human eyes, see 13:22; Gen 16:13; 32:30; Exod 20:19; Isa 6:5. It thus appears that the author of this story has Gideon seeing "Yahweh's envoy face to face," so that Gideon's invisible Lord may enter into direct negotiations with Gideon, as he had with Moses. Gideon's exclamation indicates that an encounter with the envoy could be a traumatic experience in itself, so that Yahweh is shown to be gracious and compassionate, as promised to Moses in Exod 33:19.

23. *You are safe.* Lit. "you have peace" (Heb. *šālōm*), that is, "well-being."

24a. *He creates peace.* Heb. *yhwh šlwm*, a name in which the name Yahweh still retains its original verbal force, as in *yhwh ṣᵉbā'ōt*. The naming of the altar cannot be treated apart from the total narrative. The verse indicates that Gideon now acknowledges that he has been fighting on the wrong front. For other altars with commemorative names, see Gen 33:20; 35:7.

24b. *To this day . . . Abiezrites.* The last half of vs. 24 is antiquarian anticlimax. It forms an editorial inclusio, however, with "Joash the Abiezrite" in vs. 11. The kind of cult etiological interest indicated by "unto this day" is not primary to the development of the Gideon cycle. It reflects an antiquarian's interest, not an original narrative motivation. See 1:21 and NOTE, and 1:26. In the following unit the etiological interest in Gideon's baal-name is much more generic; it is also characteristically Yahwist (vss. 25–32), as is this whole account of the origin of the historical Yahweh altar at Ophrah.

25–32. These verses make the point that new altars will not stem the tide. They are also concerned to provide a properly Yahwist etiology for Gideon's baal-name, which was, of course, given to him at birth.

25. *That night something happened.* Heb. *wayhī bal-laylā ha-hū'*, as in 7:9; II Sam 7:4, repeated exactly in I Chron 17:3; II Kings 19:35. The statement relates directly to vs. 24a, prior to the addition of the etiological note in 24b. On the introductory *wayhī*, see NOTES on 1:1 and 6:7.

that's right, the second one, seven years old. Again, Gideon is slow to get the message. The "second one" is presumably the older bull, rather than the prime bull, which would be needed for the future of the herd. It is another example of considerate and gracious administration in this story of domestic reform. We have taken the text at face value, although it seems awkward. Attempts to solve the syntax have had to repoint either one of the numerals (Alfred Guillaume, *Journal of Theological Studies*, N.S. 1 [1949], 52–53), or both of them (ALUOS^D, 12), although numbers figure prominently, especially "seven," in stories.

the Asherah. Sacred groves, or sanctuary replicas thereof, were a constant feature of Canaanite religion, variously accommodated at Israelite festival centers: Exod 34:13; Deut 12:3; I Kings 14:23; II Kings 17:10, 21:7, 23:6.

26. *this stronghold.* There follows in MT *bam-ma'ᵃrākā*, lit. "in the row." The phrase is perhaps the remnant of some information regarding alignment in the Asherah.

27. *ten.* The number was perhaps chosen for its assonance with *h-'šrh 'šr,*

"the Asherah which," and *w-yʿs k-'šr*, "and he did according as," and *k-'šr yr'*, "because he was afraid."

at night. A neat inclusio with the introductory clause in vs. 25—from hesitancy before a night vision to hesitation over the task of the day.

29. *deed.* In Hebrew simply *dābār*, with its semantic range from "word" to "thing," including "act," and formulaic use as "covenant stipulation." The phrase is repeated at the end of the verse, for emphasis and effect.

31. The questions are rhetorical and carry on a stylistic tradition reflected already in Ugaritic epics. See NOTE on 2:22. Joash is depicted as confident that Baal can take care of himself, "If he is a god." He is not so sure about his own colleagues.

prosecute. Heb. root *ryb.* The advocates of Baal are represented as threatening to take the field and press Baal's case in combat without any prior authorization from Baal, a skillful structural antithesis to the prolonged account of reluctant Gideon's authorization. In this context to "sue" for a god is to represent him at the head of the earthly forces; the outcome will be divine justice. Cf. the story of Jephthah where Israelites and their repatriated judge made an exemplary attempt to conduct Yahwist diplomacy (11:12–28). To the Yahwist narrator there could be no danger in admitting Joash's mediation. The idea that Baal might make his own defense was as absurd as the notion that God needs the legal defense of Job's comforters.

32. *He named him.* The emphasis is clear from the word order; "on that day" normally begins the sentence if its temporal force is emphasized. See "that night" in 6:25 and 7:9.

Examples of Yahwists bearing baal-names are not uncommon (e.g. Meribbaal in I Chron 8:34, 9:40; Ishbaal in I Chron 8:33, 9:39; Baal-yada in I Chron 14:7) and may here and there be taken as evidence of religious syncretism. But each case must be considered on its own merits, e.g. Baal-yah (I Chron 12:5) one of David's Benjaminite heroes. Names were, after all, bestowed by parents; in the period under consideration an "Israelite" was only recognizable by his own confession of faith in Yahweh, irrespective of his parents' religious preference.

COMMENT

By building into the introduction to Gideon an account of prophetic confrontation, the later redactor showed that by his own time (late seventh century?), appealing to Yahweh in periods of hardship had become habit. The old narrative of Gideon's enlistment, however, starts out on the other foot; the Midianite movement was of such proportions that it was assumed to be irreversible. It begins, like the preceding stories of Deborah and Ehud, with a genuine — not stereotyped — statement of crisis. This unit thus implies the preceding stories, from Othniel to Deborah, strung together to form an early epic or saga book (see COMMENT on 2:6–10, p. 72).

The antiquity of the material is further indicated by archaic elements in the Hebrew and the immediate didactic freedom with which the history of Moses is drawn upon to depict Gideon and explain his significance to the narrator's audience; for that is the purpose of ch. 6 (Gideon's enlistment) and ch. 7 (Yahweh's victory). Ch. 8 will tell the sequel in another vein.

The crucial circumstance in ch. 6 is the covenantal organization of premonarchical Israel, where the chief administrative responsibility was lodged with the judge. The judge, by definition, had the power of the Sovereign's lawsuit in both domestic and foreign affairs, after proper divine consultation. A good judge, according to this chapter was sometimes hard to find. When the state of affairs had deteriorated to the brink of anarchy, so that customary procedures for popular nomination and spiritual confirmation no longer functioned, God sent his angel, according to this enlistment story (and the one about Samson in ch. 13). Compare the enlistment of Samuel, where a "man of God" confronts the elderly Eli and prepares the way for Yahweh's interruption of the young Samuel's sanctuary slumbers (I Sam 2:27 – 3:14).

The administrative function of the Yahweh angel in these early narratives stands for Yahweh's own gracious maintenance of the realm. It is equally clear in 2:1–5, where, however, the angel sounds more like the Deuteronomic Historian himself. Comparison should be made, also, with passages like Josh 5:13–15, where the problem was somewhat the reverse; Joshua was going to be consistently loyal and amazingly successful. In his case it was commonly acknowledged that the Yahweh angel was the real commander of Israel's army.

In general we can say that the infrequent references to angels in the judges period confirms the importance of the tribal assembly in the amphictyony. The combination of procedures for popular election of the leader and the frequent recognition that the leader did indeed display the Yahweh spirit was largely sufficient for Israel's self-understanding in this period. Angels figure in the narratives of Judges only in the absence or malfunction of the tribal assembly, where the customary provisions for election of the judge did not in fact explain the rise of the judge, i.e. Gideon and Samson (ch. 13). The angel explains the inexplicable, as in the introduction to the period (2:1–5), where the assembly is gathered in lamentation and the angel's speech serves to provide yet another reason for lamenting.

Prophets, as depicted in the unpredictable and unsolicited appearances of men such as Elijah and his successors from the ninth century on, are even more of an oddity in this period (6:7–10 provides the sole example, and it uses characteristically Deuteronomic language). On the other hand, the judges as depicted in their responsibility to the oracle are the forerunners to the classical prophets.

It appears that the establishment of the monarchy in the tenth century and the emergence of the closely related cultic organization, especially in Jerusalem, brought with it a specialization of functions that was not so clear in the earlier period. Judges were now all "minor judges," with the exception of the king, the highest court of appeal. Throughout the period of II Samuel and I and II Kings, references to angels are few and far between; prophets are the conveyors of criticism. But classical prophecy entered upon a new phase, with the destruction of the nation in 587 B.C.E. Prophecy was in fact transformed and in its new form figured prominently in the apocalyptic movements of the intertestamental period and early Christianity. This was another age of crisis in political and religious institutions. References to angels multiply rapidly in the works of the apocalyptic seers such as the author of Daniel, at the close of the OT period, and in early Judaism and early Christianity.

Verse 32 bears witness to continuing popular delight that one of Israel's great saviors had a baal-name. Jerubbaal earned his given name on the day that Baal's altar came down! This verse is transitional to 7:1 which introduces a narrative segment in which the protagonist is "Let-Baal-sue, really, Hacker" (see NOTE on 7:1). The transition is interrupted for a flashback to the scene of the impending battle and the mustering of Yahweh's forces (6:33–35) and a further delay due to Gideon's protracted concern for the authentication of his role as savior (6:36–40).

If the tradition appears to be inordinately preoccupied with the call of Gideon, it must be remembered that his flair for divination at last posed a serious new crisis for Israel (8:27). He was rightly (but not uncritically) remembered as God's answer to the Midianite depredations.

XIII. The Opposition
(6:33–35)

6 ³³ All the Midianites and Amaleqites—even the Easterners!—
rendezvoused, crossed over, and pitched camp in the Valley of Jezreel.
³⁴ Yahweh's spirit clothed Gideon. He sounded the trumpet, and the
Abiezrites were called out after him. ³⁵ Envoys he dispatched
throughout Manasseh; and they, too, were called out after him. Envoys he also sent into Asher, Zebulun, and Naphtali. Then they went
up to meet them.

NOTES

6:33–35. These verses apparently have a separate source from the bulk of
the Gideon traditions. The opening clause, however, "All the Midianites and
Amaleqites—even the Easterners!" has a rhetorical relationship with the statement of the menace in vss. 3–6, reemphasizing the gravity of the situation.

34. *clothed*. On the "spirit," see Introduction, "Heaven and Earth: Yahweh's
Kingdom," and NOTE on 3:10. See the boast of Job 29:14, how he had "put
on righteousness" and worn "justice." A man can, on the other hand, also
clothe "himself with cursing," as in Ps 109:18, AB.

35. *Envoys . . . Envoys*. The construction contrasts with the story of
Gideon and the Yahweh envoy. Gideon has now taken charge and is overreacting. This narrative stratum next appears in 7:23.

This verse seems to indicate that only his own unit and wider "Manasseh"
were immediately mobilized; "Asher, Zebulun, and Naphtali" were put on
alert. Asher and Naphtali were subsequently brought into the field (7:23).
See Map 4.

to meet them. To join the battle. Gideon, however, will postpone that day
long enough to make one more inquiry.

COMMENT

After the long digression concerned with the enlistment of Gideon and the ordering of internal affairs ("judging Israel" as in 3:10; I Sam 7:6; and the notices about the minor judges in 10:1–5 and 12:8–15), these verses return to the description of the menace before unfolding the account of Gideon taking to the field. There is not necessarily a contradiction between a prophet arising in the tribal assembly (vss. 7–10), the angel's prodding to enlist Gideon (vss. 11–32), and Gideon's achievement as evidence of the Yahweh spirit.

This unit continues the dominant theme of the enlistment story in vss. 11–24; Gideon was regularly slow to respond and characteristically overreacted.

XIV. The Patience of God
(6:36–40)

6 ³⁶ Gideon said to God, "If it is true that you will rescue Israel by my hand as you have said, ³⁷ look: I am placing the woolen fleece on the threshing floor. If dew comes on the fleece alone, while all the ground is dry, then I will acknowledge that you will rescue Israel by my hand, as you have said." ³⁸ And so it was! When he got up early the next morning and wrung out the fleece, he collected enough dew from the fleece to fill a bowl with water.

³⁹ But Gideon said to God, "Do not let your wrath blaze against me; let me speak just once more! I will try just once more with the fleece. Please let the fleece alone be dry, while the dew comes over all the ground."

⁴⁰ And God did so on that same night. The fleece alone was dry, but over all the ground there was dew.

Notes

6:36–40. In these verses Gideon bids fair to assume complete command, but demands from the deity some further proof that he had really meant what he had said in the enlistment interview. The pericope picks up a theme that had been succinctly introduced at the end of Gideon's first interview, when Yahweh had said, "I will wait" (vs. 18). Cf. Jephthah's vow (11:29–31 and Note on 11:30).

36. *to God*. Notice the complete absence of the divine name in this pericope, which uses exclusively the generic noun *'ᵉlōhīm*. Like the great *E* source stratum of the Tetrateuch, this pericope displays a heightened interest in the miraculous. This is often regarded as the first clear *E* pericope to be encountered in the book, but the criterion of divine names cannot be pressed very far in this case. Cassuto's recognition of the subjective use of Elohim heightens

the impression that is clear on other grounds; Gideon is now exploiting God. See NOTE on vs. 14.

37. *will acknowledge*. The careful placement of this unit within the Gideon collection is a clue to the covenantal semantics of the Heb. *yd'* (lit. "know," "acknowledge"). See NOTE on 2:10.

38. *bowl*. Heb. *šēpel*, as in 5:25.

39. *Do not let your wrath blaze . . . let me speak just once more*. There is a nearly verbatim parallel to this petition in Gen 18:32, which is part of a *J* story, as pointed out to me by Freedman.

40. God meant what he had said. But on the basis of this assurance Gideon took to the field with a vast army; God had other expectations for Gideon.

COMMENT

That rain can fall in one place and, miraculously, leave the surrounding area dry is a frequent motif in legends of saints (as noted by Gaster in MLC, pp. 419–20, 530–31).

At this point the depiction of the judges period begins to resemble the modern theater of the absurd. Gideon had exploited his sober judicial responsibility by seeking a superfluous divine "yes" or "no" before battle. The audience of course knows, in general, that what is to follow is a sparkling account of Yahweh's victory, without Gideon or anyone else actually fighting, at first.

With the physical properties of fleece lying exposed overnight on bare rock, the differentials of condensation and evaporation necessary to give rise to the story are entirely understandable; fishermen living on one of the streamless and springless Desert Islands have obtained sufficient water for their livelihood by spreading out fleece in the evening and wringing dew from them in the morning (S. Tolkowsky, *Journal of the Palestine Oriental Society*, 3 [1923], 197–99). The true miracle is the reverse of the process, and that's what young Gideon had required.

XV. SMALL FORCE: GREAT VICTORY
(7:1–22)

7 ¹ Jerubbaal (really "Gideon") and all the people who were with him busied themselves and pitched camp by Harod's Spring. The camp of Midian was in the valley, north of Teacher's Hill. ² Yahweh said to Gideon, "The people that are with you are too many for me to surrender Midian to their power, else Israel might vaunt itself against me, saying, 'My own hand has rescued me!' ³ So announce at once within the people's hearing, "Whoever is downright afraid, let him turn back. Let him decamp from Mount Fearful!'" Twenty-two units went home and ten units were left.

⁴ Yahweh said to Gideon, "The people are still too many; make them go down to the water, and I will purify them for you there. He of whom I say to you, 'This one shall go with you,' shall go with you; but any of whom I say to you, 'This one shall not go with you,' shall not go." ⁵ So he made the people go down to the water. And Yahweh said to Gideon, "Everyone who laps with his tongue, the way a dog laps, set apart by himself; and everyone who goes down on his knees to drink water, with hand to mouth, set apart by himself." ⁶ The total of those who lapped with their tongues was three hundred men; all the rest of the people went down on their knees to drink water.

⁷ Yahweh said to Gideon, "With the three hundred men that lapped I will rescue you; I will subject Midian to your power. All the rest may go home."

⁸ They took the people's provisions and trumpets into their own hands; and all the Israelites he sent away, each to his own tent. And with the three hundred men he stood fast; Midian's camp was below him in the valley!

⁹ That night something happened! Yahweh said to him, "Get up, go down into the camp, for I have subjected it to your power. ¹⁰ If,

however, you are afraid to go down, go down with your squire Purah to the camp; you will hear what they are saying. 11 After that you will be much bolder, and you will go down into the camp." So he and his squire Purah went down to the vicinity of the armed men in the camp. 12 Midian and Amaleq—all the Easterners—lay along the valley, as numerous as locusts! Their camels were too many to count, as numerous as grains of sand on the seashore. 13 When Gideon arrived, a man was just then describing a dream to his friend. He said, "Look. I had a dream. And, of all things, a moldy barley bread came tumbling into Midian's camp. It came to the Tent and struck it so that it fell. Turned it upside down! The Tent fell!" 14 His friend replied, "This can be nothing other than the sword of Gideon ben Joash, the Israelite! God has surrendered Midian and the entire force into his power!"

15 When Gideon heard the account of the dream and its interpretation, he fell prone before Yahweh.

He returned to the Israelite camp and said, "Up! For Yahweh has surrendered the Midianite force into your hand!"

16 He divided the three hundred men into three companies and put trumpets into the hands of all of them, and empty jars, with torches inside the jars. 17 He said to them, "keep your eye on me and do as I do. And especially when I come to the outskirts of the camp, do exactly as I do! 18 When I blow the trumpet, I and all who are with me, then you blow the trumpets too, all around the entire camp; and say, 'For Yahweh and for Gideon!'"

19 Gideon and the hundred men who were with him arrived at the camp's outskirts at the beginning of the middle watch, just as they had posted the sentries. They blew the trumpets, while smashing the jars that were in their hands. 20 The three companies blew the trumpets and shattered the jars. They held in their left hands the torches and in their right hands the trumpets (so as to blow), and shouted, "a sword for Yahweh and for Gideon!" 21 They stood, each man at his post, around the camp. And the entire force awoke with a start. They yelled and they fled. 22 When the three hundred blew the trumpets, Yahweh set each man's sword against his own ally throughout the whole camp. The force fled! To Beth-shittah! Towards Zererah! To the border of Abel-meholah, near Tabbath!

NOTES

7:1. *Jerubbaal* (*really "Gideon"*). The manifest interest in the hero's baal-name connects this passage with 6:32; but the connection has been broken with the incorporation of 6:33–40 and so the name is glossed (really "Gideon"). The alternation of names is, however, not so much a sign of sources as a clue to the narrative structure. That is, the name "Gideon" (Hacker) stands for the man in all his concrete, heavy-handed individuality. The name "Jerubbaal" (Let-Baal-sue) stands for God's accomplishment through this one historical savior. We first meet "the man" in 6:11–24; then his baal-name is explained in 6:25–32. In 7:1–22 God wins the victory through "Let-Baal-sue (really 'Gideon')." Finally 7:23 – 8:27 present the man Gideon going far beyond his orders.

all the people who were with him. The story seems to envisage at the outset a muster of all the tribes of Israel. The Gideon traditions pay special attention to the relation between the judge and "all Israel." Cf. 8:27. But see below on vss. 3–6.

busied themselves. A distinctive usage which occurs again in 19:9 and 21:4. For this meaning of *škm* in hiphil see Speiser, *Genesis,* AB, vol. 1 (1964), second NOTE on 19:2.

Teacher's Hill. Presumably a place of oracular inquiry, like "Deborah's Palm" in 4:5. The place is modern Nebi Daḥi opposite Mount Gilboa in Issachar's territory. Map 4.

2. *Israel might vaunt itself.* As indeed is seen to have happened when Gideon went beyond his orders and the Ephraimites at last entered the picture (8:1–3). This is a standing theme in Deuteronomic retrospect and prospect (Deut 8:11–18; 9:4–5; cf. Isa 10:13–15).

3–6. The "census" lists of Num 1 and 26 indicate that Manasseh's quota was precisely thirty-two clan units totalling approximately three hundred men, which would represent roughly a thirty percent levy of the able-bodied men. Mendenhall, JBL 77 (1958), esp. 61–64, n. 53. Three hundred men would be a sizable army, as is clear from the ninth-century inscription of Mesha, king of Moab, who boasts of using an army of "two hundred men, all first class warriors," against the city of Jahaz. ANET[3], p. 320. It is thus clear that all of the numbers in this story originate in the early provisions and regulations for the muster of one tribe only, Manasseh, and the reduction of its force on one occasion. The reduction must have proceeded from the "full strength" quota of three hundred, so that the expeditionary force was in fact a relative handful of men, perhaps fifty or so. The tradition was subsequently enlarged by a misinterpretation of *'ᵃlāpīm* as "thousands" not "units," and the mistaken assumption that thirty-two *'ᵃlāpīm* was the entire force of the league. Freedman, private communication.

3. *downright afraid.* Heb. *yr' w-ḥrd,* lit. "fearful and frightened," synonyms which are here treated as a hendiadys, in a play upon the name *'n-ḥrd,* "Harod's Spring," and a technical term for exemption from military duty, *hyr' w-rk hlbb,* "anyone who is afraid and has lost heart." This formula appears at the end of the list of exemptions in Deut 20:5–8.

Let him decamp from Mount Fearful. Balances the opening reference to Teacher's Hill (vs. 1). See Map 4. For this solution to an extremely odd reference to "Mount Gilead" in MT, see the brilliant discussion by Burney, p. 207 f., which proposes the modern name of the Harod Spring (Ain Ĝâlûd) as preserving an ancient name, and clarified from Akk. *galadu,* "to be afraid." Similarly his appeal to Ar. *ḍafara,* "to go quickly," thus "decamp," makes it unnecessary to emend to read "Gideon tested them" (RSV). In this vignette God does the testing, and some two-thirds of those assembled by Gideon happily go home. Gideon and his suzerain are here involved in the Israelite counterpart of the Mari muster of land-grant warriors, as becomes quite clear in the next verse.

4. *purify.* Heb. *ṣrp,* commonly used of smelting metal, in an obvious word-play with *ṣpr* (decamp) in the preceding verse. There were now too many; Gideon needed a posse, not an army. The action which transpires at the water has nothing to do with mere ritual preparation for combat; nor is it a clear reflection of divinatory options allowable in the judges period. Rather the "purification" which takes place has to do with reorganization of the citizenry for military duty, as on the occasion of the old Amorite *tebibtum,* lit. "cleansing," ceremonies. Cf. the relationship between "refinement" and the raising up of "judges" in prophetic critique of eighth-century Jerusalem (Isa 1:25–26; 3:2–3).

5b–6a. The text is a jumble, due mainly, we suspect, to mutilation of the text behind MT and LXX^B *Vorlage.* The bulk of the differences, however, can be comprehended as due to well-known scribal lapses. The reconstructed text (*) is based on the longer text of LXX^A.

	MT/LXX^B	*wkl 'šr ykr' 'l brkyw lštwt*	
5b	LXX^A	*wkl 'šr ykr' 'l brkyw lštwt*	*tṣyg 'tw lbd*
	*	*wkl 'šr ykr' 'l brkyw lštwt mym bydm 'l pyhm tṣyg 'tw lbd*	
	MT/LXX^B	*wyhy mspr hmlqqym*	*bydm 'l pyhm šlš m't 'ys*
6a	LXX^A	*wyhy mspr hmlqqym blšwnm*	*bydm 'l pyhm šlš m't 'ys*
	*	*wyhy mspr hmlqqym blšwnm*	*šlš m't 'ys*

We expect the fuller statement at the outset, whereas the second can be shorter. We suspect that the key to these differences is a vertical displacement due to homoioteleuton, advancing *bydm 'l pyhm* from 5b to 6a. This in turn precipitated a haplography, due to homoioteleuton, by which *blšwnm* dropped out of MT. Six of the seventeen words in MT vs. 6 end with *mem,* a situation ripe for haplography.

The test in the story is one of alertness; the men who lap the water scooped up with their hands, instead of lying down, "show themselves more watchful and ready to meet any sudden emergency, such as an attack from the rear."

Gaster cites numerous parallels in MLC, pp. 420–22, 531. The story thus gives even greater credit to Yahweh, who chose not only a smaller force, but also those less suitable to a military enterprise.

8. *the people's provisions and trumpets.* The versions make it improbable that "provisions" was originally "pitchers" (*kaddē*) as is often suggested, although the former must be read as a construct (*ṣēdā* in MT).

he stood fast. Treating Heb. *hḥzyq* as the internal hiphil without an object.

Midian's camp was below him in the valley. Gideon was anticipating a fight to the finish. His continued reluctance called for direct intervention.

9–15a. The story of the Midianite sentry's dream is a self-contained unit which by the mere connective of vs. 15b has become a part of sustained narrative.

9. *That night something happened.* See NOTE on 6:25.

10. *squire.* Heb. *na'ar,* lit. "boy," "lad." The squire was a personal attendant and handyman, remembered especially as armorbearer (9:54; I Sam 14:1, 6). The Philistines unwittingly supplied Samson with a squire, thanks to whom that Yahwist judge worked a deliverance in his own tragic death (16:26).

11. *the armed men.* Heb. *ḥᵃmušīm.* The sentries. Cf. Josh 1:14, 4:12 where the word has to do with alignment for battle, a sense confirmed from Mari (*The Assyrian Dictionary,* vol. VI, p. 67).

12. *on.* See fourth NOTE on 5:7.

13. *a moldy barley bread.* Heb. *ṣᵉlīl leḥem šᵉ'ōrīm.* Not "unleavened" but "stale" or "moldy," relating the introductory word to Ar. *ṣalla* (became dry and cracked, was putrid, stank, had gone bad). ALUOS^D, 13. This is consistent with our interpretation of vss. 1–7, where Yahweh singles out a much smaller force, consisting of the less alert troops. The appositional phrase, "barley bread," seems to be related to the text of 5:8, which is mispointed in MT (*leḥem šᵉ'ārīm,* "bread of the gates") but which makes sense as *lāḥᵃmū šᵉ'ārīm,* "they fought in the gates." We suspect that barley bread (*leḥem šᵉ'ōrīm*) in the dream plays upon something like *loḥᵃmē šᵉ'ārim,* "gate fighters."

The Tent. A proper noun (like The Pentagon).

14. *nothing other than the sword of Gideon.* Gideon will be greatly impressed by the dream, once it has been interpreted as applying to him.

15. *he fell prone.* Heb. *way-yištāḥū.* The root is clarified from Ugaritic root *ḥwy;* and the biblical semantics are clearer also from the Amarna Letters where the vassal addressing himself to Pharaoh uses stereotyped expressions of homage, among them "I fall," "bow."

before. With LXX, which is normal idiom, as elsewhere in Judges, 2:19 *et passim.* In the beginning there was a caricature of the historical Gideon, at long last maneuvered into the field by God himself (cf. 6:22). In its present context any concern for the divine legitimation of Gideon's fighting is marginal, if indeed, it can be detected in the story at all. Rather the redactor is interested in the psychology of an historical Yahwist leader, as it was reflected in popular traditions concerning him.

15b–22. These verses describe the rout of Midian in deliberately exalted language, probably drawing heavily upon liturgical celebrations of the great

1. *The plain south of Judah, going down from Arad (1:16)*

a. The mound of Tell Arad at the northern edge of the Negeb desert, that is, the "plain south of Judah."

b. A model of the eighth-century B.C.E. Israelite border citadel at Arad, showing: (1) large open courtyard, (2) storage rooms, (3) Yahwist temple, (4) industrial area, (5) living quarters, (6) water channel.

c. The small Holy of Holies in the Arad temple. Note the two pillar bases flanking the entrance to the cella which contains a single *maṣṣēbā*, a sacred standing stone. This Israelite temple perhaps was built on an early Qenite holy place.

2. *He could not evict the inhabitants of the plain, for they had iron chariots (1:19)*

The chariots could not have been made entirely of iron, but would have had iron nails and fittings. The working of iron was a knowledge acquired by the Sea Peoples in their conquest of the former Hittite realm. Here the chariots of the Sea Peoples are under attack by Egyptian foot soldiers.

3. *Show us an entrance to the city (1:24)*

a. Perhaps an example of such an entrance, from the later period of the monarchy, is the small underground postern gate at Ramat Raḥel, a suburb of Jerusalem. The gate, built into the casemate wall, is just high and wide enough for one person to enter at a time.

b. The inner entrance to the postern gate at Ramat Raḥel.

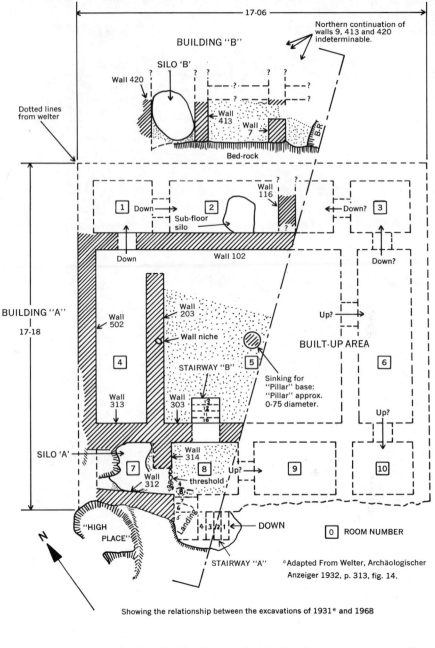

BUILDING "B"

17-06

Northern continuation of walls 9, 413 and 420 indeterminable.

SILO 'B'

Wall 420

Dotted lines from welter

Wall 413

Wall 7

B-R

Bed-rock

Wall 116

1 Down→

2

Sub-floor silo

←Down? 3

Down

Wall 102

Down?

BUILDING "A"

17-18

Wall 502

Wall 203

Wall niche

Up?

BUILT-UP AREA

4

STAIRWAY "B"

5

Sinking for "Pillar" base: "Pillar" approx. 0-75 diameter.

6

Wall 313

Wall 303

Up?

SILO 'A'

Wall 314

7

Wall 312

8

Up?→

threshold

9

10

"HIGH PLACE"

Landing

4 3 2 1 ← DOWN

0 ROOM NUMBER

N

STAIRWAY "A"

*Adapted From Welter, Archäologischer Anzeiger 1932, p. 313, fig. 14.

Showing the relationship between the excavations of 1931* and 1968

0 1 2 3 4 5 6 7 8 9 10   15

Meters

4. Jotham . . . went and stood on a promontory of Mount Gerizim (9:7)

Schematic of the Tananir Sanctuary (Building A), some 400 meters up the slope of Gerizim from Shechem, after excavation by Welter in 1931 and re-excavation by the writer in 1968. The building was destroyed by Egyptian troops in the mid-sixteenth century; it had succeeded an earlier structure, remarkably similar in plan and orientation (Building B), just one step downhill. These buildings are probably older covenant sanctuaries. (The slightly later temple uncovered at the Amman airport resembles them closely.) The overall plan of Building A is that of Welter, from the 1931 excavations. The hatched lines indicate walls that were still discernible in 1968, when Building B was first found.

5. Gaal ... went out and stood at the entrance to the city gate (9:35)

The east gate of Shechem, flanked by guardrooms, with stairs descending into the city. The four pairs of stone orthostats and connecting walls supported a massive brick superstructure, and the entire complex was roofed over. Arumah, Abimelech's residence, lies in the hills to the upper right.

6. The Navel of the Land (9:37)

The plain of Shechem, looking southeast from the foot of Mount Ebal, with the narrow east-to-west Shechem pass joining the broad north-to-south plain. The excavations of ancient Shechem are at the lower left. "Jacob's Well" and the "Tomb of Joseph" are traditional pilgrim sites of the Balatah village to the south and east of the mound. The Tananir sanctuary (white arrow) lies on the lower slope of Mount Gerizim just above the town. Arumah (black arrow) is across the plain atop the hills to the upper right.

7. Shechem's Tower ... the stronghold of Covenant God's temple (9:46)
A western view of the remains of the Middle Bronze Age Shechem temple,
after the 1962 archaeological campaign, with the courtyard rebuilt and the great
sacred stone *(maṣṣēbā)* set up again. The temple of Abimelech's day was smaller,
for it reused only sections of the walls of the massive Middle Bronze original.

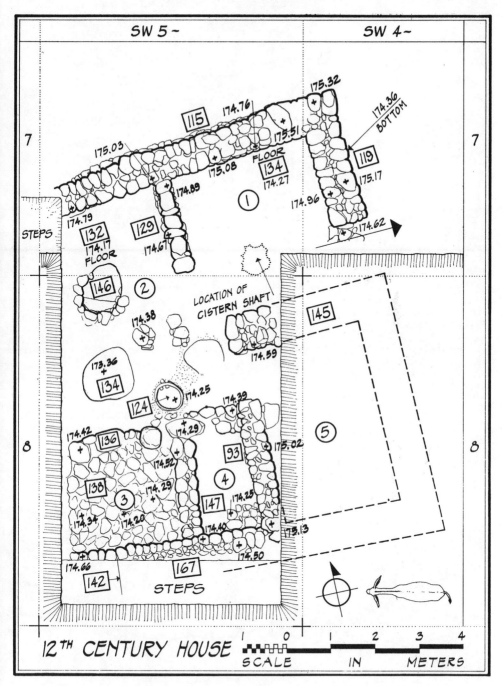

8. *Jephthah . . . his daughter came out to meet him (11:34)*

a. Plan of a twelfth-century house at Taanach.

b. A south-southwest view of the twelfth-century house at Taanach, showing curb and street surface in left foreground, oven and two pits in the court, and behind the oven a pillar of the pillared wall.

c. Reconstruction of a typical house in Old Testament times. Because there were rooms built on three sides of a court, there was plenty of space to house such animals as sheep, cows, goats. It was reasonable, therefore, for Jephthah to assume that the first creature to wander out of his house when he returned would be an animal acceptable for sacrifice, and not his daughter.

9. *Samson staged there a party for seven days (14:10)*

a. A Philistine beer jug from Tell Aitun. The Philistines consumed enormous quantities of beer, from highly decorated jugs showing their "Sea Peoples" background.

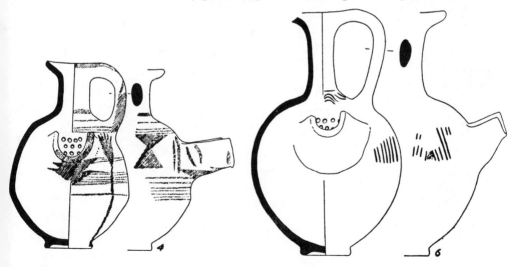

b. Philistine beer jugs like these from the tombs at Tell Fara are characterized by small holes drilled directly into the jar above the neck of the spout, forming a strainer.

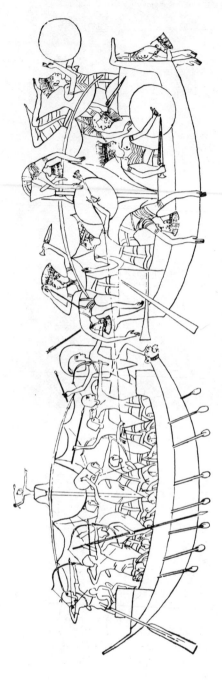

10. The Philistines dominate us (15:11)

Roughly contemporary with the Israelite invasion of Canaan from the east and the south came the Sea Peoples' invasion from the west and the north. Among the Sea Peoples were the Philistines, who would one day give their name to the land of "Palestine." Here the crew of a Sea Peoples ship, identified by their crested helmets, opposes a ship of Rameses III in a mid-twelfth century B.C.E. sea battle.

saving events in Israel's emergence as a revolutionary alliance. Cf. the importance of trumpets and shouts at the encircling of Jericho's walls (Josh 6).

15b. *"Up! For Yahweh has . . ."* Following such a proclamation the narrator's audience was prepared for a description of intense fighting (see Deborah's charge to Baraq, 4:14). Gideon has a plan, however, that deserves to be called inspired. He prepares for a sudden victory by arranging an elaborate prank, one which will stir the superstitious raiders into flight, and thus give effect to the will of Yahweh for the well-being of Israel.

your hand. LXX[B] reads "our hands."

16. *three companies.* Traditional military organization (9:43; II Sam 18:2), with antecedents at Mari. Mendenhall, JBL 77 (1958), 57–58, n. 32.

trumpets . . . empty jars . . . torches. The Israelite fighters were heavily laden with the makings of a spectacular demonstration, but little else. Repetitions in 19b and 20 add to the impression that the narrative is conflate, drawing upon parallel recitals of the story. Source analysis is, however, highly subjective. The finished narrative has an air of contrived unreality which reminds one of the account of the war against Benjamin in chs. 19–20. See NOTE on 8:27.

torches inside the jars. A tactic used by Cairo police as recently as the mid-nineteenth century. Burney, p. 216, based on Edward W. Lane, *The Manners and Customs of the Modern Egyptians* (1908), p. 123.

18. *For Yahweh and for Gideon.* A statement of the heart of Israelite social structure in the judges period. The declaration of war asserts the unity of Yahweh's action and his people's destiny, as in the stories of Ehud (3:28) and Deborah (5:8–9). A sizable number of minor witnesses read here "a sword for Yahweh and for Gideon," in conformity with vss. 14 and 20. That none of the major recensions follows suit, however, means that the shorter text must be taken seriously. See NOTE on vs. 20.

19. *the beginning of the middle watch.* The nighttime is divided into three parts according to the Book of Jubilees 49:10 and 12. "The morning watch" is mentioned in Exod 14:24 and I Sam 11:11. According to Mark 13:35 the nighttime could also be divided into four watches—evening, midnight, cockcrow, and morning—and the rabbis debated the question of whether the watches were three in number or four (*Berakoth,* 3a–b). I owe this collection of references to Freedman.

smashing. Heb. *nāpōṣ,* the infinitive absolute used as emphatic surrogate for a finite verb form. Freedman, private communication.

20. *sword.* As in vs. 14. The same word connotes "battle," as in the analogous *milḥāmā le-yahwē,* "Yahweh's battle!" in Exod 17:16. Cf. Lev 26:7, 36, 37; Num 14:3; 20:18; Josh 10:11; Job 5:20; Song of Songs 3:8; Ezek 38:4, 21; ALUOS[D], 13. The idea seems to be that Gideon and his small force will exceed the field orders; the grand demonstration was to have been sufficient (vs. 18, with no mention of fighting.)

21. *awoke with a start.* Not "ran," but "jumped up" as in Gen 25:22; Ps 18:29; Joel 2:9. ALUOS[D], 13.

22. *throughout the whole camp.* Heb. *wbkl hmḥnh,* lit. "even in all the camp"; the initial *waw* is emphatic. LXX[B], OL, and Syr. which omit the con-

junction, reflect a haplography after the immediately preceding *waw,* or else an example of the double-duty spelling practice: one consonant where morphology requires two. On the latter, see Dahood, *Psalms III, 101–150,* AB, vol. 17A (1970), pp. 371–72.

The force fled. The older literary analysis assumed a syntactic unity which simply cannot be wrung from vs. 22b, with the resultant hypothesis of "sources" brought into play. At the end of a six-page note Burney, p. 225, remarked: "we are probably justified in concluding that the variation between two narratives, as regards topography, was by no means as great as some scholars have assumed." The raiders are rather abruptly described as scattering in retreat, so that three Israelite battalions will be inadequate for the pursuit.

Beth-shittah. Location unknown but presumably somewhere in the Jordan valley across from Abel-meholah. The latter is quite possibly Tell el-Maqlub on the Wadi el-Yabis. Simon Cohen, IDB I, 5. See Map 4.

Zererah. Apparently a variant of "Zarethan," modern Tell es-Sa'idiyah in the Jordan valley, newly excavated by J. B. Pritchard. (Aharoni proposes Tell Umm Hamad as the location of Zarethan. LOB, p. 31.) See Map 4.

Tabbath. The site has not been certainly located but is surely to be sought in the mountains of eastern Gilead. Aharoni, LOB, p. 241, proposes Ras Abu Tabat on the Wadi Kufrinjeh. See Map 4.

COMMENT

These verses tell of Yahweh's victory and the rout of the Midianites. The following through 8:28 deals with Gideon's pursuit of a predatory force and reflects considerably more interest in raw historical details. Chapter 7 tells a story to provide a theological perspective for reading the events recorded in ch. 8. The story can be divided easily into three segments: 1–8, reduction of the force; 9–15, the enemy sentry's dream; 16–22, rout of the Midianites.

The fleece-test story emphasizes that it is as easy for Yahweh to save by few as by many. That there is an understandable exaggeration of the military proportions is now clear (see NOTES on vss. 3–6). There remains the problem of how to account for the consistent characterization of Gideon, who inclines regularly to the divinatory approach (6:17, 36–40), so that at last God himself must resort to "divination" to reduce Gideon's army to the size of an adequate domestic force. The actual setback to Gideon that lies behind the story is unknown. Perhaps on this occasion the assembly had responded to his call but voted "no" to the idea of massive retaliation, so that he would have to proceed with his own force. In any case, the story explains how well-being for Israel was dependent upon Yahweh's victory, and that Yahweh himself had selected the troops. But with such a limited force, Gideon was not about to take to the field until his reconnaissance assured him that the enemy could be stampeded (vss. 9–15).

It was, at last, no contest (vss. 16–22). Gideon did no fighting, and Yahweh won. The victory was strictly analogous to the one at the Reed Sea (Exod 14–15), and it made good the promise of Deut 32:36. The narrator clearly implies that with the successful deployment of his ruse and the peace secured once again, Gideon ought to have gone home. Thus one delightful story (there must have been many of them) was selected for what it communicated about the man. In its present context its purpose is to counter excessive claims about this one historical savior. The remainder of the Gideon segment is of another, more sober, literary character; the perspective on Gideon and Israel is, however, continuous.

7 23 Israelites rallied from Naphtali, from Asher, and from all Manasseh; and they chased after Midian.

24 And envoys! Gideon sent throughout the Ephraimite hill country: "Come down against the Midianites and capture the watering places from them as far as Beth-barah (and also the Jordan)." So all the Ephraimites rallied, and they captured the watering places as far away as Beth-barah and the Jordan. 25 They captured two Midianite commanders, Oreb and Zeeb. They executed Oreb at Oreb's Rock, and Zeeb they executed at Zeeb's Winepress. They chased Midian and brought the heads of Oreb and Zeeb to Gideon across the Jordan.
8 1 The Ephraimites said to him, "What's this you have done to us, by not calling us when you went out to fight Midian?" They argued vigorously with him. 2 He said to them, "What, now, have I done, as compared with you? Is not the gleaning of Ephraim better than the vintage of Abiezer? 3 Into your power has Yahweh surrendered Midian's commanders, Oreb and Zeeb. What have I been able to do, as compared with you?" When he had said this, their indignation against him subsided.

NOTES

7:23 – 8:3. It is impossible, on the basis of attitudes toward Gideon, to separate the sources. Vs. 23 appears to be the same material stratum that last surfaced in 6:35. Presumably this source too will have said something about Gideon's home-front successes, but it has been displaced by the work of a more specifically theological traditionist in the bulk of ch. 7.

7:23. This verse harks back to 6:35 where Manasseh is mobilized, with Asher, Zebulun, and Naphtali placed on alert. All of them except Zebulun now take to the field. Ephraim, only now summoned, moves at once to an accomplishment which takes Gideon completely by surprise.

rallied. With LXX, repointing as qal in both vss. 23 and 24. The Masoretes were no longer alert to the contextual implications of ṣ'q ("to appeal in person," not merely "to call"; e.g. 3:9 and NOTE), and treated the verb as passive.

24. *from them.* Heb. *lhm,* the suffix with *lamedh* in the sense of *from.* See Dahood, *Psalms III, 101–150,* AB, vol. 17A (1970), pp. 394–95.

Beth-barah. Location uncertain; perhaps to be sought in the Wadi Far'ah northeast of Shechem.

25. *Oreb* and *Zeeb.* Lit. "raven" and "wolf." For poetic expression of the tradition, see Isa 10:26 and esp. Ps 83:9–12. Neither of those passages reflects any etiological interest whatsoever. In our verse an etiological element has been exploited by the narrator so that the belatedly rallied Ephraimites can present themselves as the workers of poetic justice.

They chased Midian. With LXX, Vulg., Syr., reading the *nota accusativi* instead of the preposition *'el,* "to Midian."

and brought the heads . . . across the Jordan. Another stock device of biblical narrative, delaying the reporting of vital information until it helps to make the narrator's point. Prior to this verse we are given no indication of the whereabouts of Gideon. The arrival of the Ephraimites with their bloody trophies seems to imply that Gideon had considered the rout of Midian so complete that he took up the chase east of the river Jordan. A mighty harangue thus ensues, from which Gideon makes a quick diplomatic recovery and goes on to further exploits.

8:1. *The Ephraimites.* Characteristically they arrive uninvited (12:1) or unexpected (5:14) in the book of Judges. Here they take a stance in relation to Gideon much as they will toward Jephthah, but with entirely different outcomes, so that there is no reason to regard one or the other of the stories as secondary. They are independent witnesses to the life style of Ephraim, as a member of the old league.

2. *Is not the gleaning of Ephraim better than the vintage of Abiezer?* Is the mop-up work done by your tribe not more significant than the performance of my contingent? He is either coining a proverb or adapting an old one, more likely the latter, in view of his early education at the cult place of "Joash the Abiezrite" (6:11). The statement is perhaps deliberately ambiguous. The popular slogan itself might only strain the relationship further, unless it be provided with strictly Yahwist exegesis, which Gideon supplies in vs. 3.

3. *Into your power.* See second NOTE on 1:2.

Yahweh. Follows the uniform witnesses of the early versions, where MT reflects the more provincial collocation (a secondary northern development) of "Ephraim" and "Elohim."

COMMENT

These verses are transitional, dividing Gideon's exploits (altogether a bundle of contradictions) into two parts. Whereas he had earlier advocated total war against the new confederation (ch. 7), he later took the federal militia into the field, beyond the river, in pursuit of merely personal vengeance, as will become clear in 8:19.

This transitional unit, however, sits loose in its context. After showing the heads of Oreb and Zeeb to Gideon as proof of their prowess, the Ephraimites are talked out of their resentment against Gideon's allegedly preferential treatment of tribes. They simply drop out of the picture.

We may therefore suspect that the gap between stories about "Gideon at home" and "Gideon abroad" has given a redactor opportunity to lead into Gideon's pursuit of Zebah and Zalmunna (8:4–21) and at the same time to score against Ephraim by inserting this pericope which tells how Ephraim, too, had been very active in Israel's response to the Midianite problem. The unit may in fact preserve the memory of an attempt by Manasseh's neighbor to put a stop to Gideon's retaliatory raiding.

To the redactor, however, Gideon was put in a most curious position; for the Ephraimites had brought him the wrong heads.

XVII. Blood Vengeance
(8:4–21)

Gideon in Transjordan

8 4 Gideon had arrived at the Jordan and went on the prowl, he and the three hundred men who were with him wearily giving chase. 5 He said to the men of Succoth, "Please give some loaves of bread to the force which is in my command. They are exhuasted! I am following the trail of Zebah and Zalmunna, the Midianite kings." 6 But Succoth's captains said, "Do you already have in your possession a hand of Zebah or of Zalmunna, that we should supply bread for your army?" 7 And Gideon said, "For that, when Yahweh surrenders Zebah and Zalmunna into my hand, I will flail your flesh with the desert-thorns and thistles!"

8 He went up from there to Penuel and spoke to them in the same way; but the men of Penuel answered him exactly as the men of Succoth had answered him. 9 He said, moreover, to the men of Penuel, "When I return victorious, I will tear down this tower!"

Success at Last

10 Zebah and Zalmunna were at Qarqor, and their forces were with them, about fifteen contingents, all who were left of the entire force of the Easterners. The fallen came to a total of a hundred and twenty sword-wielding contingents. 11 Gideon went up the Trail of the Tent Dwellers, east of Nobah and Jogbehah, confronting Zebah. He attacked the camp, although the camp was undefended. 12 Zebah and Zalmunna fled, but he chased after them and captured the two Midianite kings, Zebah and Zalmunna. But the camp as a whole had panicked.

Gideon as Good as his Word

13 When Gideon ben Joash returned from the battle, from the Heres Pass, 14 he caught a lad belonging to the men of Succoth. At his request, he listed for him the commanders and elders of Succoth, seventy-seven men. 15 He went to the men of Succoth and said, "Here they are—Zebah and Zalmunna—about whom you taunted me! You said 'Do you already have in your possession a hand of Zebah or of Zalmunna, that we should supply bread for your exhausted men?'" 16 And he took the city's elders and the desert-thorns and thistles, and with them he flailed the men of Succoth! 17 Penuel's tower he tore down, and he slew the townsmen.

Vengeance

18 He said to Zebah and Zalmunna, "How about the men you slew at Tabor?" They said, "They were each one of them just like you, comparable in stature to a king's sons!" 19 He said, "They were my brothers, my mother's sons! By the life of Yahweh, if you had let them live, I would not slay you." 20 And to Jether his eldest child he said, "Take a stand and slay them!" But the boy would not draw his sword, because he was afraid, being still a youth. 21 And Zebah and Zalmunna said, "You take a stand and dispatch us, for a man is measured by his strength!" So Gideon rose to the occasion and slew Zebah and Zalmunna and took the crescents which adorned the necks of their camels.

NOTES

8:4. *Gideon had arrived.* The translation relies on context to render *way-yābō'* by an English perfect. Apparently the introduction to his exploits in Transjordan has been displaced by the other edition of Gideon stories.

went on the prowl. Repointing *'br* as infinitive absolute (MT has a participle) used as emphatic substitute for a finite verb, as in 7:19. The same consonants were probably taken as a qal perfect by the translators of the LXX (the note in *Biblia Hebraica*, 3d ed., ed. Rudolf Kittel, Stuttgart: Privilegierte Württembergische Bibelanstalt, 1937 and after, is misleading, as the Greek does not read a direct object after the verb, but the independent pronoun). Freedman, private communication. On the semantics of *'br* in the judges stories, see NOTE on 2:20. Gideon's action here sets the stage for the introduction of Gaal in 9:26.

wearily giving chase. Heb. *'ypym wrdpym*, lit. "tired and pursuing," a hendiadys. That MT is correct (the versions reflect *wr'bym,* "and hungry") is confirmed by the same words *'ypm* and *rdp* in vs. 5.

5. *Succoth.* Generally identified with Tell Deir 'Alla in the Jordan valley a short distance north of the Jabboq (Map 4), known to have been inhabited only a short time later by newcomers who were probably Sea Peoples. Wright, BA 29 (1966), 73–74. In Gideon's day it was very much within the Yahwist confederation and was remembered for exercising its own prerogatives when the savior-judge had called out the militia in order to prosecute his family's blood feud. This explains why the Succoth commanders are not ready at once to join the pursuit. On the basis of recent excavations the identification of Tell Deir 'Alla as Succoth has been seriously challenged, since it has turned out to be an undefended temple mound without sizable village occupation to the end of the Late Bronze Age. Destroyed by an earthquake, which has yielded a C_{14} date of 1180 B.C.E. ($\pm$ 60 years), the ruins appear to have continued in sanctuary usage by a new group of settlers, whose pottery tradition is not strictly continuous with the local Late Bronze material and is somewhat degenerate by comparison. Franken, *Excavations at Tell Deir 'Alla* (Leiden: Brill, 1969), pp. 4–8, 19–21. Thus an approximate date for Gideon's instruction of the men of Succoth would fall in the early decades of the twelfth century. In this period Succoth (lit. "huts") was a rural rallying point very much distrusted by the free-wheeling judge. Cf. the better known rural "amphictyonic" shrines of Tananir (see NOTE on 9:7) and Amman.

Zebah and Zalmunna. These are distorted names (like "Cushan of the Double-Wickedness" in 3:8 and NOTE), meaning "Victim" and "Protection Refused." While the original names cannot be recovered, the narrative distortions reflect early Yahwist sympathy for Zebah and Zalmunna.

6. *Do you already have in your possession a hand . . . ?* A play on the two words for "hand," *yād* (here rendered "possession" in a characteristic idiom) and *kāp.* Nothing as obviously probative as the head of a victim (Oreb and Zeeb) is demanded by the Succoth captains. On the practice of mutilation of prisoners, cf. the treatment of the lord of Bezeq in 1:5–7, and NOTE on 1:6. The question from the Succoth authorities goes directly to the heart of the matter. In eliciting wider support for his militia, the Yahwist savior-judge was supposed to have some prior success to validate his military leadership. Israel's traditionists decided that in the Midianite crisis Yahweh had saved Israel, against the reluctance of Gideon (chs. 6 and 7); and Gideon had thereafter proceeded on his own initiative (ch. 8)!

7. *desert-thorns and thistles.* Why these are seized upon is not clear unless they are supposed to evoke a connection with treaty curses involving animals, weeds, and various domestic plants. See Hillers, *Treaty Curses and the Old Testament Prophets,* p. 23. Gideon is represented as promising to take the law into his own hands as soon as events give him a reasonable pretense to do so.

8. *Penuel.* The city is mentioned in patriarchal traditions in relation to Jacob's struggle with an envoy (Hosea 12:4) in the form of a man (Gen 32: 24–32). The location is probably at Tulul edh-Dhahab, on a bend in the Jabboq that nearly encircles it, not far from Succoth, known to be occupied and easily defensible early in the Iron Age. See Map 4.

9. *victorious*. Lit. "in peace," that is, having won.

this tower. Heb. *ham-migdāl*, cf. 9:46, 49, 51. Apparently the pride of Penuel was a fortress-temple carrying the same generic designation as the massive Middle Bronze and Late Bronze Age temples at Shechem and elsewhere in the same period. See *Shechem,* pp. 94–101.

This is another point at which the narrative begins to set the stage for the Abimelech story, by singling out points of correspondence. By the kind of emphasis that is given to each one, however, the narrator indicates that Gideon's judgeship had been, by and large, beneficial.

10–12. These verses form a self-contained unit, describing Gideon's capture of the Midianite kings, presumably by a daylight surprise attack this time.

10. *Qarqor*. In the Wadi Sirḥān, east of the Dead Sea, getting close to Midianite home bases. See Map 4.

The fallen. The referent is not entirely clear. The redactor probably took it to be the scene of 7:22, where we are told that Yahweh "set each man's sword against his own ally." That pattern is similar to the internal strife of Exod 32. Such struggles could be very lethal, although there is no way of checking whether exactly "a hundred and twenty sword-wielding contingents" were rendered ineffective.

contingents. For this translation of Heb. *'elep,* see NOTE on 1:4.

11. *the Trail of the Tent Dwellers*. Another example of a preposition *b* within a construct chain, pointed out to me by Freedman.

east of Nobah and Jogbehah, confronting Zebah. With LXX^A, where *nkh zbḥ*, "confronting Zebah," has dropped out of the other recensions. The spelling of the first place name in LXX^A (Nabeth) reflects how easy it is to confuse the similar-looking letters *taw* and *ḥeth*. LXX^A omits the second place name, a haplography in its *Vorlage: lnbḥ* [*wygbhh*] *nkḥ zbḥ.* LXX^B had perhaps a mutilated Hebrew text: it omits *nkḥ zbḥ* and preserves mention of Iegebal, which looks like a corruption of *Jogbehah*. The text is a jumble, and any reconstruction must be provisional.

The location of Nobah (cf. Num 32:42) is unknown. Jogbehah (Num 32:35) is identified as Khirbet el-Ajbeihat, seven miles northwest of Amman (see Map 4).

undefended. Heb. *beṭaḥ* in the same technical meaning as its use in 18:7 to describe the unwalled city of Laish, the pre-Israelite name for the city of Dan. Freedman, private communication.

13–17. These verses continue to represent Gideon as quite a single-minded individual, once he had made up his mind.

13. *the Heres Pass*. Not to be confused with the Har-heres (Mount Heres) of western Palestine, mentioned in 1:35. This one is otherwise unknown. A provocative emendation is proposed by Burney (p. 232) who sees it as a corrupt marginal variant mentioning the ban, ḥerem, but there is no other occurrence of that word (or its related verb) in the body of the book. The ḥerem is a living institution in the Joshua generation (1:17) and is mentioned as part of tragic civil war at the end of the book (21:11); Israel's judges, on the other hand, fight defensive wars, with varying degrees of sacral legitimacy in the view of the narrators. Gideon's use of the plunder at the end of this story (vs. 27) was considered highly problematical.

14. *commanders and elders . . . seventy-seven men.* This is the first mention of a town's elders in the book. They make up the corporate governing body where there is no one called king. Some of them will also be "commanders" or past commanders, the number seventy-seven standing for the total of adult free males who are heads of families. Pedersen, *Israel* I (1959), 36; C. U. Wolf, JNES 6 (1947), 99, nn. 10–12.

15. The repetition of the taunting question in its entirety, and the use again of *'ypym* "exhausted" (twice in vss. 4 and 5) forms a strong inclusio.

16. *he flailed.* As promised with the same verb in vs. 7, another inclusio. This is the consistent reading of the versions (for Heb. *way-yādāš*), though different translation equivalents were used in LXX[A] (*kataskaino*) and LXX[B] (*aloao*) in both verses. MT reads here *way-yōda'* ("and he taught") which is also defensible (cf. the usage in 3:2 and the Philistine's taunt to Jonathon in I Sam 14:12). Very possibly these are ancient variants. LXX[A] mentions "the *arxontas* (captains?)" in addition to "the elders."

18–21. These verses comprise another unit that sits loosely in the context, although vs. 18 would follow well on the heels of vs. 12. The connection has been broken by the insertion of vss. 13–17.

18. *How about the men.* Heb. *'ēpō* nowhere means "of what sort?" Here it has deictic force rather than local. ALUOS[D], 15.

at Tabor? See Map 4. The question comes as a complete surprise to the reader, for there is absolutely nothing in the preceding Gideon materials to serve as antecedent. None of the various suggested emendations—*tabbur,* "center" (Moore, p. 228); "Thebez" (Burney, p. 234)—is based on a likely orthographic or auditory confusion. We suspect that the question is intended to be as startling as it sounds; Gideon has been pursuing a feud which has nothing directly to do with the occasion of the rout of the Midianites when he had been elevated to the highest office in Israel.

19. *brothers, my mother's sons.* It is a distinctive designation. In a polygamous society "brother" generally signified half brothers, i.e. sons of the same father. Uterine brothers were especially close (e.g. Joseph and Benjamin). They could also be very hostile (e.g. Cain and Abel, Jacob and Esau). Gideon's revenge will contrast sharply with the settlement sought by Jotham, youngest son of Gideon, in very different circumstances, following the slaughter of his seventy "brothers" (the broader sense) in the sequel to this story (9:7–21).

By the life of Yahweh. For this rendering of the oath particle *ḥay/ḥē,* see Moshe Greenberg, JBL 76 (1957), 34–39. The same expression occurs as a military oath in Lachish Letter 3:9, tr. W. F. Albright, ANET[3], p. 322. Thus at the climax of his exploits Gideon rides roughshod over a basic covenant stipulation (Exod 20:7; Deut 5:11), inasmuch as the vengeance being exacted here is strictly personal. He has usurped Yahweh's executive prerogative (Deut 32:35; cf. Rom 12:19), and he invokes a covenantal blessing for himself alone. Manfred R. Lehmann, ZAW 81 (1969), esp. 83–85. For the rarity, and therefore the enormity, of this act of private vengeance in the OT, see *TenGen,* esp. pp. 69–98.

20. *Jether his eldest child.* The narrative elicits sympathy for the eldest son here, just as it does for Jotham the youngest son of Gideon in 9:7–21, and Gideon himself at the outset (6:1–11) of his story.

21. *Zebah and Zalmunna.* The two Midianite kings are defiant to the very end, unlike the prince of Bezeq in 1:5–7, who recognized a cosmic justice in his case. The narrator here, however, does not recognize Yahweh's justice in the deaths of Zebah and Zalmunna. That was, rather, the justice of Gideon, who then collected the customary trophies of victory.

COMMENT

In this chapter the focus shifts from the rise of Gideon as the savior of Israel in the Midianite crisis, regarded as only a little short of miraculous, to a glimpse of Gideon in action. Here the chief protagonist is not Jerubbaal ("Let-Baal-sue," i.e. God's man!) but Gideon (Hacker). There is no participation by Yahweh, nor reference to him, except in Gideon's own usage (vss. 7 and 19).

The story is complete in itself, as it leads the audience from the scene of Gideon half dead from hunger and thirst at the outset, to his plundering of the royal mounts at the conclusion. Its purpose is to show what later became of the young Yahwist reformer introduced by the stories in chs. 6 and 7, and ch. 8 will conclude on the note that he almost became king.

It should probably not be read as the immediate sequel to the rout of the Midianites in 7:19–22, for Gideon's purpose in Transjordan does not become clear until 8:18–19—private vengeance. Gideon's son Abimelech will reverse the process and begin his short-lived kingship at Shechem with the liquidation of his father's house, except for Jotham, the one who got away (9:4–5).

8 22 The Israelites said to Gideon, "Reign over us! You, your son, and your grandson too! For you have rescued us from Midian's power." 23 Gideon said to them, "I will not reign over you, nor shall my son reign over you; Yahweh shall reign over you!"

24 Gideon said to them, "Let me make a request of you. Give me, each of you, the rings which you took as booty." For they had gold earrings, since they were Ishmaelites. 25 They said, "We will indeed give them." And they spread out a garment, and each man threw into it his confiscated earrings. 26 The weight of the gold earrings which he requested was one thousand seven hundred gold shekels, not including the crescents, pendants, and purple garments which were on the Midianite kings, and not including the ornaments that were on their camels' necks. 27 Gideon made it into an ephod and set it up in his own city (in Ophrah), and all Israel prostituted themselves there! It became a lure to Gideon and his household.

28 Midian was subdued before the Israelites, and they no longer raised their heads. The land was calm for forty years in Gideon's days. 29 And Jerubbaal ben Joash, went to live in his own house.

NOTES

8:22–29. The verses comprise a pair of traditional units (Gideon's refusal of kingship in vss. 22–23, and request for all the earrings in vss. 24–27). Each makes its own point, but by mere juxtaposition and editorial conclusion (28–29) they are made to serve a historian's critical purpose.

22. *Israelites said . . . "Reign over us!"* The actual offer would have been made at one of the tribal assemblies, such as figure frequently in the book (2:1–5; 4:4–5; 6:7–10; 10:10–16, 18; 20:1–11).

23. *I will not reign . . . nor shall my son . . . Yahweh shall reign.* The

threefold repetition of the verb (*mšl*) is especially solemn. Gideon's refusal of a throne and his affirmation of Yahweh's kingship may be taken as an expression of strictly orthodox Yahwism in his day, thanks to the recent volume of scholarly work on biblical covenant formulations and their contemporary political models. By admitting only this much (vss. 22–23) of the available tradition about Gideon's refusal to reign, the redactor allows Gideon to speak better than Gideon knows; that is, Gideon unwittingly anticipates the Yahwist fate of his son Abimelech in ch. 9. Cf. how Deborah is presented as speaking better than she knows in 4:9.

24. *they were Ishmaelites.* Here is a direct clue that Midian in Gideon's day was a confederation of tribal groups, just as it had been at Sinai, where certain Midianites had entered the new and rapidly expanding Yahweh confederation. Buber, *The Kingship of God,* esp. pp. 29–36.

26. *gold shekels.* The unit is here implied, as in 9:4; 16:5; 17:2, 4, 10.

that were on. See fourth NOTE on 5:7.

27. *an ephod.* The narrator holds us in suspense regarding the motivation of Gideon's request until he can juxtapose it with the results: "Israel prostituted themselves." The "ephod" here is apparently an elaborate priestly vestment, the visible heavenly glory of the invisible God of Israel. Albright, YGC, pp. 200–3. See COMMENT.

his own city (in Ophrah). Variants? LXX^A reads "Ephraim" for the latter.

all Israel. Probably hyperbole. Not again until the concluding incidents of the judges period does the narrative present "all the Israelites" as united, and then only against one of their own constituencies (20:1). The stories of Gideon and the anonymous Levite in chs. 19–20 are connected by the idea of the misuse of the Yahwist militia for personal vengeance; they are the midpoint and endpoint of the period which begins with a lament scene where the angel speaks "to all the Israelites" (2:4).

prostituted themselves. An introductory theme (2:17) which is here explicated, not in terms of trafficking with other deities, but as a matter of trusting in Gideon's divinatory guidance. See COMMENT.

It became a lure. This statement resumes another introductory theme (2:3).

28. *Midian was subdued . . . and they no longer raised their heads.* The one common denominator to a number of redactional conclusions in the book is the plain declarative statement: "the land was calm" (3:11, 30; 5:31). This is variously nuanced by accompanying comments: e.g. "Moab was subdued . . ." (3:30). The similar statement about Midian is further emphasized: "they no longer raised their heads." Here the editor's conclusion is a sorrowful one. Israelites and Midian had gone full circle since the great days of Moses and Jethro.

29. *to live in his own house.* This conclusion anticipates the antithetical introduction to Abimelech, who will return to his mother's house and become king at Shechem.

Comment

It appears that the troops have been very busy in their collection of the spoils of war. The word ḥerem is not used, perhaps because that institution is being misused here. The institution of the ḥerem had existed for the purposes of building up the league treasury and providing proper compensation for the fighters.

Gideon's soldiers have made quite a haul. They gladly hand over to Gideon, who has already declined their offer of the right to rule as king, the confiscated earrings. With the gold Gideon will make an ephod, an elaborate divinatory cloak. There was to be only one such cloak in Israel, and tightly laced to it was the "judicial breastplate" (Exod 28:15–30). References to the official ephod, therefore, will often imply also the "judicial breastplate," which is itself infrequently mentioned outside of passages giving its specifications (Exod 28) and reporting its manufacture (Exod 39), until at last it supplies a powerful theological metaphor to the apostle Paul (Eph 6:14).

Gideon refused the offer of a throne in Israel but demanded all the trappings of judge. This in turn explains why he is nowhere said to have "judged" Israel. That much was clear from the stories about him.

A savior he was indeed, according to the early narrator, who larded his message with enough historical detail to suggest that things had nearly gotten out of hand, when there was nobody left but Gideon to tell the world that Yahweh is King in Israel. But this unit sits loose in its context. I suspect that its insertion was the work of the exilic redactor who recognized a parallel to his own day: with one of Gideon's sons, "Israel" was very nearly disbanded.

8 ³⁰Gideon had seventy sons, his own offspring, for he had numerous wives. ³¹His concubine—the one at Shechem—she also bore him a son, and he named him Abimelech.

³²Gideon ben Joash died at a ripe old age and was buried in the tomb of Joash his father, at Ophrah of the Abiezrites.

NOTES

8:30. *seventy sons*. Probably a political number, as in the introductory scene with the prince of Bezeq who speaks of "seventy kings" who had once shared his table but had been mutilated by him (1:7). See also the seventy "sons" of the judge Abdon in 12:14. The evidence for such councils or bodies of advisors is extensive; Malamat, BA 28 (1965), esp. 34–50. Ahab is also credited with seventy "sons" who suffered a fate similar to Gideon's sons in Jehu's coup (II Kings 10:1–7). Many of Gideon's sons will, of course, be brothers and half brothers, "for he had numerous wives." Abimelech will slaughter his seventy brothers in 9:5, yet Jotham "the youngest" will still be alive to protest the slaughter of "my father's house . . . seventy men" (in 9:18). One is reminded of the institution of the seventy elders in Exod 24, and of the fact that the family of Jacob in Egypt consisted of seventy souls, all of whom were, like Gideon's seventy, "his own offspring" (Gen 46:27).

31. *concubine*. Heb. *pīlegeš*.

named him. Lit. "made his name" (not the usual "he called," Heb. *wayyiqrā'*) as in II Kings 17:34; Neh 9:7; Dan 1:7—all three examples of renaming. What Abimelech's mother called him, we do not know. This name is bestowed by Gideon the Yahwist.

Abimelech. It is a sentence name, "my father is *mlk*." Elsewhere the name is applied to a king of Gerar in patriarchal times (Gen 20–2, 26). The name disappears from use in monarchical times, except for one who was probably father of Abiathar (not "son," as in I Chron 18:16; II Sam 8:17; see Cross, *Canaanite Myth and Hebrew Epic* [Harvard University Press, 1973], pp. 211–14) who, however, is called Ahimelech ("my brother is *mlk*") in II Sam 8:17 and I Chron 24:6. The problem is how to read the final element of such names, which the spelling conventions of MT and the versions uniformly treat as *melek,* the common noun for "king." While the noun remained in use as "king" or "counsellor," *mlk* also became a name designating, in one form or another, particular deities: e.g. Molech and Milcom. Thus the name *Abimelech* might be classed with names such as Abijah (my father is Yah), Abiel (my father is El), Abijam (my father is Yam), and Phoenician *'b(y)b'l* (my father is Baal). It is unlikely, however, that Gideon the Yahwist reformer would have chosen a name for his son which to his mind would have carried so much pagan freight. More to the point is a comparison with such names as Ahimelech, "my brother is *mlk,*" and especially, Naomi's husband at the outset of the story of Ruth, which has its setting "in the days when the judges judged" (Ruth 1:1). His name was Elimelech, "(my) god is *mlk.*" But the name of Naomi's husband is *Abimelech* in LXX[BL] plus several other Greek manuscripts, and this is supported at several other points in Ruth 2:1, 4:3, and 9. This may be a genuine alternative reading. I owe these references to Campbell; see his forthcoming Anchor Bible commentary on the Book of Ruth. In contrast to the variation between "Abimelech" and "Elimelech" the shift from "Abimelech" to "Ahimelech" may signify an actual change of name. "Ahimelech" is a name borne by two or three contemporaries of King David and no one else in the OT! They are, in addition to "the father of Abiathar" mentioned above, a Hittite in the service of David (I Sam 26:6), and a priest of Nob (father of Abiathar?) whose assistance to David triggered Saul's slaughter of the Nob priesthood (I Sam 21:1–9; 22:9–20). I suspect that the name Ahimelech reflects the Davidic revolution and means "my confederate-brother is king." But Yahweh is officially the only King of Israel in the Gideon tradition. While the image of God as father is relatively scarce in the OT, no doubt as a reaction to the grossly literal understanding of the relationship between the deity and his or her adherents in the fertility cults, the image is nonetheless ancient in Israelite material; see especially the lawsuit Song of Moses in Deut 32:6 and 20. It is probable that in the name of Gideon's most famous son, the first element "my father" refers to Yahweh, and the second element refers to Yahweh's position in Israel as "King."

32. There was a persistent belief in ancient Israel that the mortal remains of a man, a unitary individual, "constituted the very essence of that person in death." Meyers, BA 33 (1970), 26.

COMMENT

By the mere elaboration of transitions between pericopes, a redactor could often make his point. Here the point is that one of Gideon's most fateful contributions to Israel's health and history was the siring of Abimelech. The editor was thus elaborating upon the built-in evaluation of historical Gideon in the old narrative units. That is, vss. 30–31, with parallel grammatical construction emphasizing their subjects, show no characteristic narrative connection with what precedes and follows. Their composition was an exegesis of "his own house" at the end of vs. 29; and this is confirmed by the ironic portent

of Gideon, pious Yahwist and chief Israelite oracle seeker, naming one of
his own sons My-Father-Is-King! That son would make every effort to in-
herit the kingdom in ch. 9.

Is it merely coincidental that Gideon and Samson (16:31) are the only
figures in the Book of Judges who are buried, each "in the tomb of his
father"? Gideon the reforming son of Joash (proprietor of Baal's cult place)
turned at last to the supervision of his own oracular facility, where, it was
later claimed, Israel again prostituted itself. Manoah the father of Samson
will be introduced in ch. 13 as head of his own splinter group, from which
Samson will in turn go his own way.

XX. ABIMELECH
(8:33–9:57)

Preview

8 33 When Gideon was dead, Israelites turned aside, prostituting themselves to Baal; they made Covenant Baal their god. 34 Israelites did not remember Yahweh their God, who rescued them from the power of their enemies all around them. 35 Nor did they deal faithfully with the family of Jerubbaal (that is, "Gideon") corresponding to all the good that he had done for Israel.

My Father is King

9 1 Abimelech ben Jerubbaal went to Shechem, to his uncles, and said to them, that is, to the entire clan of his mother's kin: 2 "Say to all of Shechem's lords: 'Which is better for you, for seventy men to reign over you—all the "sons" of Jerubbaal—or for one man to reign over you?' You will recall that I am your own bone and flesh." 3 So his mother's relations reported the whole proposal, on his behalf, in an audience with all the lords of Shechem. They were inclined to favour Abimelech "because," they said, "he is our own kin."

4 They gave him seventy in silver from Covenant Baal's temple. With it Abimelech hired some idle mercenaries, and they trailed after him. 5 He went to his father's house at Ophrah and slew his brothers, the "sons" of Jerubbaal! Seventy men—on one stone! Jotham ben Jerubbaal, the youngest, was spared because he hid out. 6 So all of Shechem's lords got together, everyone of Millo-house. They went and made a king of Abimelech beside the oak which survives at the palisade in Shechem.

Jotham's Message

7 When it was disclosed to Jotham, he went and stood on a promontory of Mount Gerizim. He raised his voice and shouted at them.

He said to them, "Listen to me, O lords of Shechem! And let God listen to you!

(Part I)

       (Hebrew syllable count)

8 The trees set forth determined   8 ⎫ 14
    To annoint over them a king.   6 ⎭
They said to the olive tree: 6
    Reign over us!   6
9 But to them the olive tree said: 7 ⎫ 50
    Have I ceased making my oil   7 ⎫
      Whereby gods and men are honored   14 ⎬ 31
    That I should go to sway over the trees?   10 ⎭

(Part II)

10 The trees then said to the fig tree: 11
    You come and reign over us!   8
11 But to them the fig tree said: 9 ⎫ 54
    Have I ceased making my sweetstuff   7 ⎫
      My excellent fruit   9 ⎬ 26
    That I should go to sway over the trees?   10 ⎭

(Part III)

12 The trees then said to the vine: 9
    You come and reign over us!   8
13 But to them the vine said: 7 ⎫ 53
    Have I ceased making my wine   8 ⎫
      Which cheers both gods and men   11 ⎬ 29
    That I should go to sway over the trees?   10 ⎭

(Part IV)

14 All the trees then said to the bramble: 12 ⎫ 20
    You come and reign over us!   8 ⎭
15 But the bramble said to the trees: 10
'If in good faith you are anointing me as king over you, come! Find shelter in my shade! If not, let fire break out from the bramble and devour the cedars of Lebanon!'   43 ⎬ 53

16 "If now you have acted with complete honesty in making a king of Abimelech, if you have dealt fairly with Jerubbaal and his house,

if you have done to him as his deeds merited—17 whereas my father fought for you, ignored his own life, and rescued you from Midian's power; 18 but you have risen up today against my father's house, slain his 'sons' (seventy men—on one stone!), and made Abimelech, son of his slave-wife, to be king over Shechem's lords, because he is your brother—19 if it is with complete honesty that you have dealt with Jerubbaal this day, then be pleased with Abimelech and let him be pleased with you! 20 But if not, let fire break out from Abimelech and devour the lords of Shechem and Millo-house! And let fire break out from the lords of Shechem, even from Millo-house, and devour Abimelech!"

21 And Jotham fled. He ran away, went to Beer, and settled there, on account of his brother Abimelech.

Shechemites Quarrel with Abimelech

22 Abimelech became commander in Israel for three years. 23ª But God sent an evil spirit between Abimelech and Shechem's lords, 24 to bring the lawless action against Jerubbaal's seventy "sons"—and their blood to assess—against their brother Abimelech who slew them, and against Shechem's lords who lent support to the slaying of his brothers.

23ᵇ Shechem's lords dealt treacherously with Abimelech. 25 Shechem's lords stationed men in ambush against him on the mountain tops. They robbed everyone who passed by them on the highway. And Abimelech was informed.

Return of the Native

26 Gaal ben Ebed went on the prowl in Shechem together with his brothers. Shechem's lords trusted him. 27 They went out to the field, gathered grapes in their vineyards, trampled them out, and celebrated. They went into their god's temple and ate and drank and reviled Abimelech! 28 Gaal ben Ebed said, "Who is Abimelech—and who is Shechemite—that we should serve him? Is this not the son of Jerubbaal? And Zebul is his appointee. Serve the men of Hamor, Shechem's father! Why should we serve him? 29 If only this people were subject to my authority! I would disposed of Abimelech." So he said, "Hey there, Abimelech, amass your troops and come out!"

30 Zebul, the city's commandant, heard the words of Gaal ben Ebed, and his wrath was aroused. 31 He managed by a ruse to send messengers to Abimelech. "Attention! Gaal ben Ebed and his

brothers are coming to Shechem. And listen! They are alienating the city against you. 32 Get up therefore by night, you and the force with you, and wait in ambush in the plain. 33 Then in the morning, when the sun comes up, you shall get busy and charge the city! And then, when he and the force with him are coming out toward you, you may do to him whatever opportunity offers."

34 Abimelech went up at night with his entire force, and four companies lay in wait around Shechem. 35 When Gaal ben Ebed went out and stood at the entrance to the city gate, Abimelech and the force with him got up from the ambush. 36 And when Gaal saw the people, he said to Zebul, "Look! People are coming down from the mountain tops!" But Zebul said to him, "Oh, it's only the mountains' shadows that appear to you as men." Still, Gaal kept on talking. 37 He said, "Look, a force coming down from The Navel of the Land! And one company coming from the direction of the Diviner's Oak!" 38 Zebul said to him, "Where, oh where is that bold mouth of yours? You said, 'Who is Abimelech that we should serve him?' Isn't this the force you scorned? Go out now, if you please, and fight it!"

39 So Gaal went forth, at the behest of Shechem's lords, and fought Abimelech. 40 Abimelech chased him and he fled. Many fell mortally wounded, right up to the gate's entrance.

41 Abimelech presided at Arumah, and Zebul denied to Gaal and his brothers any quarters at Shechem.

Slaughter of the Innocents

42 The next day, the people went out to the fields. They reported it to Abimelech. 43 He took the force, split them up into three companies, and waited in ambush in the fields. When he saw that the people were indeed coming out from the city, he rose and attacked them. 44 Abimelech and the company that was with him charged ahead and stationed themselves at the entrance to the city gate; the other two companies charged all who were in the fields and attacked them. 45 Abimelech fought all that day in the city. He captured the city and slew the people in it. He razed the city and sowed it with salt.

Dissolution of the New Covenant

46 When all the lords of Shechem's Tower heard, they went to the stronghold of Covenant God's temple. 47 It was reported to Abimelech that all the lords of Shechem's Tower had gotten together. 48 Abimelech and all the force with him went up Mount Zalmon.

Abimelech took his ax in hand, cut down a bundle of firewood, picked it up, put it on his shoulder, and said to the force with him, "What you have seen me do, hurry and do likewise." 49 So each of the troops cut down his own bundle; they followed Abimelech, put it against the stronghold, and set fire to the stronghold on top of them, so that all the folk of Shechem's Tower also died, about a thousand men and women.

The Last Campaign

50 Abimelech proceeded to Thebez; he encamped at Thebez and captured it. 51 Strong's Tower was inside the city, and to it all the men and women (and all the city's lords) fled and shut themselves in. They went up on the roof of the tower. 52 Abimelech came as far as the tower and fought against it; he got close to the tower door so as to set it on fire. 53 But some woman threw an upper millstone down on Abimelech's head and crushed his skull. 54 He called quickly to the squire who carried his weapons and said to him, "Draw your sword and kill me. Else they will say of me, 'A woman slew him!'" So his squire thrust him through, and he died.

Summary

55 When Israelites saw that Abimelech was dead, they went away, each to his own place.

56 Thus God requited the evil of Abimelech which he had done to his own father by slaying his seventy brothers. 57 Moreover, all the evil of the men of Shechem God brought back upon their own heads; to them came the curse of Jotham ben Jerubbaal.

Notes

8:33–35. These verses are the pragmatist's introduction to the preformed Abimelech material with which he could not take editorial liberties. The beginning is marked clearly by the introductory *wayhī* (see Note on 1:1). A redactor's inclusio is represented in "Israel" in 8:35 and 9:55. These verses comprise an indictment, for which the Abimelech story presents the evidence.

After the statement, "The land was calm for forty years," in 8:28b, we should have expected something like 3:12, 4:1, and 6:1, a statement that Israelites did evil. Indeed, that is the thrust of our unit, but it is differently formulated according to the nature of the case. Here the problem is purely an internal Israelite one; Shechem reverted to its Bronze Age governmental precedents, establishing a monarchy and recruiting supporters from the Yahwist alliance. It was nearly the end of Israel.

A key to the complex redactional history of the Gideon and Abimelech material is the alternation between the names "Gideon" and "Jerubbaal." The statement in 8:28b relates to the "Gideon" material which it concludes. Verse 29 concluded the story of "Jerubbaal." With the combination of all the "Jerubbaal" and "Gideon" materials the whole acquired a new conclusion, vs. 32, harking back to the beginning of the story of Joash and his son Gideon (6:11).

When the resulting larger Gideon sequence was combined with the Abimelech unit, the introduction to the latter (8:30–31) was dovetailed into its present position, presumably so as to introduce Gideon's family before reporting his death. In this transition (29–35) the two names appear in the same order as predominates in the redacted Jerubbaal/Gideon narratives. In vs. 35, then, Jerubbaal occurs first because Abimelech and Israelite supporters have forsaken Yahweh. This verse anticipates Jotham's logic in 9:16–19.

Thus, Abimelech's rise and fall was provided with its own theological introduction (8:33–35), corresponding to 3:12, 4:1, and 6:1, differently formulated because here the problem does not involve a foreign oppressor.

33. *Covenant Baal.* See NOTE on 9:46–49.

34. *Israelites did not remember.* For the gravity of this specification, see Childs, *Memory and Tradition in Israel* (Naperville, Ill.: Allenson, 1962).

who rescued them. As in Egypt, so in recent history. Note in this connection that Gideon is nowhere said to have "saved" Israel, or even to have "judged" in Israel. The Gideon narratives had concentrated on the hero's tragic flaws. This unit is concerned to avoid a possible misunderstanding.

35. *faithfully.* They did not do ḥesed, that is, perform in a manner expected of covenant partners. (See NOTE on 1:24.) Abimelech's new covenant-making at Shechem and the acquiescence of some Israelites was a repudiation of old covenant obligation. Note that it is with the name "Jerubbaal" (predominant in the account of Yahweh's rout of the Midianites), rather than the parenthetical "Gideon" (the name of the personal feud prosecutor through ch. 8) that the redactor links "all the good that he had done for Israel." Thus the statement implies no contradiction of the tradition, but intends to protect it from distortion, for what follows had precisely to do with the literalizing exploitation of covenantal kinship language.

9:1–6. These verses continue the narrative at the point where it was interrupted by a redactional splice at the end of 8:31. The entire Abimelech chapter sustains an interest in the meaning of names that became manifest at the climax of ch. 6, vss. 31–32. See esp. "Jotham" in vs. 5 and NOTE.

1. *Abimelech.* It is virtually impossible to exaggerate the narrative's sustained contempt for Abimelech ("My father is king." See NOTE on 8:31); the name occurs thirty-one times in the chapter.

to Shechem. See Map 4, esp. the sketch of the city-state.

2. *lords.* Heb. ba'ᵃlīm. They are the "city fathers." The same term for prominent citizens, with a sarcastic or ironic tinge, occurs in Josh 24:11; Judg 20:5; I Sam 23:11–12; II Sam 21:12.

Which is better . . . for seventy . . . or for one? A double rhetorical question (see NOTE on 2:22), implying the narrator's own answer: neither one would be *ṭwb*—not merely the comparative adjective (better) but also a term for covenantal amity. Moran, JNES 22 (1963), 173–76; Hillers, BASOR 176 (December 1964), 46–47.

reign . . . reign. Heb. *mšl*, as thrice repeated in Gideon's rejection of the offer to rule in 8:22–23. Freedman's observation.

bone and flesh. Likewise covenantal, as in Gen 2:23a. W. Brueggemann, CBQ 32 (1970), 532–42. This introduction to Abimelech's career is skillfully grafted on to the end of Gideon's story, thus posing a question of the relationship between covenant-making and kinship prerogatives.

4. *seventy.* No unit is specified; we should probably understand "seventy shekels' worth" (see 8:26 and 17:2). He received one for each life. On the round number seventy in Judges, see Note on 1:7.

idle mercenaries. Heb. *'nšym ryqym wpḥzym,* lit. "men empty and reckless." For the latter, see the characterization of Reuben in Gen 49:4.

5. The slaughter of the seventy, like the decapitation of Ahab's seventy sons in II Kings 10:1–11, clearly marks the end of an era or dynasty and the beginning of a new regime.

on one stone. The reason for emphasis here is not obvious. There is nothing else in the immediate or wider context to support it as "an instructive instance of the power of animistic superstitions" (Burney, p. 271, following Moore). Comparison with I Sam 14:33–34 suggests that it is regarded by the narrator as a particularly disastrous perversion of Yahwist sacrificial cultus: Abimelech expresses his contempt by using his own brothers as sacrificial victims at the establishment of his new covenantal relationship at Shechem. Jotham survived, however, as had Gideon at first (6:11), "because he hid out."

Jotham. Heb. *yōtām,* the meaning of which is not clear. There may be a form of the verb *tmm* involved, with the divine name omitted: thus "X is perfect." I suspect that the manner of Jotham's introduction, as the only survivor, was intended to evoke comparison with Heb. *yātōm,* "orphan." The narrative thus hints that in the situation where Abimelech was exegeting his own name to mean "My father (that is, Gideon) is king," Jotham's father was the God of Israel.

6. *everyone of Millo-house.* The phrase is appositional to "all of Shechem's lords," presumably identifying them by reference to their regular place of meeting. The Hebrew is *bēt-millō,* with the second element related to the root *ml'* "to fill." The designation may reasonably be taken to reflect a method of construction involving huge earthen platforms for large structures such as the massive fill supporting the successive Bronze Age fortress-temples at Shechem. See Map 4 and illustrations 5, 6, 7. Wright, *Shechem* (1965), esp. pp. 80–102. He compares this to the Jerusalem Millo reported to have been started by King David (II Sam 5:9) and finished by Solomon (I Kings 9:15). This parenthetical explanation anticipates vs. 20 and vss. 46–49 which employ a vocabulary that is in several ways distinct from the bulk of the chapter.

which survives at the palisade. Lit. "which is found . . ." The translation follows LXX[B], where MT and other witnesses reflect a simple haplography:

'lwn (*hnmṣ'*) *mṣb*. The meaning "palisade" for *mṣb* (probably a reference to Shechem's famous Temenos area) is clear from the parallelism in Isa 29:3. Freedman, private communication. The scribal lapse might well have been triggered by the knowledge that there had stood in the forecourt of Shechem's Late Bronze Age temple a large cultic pillar (Heb. *maṣṣēbā*) and two smaller ones. See *Shechem*, esp. pp. 80–102 and 122, discussing "Temenos 8" and "Temenos 9." The great Shechem *maṣṣēbā* is plausibly related to "this stone" in the covenant narrative of Josh 24:26. For a more complex solution to our text, which finds here another reference to "the *maṣṣēbā*," see Lawrence E. Toombs and Wright, BASOR 169 (March 1963), 28 f., n. 32.

In the introduction of Abimelech to Shechem, the narrative attains its first climax on an ominous note, with "the oak . . . at the palisade" alluding to patriarchal traditions (Gen 35:4) and in an act which now defiled a great covenant sanctuary. Enter Jotham.

7. *Jotham . . . Mount Gerizim*. See illustration 4.

a promontory. The Hebrew construct state with a proper noun as *nomen rectum* is ambiguous and in this case need not refer to "the top" of Mount Gerizim (see Map 4) from which Jotham would have been invisible to the people of Shechem. Some four hundred meters from the city, however, and situated on the lower slope of Mount Gerizim, were the ruins of Middle Bronze Age buildings recently reexcavated and interpreted as a gathering place for groups not adhering to the cult of the late Middle Bronze temple at Shechem. The Tananir ruin indeed provides a plausible setting for the acted parable of Jotham. See the writer's report, and a discussion of such structures by Campbell and Wright in BA 32 (1969), 82–116. It is no longer possible to locate with certainty a spot noted by Moore (p. 246): "Modern travellers have remarked a projecting crag on the side of the mountain, which forms a triangular platform overlooking the town and the whole valley, a natural pulpit admirably suited to the requirements of the story." Allowing, however, for the recent flurry of new housing construction in the vicinity, Tananir's uphill bedrock "cornerstone" makes it a very likely candidate for the place in Moore's note. See illustrations 4–7.

at them. With LXX[A], where *bhm* dropped out of other witnesses, in anticipation of *lhm*, "to them," two words later.

Listen to me . . . And let God listen to you. The description at this point provides a rare narrative preview of the situation which is presupposed later in Israel, when the prophet speaks uninvited and unannounced: "Thus saith the Lord!" Young Jotham is thus presented as the only likely candidate for judge in his day, but he will flee, with the sympathy of the narrator and his audience. On the diplomatic roots of the prophetic summons "Hear!" as appropriate prelude to the hearer's own confession, see esp. Julien Harvey, *Biblica* 43 (1962), 172–96.

8–15. Jotham's poetic speech is set within a prose framework. The bulk of it is developed from a poetic fable which would have been familiar to the Israelite audience. The division of the speech into four parts is based largely upon the syllable counting system of Freedman (see NOTE on 5:1), the import of which is most clearly conveyed by the brackets and totals which accompany the translation. The syllable counts are based upon the text of *Biblia Hebraica* without any alterations. Structurally Part I (14+50=64 syllables) balances Part IV (20+53=73 syllables). Parts II and III are exactly the same length, give or take one syllable. The larger sub-units of Part I (50 syllables) and Part IV (53 syllables) total 103 syllables, while the total of Parts II and III is 107 syllables.

Even though the present text is in prose form and hardly perfect, the structural pattern is quite visible. The translation has attempted to isolate the poetic dialogue, a feature common in biblical stories (e.g. Genesis, esp. chs. 1–11, but also throughout the narrative). Key elements in the pattern are the repetitions with their slight variations. These give the composition its structure, and they provide a framework in which Jotham can vary the monotony of poetic rhythm by invention.

He has adapted a fable. Scattered evidence in the OT adds up to a considerable Israelite interest in the fable form, a story involving plants and especially animals. See Eissfeldt, *The Old Testament: An Introduction*, pp. 37–38. In II Kings 14:9, which makes a point comparable to Jotham's fable, a Lebanese thistle proposes his own marriage to the daughter of the Lebanese cedar but is trampled to death by a wild beast of the steppe. It is interesting to note that in our chapter Gaal's arrival on the scene (vs. 26) will be described with the same verb that first moves the wild beast in II Kings 14:9, *'ābar!* See NOTES on 2:20, 8:4, and 9:26. Jotham, on the other hand, used the motif of rivalry between the trees for supremacy, which was a popular one in antiquity. See Gaster, MLC, pp. 423–27, 532–33.

8. *The trees set forth determined.* This line, a poetic bicolon 3:3 (8+6 syllables), is anticipatory. The verb *hlk*, "to walk," preceded by its infinitive absolute used adverbially evokes an image of persistence.

9. *Have I ceased . . . ?* Heb. *he-ḥºdaltī*, repeated in vss. 11 and 13, reminiscent of 5:6, where the caravans "ceased." The form is peculiar in these vss. We have treated it as a qal.

are honored. Reading *ykbdw* as niphal instead of piel, as do RSV and NEB by implication. For reflexive use of *kbd* in niphal, see Exod 14:4. This leaves the words *'šr-by*, lit. "which in me," unexplained. LXX[B] reads "by it" (*'šr-bw*), which is preferable here. The *y* is a third-person suffix.

That I should go to sway over. The picture is that of the king who nods, sitting above his subjects.

13. *cheers.* Regarding the significance of pagan libations, Burney (p. 274) commented "the god, as well as his worshippers, was thought to be cheered by the beverage." In its Yahwist context the fable implies that Abimelech's aspirations defied both nature (vss. 8–14) and nature's God (vs. 15).

15. That this is the prose writer's adaptation of the poetic fable is clear. Three phrases from vs. 8, which are three individual words in Hebrew — to anoint, over them, a king — are repeated here in chiastic arrangement (anointing me as king over you) to emphasize the inclusio.

in good faith. Heb. *bº-'ºmet*, lit. "in truth," a noun which is common in covenantal usage, where it stands for fidelity to an agreement.

Criticism generally distinguishes between the core fable (vss. 8–14) and its adaptation or Yahwist conclusion (vs. 15), which, it is argued, does not exactly fit either the body of the poem or the prose explication of it which follows in vss. 16–20. Especially troublesome is the last-minute mention of the "cedars of Lebanon" and the preceding invitation: "come! Find shelter in my shade!" (a three-beat colon without a parallel). But the shade of a bramble is not much of an offer, and the offer is probably calculated to jar the listeners out of the complacency induced by the familiar and the rhythmical. The narrator uses a semitechnical phrase, "a clever play on a popular expression associated with kingship. For in the royal letters of Assyria persons under the special protection of the king, or officials traveling on missions of state, are frequently said to be 'in his shadow.'" Gaster, MLC, p. 427. Comparison with II Kings 14:9 suggests that "cedars of Lebanon" was the usual metaphor for self-sufficient monarchs; in this light, the implications of "bramble" are obvious. Possible discrepancies between core fable and conclusion disappear if it is recognized that the Hebrew poet has improved upon the original by making the bramble impose covenantal blessing and curse, as no doubt Abimelech did. From this it follows that the bias expressed is not so much against monarchy as a form of government, as it is against the particular use of religious covenant by Abimelech and his associates. There is no "prophecy and fulfillment" scheme introduced by Jotham's contribution to the pericope. Rather, Jotham, by using the fable, is merely anticipating that the covenantal curse accepted by the Shechemites in connection with Abimelech was likely to be far more effective than any attendant blessings. Moore remarked that Jotham's speech is "hardly to be deemed historical" but concluded by observing that Jotham's role is what confirms the story's antiquity (Moore, p. 246). It is clear that Jotham's role is historical and that the contents of his speech had a prehistory.

16. *with complete honesty.* Heb. *be-'emet u-betāmīm,* lit. "in truth and in completeness," another example of hendiadys. The phrase is repeated in vs. 19 for emphasis. The same combination occurs elsewhere only in the covenant formula of Josh 24:14, an observation which I owe to my student, D. Roberts Burton.

as his deeds merited. With the background as provided in chs. 6–8 there can be no misunderstanding of this as Jotham's justification for the rule of Gideon's seventy sons. After all, Abimelech had already been introduced in such a way as to recognize his offer to Shechem's lords as a false posing of alternatives (vss. 1–2). Rather, the narrative promptly elicits sympathy for the brutally butchered men, sons of one who had, as a matter of fact, "rescued" (vs. 17) them, although that point is nowhere specified in the stories about him.

17. *my father.* Heb. *'ābī,* occurring twice in quick succession, surely to call attention to the first element in the name of the new king of Shechem. Abimelech is mentioned five times in this highly charged conclusion to Jotham's speech (vss. 16–20).

ignored his own life. This reading adopts the proposal of *Biblia Hebraica* to point the anomalous *mngd* as *minnegdō;* that is, he cast his life "away from himself." This reading is supported by the recognized practice of writing one sign for double use (Dahood, *Psalms III,* AB, vol. 17A [1970], pp. 371–72), in this case the initial *waw* of *wyṣl*, "and rescued." Freedman, private communication.

18. *slave-wife*. Heb. *'mh*, lit. "handmaid," a synonym of *siphā* "maid, maidservant," when the latter has the role of concubine. Gen 20:17; 21:12. The usage does not impute to her either high or low social position. The same word is used in the Shebna inscription to designate the woman who was buried in the same tomb with that high ranking official. Nigel Avigad, IEJ 3 (1953), 137–52. I owe this reference to Freedman.

20. *even from Millo-house*. Treating the initial *waw* of *wmbyt-mlw* as emphatic removes any lingering suspicion that Millo-house might not be the great El-bᵉrit temple. For Jotham is invoking the curses which, in this case, were apparently reciprocal and equal in the negotiations that culminated in coronation of Abimelech in vs. 6. That is, the Millo-house must have been house of the deity enlisted as witness to the agreement on the part of the Shechem nobility.

The clearest evidence for the prehistory of Jotham's speech in its poetic and prose versions, prior to the development of the present narrative, is the assumption that the hearers will understand what is meant by Millo-house and the curse calling for reciprocal destruction of Abimelech and Millo-house at this point.

That Millo-house was destroyed long before the Book of Judges was put together means that we are dealing with authentic early tradition at the core of Jotham's speech.

21. This verse is the narrator's wrap-up to the Jotham story, reminiscent of the beginning that is now plugged into vs. 5, where Jotham was spared "because he hid out."

22. *commander in Israel*. The sentence seems, at first, isolated in its context. For Abimelech's position has already been described at length—king at Shechem. Elsewhere in connection with Abimelech, Israel and/or Israelites are mentioned only in 8:33–35 and 9:55. The redactor thus understands that some time after Abimelech became king at Shechem (by covenant with the local nobility), he also saw active service on behalf of the Yahweh-confederation as a *śar*, "field commander"; i.e. he had tried to retain his new possession and assert his former loyalty at the same time, and God had put up with it—for three years. Cf. Hosea 8:4, "They appointed commanders (*heśīrū*) but I did not concur." It cannot be overemphasized (and at this point most introductions and handbooks need revision) that at no point in scripture is Abimelech said to be or considered to be king of Israel. Rather he was *śar*, for a while. This verse thus interprets the introductory statement of the narrative which follows, and which gives the reason for the development of the split between Abimelech and his Shechemite supporters.

23–25. The translation places vs. 24 between 23a and 23b to convey the sense of the original. The reason for the arrangement in Hebrew is not obvious. Perhaps it has to do with a redactor's theological appropriation (vss. 23a–24) of the nuclear historical tradition (vss. 23b–25).

23a. *God sent an evil spirit*. Narrative shorthand for the satisfactory resolution of a situation that was on the verge of getting entirely out of hand: "God" is the architect of estrangement "between Abimelech and Shechem's lords" (cf. the spirit volunteer in I Kings 22:21). Regarding the "spirits" and the heavenly court, see Introduction, pp. 25–26 and NOTE on 3:10. That the spirit here comes from "God," not from "Yahweh," represents a redactor's value judgment (see NOTES on 6:14 and 36). In this case, it highlights his agreement with Jotham who says "Let God listen to you!" in vs. 7. Evil spirits from the deity are, on the whole, extremely rare in biblical narratives and they stand generally for the utterly inexplicable, e.g. the near insanity of Saul, Yahweh's anointed, which is in fact handled very carefully and compassionately in I Sam 16:14.

24. *to bring . . . to assess.* With LXX, which read a causative (MT "to come") for "to bring," parallel to the active verb "to assess," lit. "to place." The purpose of the divine maneuver was to bring on both parties to the crime the appropriate consequences. Chiastic word order in the original indicates how closely bound these clauses are.

25. The narrative climax is another case of "the best laid plans. . . ." Shechem's lords placed lookouts to warn of the approach of Abimelech while they took to plundering the caravans (cf. the situation described in the Song of Deborah, 5:6–7). But someone turned informer, thanks to the "evil spirit" of 23a, with which this verse forms an inclusio.

26–41. The story of Gaal at first glance appears to intrude, without literary connections, into the chapter. Thus the older literary criticism, lending an *E* cast to the bulk of the chapter, designated Gaal's story as *J*. Yet data independently regarded as indicative of one source or another are mutually indispensable to the integrity of stories in the Book of Judges. The designation of the Gaal pericope as *J* is an argument from silence. The connection with the preceding material is implicit; for vs. 25 clearly depicts a wide-open city, ripe for the plucking by another opportunist, who does not offer even a pretension of Yahwist credentials, who indeed represents the ultimate ethnic perversion of a great covenant tradition.

26. *Gaal ben Ebed.* Another apparently distorted name (see NOTE on 3:8). The first element evokes comparison with the root *gʿl* "to abhor, loathe." The second element is "servant," "slave," as in many compound names, e.g. Obadiah, "servant of Yahweh." Cf. especially the roughly contemporary Obed, ancestor of David (Ruth 4:17, 22). LXX[B] consistently gives his name as Gaal son of *Iobel.* The latter element "Yahweh is lord" (*baʿal!*) is not pejorative, but probably reflects syncretistic usage in his day at the great Shechem temple, the house of *baʿal-berīt* (vs. 4) or *El-berīt* (vs. 46). I suspect that the two traditions MT/LXX[A] and LXX[B], have leveled throughout the narrative different selections from the same genealogy, *gʿl bn ʿbd bn ywbʿl,* selections perhaps originally triggered by a haplography.

With the shift from the son of a concubine (Abimelech) to Gaal the son of an adherent to the corrupted Shechem temple, one who in fact makes his claim to kingship in terms of long genealogical purity ("sons of Hamor"), the point is made that Shechem's lords were now scraping the bottom of the barrel. Israelites on the other hand are, by definition, free men, their Israelite identity being established by loyalty to Yahweh alone.

went on the prowl. Like the wild animal in II Kings 14:9 (where the fable is surely drawn from the same broad repository as Jotham's), and like Saul and his servants looking for the lost asses of Kish (I Sam 9:4): The traditional rendering "crossed over" requires some antecedent description and is thus unnecessary at a good many points in Judges, e.g. 8:4 and NOTE. There may be a double meaning. Without the Jotham fable as a part of preceding context, the root ʿbr could be taken here to mean "take over by illegitimate force." *Ten-Gen*, p. 140.

brothers. Marauding, mercenary confederates, according to H. Reviv, IEJ 16 (1966), 252–57. However, the notion that Gaal was not himself a close blood relative of the Shechem nobility is flatly at odds with the appeal that Gaal makes, precisely in terms of genealogy.

trusted. An extremely important covenantal act.

27. *celebrated.* Metaphorical use of *way-yaʿⁿśū hillūlīm,* lit. "made praises." The scene depicted "is similar to the classic wild western stories of the cinema. The bad men come to town and make straight for the bar, and in a drunken state begin to curse the local leander." Crown, *Abr-Nahrain* 3 (1961–62), 95. The only flaw in Crown's description is his view of Gaal as an outsider, not as a Shechemite who has come home to ask in the next verse about why "we" should serve the half-breed king.

ate and drank and reviled. The scene contrasts sharply with the standing theme of legal protection and cultic participation by the disadvantaged elements of society, required repeatedly in Ugaritic and Hebrew. See Greenfield, *Eretz Israel* 9 (1969), 65.

28. *and who is Shechemite?* Repointing Heb. *škm* as the gentilic noun *šikmī,* where LXX in both main recensions reads "son of Shechem."

Is this not . . . ? Like the question in vs. 38; here, however, only LXXᴬ has the pronoun (Hebrew equivalent, *zē*). MT may well be the remnant of something like *hⁿlōʾ[hūʾ],* "Is not [he] (the son of Jerubbaal)?" See discussion of these variants in Boling, VT 13 (1963), 479–82. Gaal thus counters Abimelech's claim to legitimacy through his Shechemite mother by pointing to Jerubbaal his non-Shechemite father.

Zebul. "Big Shot." Heb. *zebūl,* "high," "exalted," is apparently the remnant of a sentence name (the mythological creature "Sea" is "Prince Yam" [*zbl ym*] in Ugaritic).

appointee. Heb. *pāqīd,* a technical term, perhaps "recruiter," related to the verb that occurs often in the sense "to muster," with its largest concentration of occurrences in the census lists of Num 1–4 and 26. In light of the detailed records in descriptions of the military muster at Mari the verb should now be rendered "to record, enroll." Glock, "Warfare in Mari and in Early Israel," p. 200. We are thus in a better position than ever to understand the intense resentment of the Amarna period populace to functionaries like Zebul. J. B. van Hooser, "The Meaning of the Hebrew Root *pqd* in the *Old Testament*," unpublished Th.D. dissertation, Harvard, 1962.

Serve. With MT, where the Greek recensions have misconstrued the same consonants as noun plus suffix, "his servant," (*doulos autou*) in awkward apposition to "his appointee."

Serve the men of Hamor, Shechem's father. This imperative sentence supplies, in anticipation, the answer to Gaal's own concluding question: "Why should we serve him?" (that is, Abimelech). It offers the clue to the whole genealogical basis of Gaal's appeal, which is presented as the inversion of a great covenantal practice at the Shechem sanctuary, a tradition with roots going beyond the fourteenth century Apiru domination and an earlier Hivite period (see NOTE on 3:3) to still earlier Hurrian settlement. YGC, p. 271. Hamor (Ass) is the "father of Shechem" in Gen 33:19 and 34:6 ff. He had borne the honorable title of *nāśî'*, "chief," according to Gen 34:2, where he is variously identified as "Hivite" (MT) or "Horite" (LXX). At Mari the sacrifice of an ass was so much a part of contractual procedure that "to slay an ass" became an idiom for covenant making. Inasmuch as the name of Shechem's "father" would have been no more complimentary then than now, Wright argues that the men of Hamor at Shechem in Abimelech's day are heirs to a longstanding covenant tradition. *Shechem*, pp. 123–38. It remains only to be noted how Gaal's complaint represents a complete exploitation of the older covenant tradition: he appeals to Shechemite genealogy and objects to the domination of Shechem by the semi-Shechemite Abimelech. It belongs to the narrator's portrayal of absurdity that genealogy was a poor basis for the determination of loyalty. Thus, by his use of pious cliches, Gaal joins the ranks of many protagonists in Judges, who, unlike Jotham, are presented as speaking better than they know.

29. *So he said.* With MT, where LXX no longer understood the following *lamedh* vocative:

Hey there. Gaal challenges Abimelech in the snug context of the conspiratorial feast.

amass your troops. Heb. *rabbē*, not "increase your army" as in RSV. The basic idea may go back to counting or numbering, as so many of the terms connected with the military do: i.e. "make a *rab* of your army." Freedman, private communication.

31. *by a ruse.* Heb. *bᵉ-tormā* cannot be derived from *rmh*, "deceived," and mean "secretly." ALUOSᴰ, 15. RSV's emendation, "at Arumah," requires an orthographic confusion that is hard to imagine; while that place name is perfectly intelligible in vs. 41, it would fall into the category of data that does violence to the narrative structure ten verses earlier.

alienating the city. Heb. *ṣārîm 'et hā'îr.* For this sense of the verb see Deut. 2:9, 19; Esther 8:11. "Besieging the city" would normally be *ṣārîm 'al hā-îr.*

33. *charge.* Hebrew root *pšṭ.* Except for Jotham's performance, this is the closest we come in the chapter to any judicial (*špṭ*) activity. That we are justified in recognizing here a double entendre is confirmed by the same verb used twice in vs. 44.

35. *Gaal . . . city gate.* See illustration 5.

37. *The Navel of the Land.* An old poetic designation for the geography of the Shechem area, the narrow east–west pass emptying into the broader north–south plain. See illustration 6. Here it must have particular reference to one of the two mountains flanking the Shechem pass. Mount Ebal is ruled out, as it was associated, in the Israelite period, with the covenantal curses (Deut 11:29).

Mount Gerizim, the mountain of blessing, had been a holy mountain from time immemorial, as indicated by the excavations at Tananir (see above, NOTES on 9:6, 7, and Introduction, p. 21, and illustration 4. The navel of the earth was its mythographical center, the link between heaven and earth. It figures frequently in the stories of ancient and primitive peoples as "the site of their main city or principle shrine." See Gaster, MLC, pp. 428, 533.

the Diviner's Oak. See the "oak" that is plausibly associated with the Temple area in vs. 6. The place of the conversation is surely the east gate of Shechem, since the northwest gate had gone out of use in the Late Bronze and Iron I ages. See Map 4 and illustration 5. Gaal suddenly observes that exit from the city is rapidly closing, blocked by a larger "force" (*'ām*) descending the lower slope of Gerizim. They had probably climbed the back side of that spur, after crossing the plain from Arumah (*Jabal al 'Urma*) under the cover of darkness. A smaller company was deemed all that would be necessary in the narrow pass to the west of the city.

38. *bold mouth*. Heb. *pe*, used figuratively, as in Ps 49:13.

39. *at the behest of*. On this usage of the preposition *lpny*, see Speiser, *Genesis*, AB, vol. 1 (1964), p. LXVIII and NOTE on 6:11.

40. *chased him*. Subsuming the whole army under the rubric of the commander. A Qumran manuscript (1Q6) reads "chased them," which looks like a genuine variant.

41. *presided at*. Heb. *way-yēšeb b-*. For this sense of *yšb* "to sit, dwell," see the story of Deborah and NOTE on 4:5. A number of LXX manuscripts interpreted the same consonantal text as *way-yāšob* "and he returned"; *šwb*, however, is not regularly construed with the preposition *b-*, although the latter is clearly reflected in both LXX^A and LXX^B. Freedman, private communication.

Arumah. The site is *Jabal al 'Urma*. See Map 4, enlargement on the Shechem city-state.

quarters at. Heb. *šebet b-* (root *yšb*), lit. "residence in." The point is that as long as Abimelech made his headquarters at Arumah, Zebul wouldn't let Gaal use Shechem as a base of operations, i.e. a safe place to quarter his men. There is no more mention of Gaal. It appears that like Jotham in vs. 21, Gaal got away. To the narrator, Gaal was not the real problem and had served only to further heaven's judicial proceedings, which had begun with Jotham. The stage is now set for the last treachery of Abimelech, and his near escape.

42–43. This unit begins with an obvious wordplay: *hā-'ām* means "the people" in vss. 42 and 43b, but "the force" (The People, i.e. the military sense) in vs. 43a. The narrator's sympathies are with the former, the exploited common folk who on the day after Gaal's defeat assume that the crisis is past, and go out to inspect the latest damage to "the fields." Critics have found difficulty in regarding vss. 39–41 as the antecedent of "the next day." Moore assumes that this originally followed vs. 25 and that it was men coming out of ambush who were in turn ambushed by Abimelech. Such a reconstruction is possible only on the assumption that Israelite traditionists were completely ignorant of geography in the Shechem vale. However, with the recognition of vs. 41 as an editorial pause, the resumption of the narrative is entirely plausible. Once again the common folk of Shechem were victimized, with Abimelech proving as treacherous at the end as he was treasonous at the beginning, in the narrator's opinion.

43. *three companies*. See NOTE on 7:16.

44. On this verse Moore (p. 263) was surely correct in observing that "the stratagem has some resemblance to that employed at the taking of Ai (Josh 8)." There the editorial introduction attributes the idea of an ambush to Yahweh.

the company. With Vulg. and some Greek manuscripts, where MT reads plural.

45. *He captured the city*. Presumably the reference is to the lower city, as distinct from the acropolis or "temenos" area of the fortress-temple. Cf. the role of the fortress-temple at Thebez in vss. 50–51. That is, after the effective capture of the city, the people fled to the citadel, i.e. the stronghold in the upper city.

the people. An inclusio with the same phrase in vs. 42, which explains why there appears to be a redundancy in the following account of the destruction of Shechem's Tower. That is, the narrative is built up from preformed units, which a compiler did not have license to revise.

sowed it with salt. The significance of this act is not transparently clear. One possible explanation is that it signified "a means of purifying the site as an act of, or in preparation for, its consecration," that is, total destruction under the ḥerem. Gevirtz, VT 13 (1963), 52–62. This would balance, in inverted relationship, Gideon's personal appropriation of booty to make an ephod (8:22–29). The problem with such an interpretation is the uniform absence of ḥerem-language, apart from the secondary introduction (1:17) and conclusion (21:11). More likely, in razing the city and sowing it with salt, Abimelech is represented as preempting God's own prerogative, implementing a covenantal curse (see, e.g. Jer 17:6; cf. Deut 29:23). Fensham, BA 25 (1962), 48–50.

46–49. *all the lords of Shechem's Tower*. The standing designation for the Shechem power bloc, "lords" (*ba'ᵃlē*), connects this unit with the bulk of the chapter. Shechem's Tower, however, is introduced abruptly, presumably from another source, and apparently as an alternative designation for Millo-house (vss. 6 and 20), identical with Covenant God's temple. The same is called by a derogatory name, "the house of Covenant Baal," where the emphasis is upon the use that men made of the god (8:33–34). The shift from "Covenant Baal" to "Covenant God" at the climax of the chapter signals a narrator's value judgment, as in comparable variations noted repeatedly in the Gideon-Abimelech materials. See NOTE on 6:14. The narrator is thus saying that God had in fact done away with his own temple, in order to retain his own prerogatives and restore order in Israel.

46. *When all . . . heard*. Presumably, when those safely ensconced within the walls heard what had happened to the peasants in their fields, they crowded into the Shechem fortress-temple. Though the Late Bronze Age rebuild was smaller and not as strongly constructed as the Middle Bronze Age original, it would have served as a last-ditch fortress. E. F. Campbell, Jr. and James Ross, BA 26 (1963), 14 ff., reprinted in *The Biblical Archaeologist Reader* II (1964), pp. 289 ff. The overlapping of vss. 45 and 46 is readily explained; there was a

story about Abimelech's slaughter of the innocents ending with the destruction of the city (vss. 42–45). There was also a story which emphasized Abimelech's destruction of both the temple and the conspirators as his unwitting collaboration with God. The compiler has merely placed them end to end.

Shechem's Tower . . . God's temple. See illustration 7.

the stronghold. The translation follows LXX^AL and Vulg., which suggests a relationship between the rare word in MT, *ṣᵉrīᵃḥ*, and Ar. *ṣarḥ*, "a lofty building or chamber *standing apart*" (Burney, p. 286, who, however, rejected the equation in this passage). Older commentaries have taken the lead from I Sam 13:6, where the same word stands in series with "caves, thickets, rock crags . . . and pits," suggesting that the *ṣᵉrīᵃḥ* must refer to some sort of underground chamber. See S. R. Driver, *Notes on the Hebrew Text and the Topography of the Books of Samuel,* 2d ed. (Oxford: Clarendon, 1913), p. 99. But excavations have shown that no such cave or crypt existed under the temple (*Shechem,* pp. 123–28). Thus *ṣᵉrīᵃḥ* must designate some part of the temple itself, possibly as the excavators suggest, the tower portion, inasmuch as the main room (cella) of the Late Bronze temple was not as strongly built as that of the earlier temple.

Covenant God. It is an ancient, pre-Yahwistic epithet which survives here. For the recognition of "God of the Covenant," also called "El the Judge," in a Hurrian hymn from Ugarit, see Frank M. Cross, Jr., *Canaanite Myth and Hebrew Epic* (Harvard University Press, 1973), p. 39.

48. *Mount Zalmon.* The name means "dark one" and is probably a reference to Ebal, the mountain of covenantal cursing. Raymond J. Tournay, *Revue biblique,* 66 (1959), 358–68. The argument, however, cannot appeal to the convenient location of the northwest gate at Shechem, which was apparently unused in the Late Bronze and Iron I periods.

The name Zalmon is otherwise unused in connection with the Shechem vale and is to be distinguished from the "Mount Zalmon" of Ps 68:14 (Djebel Ḥaurôn in Syria). Albright, *Hebrew Union College Annual,* 23 (1950–51), 23. The best argument for identifying our Zalmon with Ebal is the poetic justice which Tournay sought to document, pointing to the Tananir ruins as the setting for Jotham's speech. Just as Jotham had accurately proceeded to the ruins of an old covenant sanctuary on Gerizim, the mountain of covenantal blessing (Deut 27:12), so Abimelech had unerringly gathered his firewood on Ebal. (Deut 27:13–26; 28:15–68.) Cf. Josh 8:30–35.

49. *all the folk of Shechem's Tower.* An inclusio with "all the lords of Shechem's Tower" in vs. 46.

50–55. The narrative transition to Abimelech's last campaign is a tight one. Mention of Strong's Tower (see NOTE on vs. 51) in which the city folk took refuge made this a natural sequel to the devastation of the Shechem temple, and the conclusion forms an ironic contrast with vs. 49. Thus the two stories were probably tied together before being written down by the compiler.

Whether or not the Thebez campaign was the immediate sequel to Gaal's rebellion (and politically connected) is another question, for which the sources fail. Abimelech's move against Thebez perhaps had no direct connection with the settling of accounts with Gaal. In any case it was a way to further enhance his prestige and position as Israelite commander (vs. 22), now that the Shechem power base was wiped out.

50. *Thebez*. The longstanding identification of ancient Thebez with modern Ṭûbās is linguistically questionable and no signs of a Late Bronze–Iron I town have been found there. Malamat suggests that Thebez is a corrupted spelling of Tirzah (Tell el-Far‘ah) still farther to the northeast of Shechem. See Map 4. See also LOB, pp. 242–43.

51. *Strong's Tower*. Heb. *migdal*, "tower"; *‘ōz*, "strong." The word *‘ōz* is a theophorous element in a number of OT proper names as well as in Canaanite, and there is no difficulty in taking it as an appellative of El. We may thus adopt the suggestion that Thebez was supposed to have had a fortress-temple as did Shechem and Penuel (the latter destroyed by Gideon, 8:9, 17), and probably a number of other towns. *Shechem*, p. 255, n. 12.

and all the city's lords. Missing in LXX[B]; MT is perhaps conflate.

53. *some woman*. Heb. *'iššā 'aḥat*, lit. "one woman." The word "one" is used in the sense of the indefinite article, e.g. I Sam 6:7, 24:15, 26:20, and in the sense of "a certain one" in I Sam 1:1; II Sam 18:10; II Kings 4:1.

threw. The statement is a hyperbole, not so surprising in this narrative conclusion. She must have "dropped" it, and probably had help, as a single individual could hardly manage to throw one.

54. *squire*. See NOTE on 7:10.

55–57. These verses are a compiler's theological conclusion corresponding to the theological introduction to the period in 8:33–35.

55. *each to his own place*. In light of the fleeting references to "Israel" in 8:33–35 and 9:22, the implication seems to be that *Israelites* were those who recognized heaven's justice in the death of Abimelech; they went home.

56–57. The function of Jotham as Yahweh's diplomat (the *rīb*-bearer), implicit in the construction of the narrative, is here explicit. But Jotham had fled. The result in Israel, when God had repudiated Abimelech's murderous leadership, was a state of leaderless disorganization. Perhaps that is why, with the following notice of the first of the great administrator-judges, Tola, the thing to be specified is that he arose "in order to save Israel" (10:1).

57. *the curse of Jotham*. That is, the covenantal curse as expounded by Jotham.

COMMENT

The introduction to Abimelech illustrates one of the pragmatist's themes in the introduction to the judges era (2:17), but at this point it capitalizes on the statement in 8:27 that "all Israel" had recently prostituted themselves at Ophrah, where there was Gideon's ephod. A situation bad enough under Gideon now took a turn for the very worst, especially since the negotiations represented the local exploitation of religious covenant-making. Those Israelites who yielded to Abimelech's pretensions about being their king had simply made Covenant Baal their god, for they no longer accepted themselves as the liberated property of Yahweh, their covenant-keeping god. This emphasis is clear from the nonparallel constructions for the possessive in the Hebrew text.

Thanks to the recent archaeological work at Tell Balata, the history of Israelite Shechem has come into sharp focus. Throughout a long and strategically successful career in Middle Bronze Age history Shechem dominated the north central hill country. See illustration 6. Israel's patriarchal tradition had a number of connections with Shechem, and it can now be recognized that covenant had played a pivotal religious role (see illustration 7) in the kingdom of Shechem. The Middle Bronze city was destroyed in at least two campaigns, about 1550 and 1543, by Egyptian forces bent on uprooting the Hyksos and reclaiming Palestine for a native Egyptian Pharaoh. It was nearly a century before Shechem recovered, but the Late Bronze city became the flourishing capital of the famous Prince Labayu of the fourteenth-century Amarna letters.

The traditions make no claim (and archaeology finds no evidence) for a thirteenth-century destruction of Shechem. This has often led to the suggestion that Abimelech's story is the Shechem conquest tradition showing how Shechem became Israelite. (Sellin, *Wie wurde Sichem eine israelitische Stadt?* [Leipzig, 1922].) This hypothesis has to make its way upstream against the explicit flow of the chapter. The narrative presupposes a prior unity—all Israel—from which Abimelech and the Shechemites and collaborating Israelites are a nearly disastrous departure.

More recently, scholars have treated the Abimelech story as recounting the first, abortive, attempt at monarchy in Israel, but this theory is unable to account for the fact that in the whole of Scripture Abimelech is nowhere said to be "king" in "Israel." All that the ancient historian could imply was that some Israelites were deeply involved in Abimelech's island of monarchy at Shechem.

With careful attention to the forms of the narrative complex and the archaeological evidence for the long-standing element of covenant in Shechemite religion we can see approximately what happened. Religious tradition had paved the way for Shechem's peaceful entry (with the bulk of her population) into the Yahwist federation. The fact that here a great city did not have to be rebuilt may have been largely responsible for its choice as the site of the revolutionaries' congress, where Joshua presides in Josh 24. There is clear evidence that Shechem continued, for a period, at least, as the site of periodic covenantal assemblies; Deut 27 is generally regarded as a piece of early Shechem liturgy, stemming from the earliest days of Yahwism's ascendancy there.

Yet it is impossible to make sense out of the welter of traditions by thinking of Israel in this early period in geographical terms. Israel is, rather, a movement straining to remake the country through individuals who have agreed to live under one law, modeled on the international order, with Yahweh as their only king and with all the uncertainty that belongs to such a style of life. This explains why actual territorial claims were later such a problem to the historians of Israel and Judah. They were an ideal which had been forever frustrated, and according to ch. 1, an ideal which probably originated in the early assembly's plans for the future.

Careful attention to the confessional politics of early Israel also helps to understand the movement of the central sanctuary away from the Gilgal base camp (2:1–5 and NOTES; notice the anti-Bethel polemic in the same context) to a more central location at Shechem. From thence, with Abimelech's destruction of Shechem, the central sanctuary seems to have moved to Bethel (20:26–28); and finally it is found at Shiloh (I Sam 1:9) where it was safely off the beaten path of armies (for a while) and visited from time to time by Yahwists of surrounding territories (21:19). No doubt the later ascendancy of Shiloh was at least in part prompted by the tradition that there Joshua and the revolutionaries had proposed (by lot) the ideal partitioning of the land (Josh 18), having already shown preferential treatment to Judah at Gilgal (Josh 15), which they honored. Many details of the lists in Josh 15 and 18 reflect later realities, as does the element of exaggeration in the claims made for historical Joshua in the first half of that book (see Wright, JNES 5 [1946], 105–14). Yet there is nothing wrong with the nuclear claims of either half of the Joshua book.

Into the picture of Shechem's role as central sanctuary city the recent excavations at Tell Balata have introduced decisively new data, namely the massive destruction debris of the early twelfth-century city, which can only be correlated with the Abimelech story. If the Shechem assembly of Josh 24 is to be dated around the close of the thirteenth century, then Shechem's role as central sanctuary town was short-lived; and we are in a better position to understand both the strategic objectives of Gideon and Abimelech, on the one hand, and the perspective of the Deuteronomic Historian in his handling of the traditions, on the other.

The objective of Gideon and Abimelech had been to weld together a nation-state centered in Shechem, which was decisively situated in the north central hill country. Thus Freedman summarizes the account in a (paraphrased) note to the writer: Gideon and Abimelech perpetuated the policy of Joshua's day, when extraordinary efforts had been made to conciliate and amalgamate the population of Shechem into the confederation. Pursuing a similar objective of taking over one Canaanite stronghold and making that the center of rule, Saul and David finally succeeded at the end of the judges era. They succeeded "at the price of giving up on Shechem entirely, and trying a different location."

Abimelech's achievement has, in other words, been played down by an extremely hostile author. What is the significance of the fact that the Book of Judges virtually centers in the story of Abimelech? It appears that a vastly disproportionate space has been given to Gideon and Abimelech, whose careers in fact ought to precede Deborah and Baraq, instead of following them. On the archaeological evidence of a late twelfth-century date for Deborah and Baraq, see COMMENT on ch. 5. This evidence favors the tradition which remembered Gideon ahead of Baraq (I Sam 12:11 LXX, Syr.; Heb 11:32).

It is interesting, therefore, to observe an arithmetical progression in the space allotted to various segments of the Deuteronomic edition of Judges. That edition (late seventh century, telling the story to the time of the great reformer,

King Josiah), we have argued, extended from 2:1 to 18:31 (see Introduction, 34 ff., and NOTES on 1:1 – 2:5). It began with polemic against the Bethel sancuary (2:1–5) and ended with polemic against the Danite sanctuary (ch. 18). In the Hebrew Bible (*Biblia Hebraica*) seven pages tell the story from 2:5 to 6:1, the beginning of the Gideon segment. Ten and one-half pages are given to Gideon and Abimelech and a mere fourteen pages to all the rest. Ch. 9 is precisely the center of the Deuteronomic edition. It is difficult to avoid the conclusion that the historian has deliberately arranged his presentation so that the period of the judges begins, centers, and ends with accounts that devalue possible competitors to the Jerusalem Temple, thus endeavoring to legitimate King Josiah's policies in the late seventh century.

Deuteronomic theology also helps to clarify the hostility toward Abimelech. Unlike King Josiah, he had become king on his own initiative. To the Jerusalem historian it meant that Abimelech had assumed the prerogatives of God and had himself brought about the ruination of the venerable covenant temple together with a mass of victimized citizens. As noted above, the heavy destruction debris found at Shechem from early Iron I (early to mid-twelfth century) is to be correlated with the Abimelech story. That the great structure was never rebuilt as a temple (but only as a sturdy granary) corresponds to the way the story about Abimelech's defiling of the place was told: Yahweh won that war (declared by his diplomat Jotham) after Abimelech had made himself lord of the covenant and went around making and breaking agreements and implementing curses.

With all that can be known today about the struggle of early Israel to actualize a new society modeled on the international order, with maximum human variety, because God alone was king, it is not difficult to see through the bias of the Abimelech narrator. What one sees is a hotbed of conspiratorial action and reaction. Abimelech had contrived to be both King of Shechem and field commander in Israel; Gaal, using a purely genealogical appeal, would be happy to be merely King of Shechem. Thus Abimelech's divided loyalty was his undoing; he wound up suing Israelite troops against Shechem, and later Thebez. Then some woman dropped a millstone on him and all the Israelites who were involved with him went home.

XXI. Two Minor Judges
(10:1–5)

Tola

10 ¹ After Abimelech, in order to save Israel, arose Tola, "son" of Puah, "son" of Dodo, a man of Issachar. He lived at Shamir in the Ephraimite hill country. ² He judged Israel for twenty-three years; when he died he was buried at Shamir.

Jair

³ After him arose Jair the Gileadite; he judged Israel for twenty-two years.

⁴ Now he had thirty "sons" who rode thirty donkeys. Thirty towns belonged to them. Their towns are called Havvoth-jair, which are in the land of Gilead, to this very day. ⁵ When Jair died he was buried at Qamon.

NOTES

10:1–5. These verses introduce the first of the minor judges. The fact that several of the same names appear elsewhere as clan designations (e.g. Tola and Puah in Num 26:23; I Chron 7:1 ff.) indicated to earlier critical scholars that the same names in Judges represent the personification of complex tribal movements, comparable to the idea that Shechem had a "father" (9:28). Moore, p. 270–71. That Tola, the first of the minor judges, is further specified as "a man of Issachar" (vs. 1) seems, however, to reflect an awareness of the possible confusion of personal and clan names.

More recently scholars working from the form-critical and history-of-traditions perspective have considered the minor judges (including Jephthah, whose career is framed by the same rubrics) to be historical figures and have in fact thought they could recognize in the reports about them the only clear reflections of the office of judge in premonarchical Israel. From this point of view, the judges of the confederation (that is, the minor judges) were either proclaimers of Israel's own sacral apodictic law or transmitters of the conditional case law which Israel inherited from all parts of the ancient Near East. Thanks to recent intense work on ancient international law we can recognize elements of historical accuracy in both of these positions and note progress all along the way.

1. *After Abimelech.* Only here is the predecessor to a minor judge mentioned with him in the same pericope. Otherwise the standing introduction is simply, "After him" (vs. 3 and 12:8, 11, 13). Thus a preformed list has been broken apart, and pieces of it used to plug gaps in the narrative presentation of the period.

in order to save. On the verb *yš'* "to save" in the sense of preserving existence, see Introduction, p. 6. Scholars who take this to mean that Tola too was a military hero normally overlook its syntax, here represented in translation as literally as possible. Rather the point is quite directly made that, in contrast with Abimelech's effort and short-lived success as king, what Israel needed was good administration, which Tola provided as "He judged Israel for twenty-three years" (vs. 2). The different locations of the length of term within the pericopes indicate that these specifications derive from the original list, not from editorial activity, as Noth rightly observed in *The History of Israel,* p. 102.

Tola. The meaning of the name is not clear; "worm" (Heb. *tōla'*) is perhaps unlikely.

"son" of. It is now quite probable that Heb. *ben* (son of) in the Chronicles census lists originates in political affiliation, and the same thing will be recognized as true in many other contexts. That this sense was obscured in later centuries is indicated in this verse by LXX^B which rendered *ben-dōdō* as "his nephew," lit. "son of his uncle." Gideon had a council of "seventy sons" which is probably a political number (see also NOTES on 17:5 and 11).

Against the oversimplification of early Israel's social organization, due to excessively literal handling of the kinship language, see Mendenhall, "The Relation of the Individual to Political Society in Ancient Israel," *Biblical Studies in Memory of H. C. Alleman,* eds. J. M. Myers, O. Reinherr, and H. N. Bream (New York: J. J. Augustin, 1960), pp. 89–108; "Biblical History in Transition," *The Bible and the Ancient Near East,* esp. pp. 32–44.

He lived at Shamir. The place is thought to be identical with Samaria (Map 4); there are other references which "suggest that certain clans from the tribe of Issachar had affinities with the Ephraimite hill country." LOB, p. 223.

2. *buried at Shamir.* The regularity of the death-and-burial notice at the end of each minor judge pericope seems also to belong to the form (and is not redactional) since there is nothing quite like it in connection with Othniel, Ehud, Shamgar, and Deborah, while the conclusions to the remaining two (Gideon and Samson) display editorial manipulation of this formal element (see 8:32; 15:20; 16:31). See also the notice of the death of Eli, after having "judged Israel forty years" (I Sam 4:18).

3. *Jair.* "He enlightens." Apparently the name of his "father" had been lost in the process of transmission, as in the case of the ninth-century prophet Elijah, another "Gileadite" without patronymic (Freedman, personal communication). Jair is a "son" of Manasseh in Num 32:41 and Deut 3:14.

4. *he had thirty "sons."* The kinship language in these pericopes seems to denote a confederate subgrouping (see Map 2, D-2). Such an approach also helps to understand the fluctuations in the number of Jair-villages across the years. LXX here credits Jair with thirty-two sons, while I Chron 2:22 credits him with twenty-three cities. The number of participating villages varies from time to time.

Thirty towns (Heb. 'ārīm) *belonged to them.* Restored from LXX. The writer has published the reconstruction, where the first half of MT is a conflation of variants, differing only in the way they referred to the number of donkeys ('*ªyārīm*): VT 16 (1966), 295–96. The Hebrew text then was ripe for haplography, leaving nine of sixteen words in sequence ending with *mem,* but obscuring the original wordplay. The wordplay with 'ārīm (towns) explains why we have the rare word for donkeys ('*ªyārīm*) rather than *hªmōr* (of covenantal usage in 9:28) or '*ªtōnōt* ("females," chosen *metri causa* in 5:10). Wordplay does not explain the use of '*ªyārīm* later in the list (12:14) where the writer is interested, rather, in Abdon's "forty 'sons'" and "thirty 'grandsons'"—an odd progression unless the words are used metaphorically of political affiliation (another seventy). Other evidence for metaphorical use is that a time when so many "sons" and "grandsons" could ride unhindered would have to be one of peace, that is, good administration. The same point is made in the note about Ibzan's success in arranging sixty marriages (12:8–9), half of them obviously outside his own primary sphere but very much, we may assume, within "Israel." To go farther afield in this period was considered to be a reckless risk to league security (ch. 21).

Pedersen rightly remarked on the special sacral significance which Israel assigned to the donkey which "was not admitted to their world in the same way as the ox." The fact that the sequel to Passover singles out the firstling asses (like the first-born sons) to be redeemed by a sheep or a kid, instead of being sacrificed (Exod 13:13; 34:20), means that "the ass has become so well established in the Israelitish world that it cannot avoid contact with the law of sanctification, but it has come too late to be sanctified by sacrifice itself . . . The firstling ass is given to holiness, but cannot be absorbed by it." *Israel III–IV,* 317–18. The only adjustment necessary today in Pedersen's description is to note not that the donkey came too late but that its social significance among the Habiru caravaneers was already too well established. This was obviously obscured in later centuries, but not completely. Exod 13:13 regards the human males to be redeemed as the first-born of '*ādām* (mankind, the species) "among your sons." That is, "sons" in the passover ritual are participants in the new humanity that becomes possible with the exodus from Egypt and the covenant in Israel. Their heritage is not genealogically determined.

Havvoth-jair. "Villages of Jair." Located in Gilead (I Kings 4:13) or Bashan (Josh 13:30). Map 2.

5. *Qamon.* Usually identified with modern Qamm, on the Jordan–Irbid road. Map 2, D-2.

COMMENT

After the sustained turmoil of the Abimelech narrative the notices about two of the minor judges provided a possibility for some uneventful peace. This has been obscured in recent discussions by a preoccupation with the idea that these notices originate in an independent archive. It is, however, an extremely odd antiquarian or administrative interest, even in antiquity, that concerns itself with the number of a man's sons, daughters, grandsons, donkeys, and weddings.

It is likely that the list of minor judges once included most if not all of the judges, but has only been cited directly, in the finished edition of Judges, in connection with the peaceful interludes of the period, and the exemplary administration of Jephthah (chs. 11–12).

The minor judges were the successful administrators in the period, whose nonviolent administrations generated no blood-and-thunder tradition. The exception is Jephthah, whose story is surrounded by the same minor judge rubrics.

XXII. What's Past Is Prologue
(10:6–16)

10 6 Israelites continued doing what was evil in Yahweh's sight. They served Baal and Astarte: the deities of Aram, Sidon, Moab, the Ammonites, and the Philistines. They deserted Yahweh; they did not serve him. 7 So Yahweh's wrath blazed against Israel, and he sold them into the power of the Philistines and Ammonites.

8 They oppressed and suppressed the Israelites that eighteenth year—all the Israelites, that is, who were beyond the Jordan in the Amorite country in Gilead. 9 But the Ammonites crossed the Jordan to fight Judah also, as well as Benjamin and the house of Ephraim. Israel was besieged!

10 The Israelites cried out to Yahweh, "We have sinned against you! Indeed, we have deserted our God and served Baal!"

11 But Yahweh said to the Israelites, "Was it not from Egypt and the Amorite alike, from Ammonites as well as from Philistines 12 and Sidonians—even Amaleq and Maon oppressed you! But when you cried out to me, I rescued you from their power. 13 But you have betrayed me and served other gods. Therefore I will no longer save you. 14 Go on! Cry out to the gods that you have chosen! Let them be the ones to rescue you in your time of trouble!"

15 The Israelites said to Yahweh, "We have sinned. Do to us entirely as you please, only please deliver us today!" 16 They removed the foreign gods from their midst and served Yahweh alone, and the plight of Israel became intolerable to him.

NOTES

10:6. *continued doing what was evil.* The same formula occurs in 3:12 (Ehud), 4:1 (Deborah), and 13:1 (Samson) and is not quite as forceful as the blanket statement that introduced the entire judges era in 2:11, 3:7, "Israelites did what was evil . . ." Among the subsequent "hero" units, that stronger form of indictment is employed only in the case of the Midianite crisis (6:1).

served . . . deserted . . . did not serve. By repeating the one verb and explicating it with the other in terms of treason, the narrator carefully prepares for the sudden resolution of the predicament in vs. 16.

Baal and Astarte. See NOTE on 2:11.

Aram. The editor's referent is presumably 3:7–11 where, we have suggested, the EVV translation "Aram" is highly problematical and probably the remnant of a place name, Armon-harim. These verses are relatively late. See COMMENT.

Sidon is the only one not mentioned by that name in the first half of the book. Moran suggests that it be taken as a synonym for "Canaan" in 4:2. *Biblica* 46 (1965), 227.

Conspicuous for its absence here is any reference to gods of the Midianites, who perhaps "go unmentioned because they were felt to be outside the immediate circle of Israel's neighbors and of less immediate concern." Moran, *Biblica* 46 (1965), 228. Actually there is nothing in the Gideon tradition to suggest that Midianite deities were ever a problem. Rather, it was the new confederation that caused concern, as a threat to Israel's very existence (chs. 6–8). The problematical deities were those associated with what Israel envied as a better existence (Caananite).

Moab. 3:12–30. See Map 2, D-5.

the Ammonites, and the Philistines. The shift from proper names to a grammatical class specification (lit. "sons of Ammon") and a gentilic (Philistines) tallies well with the archaeological data. Ammon was the last nation to emerge in Transjordan; and Philistia was, like Israel, a new establishment in Canaan. The referents of this indictment are generally taken to be the Ammonite collaboration with Eglon (3:12–13) and the Sea Peoples leadership opposing Deborah and Baraq (chs. 4–5). Repetition of the names in vs. 7 indicates that they are being singled out from the preceding peoples for special attention. Since the Philistines extended their influence into the region east of the Jordan, the link here is probably political, although the details elude us. The narrative interest is on the Ammonite side, for it was on that side that Jephthah was effective.

7. *Philistines and Ammonites.* That they are mentioned here in the reverse order to the climax of the indictment in vs. 6 is not a sign of mixed sources. It is the stylistic device of chiasmus, used to link the two statements. Freedman, private communication.

8. *that eighteenth year.* The Hebrew is ambiguous and might also be rendered "that year (eighteen years)" with the parenthesis explained as secondary. But this is no round number; and the sense "eighteenth" is supported

by parallel usage elsewhere, e.g. the "thirteenth" and "fourteenth" years in Gen 14:4–5. Since this vignette focuses upon the severity of the crisis and its resolution, the number may well refer to the final year of the Philistine-Ammonite oppression. I owe to Freedman this solution to a difficult text.

9. *Judah also.* This is the first mention of the great southern tribe, since the notices of the secondary introduction in 1:1–19, 22 (elsewhere only in 15:9–11 and chs. 17–20). The name of Judah here is as hard to dislodge from the earliest form of the tradition, as is "Philistines" in vss. 6 and 7. The clear implication from all of this is that Judah was very much a part of the league but not a noteworthy participant in its defensive wars.

Israel was besieged. As in the introduction to the first half of the book, 2:15 (They were besieged!).

10–16. Richter has coined a fitting designation for the *Gattung* represented here: a theological story in dialogue form (*Ein geschichtstheologischer Dialog*). *Retterbuches,* p. 88. It is, however, a piece without parallel.

It appears that what has happened in vss. 6–16 is that the pragmatic introduction has been further exegeted by converting a piece of the framework (which had originally taken its lead from the bare narratives themselves) into new dramatic confrontations between Yahweh and Israel, as at other key points (notably 2:1–5 and 6:7–10). The result is an effective roadblock against any merely cyclical interpretation of the presentation of the judges period, save for the sake of irony.

10. *The Israelites cried out to Yahweh. See* NOTE on 3:9.

11–12. There is historical, geographical, and social logic reflected in the grouping of seven names in this list. "Egypt and the Amorite" (vs. 11) harks back to the beginning of the story of Israel and its initial successes in Transjordan against Sihon the Amorite (Num 21:21–31). The recollection of those events will be pivotal to Jephthah's negotiations with the king of the Ammonites in ch. 11. In "from Ammonites as well as from Philistines and Sidonians" (vs .11) is summarized the recent opposition on both sides of the river. "Philistines and Sidonians" (vs. 11–12) belong together by virtue of the masculine plural endings in Hebrew; they form a north-south axis. For "Sidon" as an echo of "Canaan" in 4:2 (implying a Sea Peoples coalition) see NOTE on vs. 6. "Amaleq and Maon" (vs. 12), the last two oppressors, bring the list to a total of seven names. These two belong together by virtue of parallel form in Hebrew; and both refer to specifically nomadic groups. Amaleqites were supporters of Eglon, king of Moab, in the time of Ehud (3:13).

The verses have clearly suffered in transmission, due more to scribal accident than to editorial manipulation, to judge from the character of most textual problems in the book. The loss of verbs happened early enough for the versions to preserve a uniform attempt at improvement, reading the nouns of both verses as subject of the verb "oppressed" in vs. 11.

12. *Maon.* With MT where LXX (followed by most authorities) reads "Midian." The difference is not easily explained on the basis of epigraphy. On the other hand "Maon" is plausibly connected with the Meunites who come from the same general region as the Midianites. "The homeland of the Meunim lay to the east of the line of Edomite border fortresses protecting the eastern frontier of Edom" against invasion from the desert. Gold, IDB III, 368. We

suggest that LXX in our verse is a secondary interpretation, and probably a correct one, referring to the larger desert confederation to which Maon belonged. See Midian, Map 1.

14–15. There is no hiatus between these verses, as was supposed by older literary analysis. Rather, we have here tightly constructed rhetoric showing how Israel's experience of the first half of the period had become habit forming. But there was nothing automatic about Yahweh's response (vs. 14). They decided to trust him anyway, and he delivered them (vs. 15).

The older source-critical distinction (e.g. Moore, p. 281) between "other gods" of vs. 13 (*D*) and "foreign gods" in vs. 16 (*E*) obscures the change of speakers: Yahweh in vs. 13, a narrator in vs. 16.

15. *entirely as you please*. Lit. "according to whatever is the good (Heb. *ṭōb*) in your eyes." The next savior judge will be enlisted from the land of *ṭōb* (11:3).

16. *served*. Narrative inclusio with vs. 6.

alone. With LXX^B, a variant which makes explicit the force of the declarative sentence.

COMMENT

These verses form a theological introduction to the second half of Judges, beginning with the crisis that was finally surmounted by the leadership of Jephthah. The section displays the familiar marks of the pragmatic compiler (e.g. doing evil, external oppressor, crying out) at the outset. But it has been expanded by summary references to Israel's opponents, both past (Aram, Sidon, Moab, Ammonites, and Philistines) and present/future (Philistines and Ammonites). The reversal in the sequence of the future oppressors is the editor's way of preparing us for the reversal that takes place, a few verses later, in the encounter with Yahweh (vss. 11–16).

The speech of Yahweh in vss. 11–16 is part of the same editorial expansion. Compare the charge brought by a "prophet" in 6:7–10, by an "angel" in 2:1–5. All three are Deuteronomic contexts; whereas, on the other hand, Yahweh speaks directly to the protagonists only within the old narrative units (see especially Gideon). Here the point is emphasized that the Ammonite crisis loomed large during a vacancy in the well-established office of judge. This time, however, the machinery for nomination and oracular confirmation produced only more domestic judgment, and that was understood as the necessary prelude to any success against the Ammonites.

Lip service would not suffice. They had to put behind them the cause of their guilt and fear (see 6:7–10)—other gods. The Ammonite menace in Transjordan is here presented as the counterpart of the earlier Midianite problem west of the river in the days of Gideon. The narrative will quickly make the point that once the immobilized leaders of the east bank begin to deal again with the freebooting exile, Jephthah (11:1–11), deliverance will be on its way. Thus it looks as though this little homiletical vignette is a commentary on the old narrative of Jephthah, whose extraordinary career as judge really began when he was prejudged and driven out by his own "family."

XXIII. The Ammonite Threat
(10:17–18)

10 17 The Ammonites were mustered, and they set up camp inside Gilead; and so the Israelites gathered and set up camp at Mizpah. 18 The captains of the force of Gilead said to one another, "Who is the man who will start the fighting with the Ammonites? He shall be Head of all the inhabitants of Gilead!"

NOTES

10:17–18. These verses yield a rather direct but distorted image of the process by which one was supposed to rise to a position of leadership within the tribal confederacy. Here the captains pose the question "to one another" (vs. 18), but apparently not to the assembly.

17. The two statements here pick up the conditioned-reflex theme of vss. 10–14. The army of Ammon was "mustered" (niphal of *s‘q*), using technical military language as in Baraq's muster in 4:10 (*z‘q*, "called," is a by-form), and Gideon's muster in 6:35 and 7:23–24. The Israelites on this occasion merely "gathered." The assembly apparently failed, as due process deteriorated into haggling among the military specialists.

inside. Assuming that the text asserts that there was an invasion of Israelite territory, the preposition *b*, "inside," might also mean "against," in which case "Gilead" is a town, perhaps "Jabesh-Gilead," or "Ramoth-Gilead." See Map 2, D-3. The evidence is ambiguous.

18. *The captains of the force of Gilead*. With LXX^A. As has frequently been noted, grammatical anomaly in MT is often the result of the partial, or subsequently corrupted, combination of variants, in this case *śārē ‘am gil‘ad* (LXX^A) and *śārē gil‘ad* (MT, LXX^B). For a variety of comparable textual relationships in Joshua and Judges, see the writer's articles in VT 13 (1963), 479–82; 16(1966), 294–98.

captains. Their question is as inappropriate as the one posed at the outset of the book (1:1; see NOTE and COMMENT). The answer to their question here will be as surprising as the answer at the outset of the book (2:1–5): the new judge will not be found among the most likely prospects, the recognized military specialists.

Head. Another term for the highest tribal office in the period prior to the monarchy, with antecedent significance for military operations traceable to the Mari period. Mendenhall, JBL 77 (1958), esp. 55–58.

COMMENT

These verses comprise another preformed narrative section, as indicated by repetition of "Gilead" in each of the three sentences, and have been used intact by the pragmatic compiler. They pose the Ammonite problem from the administrative angle, whereas vss. 10–16 inserted by the later Deuteronomic editor focused, as we have seen, upon the theological implications of the crisis.

The trouble with the captains of the force was that none of them wanted to go. The implication is that the high office of judge is here regarded as a protection against the erosion of the good life enjoyed by the captains. The judge would "start the fighting" (vs. 18) and perhaps finish it.

This final narrative form balances the bumbling approach of the people in the face of the Ammonite threat (vss. 10–16) with the self-serving stance of their captains.

XXIV. The Recall of Jephthah
(11:1–11)

The Savior

11 ¹ Jephthah the Gileadite was a knight. He was the son of a prostitute. Gilead had sired Jephthah. ² But Gilead's wife also bore him sons; and when that woman's sons grew up, they expelled Jephthah and told him, "you shall not be an heir in our father's house, since you are son of another woman." ³ So Jephthah fled from his brothers and made his home in the land of Tob. And the mercenaries gathered around Jephthah. They went with him.

To The Rescue

⁴ At the end of the year the Ammonites went to war against Israel. ⁵ And it was then, when the Ammonites went to war against Israel, that the elders of Gilead went to fetch Jephthah from the land of Tob. ⁶ They said to Jephthah, "Come! Be our ruler; and we'll fight the Ammonites!" ⁷ But Jephthah said to the elders of Gilead, "Didn't you despise me and expel me from my company and send me away from you? So why have you come to me now? Because you are in trouble?" ⁸ And the elders of Gilead said to Jephthah, "Not so. We have come to you now, so that you may go with us, fight the Ammonites, and be Head of all of us—all the inhabitants of Gilead!"

⁹ So Jephthah said to the elders of Gilead, "If you take me back to fight the Ammonites and Yahweh subdues them before me, then I will be your Head." ¹⁰ The elders of Gilead said to Jephthah, "Yahweh will be witness between us; we will be sure to do as you say." ¹¹ So Jephthah went along with the elders of Gilead, and the people installed him over them as Head and ruler; and Jephthah recited all his "words" before Yahweh at Mizpah.

NOTES

11:1. *Jephthah.* A shortened form of a sentence name, like the place name involving the same verbal form, *yiptaḥ-'el*, "God opens [the womb?]" in Josh 19:14, 27.

the Gileadite. Cf. 10:3 and NOTE. Elsewhere Gilead is mentioned as "son" of Machir and "grandson" of Manasseh, but the name is also the eponym of the territory (tribe?) of Gilead in northern Transjordan. Num 26:29–30; 27:1; 36:1; Josh 17:1, 3; Judg 5:17; I Chron 2:21, 23; 7:14, 17. Josh 17:1 and 3 indicate that "Gilead" could be used for both person and territory in the same context without confusion.

a knight. Heb. *gibbōr ḥayl*, like Gideon in 6:11–12, one trained in upper-class combat, and who furnished his own equipment as well as a squire and/or a unit of soldiers.

He was the son of a prostitute. Gilead had sired Jephthah. I agree with Burney's conclusion (Burney, p. 308) that here "the *district* is personified as father of Jephthah" but suggest that it is no argument for a late date of vss. 1b–2. That "Gilead had sired Jephthah" explicates the statement that he was "son of a prostitute," father unknown. All of this explicates the opening statement about "Jephthah the Gileadite." For some reason individuals from that part of the country were often referred to without patronymic (see NOTE on the name Jair, 10:3). Jephthah *in fact* had no patronym, and no Gileadite future; this seems to be the opening thrust of the story, which proceeds from the expulsion of Jephthah by his contemporaries to the formation, around Jephthah, of an effective guerilla band.

2. There appears to be an inverted relationship with narrative elements in the story of Abimelech (ch. 9) who ascended to power at Shechem through relationship on his mother's side and by liquidating the properly constituted opposition.

3. *Tob.* Map 2, E-2. Lit. "good," but also a technical term for covenantal "amity." Tob was a Syrian town later subject, it appears, to Ma'acah in alliance with Beth-rehob, Zobah, and the Ammonites against David (II Sam 10:6–8). On its history, see Mazar, BA 25 (1962), 98–120. The name is used twice, in quick succession, calling attention to itself. Since a man with Jephthah's background and associations would scarcely have spent all his time in one place, the place name was probably selected because of its covenantal nuance. Compare Abimelech's negotiations with the lords of Shechem and his question to them in 9:2. Thus "the land of Tob" in vs. 3 offsets "Gilead" in vss. 1 and 2.

mercenaries. Cf. 9:4.

gathered around. The verb is *lqṭ* "to glean." Jephthah's partners were drawn from the dregs of society. For the iterative function of the reflexive or middle voice conjugation (hithpael) in early Hebrew narrative, see Speiser, *Genesis,* AB, vol.1, 1964, p. LXIX.

with him. An inclusio with the independent pronoun in vs. 1. Thus these verses comprise one short Jephthah story, complete in itself, and were not to be revised by a redactor in the interest of smoother transitions.

4–11. This is the old story of the recall of Jephthah. The clear implication of the narrator is that with his recall Israel was well on its way to being reconstituted in Gilead. For the title was irregularly offered and accepted, but properly concluded.

4. *At the end of the year.* Heb. *wayhī miy-yāmīm.* I owe to Freedman the pointer that *mymym* can have this meaning. He compares another Gileadite passage, I Kings 18:1, where the chronology supports this meaning for *ymym rbym* and its variant there, *mymym.*

6. *Come! Be our ruler.* Heb. *qāṣīn,* "ruler," but also a ranking officer within Joshua's organization (Josh 10:24). Presumably there was nothing in the title that was objectionable to the narrator. What was irregular, for the period, was the manner of its bestowal, which indicated that Yahweh had now been relegated to the position of confirming the elders' own selection of the highest leadership. Cf. appropriation of such traditions in the classical prophets, e.g. Isa 3:6.

7. *company.* Lit. "father's house" as in vs. 2, but here it is clearly the military unit as in 6:15. Note that in vs. 2 it was the full-blooded sons who ruled that Jephthah would not "be an heir," that is, receive land in exchange for future military service.

and send me away from you? This clause is restored from LXX, where it dropped out of MT through haplography due to homoioarkton.

8. *Not so.* With LXX^A (Heb. *l' kn*) where MT's *lkn,* "therefore," may be explained as an error, omitting the quiescent *aleph* of the negative. The diplomatic denial by the elders serves to confirm the truth of Jephthah's charge.

fight . . . and be Head of all. This forms a chiasm with vs. 6 where the order is: "Be our ruler; and we will fight." The shift from "ruler" (*qāṣīn*) in vs. 6 to "Head" (*rōš*) suggests that the elders have increased the offer. For Jephthah picks up the second proposal, not the first: namely fight now, and be established as head man later on. It may be that *qāṣīn* refers to his role as temporary field commander, while *rōš* refers to the permanent post of tribal chief.

9–11. The conclusion of negotiations is here presented as exemplary. Bestowal of the high office will indeed turn upon Yahweh's ratification of the proceedings.

10. *Yahweh will be witness.* Lit. "Yahweh will be listening between us." The construction is a little peculiar with the participle of *šm'.* This promise by the elders is another example of an echoing relationship with the Abimelech story, where Jotham shouts: "Listen to me, O Lords of Shechem; and let God listen to you!" (9:7).

For another example of the same usage of *šm'* as the desirable conclusion of diplomatic action, see vs. 28.

we will be sure. Hebrew uses *'im lō,* the emphatic affirmative, with oaths expressed or implied.

11. *his "words."* There must be a reason for the avoidance of a specific

vowing word here. Jephthah's "vow" only appears in the sequel. "Words" can stand for covenant stipulations in Deuteronomic formulations (Deut 5:22 and repeatedly). See vs. 28.

before Yahweh at Mizpah. A most surprising conclusion to the pericope, since neither the Transjordanian amphictyonic center (Mizpah, or Mizpeh as in vs. 29; also Gen 31:49) nor the historical Israel which it presupposes has been anywhere mentioned in the body of the narrative. The effect is a calculated one, as is confirmed at the outset of the next section (11:12), where Jephthah first uses "envoys," like Yahweh at the outset of Gideon's career (6:11) and later Gideon himself (6:35).

The location of Transjordanian Mizpah is uncertain, but is surely to be sought in the vicinity of Jebel Jel'ad and Khirbet Jel'ad, south of the Jabboq. Aharoni, LOB, p. 243. See Map 2, D-3.

COMMENT

In vss. 1–3 the reader is introduced to Jephthah, who is placed in conscious contrast to Gideon and Abimelech by the emphasis on his illegitimate parentage, his expulsion by his father's legitimate sons, and his mercenary associates. Merely inserting a temporal qualifier ("At the end of the year") at the beginning of vs. 4 tied vss. 4–11, originally a separate unit, tightly to the first unit. The kinship language used to describe military organization in vss. 4–11 is used literally in vss. 1–3 which are a later introduction to the older story that begins in vs. 4.

The pragmatist capitalized on the problematics of Jephthah's background by merely juxtaposing these units with the one about the captains. Thus the story about the elevation of Jephthah as judge begins on an ominous note. The first hint to dispel that feeling comes in the negotiations between Jephthah and the elders of Gilead. Notice the entirely plausible implication that when the captains were reduced to bickering inaction the elders had to take matters into their own hands (cf. 4:5). They, too, however, proceed cautiously, apparently offering Jephthah nothing more than the rewards of a successful field commander. Their new-found respect for his prowess, he indicates, is curious; and so they promptly add to the offer the title of Head of all the Gileadites. Here is another clear indication that the office of judge involved both administrative and military responsibilities.

Verse 11 is our first clear indication that, as the narrator saw it, instating Jephthah would result in justice for all parties concerned because Jephthah recited all his "words" before Yahweh. Nowhere else is there any direct mention of the judge's oath of office, although it is treated poetically in the Song of Deborah (5:7–9) and probably lies behind the sparkling conclusion to the story of Gideon's enlistment (6:22–24). The pivotal significance of the judge's direct approach to Israel's Sovereign was also regarded as the factor that at last made a judge out of Samson (15:18–20).

11   12 Jephthah dispatched envoys to the king of the Ammonites to say, "What is at issue between us, that you have invaded my land to fight against me?"

13 The king of the Ammonites said to Jephthah's envoys, "Because Israel seized my land, when they came up from Egypt, from the Arnon all the way to the Jabboq and to the Jordan! Return them now peaceably, and I will go." So the envoys returned to Jephthah.

14 But Jephthah again dispatched envoys to the king of the Ammonites and said to him, 15 Thus says Jephthah: "Israel seized no Moabite land, no land of the Ammonites. 16 For when they came up from Egypt, Israel traveled through the desert, as far as the Reed Sea, and came to Qadesh. 17 Israel dispatched envoys to the king of Edom to say, 'Let me pass, if you please, through your land.' But the king of Edom would not listen, so he also sent to the king of Moab. But he too was unwilling to allow them to cross. Israel remained at Qadesh. 18 They traveled through the desert and circled around the land of Edom and the land of Moab; they came to the east of the land of Moab and set up camp on the other side of the Arnon. They did not enter Moabite territory, for the Arnon was the Moabite border. 19 Israel dispatched envoys to Sihon, king of the Amorites, king of Heshbon; and Israel said to him, 'Let me pass, if you please, through your land to my holy place.' 20 But Sihon did not trust Israel to cross his territory. Sihon assembled his entire force, set up camp at Jahaz, and fought Israel. 21 Yahweh, God of Israel, delivered Sihon and his entire force to Israel's power, and they defeated them. Thus Israel assumed possession of all the land of the Amorites who inhabited that country. 22 They acquired possession of all the territory of the Amorites, from Arnon to the Jabboq, and from the desert to the

Jordan. 23 So now Yahweh, God of Israel, evicted the Amorites before his people Israel. Will you dispossess him? 24 Is it not right that whatever your god Chemosh expropriates for you, you should possess; and that everything that Yahweh our God expropriates for us, we should possess? 25 Now, are you any better than Balaq, son of Zippor, the Moabite king? Did he institute proceedings against Israel? Did he actually go to war with them? 26 While Israel inhabited Heshbon with its dependencies, and Aroer with its dependencies, and all the cities on the banks of the Arnon (some three hundred years!), why did you not liberate them within that time? 27 I have not wronged you; but you are doing me harm by waging war against me. Yahweh, the Judge, will decide today between the Israelites and the Ammonites!"

28 But the king of the Ammonites would not heed the words of Jephthah which he sent him.

NOTES

11:12–28. The two standing critical theories about the composition of this material are here inadequate. According to the first, presented in detail by Moore (p. 283) and more recently refined by Otto Eissfeldt in *Die Quellen des Richterbuches* (Leipzig: J. C. Hinrichs, 1925), p. 76, the negotiations were entirely with Moab, not the Ammonites. According to the second, whose principal advocate is Burney (pp. 298–305), historically the negotiations were between Jephthah and the Ammonites, with some conflation from another account of negotiations with Moab. The trouble with both theories is that this unit shows no signs of the reflective glossing that accompanied such redactional activity elsewhere in the book (e.g. 1:36); the only clearly secondary phrase is the total "three hundred years" in vs. 26.

Actually these verses represent the only narrative account of Israelite diplomacy toward a nation-state in the Book of Judges. The bulk of the unit (vss. 15–27) is one long speech by Jephthah, delivered to the Ammonite king by one of Jephthah's couriers. That the two successive delegations from Jephthah are not to be traced to separate sources follows from the character of vss. 14–27 as compared to vss. 12–13. In vss. 12–13 the first delegation addresses a brief, direct question to the king of Ammonites, receives an equally brief, direct answer, and then goes home. But in vss. 14–27 the second delegation makes a long, labored, and meticulous appeal to historical precedent in specific response to the answer given to the first delegation, and receives no reply at all (vs. 28). The unit is thus one of the earliest examples of the *Bundesbruch-rīb* (covenant-lawsuit) which later governs the prophetic critique of both Israel and the nations and which reappears elsewhere in Judges as a result of Deuteronomic redactional activity (2:1–5, 6:7–10, 10:11–16). See James Limburg, JBL 88

(1969), 297–99. As applied to the Jephthah episode, the term "covenant" lawsuit is a bit misleading, because Ammon is not a party to that treaty. Rather it is
a matter of the covenant confederation suing for peace with a nation-state, but
ready to go to war if diplomacy fails.

12. *What is at issue between us.* Lit. "What to me and to thee?" For the same
question, see II Sam 16:10, 19:22; I Kings 17:18; II Kings 3:13; II Chron
35:21.

13. *my land.* Both parties use the same expressions, in the archetypal pattern
of conflicting claims.

from the Arnon . . . to the Jabboq and to the Jordan. For the fuller, four-
point geographical description, see vs. 22 and Map 2, D-5, D-3.

The Ammonite claim is based upon their assumption of Moabite sovereignty.
Regardless of how the transfer took place (usually by conquest) the successor
inherited all rights and claims of the predecessor along with his territory.

Return them. Presumably a reference to the cities in the disputed territory.

and I will go. Supplied by LXX[B]. Its loss can be explained as due to homoioarkton in Hebrew.

So the envoys returned to Jephthah. Restored from LXX[A]. Another example
of haplography triggered by homoioarkton in Hebrew.

15. *no Moabite land, no land of the Ammonites.* Not two different territories, but land which was formerly Moabite and now Ammonite. Jephthah is
being technically meticulous. By naming "Moabite land" first, Jephthah denies
that Israel ever did anything comparable to Ammon's more recent expansion
into Moab.

17. *he too was unwilling to allow them to cross.* With some LXX witnesses,
where MT is abrupt: *wᵉ-lō' 'ābā,* "But he was unwilling. . . ." With the verb
'bh we expect the infinitive. It is, however, impossible to explain the loss in MT
by any common kind of scribal lapse.

18. *for the Arnon was the Moabite border.* In verbatim agreement, as far as
it goes, with Num 21:13. This begins a section in which the speech of Jephthah
is directly related to the epic tradition.

19–21. These verses are the same as Num 21:21–22a, 23–24a, with minor
variations except at the end, which is strikingly different and presupposes a
very different life setting. A similarly close relationship exists between the narrative in Numbers and the speech of Moses in Deut 2:26–35. The latter is by
far the latest of the three passages and is a considerably fuller account. Jephthah
confines himself to diplomatically relevant matters.

19. *Israel dispatched envoys.* Just as Jephthah is now doing. Only here is
Israel represented as performing in a manner consistent with the preconquest
organization of Israel on the move.

Sihon, king of the Amorites, king of Heshbon. See Map 2, D-4. In Deut
2:26, 30, Sihon is mentioned simply as "King of Heshbon." He is also associated
with "Og, King of Bashan" (Num 21:33–35; Deut 1:4; cf. Ps 135:11). Excavations begun at Tell Ḥesban in 1968 and resumed in 1970 have not succeeded in locating significant evidence for the Late Bronze or Iron I periods.
Siegfried Horn, BA 32 (1969), 26–41.

Let me pass . . . to my holy place. With LXX[A], where LXX[B] reads "Let us pass . . . to our holy place," and MT is contaminated, "Let us pass . . . to my holy place." The speaker is Moses, according to Num 21:22.

holy place. Heb. *māqōm,* in the sense of "sanctuary location," as in 2:5; cf. Gen 12:6; 13:3; 21:31.

20. *Sihon did not trust Israel to cross.* Heb. *l' h'myn syḥwn 't yśr'l 'br.* Wandering tribesmen taking the trouble to negotiate safe passage to their cult center were apparently difficult for Sihon to believe. The interesting reading in a number of witnesses headed by LXX^A (*wym'n syḥwm tt yśr'l,* "Sihon refused to permit Israel . . .") seems to be contaminated by a scribe's familiarity with Num 20:21, which however refers to Edom, not Sihon. I owe this suggestion to Freedman.

Jahaz. Possibly Khirbet el-Medeiyineh at the desert fringe, which early belonged to the Amorite king, then to Israel, then to Moab (Mesha stele, lines 18–19, tr. Albright, ANET³, pp. 320–21). Thus Jephthah, involved in a dispute over land which has changed hands since the wilderness period, cites how in connection with passage through another piece of land which subsequently changed hands Israel had in fact fought only when negotiations failed. Map 2.

23. *him.* Reading the ambiguous suffix of *tīrāšennū* as singular, with LXX, instead of plural ("them" or "us" in MT). Presumably the antecedent is "Israel."

Jephthah can only present the case of his sovereign, to the best of his ability.

24. *your god Chemosh.* This climax to the argument is the chief evidence for the standing critical conclusion that an "Israel versus Moab" account has been imperfectly transposed into "Israel versus Ammon." But even more surprising than the fact that the alleged revision is incomplete is the clear evidence of its ancient intelligibility; there are no harmonizing glosses. Moreover, the fluctuation between "Ammon" and "Moab" as the focus of attention in the negotiations is adequately apprehended in terms of diplomatic protocol. Everything hinges on technical questions of sovereignty. For a contemporary example, at the time of this writing, Freedman has reminded me, the U.S.A. officially recognizes the city of Jerusalem as an independent entity separate from Israel and Jordan, both of which it recognizes.

What was the history of the territory disputed between Jephthah and the king of the Ammonites? Israel's involvement in its history is witnessed by the epic tradition in Num 21, at which time Ammon had only recently emerged as a small national entity at the edge of the desert. Thus the king of Ammon in this later period can only make his claims and charges in the name of Moabite sovereignty over the disputed territory, since Israelite claims would antedate his own, but Moabite claims would antedate both parties! The Ammonites must have treated the former Moabite territory as a separate entity, administratively and diplomatically. They may even have maintained the idea that this was held in trust for Moabite claimants. Under such circumstances the jurisdiction of the god Chemosh would be generally recognized for diplomatic purposes. Just as Mesha, the ninth-century Moabite king, could say that Chemosh was angry with his people and had allowed them to be oppressed by Israel (ANET³, p. 320), so here it appears that Chemosh has been adopted by the Ammonite chancellery as god of the territory formerly within the Moabite sphere. Compare the claims that Cyrus of Persia makes for the benefactions to him of Marduk, chief deity of Babylon. From the Israelite perspective too, the deity is the one who gives the land.

for you. Reading the final *kaph* of *ywryšk* as dative suffix, in agreement with LXX^A, where the note in *Biblia Hebraica* is misleading. Freedman, private communication.

25. That is, "is your claim any better," than that of a still earlier Moabite adversary of Israel?

any better. The adjective *ṭob* is repeated in the Hebrew for the sake of emphasis.

Balaq, son of Zippor, the Moabite king. The narrative tradition is found in Num 22–24, where a ruling theme is the great labors taken to communicate with Balaq. Both content and tone of the tradition were relevant to this context which relates the prosecution of Yahweh's case against his Ammonite opponent. On the form of the "double rhetorical question," see NOTE on 2:22.

institute proceedings. Hebrew root *ryb* as in 6:31–32 and Gideon's given name, "Let-baal-sue."

26. *some three hundred years.* Adding years of oppression and successive judges to this point (not counting eighteen Ammonite or Philistine years) yields a total of three hundred and one. The figure is therefore based on the book's chronology and is probably a gloss. Moore, pp. 296–97.

why. Idiomatic use of *waw*-conjunction, which Burney (p. 317) considered a bit sarcastic, as in 6:13 (see NOTE). Here, however, it appears as part of a tightly constructed argument for peace, with every indication that hope for peace accompanied it.

liberate them. With LXX^B, reading *hiṣṣaltām* against MT's *hiṣṣaltem* (no object). That the suffix meaning "them" is masculine suggests that the antecedent "cities" (normally feminine) here stands for their populations, a usage that is quite common.

27. *Yahweh, the Judge.* This title appears to be a functional description of God the Suzerain of the universe (I Sam 24:13). The latter passage is particularly significant, as it relates an encounter between Saul and the outlaw David not long before Samuel's death. Judge Samuel had anointed both of them. David, in protesting his innocence, says: "May the Lord therefore be judge (root *dyn*) and give sentence (root *špṭ*) between me and you, and see to it, and plead my cause (root *ryb*), and deliver me from your hand" (I Sam 24:15). For more on the synonymity of *dīn* and *špṭ*, see last paragraph of COMMENT, Sec. IX.

decide. The verbal root here is *špṭ;* see the poetic equivalent *dyn* in the Song of Deborah (5:10 and NOTE; cf. Deut 32:36). It is not a prediction; not necessarily even said in absolute confidence of Israel's winning. Cf. appeal to the gods of two parties, "to judge," in Gen 31:53.

28. *would not heed the words.* The verb is *šm'* in its diplomatic usage, as in vs. 10 (see NOTE). The result is, by implication, a crisis so grave that it can only be surmounted by a demonstration of the Yahweh spirit.

COMMENT

Jephthah's claims against the Ammonites reflect a high historicity. Mosaic tradition is consistently silent on the subject of Ammonite opposition, but the silence is being broken by archaeological discovery. It is now known that there was as yet no strong nation of Ammon when the Yahweh army first appeared in Transjordan. Moab had emerged early, but by the time of the judges it was restricted to territory between the Arnon and the Zered, while the name "Moab" still was used as a geographical designation for all inhabitable land east of the Dead Sea and west of the desert. See the story of Ehud (3:12–30), whose success against Moab perhaps paved the way for Ammonite expansion.

Jephthah's arguments thus come into sharp focus. In Israel's initial negotiation with Ammon Jephthah could turn for precedents only to Israel's early relations with Ammon's neighbors, relations which the narrative affirms were diplomatically irreproachable. His claim that the Ammonites should have only the land that their god Chemosh has given them reflects the gravity of the crisis. In this period, when success in warfare was everywhere acknowledged as a sign of divine favor, the Israelite Jephthah believed an appeal to the Ammonite god's authority was important enough to risk Yahweh's wrath for talking about another god. In addition to being the crowning argument for peace, it is also a bit of gratuitous religious instruction.

That Jephthah is represented as no strict theoretical Yahwist who at all costs denies the existence of other gods is, on a later view, unorthodox but scarcely surprising. In matters of diplomacy, he was a practical Yahwist, the sort of man God used repeatedly throughout the stormy period prior to kingship, a man who would have been very dear to the heart of the pragmatic compiler.

Indeed, the pragmatic compiler might have composed this account of Jephthah's delegations to the king of Ammon, after having carefully checked his sources. The absence of any clear redactional seams and the account of strictly unimpeachable negotiations point to his authorship. However, this must remain merely a conjecture, for there is no material for comparison other than the brief description of Othniel, the first judge, and an exemplary one, in the pragmatist's edition (3:7–11).

11   ²⁹ Yahweh's spirit came upon Jephthah. He toured Gilead and Manasseh, and moved on to Mizpeh of Gilead. From Mizpeh of Gilead he stalked the Ammonites. ³⁰ Jephthah made a vow to Yahweh; he said, "If you will really subject the Ammonites to my power, ³¹ then anything coming out the doors of my house to meet me, when I return with victory from the Ammonites, shall belong to Yahweh; I will offer it up as a burnt offering."

³² So Jephthah advanced toward the Ammonites to fight them, and Yahweh delivered them to him. ³³ He defeated them—all the way from Aroer to the vicinity of Minnith (twenty cities!) and to Abel-Keramim; it was one great slaughter. Thus were subdued the Ammonites before the Israelites.

³⁴ At the moment Jephthah arrived home at Mizpeh his daughter came out to meet him with music and dancing! She was his one and only child; except for her he had no son or daughter. ³⁵ When he recognized who it was, he tore his clothes and exclaimed, "Ahh! My child! You have brought me low! You have become a stumbling block before me. You have become my great misfortune! I have opened my mouth to Yahweh, and I cannot retract."

³⁶ She said to him, "Father, if you have opened your mouth to Yahweh, do to me exactly as you promised, since Yahweh has saved you from your enemies the Ammonites." ³⁷ She said to her father, "Let this thing be allowed me; let me alone for two months, that I may go and wander on the hills and bewail my virginity, I and my dear friends."

³⁸ So he said to her, "Go." He sent her for two months. She and her friends went and bewailed her virginity, away on the hilltops.

³⁹ At the end of two months she returned to her father, and he fulfilled with her the vow which he had made.

A Note

She had never had intercourse with a man. ⁴⁰ It became a custom, year after year, that the daughters of Israel should go to mourn for the daughter of Jephthah the Gileadite, four days each year.

NOTES

11:29. *Yahweh's spirit came upon Jephthah.* This sober declarative statement corresponds to 3:10 and stands in contrast to the assertion in 6:34 that the spirit "clothed Gideon," who would over-react. Cf. the initial attack upon Samson's conscience in 13:25. It leaves no room to doubt that Jephthah's victory against the Ammonites was considered to be Yahweh's saving act on behalf of Israel. That is, the demonstration of the spirit here stands for Yahweh's gracious ratification of proceedings that had, in effect, been taking Yahweh for granted. See Introduction, "Heaven and Earth: Yahweh's Kingdom." Cf. how another outlaw, David, who was first made king by covenant with the elders, found the covenant subsequently reinforced by another one (II Sam 6–7) initiated by Yahweh.

he toured . . . moved on . . . stalked. The same verbal root is employed at all three points in the text, which may very well be considered intact, if we recognize the wordplay. For the translation "stalked," cf. 8:4, 9:26 and NOTES.

Mizpeh. The Masoretes appear to have used the spellings "Mizpah" and "Mizpeh" interchangeably, with reference to both this town and others of the same name. The location of Mizpeh in Gilead is unknown.

30. *Jephthah made a vow.* This statement in the finished form of the book surely implies a contrast with Jephthah's recital of "words" (vs. 11) and his careful negotiations with the elders before assuming his high office. The vow, as it will turn out, was hastily worded; and Jephthah is thus marked for tragedy. Equally striking is the contrast between Gideon, whose given name was Jerubbaal (Let-Baal-sue), and Jephthah who says at last to the king of Ammon, "Yahweh, the Judge, will decide . . . !" (vs. 27). Gideon was a young reformer who became a zealous diviner and energetic blood avenger. His career ended in tragedy (8:24–27), but he was not presented as a tragic hero. Jephthah is just the opposite, an exiled knight later recalled to assume public responsibilities which he handled in exemplary manner. That the vow once made must be kept is the hinge of this story, where Jephthah's only daughter brings wisdom, as does Jotham, the sole survivor of Abimelech's purge of the sons of Gideon (9:7–20).

If you will really subject. It was one vow too many. The Hebrew uses the infinitive absolute adverbially, the force of which explains the final continuity in the redacted Jephthah stories: regardless of their source, they remembered how

Jephthah had a penchant for making deals. This one presents Jephthah's tragic flaw as a failure to trust in the time-tested institutions of the federation. Cf. Gideon's fleece test (6:36–40).

31. *anything coming out the doors of my house.* On the more or less standard plan of Iron Age houses, such as to accommodate the livestock as well as the family, see Keith Beebe, BA 31 (1968), esp. 49–58. See also illustration 8. Modern villagers in the Near East use basements, flat rooftops, and structurally integrated livestock pens in the same way. Standard translations, which read "whoever comes out," resolve an ambiguity which belongs to the building of suspense. The story illustrates Jephthah's approach to the saving of Israel, as first presented in vss. 7–11, presumably out of the same concern to maintain his new-found control of Israel. Gideon's career had gone the other way, from public savior to private vengeance.

when I return with victory. Heb. *bᵉ-šūbī bᵉ-šālōm,* the same words used by Gideon in his vow to the men of Penuel (8:9).

32. *delivered them.* Lit. "gave into the hand." See NOTE on 1:2.

33. *defeated them.* Cf. 1:4 and NOTE.

Aroer . . . Minnith . . . Abel-keramim. The sites remain to be identified, somewhere in the district west of Rabbath-ammon. Aharoni, LOB, p. 243. See provisionally Map 2, E-4.

twenty cities. Cf. the exclamatory "ten contingents!" in 1:4, with which the passage shows formal and verbal similarities. The "twenty cities" were probably border forts. Malamat, *The World History of the Jewish People: First Series,* III (London: W. H. Allen, 1971), 157.

Thus were subdued. The statement here is integral to the narrative. The same assertion regarding "Midian" belongs, however, to the framework of the Gideon narrative (8:28). Gideon went far beyond his orders; in his case the tragedy was the execution of severe reprisals against a people whose history had been meshed with Israel's ever since Sinai. Here, however, the tragic figures are Jephthah and his daughter; for the defeat of the Ammonites is represented as following Yahwist procedure to the letter.

34. The story involves a calculated inversion of the traditional role of singing women on the evening after victory (Exod 15:20–21) or welcoming the heroes home (I Sam 18:6–7). Cf. 5:28–30 and the entire Song of Deborah and Baraq in its narrative setting.

Jephthah . . . meet him. See illustration 8.

except for her. With LXX, Syr.ʰ; MT reads "except for him" (!), which represents a contamination from the preceding *lō,* "to him."

35. *Ahh.* A guttural ejaculation which is here better transliterated than translated, as in the exclamation of Gideon, "Oh no!" (6:22), for the Gideon passage was intended to evoke laughter. Not so the story of Jephthah's vow.

You have brought me low. Lit. "you have driven me to my knees" (hiphil of the root *kr',* as in the account of the reduction of Gideon's force in 7:5 and 6).

You have become a stumbling block before me. This statement is supplied by LXXᴬᴸ, Vulg., and Syr.ʰ. A simple haplography, *hkr'tny (lmkšl hyyt b'yny) w't hyyt,* might explain the shorter reading. LXXᴮ, however, reflects a shorter reading which has leveled throughout the root *ʿkr* and obscured the wordplay.

misfortune. The root is *ʿkr,* a wordplay with *krʿ* "to bow down."

36. As often happens in early Israel's popular narration of history, the one who speaks wisely, when Yahweh's rule is at stake, is a woman, e.g. Deborah and Jael. Cf. Manoah's wife in ch. 13; Hannah in I Sam 1–2; Michal in II Sam 6:20–23.

since Yahweh has saved you. Lit. "after Yahweh did for you deliverance." This is a good case where the root *nāqam* means "deliverance, salvation," not "vengeance." See Introduction, "Heaven and Earth: Yahweh's Kingdom." See also *TenGen,* p. 85.

from your enemies the Ammonites. MT repeats the preposition and perhaps preserves variants, where this particular repetition is most unpoetic, unlike the remainder of the girl's speech.

37. *and wander.* Treating *yāradtī* as a biform of the root *rwd.*

my virginity. Presumably a shorthand for "my childlessness."

39. *he fulfilled with her the vow.* The statement forms an inclusio with vs. 30, leaving the last statement of vs. 39 outside the narrative unit.

She had never had intercourse with a man. As a mere explication of "virginity" in vss. 37–38, the statement would appear to be superfluous; biblical narrators were seldom so dull. We may thus suspect that a commentator in 39b–40 is exegeting the narrative units. She died childless and that was why the daughters of Israel (i.e. Yahwist women) used to mourn her formally every year.

40. *It became a custom.* It is doubtful that this is "a story based on the ancient and primitive custom of annually bewailing the dead or ousted spirit of fertility during the dry or winter season." Gaster, MLC, pp. 431–32, 534–35. More likely, in the authoritative tradition of ancient Israel, it bears a polemical relationship to such a practice, otherwise unattested in OT (see COMMENT).

COMMENT

Human sacrifice in Israel was not condoned. Neither was it unknown. It is presented as a move made in desperation (II Kings 16:3) or, indeed, as punishment ordered by Yahweh (Ezek 20:25–26, 31). The story of the near sacrifice of Isaac (Gen 22) presupposes the reader's assent to the possibility. The fact of human sacrifice in Jephthah's story is secondary to the theme of the irrevocability of the vow. In this case the vow is so worded as to be ambiguous: "anything coming out the doors of my house" (vs. 31). Had he really expected it to be a human being? (See illustration 8.) Nevertheless, the vow once made to Yahweh must be kept.

In this old narrative, developments happened rapidly. One crisis was no sooner resolved than another was introduced, to hold the attention of the audience until the shocking conclusion circled back to the foreshadowing verses at the beginning. In this case, "Yahweh's spirit came upon Jephthah" (vs. 29) and he was absolutely consistent in fulfilling his hastily formulated vow (vs. 39). The narrator does not blame either Yahweh or the Yahwist spirit for Jephthah's tragedy. He was, rather, as in nearly all the old narrative segments of the book, profoundly sympathetic with his protagonists, but all the while retained a critical perspective on the problems of public and private life. This portrayal of Jephthah's integrity in fulfilling his vow is psychologically consistent with the story of his messages to the Ammonite King (vss. 12–28); both scenes hinge on Jephthah's "words" recited to Yahweh and before the people (vs. 11).

It is often supposed that the story of Jephthah's vow is purely etiological, a tale originally told to rationalize a defunct lamentation festival (vs. 40). There is a number of parallels to the tragic sacrifice of the hero's daughter in comparative folklore, and so the question of the shaping of the record must remain an open one. That there is no other trace of such a "festival" suggests that the tale is told for other than etiological purpose. It heightens the tragic dimension in the story of Jephthah, exemplary Yahwist judge.

XXVII. Jephthah and Ephraim
(12:1–7)

Ephraim's Envy

12 ¹ The Ephraimites were mustered, and they crossed to Zaphon and said to Jephthah, "Why did you advance to fight the Ammonites without summoning us to go with you? We will burn down your house on top of you!"

² Jephthah said to them, "I was using diplomacy, I and my people. But the Ammonites answered me with oppression. I summoned you, but you did not rescue me from their power. ³ When I saw that you were no help, I took my life in my own hand and advanced against the Ammonites; Yahweh delivered them to me! So why have you come up to me today? To fight against me?"

⁴ So Jephthah assembled all the men of Gilead and fought Ephraim. The men of Gilead defeated Ephraim. For the fugitives of Ephraim said: "O Gilead, you are in the midst of Ephraim and Manasseh!"

The Shibboleth

⁵ Gilead captured the Jordan's fords to Ephraim. When any Ephraimite fugitives said to them, "Let me cross over!" the men of Gilead said to him, "Are you an Ephraimite?" and he would say "No!" ⁶ But they would say to him, "Please say 'shibboleth,'" and he would say "sibboleth," for he was not prepared to pronounce it correctly; whereupon they would seize him and slaughter him, right there at the Jordan's fords. There fell at that time some forty-two Ephraimite contingents.

⁷ Jephthah judged Israel six years. When Jephthah the Gileadite died, he was buried in his own city in Gilead.

NOTES

12:1. *The Ephraimites were mustered.* They arrived too late for the action; the redactor understood that this is at least two months later (11:38–39). They claim to have been uninformed (as in the similar case of Gideon against the Midianites in 8:1).

Zaphon. The site is probably Tell el-Qos on the northern edge of Wadi Rajeb, commanding a sweep of rich lowlands not far from the valley road about midway between Succoth and Zarethan (Map 2, D-3). The name suggests that it was a Yahwist town formerly sacred to Baal-zaphon, center of a small principality having a "princess" in the Amarna period and mentioned in Egyptian records from the Nineteenth Dynasty. The narrator, unfortunately, assumed that the mere place-name would be significant enough. Perhaps the Ephraimites met up with Jephthah at Zaphon on one of his tours as circuit riding judge (11:29; cf. I Sam 7:15–17).

We will burn down your house. Later a Philistine threat in 14:15, with Philistine fulfillment in 15:6.

2. *I was using diplomacy.* Lit. "I was a *rīb*-man, I and my people!" Implicit is the accusation that Ephraim, by contrast, would fight first and negotiate later.

answered me with oppression. Restoring '*innūnī* (Syr.ʰ, OL) which was lost by haplography after '*mwn*.

I summoned you. The stories preserve no clear description to support his claim. The statement may simply take for granted that there had been captains from Ephraim participating in the scene with "The captains of the force," in 10:18. Jacob M. Myers, *The Interpreter's Bible,* II, eds. George Arthur Buttrick et al. (New York and Nashville: Abingdon Press, 1953), 773.

3. Jephthah is represented as dealing with internal affairs in the same way that he had handled the Ammonite threat—diplomacy first. Again, except for the fuzzy antecedent of the claim in vs. 2b, his approach is presented as impeccable. The argument ending in a query (To fight against me?) has the same effect as the concluding query addressed to the Ammonite king (11:26), where it was followed by Jephthah's readiness to let battle establish the rightness or wrongness of his case (11:27b).

4. *Jephthah . . . Ephraim . . . Ephraim.* An inclusio with vs. 1. Verse 4a is the denouement of a brief, tightly constructed narrative unit.

O Gilead. The meaning of the taunt is obscure. It is missing from a number of Greek manuscripts and its origin may have been a partial dittography of vs. 5. Moore, p. 307, and Burnrey, p. 327.

5–6. This unit, capping the career of Jephthah with the disabling of "forty-two Ephraimite contingents," is one of the most puzzling in the book. It is treated here as sequel to the events of vss. 1–4 merely by virtue of its position.

5. *fugitives.* Escapees, apparently from the battle of the preceding verse.

6. *shibboleth . . . sibboleth.* The test does not turn upon the meaning of the word, which may be either "ear of corn" (Gen 41:5–7; Ruth 2:2) or "flood, torrent" (Ps 69:3, 16; Isa 27:12). The latter is more appropriate to the occasion, but both may have a common etymological origin, as pointed out by Speiser, *Oriental and Biblical Studies: Collected Writings of E. A. Speiser,* eds. J. J. Finklestein and Moshe Greenberg (University of Pennsylvania Press, 1967), pp. 143–50. Speiser argues that the merging of the spirant *t* (*tha*) and the sibilant *š* (*sha*), attested for Phoenicia as early as the eleventh century, must have occurred at about the same time in western Palestine. There was, however, a lag in Transjordan; the merging of these vocables is incomplete in Arabic even today. Analogous spelling practice is well-known from Old Akkadian, Nuzi, and Amarna; "where a distinction between original *t* and *š* is maintained orthographically, it is the spirant that is written invariably as *š,* whereas the sibilant may appear either as *š* or *s*" (Speiser, p. 149 and note). Speiser concludes, "In short, *t* had to be written *š.* It could not be set down as *s* unless such a writing was meant to express an unsuccessful imitation of the required sound, which is exactly what happened." There remains only to point out that the distinction between the letters *shin* and *sin* would not be clear prior to the invention of pointing systems. And this explains why the Ephraim-ite pronounciation is unambiguously represented by the letter *samek.*

he was not prepared. Heb. *lō' yākīn,* in a frequently attested sense of the verb, "to prepare, be ready" (*A Hebrew and English Lexicon of the Old Testament,* eds. F. Brown, S. R. Driver, C. A. Briggs [Boston: Houghton-Mifflin, 1906], pp. 465–66), which is supported by the alternate reading of a dozen manuscripts: *lō' yābīn* "he did not know how," which seems to have arisen in the similarity of written *kaph* and *beth.*

7. This rubric is drawn from a skeletal list of data regarding the early federal administrators (see NOTES on 10:1–5).

in his own city in Gilead. MT, "in the cities of Gilead," is impossible and probably represents a mispointing of the third person suffix spelled with *yod.* Dahood, *Psalms II, 51–100,* AB, vol. 17 (1968), p. xxv. LXX and OL support the interpretation as third person. They also repeat the preposition, suggesting that the single occurrence in MT does double duty, as very often in poetry. Mitchell Dahood and Tadeusz Penar, *The Grammar of the Psalter,* ch. VII, section 13e, in Dahood, *Psalms III, 101–150,* AB, vol. 17A, 1970.

COMMENT

These final episodes reported from the career of Jephthah are only loosely joined to the preceding. They are another pair of narrative units which had already taken shape and were used as building blocks in compiling the Book of Judges. In both chs. 11 and 12, the unit in which Jephthah is diplomatic ad-ministrator is placed first (11:12–28; 12:1–4), immediately followed by the section describing the warfare (11:29–40; 12:5–6). Probably both belonged to the pragmatist's history of the judges.

The account of Ephraim's expedition against Jephthah sustains the implicit comparison of Jephthah and Gideon (7:24 – 8:3). Gideon's problem with the

Ephraimites stemmed from his being a west bank judge who had become an east bank feudalist. Jephthah's problem with the Ephraimites no doubt stemmed from his east bank prominence and the consequent threat to Ephraim's prior west bank influence within the confederation. Given the widespread devastation and power vacuum which Abimelech created in a few years at Shechem, it is not surprising that the center of early resistance to the Ammonite challenge shifted to Gilead, with tribal politics taking on a whole new configuration.

The contrast with Gideon (Let-Baal-sue) is also sustained by the narrator's concentration on Jephthah's diplomacy. Jephthah had earned the distinction of being a *rīb*-man (See NOTE on vs. 2), an Israelite judge with responsibility for foreign affairs as well as domestic. The sequel to Jephthah's great victory at the head of the Israelite confederation was remembered as precipitating another small civil war.

Verses 5–6 is an extremely difficult unit to focus. It makes no mention at all of Jephthah. Instead, it describes a situation of continuing tribal strife despite Jephthah's successes, and thus it provides a rough transition to the sketchy notices about the next three judges.

The strategy employed by the soldiers at the fords is also known from the late Middle Ages; Gaster cites three strictly comparable examples in MLC, pp. 433, 535. I am told that in World War II the Dutch underground was able to screen out German spies by making them pronounce the Dutch city name Scheveningen, which only the Dutch can do properly.

All in all the pragmatic compiler leaves us with his impression that within his anxious limitations (11:30–40) Jephthah was a good judge, the best since Othniel. With his death, however, the judgeship returned to the west bank.

The brief "minor judge" style notice about Jephthah in vs. 7 has been superimposed upon epic sources showing an effective Yahwist judge dealing with both foreign (11:1–40) and domestic (12:1–6) crises. The result is a forceful contrast between Jephthah's exemplary judgeship and the tragedy of Samson's wasted charisma which comes next (chs. 13–15) in the earliest collection of judges stories.

XXVIII. THREE MINOR JUDGES
(12:8–15)

Ibzan

12 8 After him, Ibzan of Bethlehem judged Israel. 9 He had thirty "sons." Thirty daughters he sent away and thirty daughters-in-law he brought in from the outside for his "sons." 10 He judged Israel seven years. When Ibzan died, he was buried at Bethlehem.

Elon

11 After him, Elon the Zebulunite judged Israel. He judged Israel ten years. 12 When Elon the Zebulunite died, he was buried at Aijalon in the land of Zebulun.

Abdon

13 After him, Abdon ben Hillel the Pirathonite judged Israel. 14 He had forty "sons" and thirty "grandsons," who rode on seventy donkeys. He judged Israel eight years. 15 When Abdon ben Hillel the Pirathonite died, he was buried at Pirathon in the land of Ephraim, in the Amaleqite hill country.

NOTES

12:8–15. These verses continue the bare list of early federal administrators, resumed in vs. 7 after the long interruption by the old epic material which gave the clearest picture of all in the precise terms of Israel's covenant constitution. For an interpretation of the redactional use of the skeletal list to represent generally peaceful interludes, see NOTES on 10:1–5.

8–10. *Ibzan.* "Swift (horse?)." The name is otherwise unknown.

8. *Bethlehem.* Location uncertain. The town in Judah has been considered least likely and the northern Bethlehem in Zebulun close to the border of Asher more likely, simply because of a notion that the book is superficially

organized around twelve judges (one per tribe). Thus "Ibzan" perhaps stands for Asher's great federal judge. See Map 2, C-4, C-2.

thirty "sons." See NOTE on 10:1. Numerous "progeny" in such a context is no necessary indication of wealth, but stands for large administrative responsibility as clan head. Thirty is a political number, as in 10:4.

11–12. *Elon.* "Oak" or "Terebinth." Elon is a "son" of Zebulun (Gen 46:14; Num 26:26), an eponym.

12. *Aijalon.* Near Rimmon; see Map 2, C-2. Spelled the same as Elon in the early unpointed script. This brief notice of the historical judge may be etiological, explaining his name from that of the town which produced him. If so, "Elon" is another hint of the administrative takeover by Yahwists of the old oracular shrines, many having a tree that was famous for the oracular activity which transpired there, e.g., Deborah in 4:5, Gideon in 6:11, Abimelech in 9:6.

13–15. *Abdon.* He is otherwise unknown. The name perhaps means "service." That he had "forty 'sons'" but only "thirty 'grandsons'" (vs. 14) is a most surprising progression unless "sonship" is here understood politically. The total of seventy must be related to other uses of that number to represent the council composed, insofar as possible, of relatives of the ruler. Cf. Gideon's seventy "sons" (8:30 and NOTE). This brief notice about the administration of Abdon thus allows for a contrast with the new separatism expressed in the introduction to Samson.

15. *Pirathon . . . Ephraim.* The latter has geographical sense, if the location of Pirathon near the southern border of Manasseh is correct. Map 2, C-3.

COMMENT

It was an uncertain peace that Jephthah willed to Israel, yet three judges (twenty-five years) came and went before any strife occurred that was serious enough to be recorded.

13 1 Israelites continued doing what was evil in Yahweh's sight, and Yahweh subjected them to Philistine power for forty years.

2 There was once a man from Zorah (from the clan of the Danites) by the name of Manoah. His wife was barren and childless. 3 But Yahweh's envoy appeared to the woman and said to her, "Look here! You have been barren and childless. But you will be pregnant, and you will bear a son. 4 Be careful now. Drink no wine or beer, and eat nothing unclean. 5 Actually, you are already pregnant and bearing a son. And no razor shall come upon his head. Indeed, the boy will be God's Nazirite from the womb. And he shall begin to liberate Israel from Philistine power."

6 So the woman came and said to her husband, "A man of God came to me! His appearance was just like that of God's envoy—very awesome! I did not inquire whence he came, and he did not tell me his name. 7 But he said to me, 'You are pregnant and bearing a son. Therefore, drink no wine or beer, and eat nothing unclean. Indeed, the boy will be God's Nazirite, from the womb to the day of his death!' "

8 Manoah then prayed to Yahweh and said, "Pardon me, Lord, but let the man of God whom you sent come to us again and instruct us in what we shall do for the boy who is to be born."

9 God granted the request of Manoah; and God's envoy came again to the woman, as she was sitting in the field. Manoah her husband was not with her. 10 So the woman ran in haste, informed her husband, and said to him, "Look! He has reappeared—the man who came to me that day!" 11 So Manoah got up, followed his wife, and came to the man.

He said to him, "You are the man who spoke to this woman?"

12 And he said, "I am." So Manoah said, "Well now, let your words come true! What will be the judgment of the lad and his work?"

13 And Yahweh's envoy said to Manoah, 14 "Of all that I said to the woman let her be mindful. Of all that comes from the vine let her consume nothing. Wine and beer let her not drink. Let her eat nothing unclean. All that I have commanded her let her observe."

15 Manoah said to Yahweh's envoy, "Please let us detain you and we will prepare a kid for you." 16 Yahweh's envoy said to Manoah, "If you detain me, I will not eat your food. But if you want to prepare a burnt offering for Yahweh, offer it up!" For Manoah did not know that he was the Yahweh envoy.

17 Manoah said to Yahweh's envoy, "Who . . . ? Your name? When your words come true, we will honor you!"

18 Yahweh's envoy said to him, "To what purpose is this? You ask for my name? It is wonderful!" 19 So Manoah took the kid and the grain offering and went up to the rock, to Yahweh, making ready for Yahweh, the wonder worker. 20 And as the flame ascended upwards from the altar, Yahweh's envoy also ascended in the altar flame, while Manoah and his wife looked on. Then they fell face down on the ground!

NOTES

13:1–20. Following the editorial rubric in vs. 1, an entire chapter is given over to the old story of the birth of Samson. That Samson became a judge was nothing short of wonderful, according to the narrator. See vss. 18 and 19.

1. *continued doing what was evil.* See NOTE on 3:12.

Philistine. Not their first appearance in the book. See NOTES on 1:19, 3:31, 10:6–7, and illustrations 2 and 10. Their arrival in Canaan dates roughly half a century after that of Israel, and their presence has been assumed throughout the book (see esp. the interpretation of Sisera as one such Sea Peoples chieftain heading the northwest coalition against Deborah and Baraq in chs. 4 and 5). The editorial headings to the individual judges do not represent the introduction of new population groups (and thus a "cyclical" view of early Israelite history); rather they interpret the repeated encroachments of various historical oppressors in terms of Yahweh's freedom of choice. In doing so they were interpreting a theme that is integral to the theology of the narrative units and which is indeed a controlling motif in the story of Samson's birth.

2. *There was once.* Introductory *wayhī;* see NOTE on 1:1.

Zorah. See Map 2, C-4. The town is assigned to Dan (on its border with Judah) in Josh 19:41, and it is given as the point of departure for the Danite migration in 18:2, 8, 11. It belongs to Judah in Josh 15:33. The lists thus reflect the reality of the migration tradition. The place changed hands. The site is identified as modern Sar'ah, on a summit dominating the Valley of Soreq (Vineyard Valley) from the north. That he is introduced as a man "from" Zorah implies that he had gone away to live with his wife somewhere else. The new location was not considered important. See below on vs. 12. Only the general vicinity of Manoah's tomb was known (16:31).

clan. The parenthesis is not to be taken as a marginal comment, since it uses the word *mišpāḥā* (generally "family" or "clan") for a smaller social grouping that had not attained the strength and stature of a later "tribe." Cf. 17:7.

Manoah. The name means "rest" ("Noah" involves the same root) and is probably the shortened form of a sentence name standing for security as God's gift. This story, however, is not an etiology of the name; Manoah is an active and busy man.

3. *Yahweh's envoy.* For another encounter with this bearer of good tidings, but with a different response, see 6:12. The angel's remarks here are extremely polite (Heb. *hinnē-nā*, "Look here!"), in gentle contrast with the blunt announcement to Gideon (6:16 uses a quotation from the enlistment of Moses!).

You have been barren. EVV heighten the miraculous element prematurely and unnecessarily by ignoring the sequence of tenses in Hebrew and rendering everything in the announcement as present tense. The narrator, however, has carefully described the situation in such a way that the happy woman can regard her change of fortune as the miraculous thing. From the standpoint of the narrator, the miracle is Yahweh's ability to create joy. But this is only latent at the outset. The husband was not immediately persuaded; Manoah is, in fact, presented as remarkably slow of discernment.

you will be pregnant, and you will bear a son. Against the view that the text here and in vs. 5 is redundant and conflate (Burney, pp. 341–42, on the basis of LXX[B], where, however, the *Vorlage* of vs. 3 shows a transparent haplography). This combination of verbs is traditional (Gen 16:11; Isa 7:14). We need only assume initial surprise plus the ambiguity of mere conception; what was needed was "a son."

4. *no wine or beer, and eat nothing unclean.* Since wine is specifically mentioned, the second term *škr* must be beer, as there is no evidence for distilled liquors in ancient times. Since wine was the ordinary drink and always mixed with water, beer was often stronger in alcoholic content and was reserved for parties and celebrations. The Philistines used an awesome amount of beer, as indicated by so much of their distinctive pottery with strainers. See illustration 9. In this passage the rule of the Nazirite (Num 6:1–8), formulated for those who will enlist on their own initiative, is delightfully adapted as highly desirable prenatal care. For example, the admonition to stay clear of the uncleanness that emanates from a dead body (Num 6:6–7), which is surely beyond the control of the fetus, is displaced by the instruction to the mother to "eat nothing unclean," like any other Israelite (Lev 11; Deut 14).

It should be noted that the rule of the Nazirite is itself rooted in the regulations for the ritual purity of the fighting man as reflected in tradition stemming from the Mosaic period; Deut 29:6 cites "no wine or strong drink" as part of the preparation for Israel's first real victories, against Sihon and Og.

5. *Actually, you are already pregnant and bearing a son.* The shift in verb forms (perfects in vs. 3, participles here) is entirely in order, following the double asseverative *kī hinnāk.* For the same pattern but with a single asseverative, see Gen 16:11, which explicates the preceding verse. In Isa 7:14, where the same formulaic elements occur, there appear to be successive changes of tense: "has conceived, is bearing, and will call . . ." In vs. 24 we will be told simply that "she bore a son," fulfilling the promise, not a daughter.

God's Nazirite . . . begin to liberate. Any Israelite, male or female, taking special vows of consecration to God according to rules such as survive in Num 6:1–21 was known as a Nazirite. The Nazirites were highly militant and tenaciously conservative of the early Yahwist life-style.

God's plot, this time, is to make the man a "Nazirite from the womb," to be doubly sure that this one does not get away, so that "he shall begin to liberate." There is a close formulaic parallel between LXX at this point and Matt 1:21. "Jesus is, according to the writer of the first Gospel, a second Samson, who comes to play the role of 'judge' or deliverer." F. W. Danker, *Multipurpose Tools for Bible Study* (St. Louis: Concordia, 1966), p. 92. Danker also observes a typological treatment in the ridicule of Samson (16:25) and the mocking of Jesus (Matt 27:29, the same Greek verb), the positioning of Samson between two pillars and Jesus between two thieves; "the blows dealt their respective enemies in the hour of their death are more devastating than in their lifetimes."

In Samson's case both the narrator and the audience know how the story in general turns out. Samson will begin the liberation but it will be up to Yahweh to finish it. That is, the angel, not yet fully recognized as such, makes a prediction that stands in contrast to the panicked "captains of the force" in 10:18 who asked: "Who . . . will start . . . ?" To judge from 13:25 and 16:22, it is likely that the narrator has here chosen his words very carefully (contra Moore, p. 317).

6. *A man of God . . . God's envoy.* As repeatedly in the other envoy story (6:11–24), the participants are shown as speaking better than they know. That the woman speaks of a "man of God" and "God's envoy" in the same breath is not a sign of different literary or traditionary sources but belongs to the structure of this recognition story. As often elsewhere, the divine name is used in narrative description, and the generic noun "God" is used to signal a subjective conviction. Thus there is irony in saying that the man of God (previously introduced by the narrator as "Yahweh's envoy") looked just like God's envoy.

whence he came. The interrogative is identical with that used by the sailors questioning the reluctant prophet in Jonah 1:8. Freedman has called my attention to the latter and suggests that there may be an intentional overtone to the assertion of Manoah's wife. She might have been surprised at the answer about the envoy's origin. The narrator, in other words, has Manoah's wife come very close to the truth in her groping way, thereby entertaining the reader, who already knows better.

7. *to the day of his death.* A detail not supplied in the initial description of the interview, but consistent with other instances of anticipation in this story. To those who knew the story of ch. 16 in one form or another, Manoah's wife would again be speaking better than she knew.

The woman's breathless recapitulation of events to Manoah fails to mention the prohibition of haircuts (that much could be assumed, for a Nazirite), and makes no mention of the eventual liberation of Israel. Rather the narrative skillfully concentrates on what the announcement means for her, a proposal to cooperate with Yahweh and go the Nazirite rule one better. A reason for her failure to mention one of the main qualifications of the Nazirite, the long hair, will appear later in the cycle; the cutting of the Nazirite's hair belonged to the completion of his "consecration," his mustering out, the return to "secular" life (Num 6:18–20).

Contrast the announcement to Samuel's mother, where a sanctuary setting is part of the given, with Hannah's promises (I Sam 1:11) that her son will be both priest and Nazirite, with the climactic result that "There they worshipped Yahweh!" (I Sam 1:28b).

8. Caution about the testimony of women is a recurring phenomenon in biblical narrative, all the way from Gen 3 to the resurrection stories. Manoah's caution is thus part of the author's buildup. The woman doesn't really know what she is saying, though she is dropping hints all along the way. The narrator thus seeks to stir up the reader, who must become impatient with these two people.

Pardon me, Lord. Cf. "Pardon me, sir" (6:13, 15), and NOTE on 6:13.

9. *God granted the request of Manoah.* The generic noun "God" here stands for the narrator's agreement with the identification proposed by the woman. In other words, his own convictions in the matter are not explicitly injected until he has elicited full sympathy for the plight of his characters and some considerable desire, on the part of his hearers, for a solution that is both entertaining and edifying. This initial emergence from mere narration to the narrator's own affirmation of reality is sustained precisely long enough for the crucial question concluding vs. 12.

10. *that day.* LXX^A reflects the demonstrative pronoun *hhw'*.

11. *this woman.* The definitive article often has demonstrative force as in the shorter text of vs. 10, "that day."

12. *let your words come true.* The syntax of the Hebrew is odd for the temporal qualifier (EVV), but transparently jussive. Manoah's enthusiasm about becoming a father is matched only by his eagerness to make the most of this private audience.

the judgment. Heb. *mišpāṭ,* as in 4:5, where Israelites approach Deborah for "the judgment." General observations about the origins of law in customary procedures do not alone determine the semantics of *mišpāṭ* in the Book of Judges. The reader is now in a position to see how the narrator has depicted Manoah as a man who thought of himself as all that was left, head of a one-clan Israel, making his inquiry regarding the promised son. What sort of career will he have? or What will be his style and achievement?

14. With MT, where LXX has masculine instead of feminine forms of the verbs. That is, the LXX reflects a tradition which explicitly anticipates that Samson will be subject to the Nazirite rules. MT focuses attention upon the mother. The envoy ignores Manoah's question (which any member of the audience could answer) and indicates simply that he had meant what he had said nine verses earlier. Similarly the protracted scene involving Gideon and the Yahweh angel, in 6:11–24, makes the point that Gideon had from the outset all the information that he needed. At this point the text reverts to the use of the divine name, "Yahweh," holding this one man in check, because Yahweh had intended to save Israel.

15. *Please let us detain you.* Echoes of Gideon again? See 6:17–18.

16. *For Manoah did not know . . . envoy.* The reminder seems superfluous, but it is important to remind the reader that he is privy to information which Manoah does not have or truth which he does not recognize.

17. *Who . . . ? Your name?* Manoah uses the wrong pronoun for "what is your name?" (Gen 32:28; Exod 3:13). Rather, he is momentarily reduced to stuttering but promptly recovers. The partial similarity to the question in Exod 3:13 prompts another comparison. There the order was given to "honor God on this mountain"; it was to be a "sign." Manoah, on the other hand, makes the honoring of the angel contingent upon the truth of his announcement; like Gideon (6:36–40), Manoah requires a sign.

18. Literal rendering in a very difficult passage, which continues the inverted relationship with the disclosure of divine names to Moses in Exod 3.

It is wonderful. Heb. *pl'y.* That is, beyond comprehension. Yahweh is "Wonder-Worker" in the Song of Miriam (Exod 15:11).

19. *the kid.* Reminiscent of Gideon's divinatory offering of a kid and unleavened cakes in 6:19. Gideon was directed to "put" (*hnḥ,* from the same root as Manoah) his offering on "the rock" (6:20).

grain offering. Heb. *minḥā,* a departure from the Gideon parallel (*maṣṣōt,* 6:19), because the former provided a play on the man's name *manoᵃḥ,* alerting the reader to the upcoming play on the root *pl'* "be surpassing, extraordinary," hiphil "work a wonder."

making ready for Yahweh, the wonder worker. The obscurity of this passage is mostly removed by restoring the divine name with LXX[AL] and other witnesses, lost through haplography in MT and LXX[B]. The verb *'śh* has precisely the same sense in the Gideon parallel, "prepare," "make ready" (6:19). There remains only to underscore the chiastic word order in the full text, lit. "he went up—to the rock—to Yahweh: to Yahweh—who works a wonder—to prepare." This use of "wonder worker" in strict grammatical parallelism with "the rock" brings out the double meaning of the latter (see 6:21). With this climactic allusion to the God of Israel as "the Rock" and "Wonder Worker," the reader is prepared for the denouement.

20. *flame ascended . . . they fell face down.* While the "flame" and "envoy" go "up," "Manoah and his wife" go "down." Cf. Gideon (6:24), and all

Israel in the encounter with the Yahweh angel which introduced the period (2:5; cf. I Sam 1:28b). They affirm their ultimate allegiance once again.

An additional comparison between Gideon and Manoah seems to be in order. While the tendency to regard such materials as sanctuary legends undoubtedly has its justification in terms of the institutional custody of much tradition that survived, the specific understanding of them as "foundation legends" has seriously curtailed the exegesis of their own integrity. Especially is this true in the case of Manoah, who is represented as a one-man assembly conducting his own cultus wherever it was that he lived. The location was regarded as unimportant. "Signs and wonders" are used to apply the Mosaic heritage in an analysis of two very different individuals. Gideon, with his personal penchant for divination, asked for a sign from the envoy, but got one from Yahweh. Manoah was reluctant to take the envoy at his word but promised to honor him if and when the wonderful thing happened. The result was something to make him behave like a loyal vassal.

COMMENT

In the case of Samson we are confronted by material without close parallel in the preceding chapters. The differences, however, are concentrated in the characterizations of Samson and his parents. On the other hand, there are many evidences of stylistic continuities, especially with the Gideon and Jephthah materials, as was indicated in NOTES on vss. 1, 17, 19, 20. We have concluded, therefore, that at least Samson's birth and enlistment (chs. 13–15) belonged to the earliest edition of the pragmatist's book. Closer contacts with the Deborah material occur in chs. 14–16.

Scholars often despair of saying anything at all about the historical Samson, because of the high degree of legend in the narrative. Yet it is doubtful in the extreme that any ancient historian could have arbitrarily promoted Samson or anyone else to such office given the great amount of tradition still alive in the later period. Gaster, in MLC, p. 434, has put the matter most succinctly:

in the extravagance of its colouring the picture of Samson owes more to the brush of the story-teller than to the pen of the historian. The marvellous and diverting incidents of his career probably floated about loosely as popular tales on the current of oral tradition long before they crystallized around the memory of a real man, a doughty highlander and borderer, a sort of Hebrew Rob Roy, whose choleric temper, dauntless courage, and prodigious bodily strength marked him out as the champion of Israel in many a wild foray across the border into the rich lowlands of Philistia. For there is no sufficient reason to doubt that a firm basis of fact underlies the flimsy and transparent superstructure of fancy in the Samson saga. The particularity with which the scenes of his life, from birth to death, are laid in definite towns and places, speaks strongly in favour of a genuine local tradition, and as strongly against the theory of a solar myth, into which some writers would dissolve the story of the brawny hero.

The tradition, to be sure, was preoccupied with matters which frustrate our passion for dating. Since the Philistine occupation of towns such as Ashdod is datable on archaeological evidence to the second quarter of the twelfth century, whereas the northward migration of Dan belongs probably to the early eleventh century, Samson's precise dates are not surely known. We must be content, therefore, to place him somewhere within the span between c. 1160–1100.

The whole structure of the Samson segment is different from that of the other judges. There is no participation by Israelites in his elevation to judge and no mention of Israelites taking the field behind him. Yet there is clearly an intention on the part of the writer to substantiate the claim that Samson judged Israel (15:20). This indicates that the segment was probably included by the pragmatic historian. Further proof is that above all the pragmatist was concerned to delineate Israel's life with the judges, not to exalt the protagonists, and Samson is here rigorously scrutinized. Indeed, among the points made in ch. 13 is that the historical Samson was a most unlikely prospect for the judgeship of the federation. Jephthah, the disowned, outlawed adventurer was, to be sure, a surprise. But the son of a secessionist? That such a man became judge could only be the result of a conspiracy between Yahweh and the boy's mother. Cf. the story of Samuel's birth and early years (I Samuel 1–2), in a later Philistine crisis.

As an added dividend we have here a colorful reflection of life on the Philistine frontier, sure to be illuminated in considerable detail by continuing archaeological work. See e.g. Wright, BA 29 (1966), 70–86; and Dothan, "Ashdod of the Philistines," *New Directions in Biblical Archaeology* (Garden City, N.Y.: Doubleday, 1969), pp. 15–24.

XXX. The Messenger Is for Life
(13:21–25)

13 21 Yahweh's envoy did not reappear to Manoah and his wife. Then Manoah acknowledged that he was Yahweh's envoy. 22 And Manoah said to his wife, "We are going to die! We have actually seen God!"

23 But his wife said to him, "If Yahweh had desired to kill us, he would not have accepted a burnt offering and grain offering from our hands, or shown us all these things, or just now announced to us such a thing as this."

24 So the woman bore a son and named him Samson. The boy grew, and Yahweh blessed him. 25 The Yahweh spirit began to arouse him at a Danite camp between Zorah and Eshtaol.

NOTES

13:21. *envoy did not reappear . . . Manoah acknowledged*. For this use of *yd‘*, "acknowledged," see 4:9 and NOTE. The latter part of this verse picks up the statement in 16b, and neatly reverses it. What he did not know then, when the envoy was present, he later "acknowledged," when the "envoy did not reappear."

22. *We are going to die*. Manoah draws the dreadful consequence. Cf. 6:22–23. This unit displays a skillful antithesis to the preceding one, where the unnamed wife was shown to be on the brink of an identification that would require a miracle to convince her husband.

23. Her argument is a practical one, countering the popular idea that to look directly upon God or his angel must be fatal.

24. *Samson*. The name is clearly related to Heb. *šemeš* (sun), and means "(Man of) Shamash" or the like. It remains an open question whether the ending is the Hebrew diminutive, "little sun," or adjectival, "solar." The ending may belong to a class of Ugaritic personal names, ending in *-yanu*. For additional, but more remote, possibilities, see Kraft, IDB IV, 198–99.

A number of similarities to the traditions of chs. 4 and 5, noted below, suggest that the narrator believes that Samson as a judge was several cuts below Deborah; see esp. the conclusion to the Song of Deborah (5:31).

The boy grew, and Yahweh blessed him. Cf. I Sam 2:26 and Luke 2:52.

COMMENT

This sequel to the scenes involving the heavenly messenger is brief by comparison, but it continues the ruling ideas. The plodding confidence of the unnamed Yahwist woman dominates the conclusion of the chapter as it does the beginning.

The concluding reference to Samson's display of the Yahweh spirit is anticipatory. It will be explicated by the incidents of ch. 14, which mark him as having excellent potential for the office of military leadership, in terms of physical prowess.

XXXI. Frontier Life
(14:1–20)

Samson Aroused

14 ¹ Samson went down to Timnah. At Timnah he noticed a certain woman among the daughters of the Philistines, and she was the right one in his eyes. ² He came up and told his father and mother, "At Timnah I noticed a certain woman among the daughters of the Philistines; get her for me now, as my wife!"

³ His father and mother said to him, "Is there no woman among the daughters of your brotherhood, or among all my force, that you must go get a wife from the uncircumcised Philistines?"

But Samson said to his father, "Get her for me, for she is the right one in my eyes!"

Note

⁴ Now, his father and mother did not realize that it originated with Yahweh, that he was looking for some occasion from the Philistines. The Philistines at that time dominated Israel.

To Timnah Town

⁵ Samson went down to Timnah with his father and mother. He turned aside and went into the Timnah vineyards, where suddenly a young lion came roaring to meet him. ⁶ But Yahweh's spirit empowered him, and he tore it open—like tearing a kid!—barehanded. But he never disclosed to his father and mother what he had done. ⁷ He went down, then, and spoke to the woman. She was, in Samson's eyes, the right one.

⁸ Some time later, when he returned to get her, he turned aside to look at the lion's remains. And to his surprise, there was a swarm of bees in the carcass of the lion—and honey! ⁹ He scraped it into his hands and was on his way, eating as he went. When he rejoined his

father and mother, he gave some to them, and they ate too. But he did not let them know that it was from the lion's carcass he had scraped the honey. 10 So his father went down to the woman.

The Big Spender

Samson staged there a party for seven days, because that is what the elite fighters used to do. 11 Because they were afraid of him, they arranged for thirty friends to be with him. 12 Samson said to them, "Let me propound you a riddle. If you can fully explain it for me within the seven days of festivity—if you can solve it—then I will give you thirty linen garments and thirty changes of fine clothing. 13 But if you cannot explain it for me, then you will give me thirty linen garments and thirty changes of fine clothing."

They said to him, "Propound your riddle. Let's hear it." 14 So he said to them:

> Out of the eater came something to eat,
> And out of the strong came something sweet.

But they could not explain the riddle even three days later. 15 So, on the fourth day, they said to Samson's bride, "Either wheedle your husband to let us know the riddle, or else we will burn you and your father's house! Have you invited us here to impoverish us?"

16 So Samson's bride shed tears before him and said, "You simply hate me! You do not really love me! You have told a riddle to my countrymen, but you have not let me know!"

And he said to her, "Look here, I have not even told my father and mother. So should I tell you?" 17 So she cried on his shoulder for the seven days that they feasted, and on the seventh day he told her because she had nagged him. Then she explained the riddle to her countrymen.

18 The townsmen, then, said to him on the seventh day, before the sun had gone down:

> What is sweeter than honey?
> And what is stronger than a lion?

And he said to them:

> If you had not plowed with my heifer,
> You would not have solved my riddle!

19 And the Yahweh spirit suddenly empowered him, and he went down to Ashqelon, struck down thirty of their men, took their gear,

and gave the clothing to those who had explained the riddle! Then, his anger blazing, he went up to his father's house. 20 And Samson's bride became the wife of his best man, whom he had befriended.

NOTES

14:1–20. This chapter divides naturally into three main segments. The first (vss. 1–3) comes to a peak with Samson's point-blank directive to his parents; "get her for me" (vs. 3) forms an inclusio with "a certain woman" (vs. 1). Verse 4 is a rather cumbersome explanation inserted between story segments. Verses 5–10a belong together by virtue of the inclusio in which first Samson and finally his father "went down," and vss. 10b–20 show how the problematical marriage was annulled by the young man's unexpected display of the Yahweh spirit.

1. *Timnah.* The site is identified with Tell el-Batashi, four miles northwest of Beth-shemesh, "House or Temple of the Sun-god," in the Wadi es-Sarar. See Map 2, B-4. The name means "allotted portion," and the earliest hearers of the story would have been alert to the institutional relationship between military service and land tenancy in early Israel (see NOTE on 1:3).

and she was the right one in his eyes. With LXX^A restoring *why' yšrh b'ynyw*, which was lost by haplography due to homoioarkton in Hebrew. The phrase forms an inclusio with the end of vs. 3. On the variation in Greek equivalents for *b'yny* (*enopion* in vs. 1, *en ophthalmois* in vs. 3), see Appendix A, point 13.

This is the reader's first exposure to a phrase that is reiterated in the Deuteronomic climax (17:6) and the later Deuteronomistic conclusion (21:25) to the book.

3. The parents object to the declaration of independence implied by Samson's not only choosing his own wife, but choosing a non-Israelite one. The "brotherhood" are those who have cast their lot with Manoah; they comprise his fighting "force" (*ām*, as repeatedly in Joshua and Judges). The "brotherhood" would doubtless begin with blood relatives, and the rest would quickly acquire relationship through marriage, as Freedman has reminded me.

my force. This assumes that the father speaks for both parents. LXX^L, Syr. "your force" may be understood as contamination from the preceding, "your brotherhood."

uncircumcised Philistines. Again in 15:18; I Sam 14:6; 17:26, 36; 31:4; I Chron 10:4. In the matter of circumcision Israel participated in the wider culture, the Philistines being, so far as we know, the sole uncircumcized people in Israel's vicinity. In this case the reason for opprobrium is not the absence of the rite, but the dual loyalty which such a marriage would involve, as becomes clear in the third vignette of the chapter. Compare the problem of "wives for Benjamin" in ch. 21.

4. This verse falls between preformed units which are marked by inclusios (1b and 3b, 5a and 10). The verse is interpreted as a compiler's transition, comparable in purpose to the remarks of 13:16b. In this case it was important to explain that an action contrary to the basic standards of Israelites was actually part of the divine plan.

Yahweh . . . looking for some occasion. That is, some legitimate opportunity, excuse, whereby he could seek satisfaction from the Philistines.

dominated. Heb. *mšl,* as in Gideon's refusal of the throne (8:22–23) and in Abimelech's rationale (9:2).

5. *He turned aside and went into.* Heb. *wysr wybw'.* Another example where attention to major recensions yields a text that is better than any one of them. The key is LXX^A which preserved the first verb but lost the second one. LXX^B omits the first verb and reads the second one as singular, "he entered." MT reflects an attempt at correction after the lapse: "they entered." The restoration of *wysr* uncovers a wordplay with *wtyšr* "she was the right one."

6. He was a man whom Yahwism could equip to handle any physical threat to himself.

like tearing a kid. That is, the way a lion would tear a kid apart. Or possibly, as though the lion were a mere kid.

But he never disclosed to his father and mother what he had done. This comment is often regarded as an interpolation based on vs. 16. It belongs, however, to the building of suspense. The implication is that, if he had leveled with his parents, his mother at least might have done something about him, based on her experience at the outset of Samson's story.

7. *in Samson's eyes, the right one.* He had not changed. See NOTE on vs. 3.

8–10a. *bees . . . honey.* Heb. *deborīm,* "bees." The scene in vss. 8–10a evokes comparison with the name "Deborah" who was consulted for a sign or oracle in the face of the Sisera crisis, which likewise stemmed from Philistine or Sea Peoples oppression. The frequency with which so many narrative elements from earlier stories reappear in inverted relationship in the Samson stories is indeed striking. Why did the redactor fill one whole chapter with the story of the honey? Honey was renowned for special qualities. The Mesopotamian could use a mixture of milk, honey, and other components to ward off a devil causing "fever-sickness"; the mixture was to be burnt. R. C. Thompson, *The Devils and Evil Spirits of Babylonia,* II (London: Luzac, 1904), 43. In Israel honey was not to be used in burnt offerings (Lev 2:11). Especially interesting are a Mesopotamian offering of "a mash of honey and milk" and a "libation of (honey), milk, wine, oil . . ." as part of the preparation for battle. Heinrich Zimmern, *Babylonische Religion: Ritualtafeln,* (Leipzig: Hinrichs, 1901), Text No. 57, p. 173. In Israel it was widely understood that honey held enlightening and courage-producing potential, as in the story of Jonathon (I Sam 14:24–30). Cf. also the "jar of honey" presented to the blind prophet Ahijah by King Jeroboam (I Kings 14). This data suggests that Samson's discovery of the congregation (Heb. *'ēdat*) of bees and the honey might have been a sign to him, especially if he had described the source of it to "his father and mother" (vs. 9). Either he missed the sign or else he suppressed it, and "his father went down" (vs. 10a) presumably to complete the negotiations.

9. *scraped*. With LXX which interprets *rdh* as "to remove, lift out." The verb is used twice in a wordplay with *yrd* "go down" at the beginning of vs. 10.

10. *Samson staged . . . seven days*. See illustration 9.

a party. Heb. *mšth*, a drinking bout.

for seven days. With LXX and Syr.

elite fighters. Heb. *baḥūrīm*, not simply "young men" (EVV), but "chosen" or "choice" ones. See Benjamin's left-handed fighters (20:15–16). The military usage is preferable here as background for the statement that follows in vs. 11.

11. *Because they were afraid*. The scene begins abruptly, with the antecedent of the pronoun subject "they" left obscure. Presumably it refers to the Philistine family. The translation follows LXX^A, Syr.^h, OL^L (Codex Lugdonensis), which reflect a preposition *b/k* with suffixed infinitive *yir'ātām* (against MT *kir'ōtām*, "when they saw"). The forms of *yr'*, "to fear," and *r'h*, "to see," were often ambiguous, and sometimes the ambiguity may have been deliberate. Freedman, private communication.

thirty friends. The expression is perhaps a double entendre based on the wide use of "the thirty" as a designation of "a circumscribed body of public functionaries," known both from the Bible and from Egyptian sources. See Talmon, BASOR 176 (December 1964), 33, who compares David's "thirty" (II Sam 23:13; I Chron 11:15). Burney (p. 361) on the other hand, compares a similar custom in peasant marriages of modern Syria.

12. *propound you a riddle*. Hebrew uses a cognate accusative, "Let me riddle you a riddle," a forceful device of popular narrative.

if you can solve it. MT perhaps preserves variants here.

14. The riddle is a precisely balanced bicolon (3+3).

15. *the fourth day*. With LXX, Syr., OL, where MT reads "seventh," which involves a displacement of only one letter in the Hebrew, an easily understandable scribal lapse in view of "seven" in vs. 10 and "the seventh" in vs. 17.

bride. Hebrew vocabulary makes no distinction between "wife" and "woman"; both are *'šh*. The status of bethrothed women was almost identical to that of married women. Gen 29, esp. vss. 23 and 27, indicates that a marriage was consummated on the first day of the seven day feast.

here. Reading *hᵃlōm*, with five manuscripts, for *hl'* (interrogative and negative) which dangles at the end in MT.

to improverish us. With LXX^A which reflects the hiphil, against MT's qal form "to take possession of us."

16. *simply*. Heb. *raq* has asseverative force, as in Gen 20:11; Deut 4:6; I Kings 21:25; Ps 32:6. Burney, pp. 364–65.

17. *the seven days*. That is, the rest of the seven days, since the nagging did not begin until the fourth day. But the number seven was the symbolic figure, overruling chronological precision at this point in the story. Cf. the number *seven* in 16:7–19.

18. *before the sun had gone down*. Hebrew uses a rare word for "sun" (*ḥrsh*, the final *h* may or may not be a feminine ending; perhaps it stands for a secondary helping vowel), apparently to avoid confusion with *šmš*,

chief element in Samson's name. At the very last minute they came up with the solution to the riddle.

19. *their gear.* Heb. *ḥlyṣwtm,* lit. "their harnesses" (cf. II Sam 2:21, RSV, "spoil"), the outer equipage, including the outer garment and the belting from which weapons and adornments were hung. Presumably "the clothing" (*ḥlypwt*) is used as a synonym.

20. *his best man.* Lit. "his friend," who is similarly described as "your best man" in the sequel to this story (15:2). He is presumably a different person from any of the "thirty friends" who had been selected for Samson, as indicated by the final clause "whom he had befriended," that is, chosen for himself, if we have rightly divined the antecedents of pronoun subjects and objects in the sentence.

Probably the "best man" was also a Timnite. In any case it was considered a legal marriage, for when the woman was abandoned by Samson they were legally divorced, as will become clear in the sequel.

COMMENT

The heavenly envoy's plan nearly founders on the liberal allowance, in Yahwist law, for exemptions from military service. The man who was newly married was allowed to go directly home from the scene of the muster, leaving the business of warfare to others (Deut 20:7, 24:5). The plot thickens.

On the other hand Manoah's parental opposition has nothing to do with ethnic dogma; as at Mari, foreign wives were regarded as prejudicial to state security. Samson's marriage with a Philistine was Yahweh's provision for the well-being of Israel, which was more severely threatened than Manoah himself was aware. The marriage was annulled in such a way that Manoah is given no opportunity to say "I told you so," for the evidence of the Yahweh spirit is regarded in this early period as unpredictable. By a public display of faith and prowess a man could give evidence that he was to be judge (3:10; 11:29), and on occasion a demonstration of the spirit might be too compulsive (6:34). But the display of the Yahweh spirit could cease, or that spirit be displaced by an unhappier spirit (I Sam 16:14).

The Samson stories swarm with reminiscences and allusions to virtually all of the great protagonists from Deborah to Jephthah (see NOTES). This can scarcely be accidental. The pragmatic compiler has strung together the stories about the judges from the Southerner Othniel, in the very earliest period when Canaan was being reorganized as Yahweh's kingdom, to the Danite Samson, whose career he places in the troublesome days when Philistine pressures were in process of forcing a reorganization of the federation. The inroads of Philistia and the isolationist response of Manoah were probably paralleled elsewhere in the country (cf. chs. 17 and 18). But Manoah claimed the name of Israel for his followers, and the narrator claimed that, in Samson, Yahweh had found a judge to function between the Philistines and Manoah's "Little Israel."

The redactor of the stories, however, understood that Samson had judged the larger confederation for twenty years (15:20), and arranged materials so as to underscore that claim. Chapter 14 makes it clear that Samson has the requisite strength. What will be lacking is administrative charisma and this will make him a tragic figure (ch. 16). In the meantime he must ascend to the high office of judge.

15 ¹ After some time, during the season of the wheat harvest, Samson visited his bride with a kid. He said, "Let me go in, to my bride! Into the bridal chamber!"

But her father would not permit him to enter. ² Her father said, "What I say is that you in fact divorced her; and so I gave her to your best man. Is not her younger sister better than she? Take her, if you please, instead."

³ And Samson said to him, "This time I am innocent in regard to the Philistines when I do them injury!"

⁴ Samson went away and caught three hundred jackals; he took torches, turned them tail to tail, and put one torch between each pair of tails. ⁵ When he had set fire to the torches, he drove them into the Philistines' standing grain and burned everything, both stacked grain and standing grain, vineyards and olive orchards alike.

⁶ The Philistines said, "Who did this?" And they said, "Samson, the Timnite's son-in-law, because he took his bride and gave her to his best man." The Philistines then went up and burned her and her father's household.

⁷ So Samson said to them, "If this is the sort of thing you do, I swear I will be vindicated against you! But thereafter, I quit!" ⁸ So he struck them leg on thigh—a tremendous slaughter. Then he went down to stay in a cave of the crag Etam.

NOTES

15:1. *with a kid.* Perhaps the ancient counterpart of the box of chocolates. Samson suddenly shows up in Timnah, assuming that nothing has changed.

2. *What I say.* Hebrew infinitive absolute plus finite form, a most emphatic

declaration, as in the following "you in fact divorced her" (root *śn'* "to hate").
The latter is based on the technical term used in matters of divorce (Deut
24:3). This explains the father's ungovernable rage. He has performed an
irreparable act in giving his daughter to another man, and she cannot return
to Samson under any conditions (Deut 24:1–4). His only hope of salvaging
anything from the situation is to offer "her younger sister." But Samson
wants the elder one, and to deny that he had divorced her would only compound the hopelessness of the situation by making her an adulteress.

3. *to him*. With LXX^A, OL^L, where MT reads a plural, presumably as a
result of contamination from the object of Samson's threat, "Philistines . . .
do them injury."

4. *jackals*. Not foxes. See G. R. Driver, *Hastings Dictionary of the Bible*, 2d
ed. (New York: Scribner, 1963), pp. 652–53.

torches. The root is *lpd*, as in the name of Deborah's husband (4:4).

5. *both . . . alike*. I owe to Freedman the recognition of the chiastic
arrangement here, which requires only the reading of *mem* as a double-duty
consonant:

$$miggād\bar{i}š \; w^{e\text{'}}\bar{a}d\text{-}q\bar{a}m\bar{a}$$
$$w^{e\text{'}}ad\text{-}kerem \; (miz)\text{-}zayit.$$

6. *Who did this*. Cf. the inquiry in 6:29.

household. With LXX, Syr., and many Hebrew manuscripts where *bēt*
(house of) has dropped out of MT by homoioteleuton.

7. *vindicated*. Passive of *nqm;* Samson trusts in the necessary executive
action by Yahweh, where there is no court to settle the case. See *TenGen*,
pp. 92–93.

But thereafter, I quit. It adds suspense.

8. *leg on thigh*. The phrase appears to be explicated by the following
appositive, "a tremendous slaughter." He left them a tangle of legs and thighs.

leg. Heb. *šōq* is not "hip" (for which *yārēk*, "thigh," can do double duty),
but the shank from knee downwards, according to Burney (p. 370), who sus-
pects that the narrator uses a wrestler's term which would have been familiar
enough to his audience. Indeed, there were probably feats of strength to be
witnessed on the same occasions when folk assembled to be entertained and
edified by such material as the Samson cycle.

crag. Heb. *sela'*. Another point of lexical overlap with the enlistment of
Gideon (6:20).

Etam. "Place of birds of prey" (?). The meaning may be more important
than the place, which cannot be located with certainty.

COMMENT

Some time later Samson shows up in Timnah once again. The girl's father
explains that it had looked like divorce to him, but will try to make the best
of a bad situation by suggesting that the younger sister is, after all, better.
But it has been clear from the outset of his story that no one can tell
Samson how to choose a wife.

For the background of the practice involving jackals and torches (*lappīdīm*) two possibilities present themselves. Some scholars recognize here the signs of a ritual practice to remove mildew from the fields. Others see in Samson's exploit a piece of guerilla strategy. (MLC, pp. 434–35, 536, cites the parallels to both.) The latter is more plausible. Samson is the guerilla fighter par excellence but a very poor follower or organizer. He is a complete antithesis of the great judges whose stories were placed ahead of his, especially Gideon and the team of Deborah and Baraq. The unit thus concludes with Samson hiding out somewhere in the southern hills. Like Baraq, who had been far away to the north and was recalled to go into the field when the people rallied around Deborah, Samson will have to be extradited if he is to fulfill the promise of 13:5.

XXXIII. Yahweh Is for Life
(15:9–20)

15 ⁹ The Philistines went up, encamped in Judah, and deployed themselves against Jawbone. ¹⁰ When the Judahites asked, "Why have you come up against us?" they said, "It is to tie up Samson that we have come, to do to him exactly as he did to us."

¹¹ So three contingents from Judah went down to the cave of the crag Etam and said to Samson, "Don't you know that the Philistines dominate us? What is this, then, that you have done to us?"

He said to them, "What they did to me balances what I did to them."

¹² Then they said, "We have come down here to tie you up, to surrender you to the Philistines."

And Samson said to them, "Swear to me that you personally will not try to harm me."

¹³ They said to him, "No. We will tie you securely and surrender you to them. We will not kill you." And they tied him with a pair of new ropes and brought him up from the crag.

¹⁴ He approached Jawbone, and the Philistines came shouting to meet him. Then Yahweh's spirit empowered him! The ropes on his arms became like flax that is set on fire, and the bonds disintegrated from off his hands! ¹⁵ He found a fresh donkey jawbone, reached out and grabbed it, and with it laid low a whole contingent. ¹⁶ And Samson said:

> With the donkey jawbone,
> One heap! Two heaps!
>
> With the donkey jawbone,
> I laid low a contingent!

17 When he had finished reciting, he threw the jawbone away, naming that place Jawbone's Height.

18 He was very thirsty, and so he cried out to Yahweh, "You have granted by your servant's hand this great deliverance. Shall I now die of thirst and fall into the hand of the uncircumcised?" 19 And God broke open the Mortar which is at Jawbone. Water flowed out of it and he drank. His spirit revived and he came alive!

Note

[That is why it is called "Spring of the Caller," which is at Jawbone to this very day.]

20 He judged Israel, in the days of the Philistines, twenty years.

Notes

15:9. *Jawbone.* Heb. *lᵉḥī.* The site is probably to be sought in the vicinity of Beth-shemesh (Map 2, B-4).

10. *Judahites.* Except for the birth narrative, this is the first hint given in the separate exploits of Samson that there was more at stake than the history of one man's family. Judahites are here regarded as constituent members of the Israel whom it was God's intention, one way or another, to rescue from the Philistines (13:5). Samson has left home, plundered Philistines, and found a hideout in territory belonging to Judahites; they are the ones who must handle the problem of extradition.

11. *contingents.* The recovery of the old military usage, later obscured as "thousands," once again brings a popular story into the realm of the plausible (see NOTE on 1:4).

dominate. See 14:4 and NOTE.

11–13 *What they did to me balances what I did to them* (vs. 11b). Samson explains his behavior as though he were the one who could decide what is just, again speaking better than he knows. For here at last Samson is the man in the middle, contending with both Philistine belligerence and Judahite servility. He extracts a promise that they will not harm him; that is, he makes a minor covenant which reaffirms his Yahwist identity, and lets them tie him "securely" (Hebrew infinitive absolute, vs. 13), willing to take his chances with the Philistines rather than exercise his enormous strength against his confederate brothers.

14. *He approached Jawbone, and the Philistines came shouting.* The narrator implies that the place was not inappropriately named, as he pictures Samson with his hands tied walking straight into a pack of Philistines clamoring for revenge.

Then Yahweh's spirit empowered him. As in 14:6. There the demonstration of the spirit was providential, but Samson had either missed the point or suppressed it. Here again the Yahwist spirit is salvific; it is to keep Samson in one piece.

15. *fresh . . . jawbone.* One that was still strong, not dry and brittle.

16. The little Song of Samson is an archaic poetic fragment, a tightly constructed pair of bicola, with repetitive parallelism, in the pattern 2+2/ 2+2. It was older than the finished story of Samson and is treated as such by the narrator.

One heap! Two heaps! Wordplay involving the words for donkey and heap, which are identical, *ḥmr*. The second line of the poem is an example of archaic poetic progression, to convey impassioned speech. For the same construction of absolute followed by dual to achieve the same effect, see "one or two girls" and the repetition of "dyed stuff" in 5:30. An alternative solution, though it involves repointing, is to read the infinitive absolute followed by the qal perfect plus enclitic *mem:* "have I mightily raged." YGC, p. 22. Cf. LXX, OL, and Vulg. Here is another striking sign of the continuity of Deborah and Samson traditions.

17. *Jawbone's Height.* Samson gives an explanation for the name of the Lehi suburb (*rāmat-leḥī*) where the fight took place. Military action usually occurred on or at a height, as in the Song of Deborah (5:18), and David's Lament (II Sam 1:21). Yet it cannot be the story's primary purpose to legitimate the name, as the one thing left unexplained is how the suburb acquired its distinctive characteristic, "Height." Rather, the story plays on the name of a town and neighborhood in order to make a point about Samson's exaltation (Heb. *rūm*). With all his fighting and singing he had gotten quite thirsty, and that common physical need was what finally enlisted him. This unit (vss. 9–17) is incomplete and not primarily etiological. On the role of water in the process of enlistment for military duty, see Introduction, pp. 16–17, and 7:1–8.

18. *and so he cried out to Yahweh.* The verb here is not the technical one "appealed" or "rallied" (Heb. *ṣ/z'q;* see NOTE on 3:9), but *qr',* the ordinary word for "calling." The implication is that Samson's speech to Yahweh was more an impudent harangue, but it was also, at last, direct address. Cf. his cry, after being tortured, in 16:28, a plea which corresponds structurally to this climax of "Samson, Part I."

your servant's hand. At first glance it appears to be polite address, mere formality, which scarcely fits the circumstances and tone of Samson's plea. He is the only one in the book to speak this way and the results are impressive. Is he speaking better than he knows? On the possible background of his servant claim in the obscurity of a Mosaic office, see 2:8 and NOTE.

the uncircumcised. Suspense is sustained to the very end as Samson uses the language his father taught him (14:3) in returning to the Philistines insult for insult (15:6). But here the fighting is past and Samson is, in a way, pleading for life. That is what he gets.

19a. *God broke open the Mortar.* Note the switch from "Yahweh" in the preceding description to "God" in the narrator's own judgment (see NOTES on 13:6–23, especially what happened "when God heard the voice of Manoah" in 13:9).

the Mortar. Heb. *maktēš* as in Prov 27:22. Here it apparently refers to a rocky spring, presumably so called for its peculiar form. Moore, p. 346. There was also a *maktēš* in Jerusalem (Zeph 1:11).

his spirit. Surely an intended contrast to his sporadic display of the Yahweh spirit.

and he came alive. Heb. *way-yeḥī,* the very last word about Jawbone (*leḥī*). The concluding paranomasia indicates interests more poetic than etiological. It is now clear why in the case of Samson the judge formula only occurs for the first time in 15:20. That is, all of the Samson stories to this point have been concerned with his becoming really "alive," his enlistment as Yahwist judge.

19b. *That is why.* Heb. *'al kēn,* lit. "therefore," a very different formulation than the consecutive-imperfect in the statement of vs. 17b. This verse is, rather, a late etiological comment.

Spring of the Caller. Heb. *'ēn haq-qōrē,* originally "Partridge Spring."

to this very day. See NOTE on 1:21. The climax and conclusion of the Jawbone story were obscured by this insertion, which intervenes after the antecedent of the initial verb in vs. 20, "He judged."

20. See COMMENT.

COMMENT

These verses present two themes closely bound together; that Samson's single-handed victory against an entire Philistine contingent was the last chance to make a judge out of him, and that the need for water finally won him over. (Cf. the near rebellion due to a water shortage in Exod 17:1–7.) Both themes terminate in an etiological statement, and together they demonstrate the complexity of redactional problems involved in such materials, as indicated in NOTES on vss. 17–19.

It can now be observed how everything that transpires in chs. 14 and 15 is oriented toward the confrontation between Samson and Yahweh that occurs in vs. 18, concluding with the exclamation that, at last, "he came alive!" (vs. 19).

In its brevity, vs. 20 is another variation upon the minor judge rubrics (see NOTE on 10:1–2). It indicates that an early edition (by the pragmatic historian) concluded Samson's career at this point.

It is not clear who arose after Samson in the pragmatist's work. Perhaps that compiler turned directly to the careers of Eli and Samuel, and the transition to kingship in Israel. The connections, in any case, have been broken by the process of redactional activity which added a series of supplements to the old book.

Why did the pragmatist not include all of the Samson tradition, especially if the cycle was already somewhat unified (see NOTES on 16:15–17)? Presumably the same purpose is at work here as in the case of Othniel, where the pragmatist confined himself entirely to rubrics. Othniel was the "model" judge at the beginning of a period which would end with Israel on the verge of dissolution. Samson toward the end of that period was truly remembered as a judge, despite all the wild stories about him. It had to be borne out that from first to last Yahweh had in truth ruled Israel through his judge, so the pragmatist used the popular stories to explore the implications of that pivotal conviction. Apparently it was also his last word on the period prior to Samuel.

SUPPLEMENTARY STUDIES

XXXIV. Samson: The Message of His Death
(16:1-31)

The Gaza Affair

16 1 Samson went to Gaza, saw a prostitute there, and went indoors. 2 When it was told to the Gazites, "Samson has come here!" they gathered around and waited in hiding for him all night in the city gate. They kept quiet all night, thinking, "When daylight arrives, we will kill him!" 3 But Samson lay low until midnight. And at midnight he got up, took hold of the doors of the city gate and the two gateposts, pulled them up—bar and all—lifted them to his shoulders, and carried them up to the top of the hill that faces Hebron!

The Double Agent

4 Later on he fell in love with a woman in Vineyard Valley. Her name was Delilah. 5 The Philistine tyrants approached her and said to her, "Entice him! Find out how his strength became great, and how we can overcome him and tie him up to torture him! We will give, each man's unit, one hundred in silver."

6 So Delilah said to Samson: "Please tell me the secret of your great strength and how you might be tied up, that one could torment you."

7 Samson said to her, "If they were to tie me up with seven pieces of fresh gut which had not been dried, then I would become weak and be like any other human being."

8 So the Philistine tyrants brought her seven pieces of fresh gut which had not been dried, and she tied him up with them. 9 The delegation was waiting for her in the inner room. And she said to him, "Philistines are on you, Samson!" But he snapped the cords, the way a strand of tow snaps when brought near the fire. The cause of his strength was not made known.

10 Delilah said to Samson, "Look here, you have teased me and told me lies. Please tell me now what is necessary to get you tied up."

11 And he said to her, "If they were to tie me securely with new ropes that had not been used for work, then I would become weak and be like any other human being."

12 So Delilah took new ropes and tied him with them and said to him, "Philistines are on you, Samson!" (The delegation was waiting in the inner room.) And he snapped them off his arms like a thread!

13 Delilah said to Samson, "You have been teasing me, up until now, and telling me lies. Tell me what is necessary to get you tied up!"

And he said to her, "If you were to weave the seven braids of my head with the web and beat up with the pin, then I would become weak and be like any other human being."

So, when she had put him to sleep, Delilah took the seven braids of his head and wove them with the web 14 and beat up with the pin, and then said to him, "Philistines are on you, Samson!" He awoke from his sleep and tore loose both loom and web!

15 She said to him, "How can you say 'I love you,' when you do not trust me? These three times you have teased me and have not told me what is the secret of your great strength."

16 And so, when she had nagged him with her words day after day, and pressured him, he was exasperated to the point of death; 17 and he told her his whole mind! He said to her, "A razor has never touched my head, for I have been God's Nazirite from conception. If I were to be shaved, my strength would leave me; I would become weak and be like every human being."

18 When Delilah saw that he had told her his big secret, she sent and summoned the Philistine tyrants with the message, "Come up once more, for he has told me the whole truth." And the Philistine tyrants came to her. They came with money in hand. 19 She put him to sleep with his head on her lap and called to the man. She snipped off the seven braids of his head. Then she began to torment him; his strength had left him.

20 When she said, "Philistines are on you, Samson!" he awoke from his sleep and said, "I'll go out—as I did before—and shake myself free!" He did not recognize that Yahweh had turned away from him. 21 The Philistines seized him, gouged out his eyes, and took him down to Gaza.

They bound him with bronze shackles, and he became a grinder in the prison. 22 But the hair of his head began to grow again after it had been snipped off.

After the Fall

23 The Philistine tyrants assembled to offer a great sacrifice with joy to Dagon their god. They said:

> Our God has given us
> Samson our enemy!

24 And when the populace saw him, they, too, shouted praise of their god. Indeed, they said:

> Our God has given
> to us our enemy,
>
> Our land's devastator,
> He piled high our slain.

25 Then it happened. When they were good and jolly, they said, "Summon Samson! Let him entertain us!" And they summoned Samson from the prison, and he performed before them. When they made him stand between the pillars, 26 Samson said to the lad who had hold of his hand, "Place me so that I may feel the pillars on which the building rests, so that I can lean on them." 27 The building was filled with men and women. All the Philistine tyrants were there. (On the roof there were about three thousand men and women looking on while Samson entertained.)

28 Then Samson cried out to Yahweh, "Lord Yahweh! Please remember me! Please strengthen me! Just this once! God! Let me deliver myself with one deliverance—on account of my two eyes—from the Philistines!"

29 Samson reached around the two middle pillars on which the building was supported, and leaned forward against them, one at his right hand, the other at his left. 30 Then said Samson, "Let me die with the Philistines!" and pushed with all his might. The building collapsed upon the tyrants and all the people inside it. Those whom he killed at his death were more than he had killed in his lifetime.

31 His brothers went down, and all his father's household, and claimed him. They brought him up and buried him between Zorah and Eshtaol in the tomb of his father Manoah. He had judged Israel twenty years.

NOTES

16:1. *prostitute.* Heb. *'iššā zonā.* Lit. "a harlot woman." The woman was going about her publicly recognized business; the judge of Israel was not going about his publicly recognized business.

2. *When it was told.* The verb is missing in MT, which has a sentence fragment; restored from LXX.

waited in hiding . . . in the city gate. Excavations have contributed greatly to the clarification of both the architecture and the semantics of "the city gate," which was the setting of so much legal activity throughout the biblical period. The city gate, where it has been discovered in early Iron Age sites, was an elaborate complex, at least two stories high, with guardrooms flanking the tunnel-like opening. For one of the best known, see *Shechem,* ch. v, esp. pp. 71–79. Any Iron Age Palestinian would easily comprehend how Samson might slip past the Gazites at the gate because the latter had assumed that they could wait "in the city gate," that is, indoors, until morning.

3. The plausibility of vs. 2 is the necessary presupposition for this resolution of Samson's plight, where the point of the story is to emphasize with deliberate exaggeration Samson's enormous strength.

Hebron. At the southeast corner of the land, Hebron was a long way from Gaza at the southwest corner (Map 2, C-5, A-5). The two names, in vss. 1 and 3, form an inclusio, closing off the unit (Freedman, private communication). The name "Hebron" in later centuries carried a lot of traditionary freight as the scene of David's elevation to kingship after nearly being forced into the role of Philistine vassal. Wright, BA 29 (1966), esp. 80–82.

4. *Later on.* Hebrew uses the introductory *wayhī* (see NOTE on 1:1) and *'aḥªrē kēn,* "afterwards," which leaves the precise temporal reference to be determined from context. Verses 4–21 were apparently referred by the compiler to the close of Samson's long career, thus balancing the story of vss. 1–3, which he related to Samson's early administrative years.

Vineyard Valley. Lit. "wadi (*naḥal*) of choice vines." It is the modern Wadi-es-Sarar, which begins about thirteen miles southwest of Jerusalem, guarded in ancient times by the town of Beth-shemesh (Map 2, B-4). That the woman is identified by wadi and not by home town suggests a narrative interest in another *nḥl*-word (Timnah, "allotted portion," in 14:1 is a synonym) which stood for the warrior's plot of ground held by virtue of service to his sovereign (see NOTE on 18:1; cf. 1:3 and NOTES).

Delilah. "Flirtatious," the name being best explained as related to Ar. *dallatum,* "flirt," yielding a sense quite congenial to the narrative structure. Recourse to Babylonian proper names (Burney, p. 407) is unnecessary.

5. *tyrants.* This is a technical political title that connects the social organization of the five great Philistine cities on the southern coastal plain with an Aegaen homeland. See 3:3.

Find out how . . . great. Lit. "see in what his strength is great."

each man's unit, one hundred. This translation is based on a redivision of

MT, without consonantal change, detaching the conjunction *w* from the number and reading it as suffix with the preceding, thus *'alpō,* "his (military) unit." MT reads "we will each give you eleven hundred," which multiplied by five for each of the tyrants, is a bribe of five thousand five hundred shekels. Such a figure is incredible, when it is recalled that the total of confiscated rings taken from the Midianites/Ishmaelites in 8:26 was only "one thousand seven hundred shekels." While prices obviously fluctuated, it is worth comparing the four hundred shekels which Abraham paid for a family burial place (Gen 24:15, 19), the fifty shekels which David paid for the oxen and threshing floor of Araunah (II Sam 24:24), the seventeen shekels that Jeremiah paid for a piece of property (Jer 32:9), and the thirty shekels which the covenant code sets as the value of a slave (Exod 21:32).

The source of the "eleven hundred" in this verse is probably the story at the outset of the next chapter, where "eleven hundred of silver" is more plausible as an item budgeted by Micah's mother for the manufacture of a sculpture in metal (17:2). Following the restitution of the "eleven hundred of silver," Micah hires a Levite for only "ten of silver per year" (17:10).

I owe to Freedman the suggestion which leads to a solution, reading "eleven hundred" in our passage as due to a misunderstanding of *'elep,* a term for the military district of which each tyrant was leader. The offer is still exorbitant and naturally exaggerates the value of a hero like Samson.

6–17. Samson's proffered explanations of his strength move from magic (6:14) to reality (15–17); the last explanation is true. His treason is the betrayal of state secrets and the tragic squandering of his great strength, because he could not believe, as in the wedding story, that the woman would betray him.

7. *seven pieces of fresh gut.* There must be some obscure reason for using the physically inferior, unprocessed gut. This is the first of several answers proposed as mere magic. Is he demeaning the maledictory elements in his oath of office? Cf. the Hittite "Soldier's Oath" (ANET[3], pp. 353–54) where, in the middle of a maledictory marathon the official throws "sinews and salt . . . on a pan" and speaks as follows: "Just as these sinews split into fragments on the hearth—whoever breaks these oaths . . . let the oaths seize him. . . ." Samson is going to be dishonorably discharged from military service.

10–12. New gut failed? Try new rope! The new ropes have been anticipated by the extradition scene with the Judahites (15:13). There also Samson had displayed the Yahweh spirit and threw them off with ease.

13–14. The most curious of all the proposals. It is apparently a return, this time, to stronger magic.

Between the two references to *the web* the intervening details were lost by haplography in MT but survived with variations in the versions. The translation follows the widely accepted reconstruction of Moore, based on LXX[B]: . . . *hmskt* (14) *wttqʻt [bytd wḥlyty whyty kʼḥd hʼdm wyhy bškbw wtqḥ dlylh 't šbʻ mḥlpwt rʼšw wtʼrg bmskt wttqʻ] bytd.* . . . LXX[A] differs in the latter half and resists explanation in terms of a common Hebrew prototype, reading: "['. . . be like any other human being.' And Delilah put him to sleep and wove the seven braids of his head while he slumbered (?) and beat into the web] with the pin. Then she said to him. . . ."

Moore's explanation is worth quoting at length:

> We are to imagine the simplest kind of an upright loom, in which an unfinished piece of stuff was standing. While Samson sleeps on the ground with his head close to the loom, Delilah weaves his long hair into the warp with her fingers, and beats it up tight and hard. He was thus most securely fastened, in a prostrate position, to the frame of the loom, the posts of which were firmly planted in the earth. Moore, p. 354.

15–17. A return to reality, and this time the truth.

15. *you do not trust me.* Lit. "your heart," locus of mind and will, "is not with me."

16. *exasperated to the point of death.* Heb. *wat-tiqṣar napšō lā-mūt,* "and his life was shortened to die." This is comparable to the feelings of Elijah in I Kings 19:4 and Jonah in Jonah 4:8, where those prophets were so exasperated with God that each requested *napšō lā-mūt* "his life to die." I owe these references to Freedman.

17. *his whole mind.* "All (that was in) his heart."

God's Nazirite from conception. Cf. 13:5, 7. Apparently the true Nazirite had to do his own volunteering. Here the rule of the Nazirite warrior means so little to Samson that he can put it in the same category with certain common and unauthorized superstitions. There is, on the other hand, nothing superstitious about the cutting of Samson's hair, since this symbolizes his discharge from active duty according to the legislation in Num 6:13–20. The plot revolves not so much around a broken vow (Blenkinsopp, JBL 82 [1963], 65–76), as it does around a vow that had never been taken seriously. This story has numerous parallels in "the widespread belief that the strength, or very life of men (especially of heroes), resides in their locks." Gaster, MLC, pp. 436–43, 536–38. But the story makes its own point and presents its own peculiar antisuperstition polemic.

19. *called to the man.* Apparently the man brought her the razor, and perhaps assisted by holding his head.

She snipped. It is rather to be doubted that they could have "shaved" him in such circumstances, as he was easily awakened. Cf. the scene in the tent of Jael (5:24–27).

20. Contrast the Song of Deborah, "When they cast off restraint in Israel" (5:2), and "Awake, Deborah!" (5:12). Samson, however, has been released from duty.

He did not recognize. This comment, like 13:16b and 14:4, makes explicit what is essential to the story.

22. *began to grow again.* He could enlist once again upon proper application (vs. 28).

23. *god.* There is pronounced sarcasm in the narrative. Yahwists have already been advised that it was Yahweh who had surrendered Samson.

Dagon. The name means "grain." Dagon's temples are mentioned at Gaza and Ashdod, and his cult and mythology have been brilliantly illuminated by discoveries at Ugarit (a temple, stelae, a number of texts); he was once known as the father of Baal. See Ginsberg, *Orientalia* 7 (1938), 1–11. Cf. the sparkling story of the Ark of the Covenant in Dagon's temple at Ashdod (I Sam 5:1–5). In our passage, however, the name is perhaps an antiquarian's gloss, since Dagon in the story explains nothing and is not mentioned again, nor even alluded to. All that the annotator knows is that what used to be a deity is now his word for "grain." The original narrator was wrestling with his own problem of comparative religion, and in his own way.

Our God. The common noun for deity that, elsewhere in the book, often signals someone's value judgment, as distinct from mere reporting. See e.g. 13:6–10 and Note. Here the Philistines unwittingly praise the God of Israel. The little proclamation is poetic (a standard bicolon, 3+2, omitting the sign of the accusative).

24. *their god . . . Our God.* As though trying to be doubly sure that no one missed the point, the cues are repeated in close sequence: "their god" and "Our God." The popular response revives a poetic couplet (2+2//2+2, omitting the relative pronoun and sign of the accusative as secondary accretions), with rhyme that successfully evades this translation.

> *nātan 'elōhēnū beyādēnū 'oyebēnū*
> *maḥrīb 'arṣēnū hirbāh ḥalālēnū*

25. *Then it happened.* Introductory *wayhī*, arresting attention and alerting the listeners.

When they were good and jolly. Reading the qere, *ke-ṭōb libbām* "when their heart was amiable." For the double entendre, see Notes on 9:2 and 11:3 (*ṭōb* as covenantal amity) and 5:9 (the "heart" in judicial activity). Bring out the judge! The situation will be echoed in 19:22.

26. *the lad.* Heb. *na'ar,* the word denotes the field commander's squire as in the stories of Gideon (7:10) and Abimelech (9:54, where Abimelech commands his squire to put Abimelech out of his misery; cf. I Sam 31:4). Here "the lad" is the one assigned to lead the blind captive, Samson.

Place me so that I may feel. The Hebrew is paratactic but the sense is clear. Lit. "Place me and cause me to touch."

27. With so many indications of a narrator straining for credibility, we are forced to seek an explanation for the reference to "the roof." It is not mentioned again, nor is the figure "three thousand" repeated, suggesting that this is an intrusive element. The *gāg,* "roof," where they stood probably refers not to the temple but to some unspecified structure, or perhaps even a nearby hill, from which the bulk of the crowd watched the proceedings. The narrative gives no hint to the total of fatalities. Freedman, private communication.

28. The disjointed Hebrew syntax is surely by design.

Lord Yahweh. See the confession initially wrested from Gideon (6:22).

God. Samson in person appeals to his Sovereign for vindication (*nāqam*)—the exercise of God's prerogative—not vengeance. See Introduction, "Heaven and Earth: Yahweh's Kingdom."

Let me deliver myself. The niphal cohortative here may be translated either as passive, "Let me be delivered," or reflexive as above. The latter seems best, as in Isa 1:24 where the reflexive sense is clear, as pointed out to the author by Freedman. See now *TenGen,* p. 93.

29. *the pillars.* The main hall of a recently excavated Philistine temple is "a long room whose roof was originally supported by two wooden pillars set on round, well-made stone bases, placed along the center axis." Amihay Mazar, "A Philistine Temple at Tell Qasile," BA 36 (1973), 43.

30. *Let me die with the Philistines.* The tragic inversion of the high prospects which had accompanied his entry upon the judicial office: then "he came alive!" (15:19).

more than he had killed in his lifetime. Such tragedy was not an occasion for assigning blame or credit: not to Samson, nor to Philistines. All parties concerned had submitted their case, and God had returned a decision.

31. It was the end of an era. It is interesting that, as in the case of Gideon, Samson has no tomb of his own but is "buried in the tomb of his father." See COMMENT on 8:32.

He had judged. Notice the use of the perfect tense. Elsewhere the verb is regularly imperfect, "he judged," as in 15:20. The literary device of repetitive resumption has been studied by Shemaryahu Talmon, who recognizes here a recurring device by which self-contained units were incorporated into narrative texts. Talmon includes Judg 15:20 and 16:31 with numerous other examples discussed in 1970 meetings of the Biblical Colloquium. Judg 16:31 he regards as the contribution of the redactor of ch. 16. The redactor, when he repeats, frequently inverts elements (cf. 2:6–9 and Josh 24:29–31) or revises slightly (e.g. the verb form in 15:20 and 16:31).

COMMENT

The older pragmatic edition of the story of Samson had answered the question: What became of Samson the prodigal son of Manoah? It had left unanswered the question: What became of Samson the Israelite judge? The Deuteronomic Historian, however, seldom left such questions unanswered unless his sources failed him, so this chapter may safely be attributed to him. Here the career of the hero is reviewed by juxtapositing two popular stories from the Samson tradition: the Gaza girl (vss. 1–3) and Delilah (4–22). The stories are shaped by the tradition's uniform characterization of Samson; but they are not two versions of the same story, as is clear from the very different settings and the anonymity of the prostitute in the first story contrasting with the high social status of Delilah. The compiler is implying that judge Samson learned nothing from his near fatal Gaza escapade, but nearly destroyed Israel as a result of the Delilah affair.

On that occasion Yahweh had in fact allowed him to be discharged from military service, so that Israel was left for a while without a judge to lead them against the Philistines. The final story to be told about him (vss. 23–30) centers on his last-minute reenlistment and a momentary settling of the Suzerain's accounts with both the Philistines and the Israelites.

The Deuteronomic Historian, who lived during the great religious reformation of King Josiah's reign (late seventh century B.C.E.) saw how relevant this last Samson story would be to his own time. That is, Israel will be safe as long as Israel's leaders truly turn to Yahweh, a point on which the Deuterono-mist's source is in climactic agreement with the earlier book, which had con-cluded one segment with the enlistment of Samson (15:18–19).

The chapter concludes with a reformulation of the earlier "minor judge" rubric (15:20); "he had judged" in vs. 31b. It can therefore be seen that the Deuteronomic redactor divided Samson's career into two segments: his rise as judge (13:1 – 15:20), and his tragic end. It may be purely accidental that the surviving information about judge Samson deals exclusively with his private life, not his public responsibilities. The narrative makes the point that, while he ran afoul because of his own lusty self-interest, the consequent suffering evoked a new confession from him and he died honorably in the act of effecting Yahweh's justice toward Philistia. It was an instructive precedent for the king-dom of Judah as long as King Josiah was alive and while the decisive shifts in the balance of international power which led to Judah's destruction (early sixth century) were still in the future.

XXXV. A LOCAL SHRINE
(17:1 – 18:1)

Micah's Place

17 ¹ There was a man of the Ephraimite hill country whose name was Yahweh-the-Incomparable. ² He said to his mother, "The eleven hundred of silver which was taken from you and about which you swore an oath, and said it in my hearing—look, I have the money. I took it. But now I will return it to you." And his mother said, "My son is blessed by Yahweh!" ³ He returned the eleven hundred of silver to his mother, and his mother said, "I had wholly consecrated the money to Yahweh from my own hand my son, to make a molten figure."

⁴ He returned the money to his mother, and his mother took two hundred of silver and gave it to the smith, and he made of it a molten figure. There it was, in the house of Yahweh-the-Incomparable!

Summary and Transition

⁵ That man was Micah. He owned a shrine. And he made an ephod and teraphim and installed one of his "sons" who became his priest. ⁶ In those days there was no king in Israel. Each one did what was right in his own eyes.

Micah's Priest

⁷ There was a young man from Bethlehem in Judah (from the clan of Judah). He was a Levite and a resident alien there. ⁸ That man pulled out of the town (from Bethlehem) in Judah, to settle wherever he could find something. He penetrated the hill country of Ephraim as far as Beth-micah, making his own way. ⁹ Micah said to him, "Where do you come from?" And he said to him, "I am a Levite from Bethlehem in Judah. I am on the move, going to settle wherever I can find something."

10 Micah said to him, "Stay here with me. Be father and priest to me. I will give you ten of silver per year, the necessary clothes, and your sustenance."

11 The Levite agreed to move in with that man. And the young man belonged to him as one of his "sons." 12 Micah installed the Levite; the young man became his priest. It happened at Beth-micah. 13 Micah said, "Now I know for sure that Yahweh will favor me, for I've got the Levite as priest!"

Summary and Transition

18 1 In those days there was no king in Israel; but in those days the Danite tribe was seeking for itself a place to live, since no plot had as yet fallen to it among the Israelite tribes.

NOTES

17:1–13. This chapter introduces the exploited, and thereby corrupted, hero of the story, a young Levite who is dissatisfied with his prospects at Bethlehem in Judah (vss. 7–13). He is presented as one man doing what was right. But this only becomes clear from the introductory study of Micah, who does only what is cultically selfish. The introduction to Micah through his mother forms a calculated contrast to Samson and his mother. As companion piece to the Deuteronomic supplement on Samson, the rebellious ingrate, the same redactor added the story of Micah, the cultic opportunist.

1. *There was.* Introductory *wayhī.* See NOTE on 1:1.

Yahweh-the-Incomparable. Literally, Micah's name means "Who is like Yahweh?" The name is paraphrased in translation of the pericope, to give due force to the ironic conclusion in vs. 4.

2. *eleven hundred in silver.* A unit of weight is implied here as in 9:4, probably "shekels" as in 8:26. The figure "eleven hundred" is extravagant but not incredible, as the amount budgeted by a prosperous woman for contribution to a Yahwist sanctuary in the form of religious art. As noted above, this figure has influenced the description of individual contributions to Delilah's fund (16:5 and NOTE).

from you. The preposition is *lᵉ,* in an archaic sense, rendered certain here by the similarly archaic spelling of the pronoun *'attī,* "you," in the next clause.

and said. The verb *'āmart,* "you said," is awkward. Commentators usually insert here some form of the vow now found in vs. 3 (Myers, *The Interpreter's Bible,* II, 799). Unfortunately the uniform support of the versions for MT at this point forces any reconstruction to proceed without controls. The translator has concluded that the narrator presents Micah on this embarrassing occasion as having difficulty forming his sentences.

But now I will return it to you. This statement is restored from the end of vs. 3 in MT, where it appears, instead, to be a statement made by the mother. I suspect that the displacement was triggered by confusion of "archaic" and "modern" uses of prepositions.

My son is blessed by Yahweh. For the formula, cf. Melchizedek's blessing of Abram in Gen 14:19. Like a doting mother she forgets the crime in her response to the confession. This is traditional. Freedman compares the parable of the Prodigal Son (Luke 15:11–32), which makes the same point.

3. *my son.* Heb. *lbny.* The *lamedh* is vocative, which is not surprising in a context which also uses the same element in another archaic sense "from" (vs. 2).

molten figure. Heb. *pesel u-massēkā,* lit. "sculpture and something poured out," an example of hendiadys. The hendiadys explains the much discussed singular form of the next main verb. Scribes of later centuries were no longer alert to the early methods of composition. Since images of any sort are strictly proscribed by the commandments (Exod 20:4–6), the story presupposes a falling away from the Mosaic system, apparently a local syncretistic variety of early Yahwism at a secondary shrine.

4. The style of this unit is complex, because the narrator begins well past the midpoint in the action. Both what the son did in returning the money (vss. 2a–b, 3a, 4a) and what the mother said (vss. 2c and 3b) needed emphasis so that the reader would observe what she did (vs. 4b) and ask himself: What became of the other nine hundred?

There it was. Heb. *wayhī,* arresting attention and forming a tight inclusio with vs. 1.

5. This verse is anticlimactic. It is treated here as a collector's comment anticipating the story that begins with vs. 7 and extends to the end of ch. 18, and to which the ephod and teraphim are integral. See NOTE on 18:14.

ephod. An elaborate priestly vestment. Gideon had made one for himself, and that was regarded as an especially unfortunate act (8:24–27).

teraphim. Divinatory equipment, apparently synonymous, in this context, with "molten figure." Cf. Gen 31:19, 34–35; I Sam 19:13; II Kings 23:24; Ezek 21:21; Hosea 3:4–5; Zech 10:2.

installed. "Filled the hand of"; Exod 28:41; 29:9, 29, 33, 35; Lev 8:33; 16:32; 21:10; et passim. This is not a sign of priestly redaction, but merely an indication that Micah used the proper routine.

"sons." Cannot have its familiar sense here, as is clear from the following account of how Micah hired his priest. The Levite became Micah's "son" by contractual arrangement.

6. *right in his own eyes.* Cf. 14:1, 3; 21:25. This important verse is not a sign that the book once concluded at this point. Rather it is, together with vs. 5, the redactional pivot separating stories of one cultic opportunist (Micah) and one aspiring careerist ("his" Levite). The supplementary stories that conclude the book deal with the cultic manifestation of the anarchy which preceded the careers of Samuel and Saul. This obervation in vs. 6 begins to force the question of how God was going to do anything about Micah, which will be answered in ch. 18.

7. *There was.* Introductory *wayhī,* which will form an inclusio with the

twice repeated *wayhī* of the conclusion (vs. 12; see NOTE). We are thus better equipped to understand the differences between vss. 1–4 and all that follows in chs. 17–18; the narrative is built up almost entirely of preformed units, with which the compiler did not choose to tamper. He strung them together using connectives such as vss. 5–6.

from the clan of Judah. This seems to be a restrictive note, referring the story to the very early period, prior to Judah's consolidation as the mighty southern "tribe." Note the similar restrictive use of *mišpāḥā,* "clan," to refer to Dan in the premigration setting of the Samson stories (13:2).

He was a Levite and a resident alien. The term *gēr,* "alien," in this description reflects the view that the Levites were considered technically aliens, resident in different tribal allotments, but with none of their own. The term "Levite" describes his occupation and, as he himself states, is adequate explanation of his movements in search of employment (vs. 9).

8. *find something.* That is, discover new opportunity, to judge from the vagueness of the Heb. *yimṣā'* (lit. "find").

Beth-micah. That the story attempts, in part, to explain a place name, is confirmed by the plural, "buildings," in 18:14. The location of Beth-micah is unknown, but it is probably somewhere in Ephraim.

making his own way. The Heb. *la-ʿᵃśōt darkō* is unusual and may mean "in the course of his journey."

10. *father.* A title which apparently emphasizes the priest's role as cultic diviner, responsible for "yes" or "no" oracular advice (as in 18:4–6). The equipment of Micah's shrine suggests that it was noteworthy for this reason. See the numerous references and allusions to the importance of proper Yahwist inquiry in the period. Later the title, "father," and the oracular responsibility belonged to prophets during the monarchy (II Kings 6:21; 8:9; 13:14). The characterizations before us suggest that in the case of Micah's Levite and the Danites, the weighty responsibility of the "father" is being exploited. Deborah was renowned as " 'mother' in Israel" for having produced the right answer (5:7).

ten of silver. A unit of weight, perhaps the shekel, is implied, as in vss. 3–4.

your sustenance. Heb. *miḥyātekā,* lit. "your living." An inverted image relationship with the Samson narrative is thus sustained, where for a period Samson "came alive!" (15:19) so it could be said that he "judged" (15:20). Micah will offer the young man "a living" and bestow the title "father" in order to have control of him and his divinatory skills.

Verse 10 concludes abruptly in MT, "And the Levite went" (*wylk hlwy*), which looks like a partial dittography of the following *wyw'l hlwy,* "the Levite agreed."

11. *agreed.* An echo of the Moses-Jethro agreement in Exod 2:21. Umberto Cassuto, *Exodus,* tr. Israel Abrahams (Jerusalem: Magnes, 1967), pp. 25–26.

"sons." That the use of this word (as in vs. 5) belongs here to careful and disciplined description (not to sentimentality) is clear from Micah's own avowal in the punchline (vs. 13).

12. *became . . . happened.* Heb. *wayhī* twice in abrupt sequence; inclusio

with vs. 7. The limits are set even more clearly by the repetition of the place name, Beth-micah, in vss. 8 and 12.

18:1. *In those days . . . no king in Israel.* That the summary fails to specify that "each one did what was right, as he saw it," but proceeds immediately to introduce the story of Dan's migration, indicates that what is lamented is the lack of acknowledgment of Yahweh's kingship in Israel. That is, the Danite migration is presented as the providential solution to the problem of Micah's establishment.

tribe. Here reference is to the eventual consolidation of Dan's power and prestige in the far north, which began, however, with the military expedition of a mere six hundred (vs. 11). Cf. the designation of Dan as a "clan" on the Philistine frontier in the Samson cycle (13:2), as here in the old preformed unit which the redactor takes up next (vs. 2).

seeking for itself a place. The last is *naḥ^elā*, "plot," the technical term for a soldier's landholding, granted with his pledge of future military services. See NOTES on 1:3, and 2:6. The redactor thus hints that the Danites were reversing the usual order, yet God was able to make administrative use of their migration.

no plot . . . fallen. The final word in Hebrew, "plot," must be the subject of the sentence. It is placed last for emphasis and identified as subject of the verb at the beginning of the long clause by use of the particle *b* (called the *beth essentiae*). Freedman, private communication.

COMMENT

The redactor who added chs. 17 and 18 to the book had been profoundly influenced by the destruction of the northern kingdom in 721 B.C.E. These chapters continue the "Supplementary Studies" which the Deuteronomic Historian appended to the earlier edition of the pragmatist's book. They preserve the memory of Dan's migration in the early eleventh century B.C.E. from the fringe of southern Philistine territory to the northern limit of the country (Map 2, B-4, D-1). The result was the establishment of a Yahweh cultus at Dan (formerly Laish) which was later viewed with a jaundiced eye by the administration in Jerusalem. That Judges was updated to include this story, which effectively counterbalances the polemic against the other great border temple of the northern kingdom, Bethel (2:1–5; Map 2, C-4), suggests that both sections can be attributed to the Deuteronomic Historian.

Verses 1–4 comprise a preformed narrative unit which has its pivot in the meaning of Micah's name, "Yahweh-the-Incomparable," which appears only here in its full spelling, obviously to attract attention to itself. It appears that the redactor was almost saying, "Think of it. Images! And with a name like that."

Verses 7–13 comprise another preformed narrative unit bearing more details about the historical Micah. This unit shows that the selfishness of the delinquent boy persisted even when he had grown into manhood.

Apparently there were two Micah stories which were combined long before the time of the Deuteronomic Historian (cf. the difference in Gideon stories:

chs. 6–7 and 8), for vss. 5 and 6 make excellent sense as the early connective. "Sons" (vs. 5) is used in its political connotation to exegete the political nuance of "clan" in the unit following. This explains how the same "young man" can be a Levite and also be traced to the Judahite cluster. That Judah is not called a "tribe" conforms to the overall impression that the story originated in a very early (premonarchical) period.

The transition in vss. 5 and 6 is carefully written so as to leave the matter of Micah's shrine as an unresolved item on Heaven's agenda, while the alternative introduction to Micah (short spelling from vs. 5 on) adds more nuances and facts. Finally in vs. 13 Micah clinches his deal with the Levite in the belief that he has also "bought" Yahweh, and it is time for a resolution.

The purpose of 18:1, another connective (probably Deuteronomic), is to remark how providential it was that in those days, when Micah had proclaimed his firm grip on God, and there was no judge in office (the word *dan* means judgment) and not yet a monarchical government, the Danites had been interested in migrating to find or take a plot of its own. What would be more just than for the Danites to execute Yahweh's judgment against the proud Ephraimite Micah, thereby accomplishing their purpose and Yahweh's both at the same time?

XXXVI. The Danite Migration
(18:2–31)

The Trouble With Spies

18 2 The Danites dispatched five prosperous men from their clan (from Zorah and Eshtaol), to reconnoiter and explore the land. They said to them, "Go, explore the land!"

They penetrated the Ephraimite hill country as far as Beth-micah and camped there overnight. 3 They were in fact very close to Beth-micah, and they recognized the accent of the young Levite. So they turned aside there and said to him, "Who brought you here? What are you doing in this place? What business have you here?"

4 He said to them, "This is what Micah did for me! He has hired me and I have become his priest."

5 So they said to him, "Inquire of God, please, that we may know whether the mission that we are on will be a complete success."

6 And the priest said to them, "Go confidently! The mission that you pursue has Yahweh's approval."

7 The five men departed and went to Laish. They observed the folk who were there, living securely, according to "Sidonians' Rule"— calm and confident—without anyone perverting anything in the territory or usurping coercive power. They were far from the Sidonians, however, and they had no treaty with Aram.

The Assembly

8 They came to their brothers at Zorah and Eshtaol. Their brothers said to them, "What do you . . . ?"

9 And they said, "Up! Let's attack them! For we have seen the land! And, indeed, it is very good! But you are doing nothing about it. Don't be so slow about setting out to invade and take possession of the land! 10 When you arrive, you will come to an unsuspecting folk.

And the land is very broad. Indeed, God has handed it over to you, a place where there is no lack of anything on earth!"

Establishing a Beachhead

11 Six hundred men of the Danite tribe set out, fully armed, from Zorah and Eshtaol. 12 They went up and pitched camp at Qiriath-jearim in Judah.

(That is why that place is called Dan's Camp to this very day. It is west of Qiriath-jearim.)

13 From there they passed through the Ephraimite hill country and came as far as Beth-micah.

14 The five men who had gone to reconnoiter the territory (Laish) spoke up and said to their brothers: "Do you realize that there are in these buildings an ephod as well as teraphim and a molten figure? Make up your mind, now, what you are going to do."

15 They turned aside there and came to the house of the young Levite at Beth-micah and inquired after his health. 16 The six hundred fully armed men had stationed themselves at the entrance of the gate. 17 The five spies who had gone to reconnoiter the land approached, went in, and took the figure, the ephod, the teraphim, and the mold. (The priest stood at the entrance of the gate with the six hundred fully armed men.) 18 These went into Beth-micah and took the figure, the ephod, teraphim, and the mold. And the priest said to them, "What are you doing?"

19 And they said to him, "Be quiet! Put your hand on your mouth and come along with us. Be father and priest to us. Which is better: for you to be priest to one man's household or for you to be a priest to a tribe and clan in Israel?" 20 And the priest was so pleased that he took the ephod, teraphim, and the molten figure, and he went into the midst of the force.

The Conquest of Micah

21 They turned away and moved out, putting the youngsters, the cattle, and the heavy stuff in front of them. 22 They had made good distance from Beth-micah when Micah and the men who were in the houses in the vicinity of Beth-micah were finally mustered. But they overtook the Danites. 23 They shouted to the Danites, who turned around and said to Micah, "What is the matter with you, that you have mustered your men?"

24 He said, "My God—which I made—you have taken! And the

priest! And you have gone away! What do I have left? How can you say to me, 'What is the matter with you, that you have mustered your men?'"

25 But the Danites said to him, "Do not shout at us, or some fiercely unhappy men will attack you, and you will die along with your household!"

26 The Danites went their way, and Micah, seeing that they were stronger than he, turned back and went home.

Fiercely Unhappy

27 They took the thing Micah had made and the priest who had belonged to him and came to Laish, to a calm and unsuspecting people. They put them to the sword and burned the city.

28 There was no deliverer, because it was far from Sidon and they had no treaty with Aram.

(It was in the valley that belongs to Beth-rehob. 29 When they rebuilt the city and settled there, they named the city Dan in honor of their ancestor, who was born to Israel. But the city's name originally was Laish.)

30 The Danites erected for themselves the figure.

(Jonathan ben Gershom ben Moses and his descendants were the Danite tribe's priests down to the day of the land's captivity.)

31 They set up for themselves the image which belonged to Micah, who had made it, throughout the period that the house of God was at Shiloh!

NOTES

18:2–3. The story of the Danite migration and the rival temple in the far north is much older than the Deuteronomic redaction and needed no polemical retouching. The original polemics are aimed at the persons involved, not at this or that cult place.

2. *prosperous men.* Heb. *'anšē ḥayl* (the same as *gibborē ḥayl.* See 6:12; 11:1).

from their clan. With MT, preserving the singular where early versions read plural, a harmonization with vs. 1. Prior to the sixth century B.C.E., the forms were spelled alike. The translation omits *miqᵉṣōtām* (from their totality), probably a variant (missing in LXX^BN, Syr.).

explore the land . . . explore the land. The single-minded repetition emphasizes what the Danites charged them to do. It is essential narrative preparation for their casual inquiry (and equally casual response) in the middle of vs. 3.

3. *they recognized the accent.* An entirely plausible note; his speech was Judahite (southern) like their own, not Israelite (northern).

the young Levite. Heb. *han-na'ar hal-lēwī.* Not a conflation of sources, as proved by the subsequent contrast with "a man, a Levite" (19:1).

they turned aside. They departed, briefly, from their established purpose. They will request an oracle and be told what they want to hear.

Who . . . What . . . What . . . On double and triple questions as a stylistic heritage from pre-Yahwist Canaan, see NOTE on 2:22.

4. *This is what . . . for me.* That is, "so on and so forth." His answer was a ramble.

He has hired me and I have become his priest. This is the only information important to the soldiers. It thereupon occurs to the spies to seek an oracular legitimation of their objective. But that should have taken place before they were even dispatched. The perspective here is in agreement with the introduction in 1:1 – 2:5; the same problem will be explored at length in chs. 20 and 21, the Deuteronomistic conclusion.

5. *Inquire of God.* It is subjective; they really want to know.

will be a complete success. The verb is *taṣlīᵃḥ* with no object, an example of the hiphil elative, used to give emphasis to the root idea. There is no need to emend, with the versions, to read a qal form. Freedman, private communication.

6. *Yahweh's approval.* "Your way is in front of Yahweh." Abrupt shift to descriptive use signals that he who had made "his own way" (17:8) glibly pronounces about theirs. That is, the young Levite, perhaps without even using his divinatory gear, assures them of their God's concurrence. And thus they will rationalize the tragic slaughter of the inhabitants of Laish (vs. 10).

7. *Laish.* The name means "Lion." Dan on Map 3.

living securely. Cf. 8:11. Here it probably means "without defenses." This interpretation is borne out by excavations, which have indicated that the city was unwalled, the inhabitants in the early Iron Age relying on the old dirt ramparts which had been built early in the Middle Bronze II period. Biran, IEJ 19 (1969), 122–23.

Sidonians' Rule. An obvious double entendre, recalling the Yahwist's public allegiance to the "ruling" of the Yahwist judge, and the wider sociological nuance of *mišpaṭ* as "custom." What they saw was, in the narrator's judgment, more to be envied than overpowered: a situation "without anyone perverting anything in the territory, or usurping coercive power." Although the versions later had difficulty with it, emendations are unnecessary.

treaty. Heb. *dābār,* "word" in the sense of contractual stipulation. See NOTES on 11:11 and 28.

Aram. With some recensions of LXX, OL, Syr., reading *'rm* for *'dm* (man); the latter leaves MT unintelligible, whereas *d* and *r* were easily confused. The last line elucidates the "calm and confident" situation; the town was far enough removed from effective interference by either the coastal cities or the great caravan crossroads of Syria. Left alone, they had developed an enviable way of life.

8. The verse concludes with a sentence fragment, unless *mā 'attem* means

"How have you fared?" as proposed by ALUOS[D], 18–19. That the statement is incomplete is urged by the versions, which offer a variety of solutions. Perhaps it indicates that the spies are so enthusiastic and impatient for the enterprise that they interrupt the proceedings. Orderly deliberation never returns, and the Danites go on the warpath.

12. *That is why.* A late etiological and extranarrative note identifying as Dan's Camp a place near better-known Qiriath-jearim (city of forests?). See Map 2, C-4.

14. *Laish.* Missing in several Greek manuscripts; MT often preserves variants.

The spies now remind their confederates ("brothers"; cf. brotherhood in 14:3) what they had observed here, mentioning first the oracular device ("ephod," cf. 8:27) that had spurred them on (vss. 5–6). Next are mentioned also, for the first time in narrative context (see 17:5, which is redactional), the "teraphim." These are probably smaller representations of deity (see COMMENT). Finally the text lists *pesel u-massēkā,* "molten figure" as in the introductory Micah story (17:4). The teraphim and the molten figure are probably traditional variants; when it comes to a showdown, Micah will object to their theft of "My God" (vs. 24)!

15. *at Beth-micah.* In MT the preposition *b-,* meaning "at," was lost by haplography, if it was not in fact implicit from the beginning.

inquired after his health. The normal greeting. They asked about his *šlwm;* more than simple physical health, it is general well-being.

16. *at the entrance of the gate.* Omitting the phrase which follows in MT, "who were of the Danites," which is clearly out of place.

17. I owe to Freedman the recognition of an envelope construction here, in which the hendiadys of the first Micah story in 17:1–4 (*pesel u-massēkā,* molten figure) has been broken open to frame the pair that is first introduced in 17:5, "ephod and teraphim." This will also account for the redundancy in vss. 17 and 18. The last part of 17 is explanatory in order to place the various groups and the priest. Verse 18a must then repeat the action of 17a in order to provide a setting for the priest's question.

19. *a tribe and clan.* In Num 26:42 the "tribe" of Dan consists of a single "clan."

20. *the ephod, teraphim, and the molten figure.* With LXX[AB], where MT has lost the last in the series, *w't mskh,* by haplography due to homoioarkton.

Apparently he retrieved the items from the five with his decision to go along, and took up a safe position surrounded by the troops.

21. *heavy stuff.* Heb. *kebūdā* occurs only here; but cf. the masculine form in Gen 31:1; Isa 10:3; 61:6. LXX[B] read the nuclear sense of *kbd* and rendered *baros,* "heavy stuff." The idea was to keep the warriors between the loot and the victims who might give chase.

22. *Micah and the men.* With LXX, restoring the name where it has dropped out of MT.

23. *They shouted to the Danites.* Missing in LXX, which in some manuscripts also omits the last verb in vs. 22, thus reflecting a shorter recension in which ". . . the men of Micah's neighborhood were mustered in pursuit of the Danites, who turned back and said . . ."

24. *My God.* Micah speaks from the heart. He is talking about his image and the whole collection of three or four items, for which his group title was "God." Of highest priority to both Micah and the narrator is the molten figure contributed by his mother, later to adorn the Danite sanctuary.

that you have mustered your men. With LXX, missing in MT.

25. *fiercely unhappy.* Lit. "bitter of soul," like a bear robbed of her cubs in II Sam 17:8.

you will die along with your household. Lit. "you will gather in your life and the life of your household," a vivid idiom, equivalent to "cash in your chips." Freedman, private communication.

26. *Micah . . . turned back and went home.* He was an Israelite once again. Cf. the behavior of Israelites in 9:55.

It is instructive after all of this to compare the Testament of Jacob, Gen 49:16–18:

> Dan shall judge (root *dyn*) his people
>   as one of the tribes of Israel.
> Dan shall be a serpent in the way,
>   a viper by the path,
> that bites the horse's heels
>   so that his rider falls backward.
> I wait for your salvation, Yahweh!

(Adapted from RSV.) This poetic (and linguistically archaic) treatment of "Dan" is the mirror image of the prose account of Dan's instrumentality in heaven's justice for Micah, on the way to Dan's own treacherous achievements elsewhere.

27. Some scholars find this verse to be a description of the ḥerem, in a story which represents Dan as conducting a one-tribe (and therefore not authentic) holy war. McKenzie, *The World of the Judges*, pp. 162–63. Actually this is only the prelude to the reappearance of the ḥerem in 21:11, after dropping from view with the passing of Joshua's younger contemporaries (1:17 and 8:24–27; Gideon's date is early!). The "holy war" construct is inadequate here, where Micah's unholy cult is unwittingly "judged" yet intentionally exploited by the Danites on their way to the slaughter of the inhabitants of Laish and the founding of an illegitimate sanctuary. This constitutes one of the poles of the tragedy with which the book now concludes. The other pole is represented by the way the confederation was at last reduced to the handling of purely internal affairs (chs. 19–21).

28. This verse concludes with a marginal comment continuing in vs. 29, indicating the imprecision of the reference to the newly emerging Aramaean kingdoms late in the period. The territory in question was eventually controlled from Beth-rehob.

29. *Dan . . . who was born to Israel.* Gen 49:2.

Laish. Verses 28b–29 and 30b interrupt the flow of the narrative and are best understood as historical comments in the Deuteronomic (late preexilic) edition of the book.

30. *The Danites erected for themselves the figure.* The statement is fol-

lowed by another commentator's interruption, proposing the identification of the anonymous Levite with Jonathon, grandson of Moses. Here we must read the name of the founder (with the versions), where in MT a *nun* has been inserted (Manasseh), apparently so as to eliminate reference to Moses in a text which could not be changed by deletion or alteration of any of its letters.

the land's captivity. Probably a reference to the end of the northern kingdom and the removal of the Danites from that location after 721 B.C.E.

31. This verse concludes the story of Dan's migration with a narrator's value judgment.

house of God. In agreement with the subjective use of *'elōhīm* in vss. 5 and 10. The narrator's historical interest in the period of the early sanctuary at Shiloh brings us down to the middle of the eleventh century. There is nothing in the story to delay its complete formation in the amphictyonic period and hence no need to seek a later cult etiological explanation, contrary to Noth, who sought to understand the story as the work of Jeroboam's non-Levitical priests at the Danite sanctuary, ridiculing their Levitical predecessors of the amphictyonic period. See *Israel's Prophetic Heritage,* eds. Bernhard W. Anderson and Walter Harrelson (New York: Harper, 1962), pp. 68–85. Actually the young Levite does not earn much of either praise or blame as the story unfolds; what it is concerned to legitimate is not a priestly prerogative, but the Yahwists' claim to have been ruled by Yahweh.

COMMENT

With the recent and continuing excavations at Tell Dan the historical setting of these chapters is rapidly coming into focus. The great Middle Bronze city was violently destroyed around 1600 B.C.E. Its Late Bronze Age revival (evidenced chiefly in tomb materials) indicates a flourishing commercial contact with Cyprus and the Aegean world in the fourteenth century and later. Reference to a Sidonian standard of living is therefore not at all far-fetched. In addition to the discovery of a later Israelite "High Place" on the northwest corner of the tell, "there is evidence to indicate that already at an earlier period the site was in use." News Release, Israel Department of Antiquities and Museums, July 21, 1969. See also Abraham Biran, IEJ 19 (1969), 240–41.

Although the separate Micah materials were conveniently kept apart in ch. 17, they have been just as conveniently combined in this chapter, where the translation makes liberal use of parentheses to set off explanatory expressions. There is little to be gained from another source-critical analysis of the chapter (Burney, pp. 412–13, remains the best judicious attempt).

The narrator sets out presumably to describe Dan's conquest of territory in the far north. The careful reconnaissance, reminiscent of Jericho, is designed to build suspense: will the Danites in fact go by the rules? No, they will not. The assembly will be stampeded by the report of the spies, so that what begins with the prospect of a peaceful settlement in the north becomes, first of all, Yahweh's conquest of Micah's establishment (without bloodshed), followed by the unnecessary and unauthorized slaughter of the unsuspecting folk of Laish.

The Deuteronomic conclusion is an ironic one: for all that time Yahweh's legitimate central sanctuary had been at Shiloh (Map 2, C-3). The irony was subsequently obscured by commentators who contributed the legitimizing vss. 29 and 30b. Without these two verses, the chapter belongs to the late preexilic analysis of Israel's life in the covenant with Yahweh. What is most striking is that the historian was content to leave unrevised the critique supplied by the people themselves in their stories about the days when the judges ruled. In the case of Micah, Yahweh had assumed the role of judge, while Dan, whose name means "judgment," went on to commit atrocity.

Allowing wide margins for the exaggeration that is often necessary to tell an effective story, there can be no doubt that the record of Micah and the Danites illustrates the spiralling anarchy and ineffective tribal organization that led to the Samuel compromise, that is, the elevation of Saul and the transition to monarchy in Israel. And thus we need not wonder why the record, at this point, fails to describe Dan's denouement, for the historian was certainly an advocate of Yahweh's world government, and could confidently leave such matters to the course of subsequent history.

THE END

XXXVII. The Gibeah Outrage
(19:1–30)

Hospitality

19 1 In those days, when there was no king in Israel, there was a man, a Levite, living as a resident alien in the remote hills of Ephraim. He took to himself a concubine, a woman from Bethlehem in Judah. 2 But his concubine became angry with him and ran away to her father's house at Bethlehem in Judah. She was there some four months. 3 Then her husband got ready to go after her, to speak intimately to her and bring her back. He had with him his servant and a pair of donkeys. When he came to her father's house, and the father of the young woman saw him, he was delighted to meet him. 4 When his father-in-law, the father of the young woman, prevailed upon him, he stayed with him for three days; and they feasted and drank and passed the nights there.

5 Then on the fourth day, when they got up early in the morning and prepared to go, the father of the young woman said to his son-in-law, "Fortify yourself with a bit of food and afterwards you can go." 6 So they sat down, and the two of them ate and drank together.

And the father of the young woman said to the man, "Please be my guest. Spend the night and enjoy yourself!" 7 When the man got ready to go, and his father-in-law still urged him, once more he spent the night there.

8 And on the fifth day, when he got busy in the morning to depart, the father of the young woman said, "Please fortify yourself." They argued back and forth for most of the day. And the two of them feasted and drank.

9 Finally, when the man and his concubine and servant got ready to go, his father-in-law, the father of the young woman, said to him, "The day is getting along toward evening, so remain for the night. Since the day is done, spend the night here and enjoy yourself. To-

morrow you can busy yourselves for your journey and depart for your
own tent."

One Law, for You and the Sojourner

10 The man was unwilling, however, to spend the night; and so he
got ready, departed, and arrived opposite Jebus, that is, Jerusalem. He
had a pair of saddled donkeys, and his concubine and his servant were
with him. 11 As they were near Jebus and the day was far spent, the
servant said to his master, "Please, let's turn to this city of the Jebusites and spend the night in it."

12 But his master said to him, "We will not turn to a foreigner's
city. We will go on to Gibeah." 13 He said to his servant, "Come on,
let's move ahead to one of these places: let's spend the night either at
Gibeah or at Ramah." 14 So they moved on. They went their way,
and the sun went down on them in the neighborhood of Gibeah,
which belongs to Benjamin. 15 They turned there to go in and
spend the night at Gibeah.

When he went in, he sat down in the town plaza, since no one
would take them home to spend the night. 16 But there was an old
man coming in from his work in the field at evening, and the man
happened to be from the Ephraimite hill country. He was a resident
alien at Gibeah, whereas the men of the place were Benjaminites.
17 When he looked up and saw the traveler in the town plaza, the
older man said, "Where are you going, and where do you come
from?"

18 And he said to him, "We are passing en route from Bethlehem
in Judah to the remote hills of Ephraim. I come from there. I have
traveled to Bethlehem in Judah and I am going to my own house.
19 But no one invites me to his house, although we have both straw
and grain for our donkeys, as well as bread and wine for myself and
your maidservant and the lad who is with your servant; there is no
need for anything."

20 But the older man said, "Be at ease! All your needs are my responsibility. You simply must not spend the night in the plaza."
21 So he took him home and foddered the donkeys. And they washed
their feet, dined, and drank.

Rising to the Occasion

22 They were becoming more and more convivial, when the local
hell-raisers surrounded the house, pounding repeatedly at the door.

They said to the master of the house, the old man, "Bring out the man who went into your house. We would get to know him!"

23 But the master of the house went out and said to them, "No, my brothers! Do not commit such outrage, inasmuch as this man has come into my house! Do not commit this senseless disgrace. 24 Look, my virgin daughter, and his concubine—let me bring them out now. Ravish them. Do to them as you please. But to this man do not do this senselessly disgraceful thing!"

25 The men were unwilling, however, to listen to him. So the man seized his concubine and forced her out to them, and they got to know her. They vilely mistreated her all night long. They released her at the approach of dawn. 26 The woman came as the morning approached and fell at the door of the man's house where her master was till it was light.

27 Her master got up in the morning, opened the doors of the house, and went out to proceed on his way. And there was his concubine, prostrate at the door of the house with her hands on the threshold. 28 "Get up," he said to her, "and let's be going." But there was no answer, for she was dead.

So he lifted her onto the donkey and set out to go to his own place. 29 When he arrived at his "house," he took the knife, got a firm hold on his concubine, and systematically dismembered her, cutting twelve pieces; he sent her throughout all the Israelite territory. 30 And the men whom he sent he commissioned as follows: "Thus you shall say to every man of Israel, 'Has there ever been such a thing as this from the time the Israelites came up from the land of Egypt to this day? Put your mind to it! Take counsel and speak!'"

NOTES

19:1. *In those days, when there was no king in Israel.* Yahweh was in fact King. This will be the thrust of the final chapters. The story itself stems "from the period prior to the founding of the state," Alt, *Essays on Old Testament History and Religion*, tr. R. A. Wilson (Garden City, N.Y.: Doubleday, 1967), p. 251.

1. *a man, a Levite.* Conscious contrast (narrative inversion) to the preceding story of "a young Levite" (18:3). This one resides in the north and acquires a concubine from the south, a partial antithesis of Micah's "priest" (17:7–12).

2. *became angry with him.* This follows LXXᴬ which reads *orgisthe auto*, where MT and other witnesses have *wtznh 'lyw*, "she became a prostitute," i.e. was unfaithful, "against him." But it is strange that the woman would become a prostitute and then run home. Moreover the verb *znh* is not elsewhere con-

strued with *'l* in this sense. The Hebrew behind LXX^A (preferred by both RSV and NEB) is not entirely clear. The verb *orgidzein* is normally rendered *ḥrh 'p* in Judges (2:14, 20; 3:8; 6:39; 9:30; 10:7; 14:19), which however would never be confused with *znh*. This leaves *z'p* (which is construed with *'l*), *z'm*, or the obscure *znḥ* of Hosea 8:5 (all called to my attention by Freedman). While the last would be the easiest to explain in terms of scribal error, the first remains the most likely. MT is interpretive. As Israelite law did not allow for divorce by the wife, she became an adulteress by walking out on him. This is the reverse of Samson's predicament in 15:1–3.

3. The Levite's concern to recover his concubine suggests that she, not he, is the offended party. That he will seek a reconciliation elicits the reader's respect for the Levite at the outset of the story.

his servant and a pair of donkeys. The servant and asses show that the Levite gives every appearance of being self-sufficient (vs. 19).

When he came. With LXX^AL, Syr., where MT requires that we presuppose that upon arrival the concubine met him and "brought him" to her father's house. The difference may go back to oral variants.

he was delighted to meet him. The pronoun antecedents are thoroughly scrambled. Perhaps it means that the "father-in-law" was relieved that the man was actually going to reclaim the runaway daughter.

4–9. *his father-in-law, the father of the young woman.* This long title is usually treated as a sign of mixed sources, here and in vs. 9. However it forms a neat inclusio around the story of the visit. The construction is pyramidal, with the double title in vss. 4 and 9, "the father of the young woman" in vss. 5–6 and 8, and "his father-in-law" in vs. 7. Thus there is no need to posit different traditions. Repetition is common in Hebrew narrative, but normatively with slight and sometimes significant variations in forms and words. The double identification at the outset is necessary because of the ambiguity of unpointed *ḥtn* which may be either "father-in-law" or "son-in-law." Freedman, private communication.

This unit with its concentration upon the father-in-law likewise emphasizes his orthodox behavior. The father will be enormously relieved to see the young woman off with her husband once again. But his lavish hospitality in the meantime will create a new crisis. At the same time emphasis upon his position as father of the young woman prepares for a sharp contrast with the way another one will rise to the occasion amidst lavish hospitality, in vs. 24. In all of the dealings between the Levite and his father-in-law the question of original grounds for the young woman's anger and her flight home, indeed all interest in the young woman herself, gets lost in the shuffle.

4–5. *three days . . . on the fourth day.* Cf. the story of Samson's riddle (14:14–15). This is a narrative device by which the narrator begins at the climax; that is, the reader of the Levite's story will expect that he will now make his departure. But the Levite and his father-in-law are somewhat extraordinary. They will feast another two days.

5–9. It was a man's world. There is no mention of the interest of the girl in rejoining her husband, nor of what the womenfolk did while the two men celebrated for most of a week.

It has been argued that the repeated postponement of the departure is due to the merging of traditional variants reflected in the forms for "fortify" (*se'ad* in vs. 5 but *se'ad-nā'* in vs. 8) and "yourself" (*libbekā* in vss. 5 and 6, but *lebabkā* in vss. 8 and 9), and in the verbs (predominantly plural throughout vs. 6, but singular thereafter). But repetition with variation is characteristic of Hebrew narrative.

8. *They argued back and forth*. Heb. *htmhmhw*. See NOTE on 3:26.

and drank. With LXX, where the verb was lost through haplography due to homoioarkton.

9. *busy yourselves*. For this sense of *škm* in the hiphil (elative) and without prepositional modifier, see 7:1 and NOTE.

tent. At last the Levite's circumstances become clear. When he leaves this lavish setting it will be to return to a tent, not a house.

10–30. The remainder of the chapter is concerned to make the point that Israel in this period could no longer accommodate her intraterritorial travelers. "Sojourners," especially in Benjamin, must stick together.

10–15a. These verses are a unit set off by repeated emphasis on the need for a place to "spend the night" (vss. 10, 11, 15).

10. *Jebus*. A pre-Israelite name of Jerusalem, as in 1:21.

and his servant. With LXX, lost in MT by a haplography. The servant plays a pivotal role.

11. *far spent*. Heb. *rad*, lit. "has gone down," may be recognized as a biform of *yrd*, as in Ps 23:6 which has *wšbty* for *wyšbty*. See Dahood's analysis, *Psalms I, 1–50* (AB, vol. 16), p. 148.

12. *a foreigner's city*. MT continues "who are not of the Israelites," which may be best understood as the remnant of a variant which specified "a city of foreigners."

14. *the sun went down*. But they were safe. Safe in Benjamin will be presented as a contradiction in terms, for this period, as the story proceeds.

15b–21. These verses make the point that there is really nothing wrong with the law of hospitality. From the initial reversal of fortune in 15b, the story steadily moves uphill; the Levite will meet with the same hospitality he received from his father-in-law in Bethlehem.

16. *man . . . from the Ephraimite hill country*. Another sojourner from Ephraim. It is clear that the writer of the story was not a Benjaminite. He not only wishes to make it clear to his audience what the ethnic situation was, but also anticipates what follows by emphasizing that the territory involved was Benjaminite.

18. *to my own house*. With LXX. MT has a reference to "the house of Yahweh," presumably the Shiloh tabernacle, which must represent a scribal misunderstanding of *byty*, "my house," as an abbreviation of *byt yhwh*. Moore, pp. 415–16.

19. *your servant*. The man has just referred to his concubine separately. MT reads plural, "your servants," but preponderant textual evidence is for the singular (many Heb. manuscripts, Vulg., Syr., Targ.). The plural of MT may be singular in meaning, just as we have the plural form of *ba'al* and *'ādōn* when

these are used in legal texts, in both cases referring to the singular "master."
Freedman, private communication.

That he is going home to a "tent" (vs. 9) is here suppressed, as he puts his
best foot forward, indicating how he has plenty of provender for his donkeys,
and food and wine for his entire party. All he needs is a roof.

20-21. It worked. And he let the old man do the foddering, after which they
feasted.

22. *more and more convivial.* Lit. "they made their hearts feel good," plying
themselves with food and drink: a warm, comfortable feeling. The expression
is a clear verbal echo of 16:25, where the Philistine crowd demands that
Samson (who never wanted to be judge) entertain them. The Levite in contrast will set himself up as judge at the end of this chapter.

the local hell-raisers. Lit. "the townsmen, sons of Belial," (*'anšē*) *b*e*nē*
*b*e*līya'al.* Here *'anšē* must be either a variant for *b*e*nē* or a scribal lapse
anticipating *'*a*našīm b*e*nē b*e*līya'al* in 20:13, contaminated by another *'anšē*
two words earlier.

"Belial" was one of the most maleficent characters of the mythic under-
world; Ps 18:4-5 (Same as II Sam 22:5-6), where RSV renders "perdition."

we would get to know. The verb *yd'*, "to know," has a wide range of meaning and is used euphemistically to denote sexual intercourse. However, it is
never unambiguously used of homosexual coitus. The idiom "to lie with" is
far more common for all varieties of sexual intercourse. Here, *yd'* is
deliberately ambiguous. With the offer of the young women (vs. 24), the
ambiguity disappears. As in Gen 19, the initial and determinative offense is a
violation of the law of hospitality.

23-24. Do not mistreat my guest. Take our women instead. This is Israel?
The question will be answered by the last chapter of the book.

24. *them.* The apparent grammatical anomaly involving masculine plural
suffixes, with the two girls as antecedent, may be resolved by treating the final
mem in all three occurrences of the plural suffix here as dual. Freedman,
private communication. For the same phenomenon of the dual with feminine
antecedents mispointed as masculine plural suffix, see the story of Ruth (esp.
1:13-22), which has many points of relationship with this concluding material
in Judges.

25. *the man seized his concubine.* Which man did this is not clear. It is
probably the Levite, whose story is being told. Other protagonists—the father-
in-law, the master of the house—are regularly identified by some such title.

28. *for she was dead.* With LXX, lost through haplography due to homoioteleuton in MT: *'nh [ky mth].*

29. *house.* The word is apparently used sarcastically; vs. 9 has described his
house as in fact a tent.

systematically dismembered . . . twelve pieces. Lit. "he cut her up according to her bones in twelve pieces." All very businesslike. Cf. I Sam 11:7
(Saul) and I Kings 11:30-39 (Ahijah of Shiloh). Evidence for the pre-Israelite
and non-Israelite use of a twelve-piece sacrifice for ritual healing attests to the
highly folkloristic character of this narrative according to Gaster, MLC, pp.
443-44, 538. The use of the story here, however, is rhetorical. It counter-

balances treatment of the Lord of Bezeq in ch. 1. This time the aim is to mobilize the confederacy, not to demoralize the opposition. There it was one man against Israel. Here it is all Israel on behalf of one man. In itself the Levite's story involves a calculated inversion of elements in the story of Lot, of whom the locals complained: "This fellow came to sojourn, and he would play the judge" (Gen 19:9, RSV). However exaggerated the story may be in detail, it is firmly rooted in historical events as the following chapter will show.

30. This verse follows LXX where MT, omitting entirely any words of instruction to the messengers, concludes abruptly with a declaration, perhaps originally the answer to the question put in LXX: "And all who saw it said, 'Such a thing as this has never happened—never been witnessed—from the time the Israelites came up from the land of Egypt till this day. Apply yourselves to it! Take counsel and speak!'" In MT these imperatives can only be construed as the Israelites' address to one another. Since LXX and MT cannot be harmonized, the original was probably longer than either variant.

Similar practices for the raising of an emergency muster are known from Mari, where Bahdi-Lim suggested to Zimri-Lim that a prisoner be slain and his head paraded throughout the Hanean territory in order to stimulate enthusiasm for sending in the requested quota of troops. *Archives royales de Mari*, II, 48.

COMMENT

It is impossible to do justice to this story without looking ahead to the last two chapters of the book, for the finale (chs. 20–21) represents the confederacy as utterly leaderless. The Israelites will overreact to one case of injustice in such a way as to compound the tragedy a thousand times over, and permit the situation to develop into a full-scale civil war. The reason is given in the opening sentence of this chapter: Israel has been too busy ordering its affairs to have more than random regard for Yahweh. Therefore, in the warfare that develops (ch. 20) for the purpose of avenging the alleged victim (ch. 19), nearly everything done is strictly proper. Indeed, ch. 20 contains one of the few examples of military efficiency in the book. However, the conduct of the war follows too closely the outdated institutions. Even the ḥerem is revived; had it not been for the shrewd thinking of the elders and the administrative grace of Yahweh, it would have utterly destroyed the Benjaminites. The final scenes (ch. 21) are lively vignettes showing all Israel hard at work trying to avoid the consequences of having relied on archaic institutions. The book concludes with the thought that, in this war of brother against brother, the true victor was Yahweh. And everyone goes home.

The civil war had taken a tragic toll. But by the time the story became part of the Book of Judges, the war was far in the past. The story is presented in the genre of the tragicomic. The writer has it carefully crafted.

The evidence of his skill is there to be seen in the compounded dramatic ironies. It is the hospitable and courteous urgings of the Levite's father-in-law which cause the delay in departure that prevents the party from reaching the safety of Ephraim by nightfall. The servant's advice to stop for the night in Jebus (a city outside the Israelite alliance) would if followed have averted the calamity. The disgraceful lack of hospitality by the Benjaminites is repaired through the offer of possibly the one man in town the sanctity of whose hearth and board is not protected by fear of reprisal through blood-kinship and political ties within the city.

(S. D. Currie, "Biblical Studies for a Seminar on Sexuality and the Human Community," *Austin Seminary Bulletin* 87 [1971], 14.)

The story of the Gibeah outrage and the civil war against Benjamin is a rich mine of data on Israel's premonarchical organization, and the most explicit in the book. Noth treated the events in these chapters as accurately reflecting a military expedition of the twelve-tribe organization against one of its members, in the clearest narrative depiction we have of Israel in the pre-Davidic era. But he failed to grasp the tragicomic vein of the narrative (*The History of Israel,* pp. 104–6). The fact that only Judah and Benjamin figure prominently indicates that the account was neither pragmatic nor Deuteronomic in origin. Rather, it was probably appended during the Babylonian exile, when Judah and Benjamin had been, until recently, all that remained of the old federation. The reconciliation of Benjamin and the other Israelites was used by the exilic redactor to conclude Judges because it balances the introduction (ch. 1). The introduction had been tacked on by this exilic redactor specifically to show Israelites living together and with foreigners as stemming from Judah's success in capturing the western hill of Jerusalem (1:8), whereas Benjamin had failed to oust the Jebusites from the old city on the eastern hill (1:21). The redactor in lively narrative form thus reminds discouraged exiles that Israelites had throughout their entire history lived among other nations. He was then able to plead for a united Israel according to the Mosaic ideal, while showing how the loosely organized tribal confederation had become antiquated and been replaced by the monarchy. In his day, he believed, God had dismantled even the monarchy. It was therefore as true as it had ever been that Israelites were men who did what was right as they saw it.

The high affirmation of Yahweh's universal sovereignty in these chapters has regularly been obscured by the low morality that pervades the events. Scholars have been simultaneously convinced of the story's antiquity in its essentials (*J*) and repulsed by the finished product, with "all the marks of the extreme decadence of Hebrew literature, and is a product of the 4th century B.C. . . ." (Moore, p. xxxi.). Moore was quite unprepared to deal with features which, at point after point, he labelled "absurd," but which contribute materially to the structural integrity of this version of the Benjaminite War. It is difficult to find any basis any more for that chronological conclusion, and there is none for the value judgment. The value judgment is rooted in the older literary analysis which regularly denied to the ancient writers anything resembling a Mosaic conscience. For example, Wellhausen regarded the finale to the Book of Judges as a late imitation of the story of Lot (Gen 19) and arbitrarily dismissed it as having no positive value (Julius Wellhausen, *Prolegomena to the History of Ancient Israel,* tr. W. Robertson Smith [New York:

Meridian, 1957], pp. 235–37). A glance at Gen 19:9 will suffice to indicate why a literary relationship exists. There the citizens of Sodom accuse Lot the newcomer of setting himself up as judge when he tries to protect his guests. In Judg 20–21 this theme is completely reversed. The amphictyonic office is demeaned by the performance of the Levite who sets himself up as judge and rallies the whole league to avenge his personal loss (cf. ch. 8, Gideon's revenge). Once the machinery for massive retaliation has been set in motion, there will be no more mention of the Levite. As self-styled judge he has done his work, and it will be up to Yahweh to maneuver the tribes into a costly but reliable peaceful settlement.

This story of civil war and its sequel, which the final editor placed as conclusion to the Book of Judges, balances the introduction in ch. 1 with which there are many rhetorical connections. Like much of ch. 1 this story actually stems from events that occurred early in the period of the judges. The account correlates with the evidence from excavations at Gibeah (W. F. Albright, "A New Campaign of Excavation at Gibeah of Saul," *BASOR* 52 [December 1933], 6–12; Paul W. Lapp, "Tell el-Fûl," *BA* 28 [1965], esp. 2–5). The first occupation of Gibeah was apparently not much more than a village. It was destroyed by fire early in the twelfth century and abandoned or only lightly occupied throughout the period of Philistine pressure, until Saul rebuilt Gibeah as his rustic headquarters (c. 1020).

The fact that in the finished story Gibeah has become a sizable town is in keeping with the nation-state dimensions of the later monarchy, which (in the exilic editor's experience) had disappeared altogether. That is what had nearly happened at the outset, with the Gibeah outrage.

XXXVIII. All Israel
(20:1–48)

The Great Assembly

20 ¹ Then all the Israelites came forth. The assembly gathered around Yahweh at Mizpah—from Dan to Beersheba including the land of Gilead—as one man! ² The leaders of all the people (all the Israelite tribes) stationed themselves in the assembly of God's people, four hundred contingents of sword-bearing foot soldiers!

³ The Benjaminites heard that the Israelites had gone up to Mizpah.

The Israelites said, "Speak out. How did this vile thing happen?" ⁴ And the Levite, husband of the murdered woman, answered, "My concubine and I came to Gibeah, which belongs to Benjamin, to spend the night. ⁵ And the nobility of Gibeah rose against me; they surrounded the house all night because of me. It was I they intended to kill, but my concubine they so ravished that she died. ⁶ So I took hold of my concubine, cut her in pieces, and sent her throughout all the territory of Israel's inheritance, for they have committed a deliberate and senseless disgrace in Israel. ⁷ Therefore, all you Israelites, give your word and counsel, right here!"

Attempt at Extradition

⁸ Then all the people arose as one man to say, "We will none of us go home; we will not one of us turn back to his own house. ⁹ This is what we will do now to Gibeah: we will go up against it by lot. ¹⁰ We will take ten of every hundred men of all the Israelite tribes (and a hundred of every thousand, and a thousand of every ten thousand) to carry provisions to the force, to those setting forth to render to Gibeah of Benjamin exact retribution for the senseless disgrace which they committed in Israel." ¹¹ All the men of Israel were assembled at the city, uniting as one man.

12 The Israelite tribes sent couriers throughout the tribe of Benjamin, saying, "What is this evil that has occurred among you? 13 Surrender the men at once, the hell-raisers who are in Gibeah. We will put them to death and burn the evil out of Israel."

But the Benjaminites would not heed the voice of their brothers the Israelites. 14 Rather the Benjaminites were rallied out of all the cities to Gibeah, to go to war against the Israelites. 15 On that day the Benjaminites mustered out of their cities twenty-six sword-bearing contingents. Without including any citizens of Gibeah, they mustered seven hundred elite soldiers. 16 From all this people were seven hundred elite soldiers, each restricted in his right hand; and each one could sling a stone at the hair without missing! 17 Now the men of Israel, not including Benjamin, mustered four hundred sword-bearing contingents, all of them warriors.

The Lots

18 They arose and went to the sanctuary to inquire of God; the Israelites said, "Who of us shall go first to the battle with the Benjaminites?"

And Yahweh said, "Judah will go first."

Initial Failures

19 The Israelites got up the next morning and encamped against Gibeah. 20 The men of Israel marched forth to the battle with Benjamin. The men of Israel aligned for battle with them at Gibeah. 21 When the Benjaminites marched forth from Gibeah, on that day they ruined twenty-two Israelite contingents on the ground.

22 But the force (the men of Israel) recovered and resumed the battle alignment at the place where they had lined up the first day. 23 That is, the Israelites went to the sanctuary and wept before Yahweh until evening. And they inquired of Yahweh, "Shall we again approach for battle with the Benjaminites our brothers?" And Yahweh said, "Attack them!"

24 The Israelites advanced toward the Benjaminites on the second day. 25 And when Benjamin marched forth from Gibeah to encounter them on the second day, they ruined on the ground eighteen more Israelite contingents; all these were swordsmen.

Success

26 Then all the Israelites (the whole force) went up and arrived at Bethel, to weep and sit there before Yahweh. They fasted that day

until evening and presented burnt offerings and peace offerings before Yahweh.

27 And the Israelites inquired of Yahweh (there is where the Ark of God's Covenant was at that time. 28 And Phinehas ben Eleazer ben Aaron was stationed before it at that time), saying: "Shall we again resume the march to battle with the Benjaminites our brothers? Or shall we quit?" And Yahweh said: "Attack! For tomorrow I will surrender them to your power."

Victory at Last

29 So Israel stationed men in ambush all around Gibeah. 30 When the Israelites advanced to the Benjaminites on the third day, they aligned themselves against Gibeah as on the previous occasions. 31 And when the Benjaminites marched forth to encounter the force, they were drawn away from the city. They began to strike down some of the troops, as on previous occasions, on the main roads, one of which goes up to Bethel, and one to Gibeah, about thirty men of Israel.

32 The Benjaminites boasted, "They are put to rout before us, as at first!"

But the Israelites said, "Let's retreat and draw them away from the city to the main roads." 33 So every Israelite rose from his position; and they deployed at Baal-tamar, while the Israelite ambush erupted from its position west of Gibeah.

34 Ten choice contingents from all over Israel arrived before Gibeah. The fighting was fierce. They did not realize that disaster was overtaking them; 35 Yahweh put the Benjaminites to rout before Israel! And the Israelites felled that day twenty-five contingents (one hundred men) of Benjamin; all these were swordsmen. 36 So the Benjaminites saw that they were defeated.

The men of Israel had given ground to Benjamin, because they relied on the ambush that they had laid for Gibeah.

Correction

37 The ambush scrambled to make a dash to Gibeah. The ambush spread out and put the entire city to the sword.

38 The Israelites' strategy with the main ambush was for them to send up the smoke signal from the city, 39 whereupon the men of Israel would turn in battle. Benjamin began by striking down about

thirty men of Israel. Indeed they boasted, "They are utterly and completely routed before us, as in the first battle!"

40 Then the signal began to go up from the city—a column of smoke. When the Benjaminites looked behind them, there it was, the whole city going up in smoke!

41 When the men of Israel turned back, the men of Benjamin panicked, for they saw that disaster had overtaken them. 42 So they turned in face of the Israelites toward the wilderness route. But the battle moved with them. . . .

43 (They surrounded the Benjaminites. They pursued them vigorously from Nohah and completely subjugated them, as far as a position opposite Geba to the east.)

Survivors

44 Eighteen Benjaminite contingents fell, all of them prosperous men.

45 They turned to flee to the wilderness, to the Rimmon Rock; they picked off five contingents of them on the main roads. They chased after them until they were cut off; they struck down two contingents of them.

46 The total of Benjaminites who fell that day was twenty-five sword-bearing contingents, all of them prosperous men.

47 But six hundred men turned and fled to the wilderness to the Rimmon Rock. They stayed at the Rimmon Rock for four months.

48 So the men of Israel returned to the Benjaminites and put them to the sword—from each city, men and beasts and all that were found. And all the cities that were implicated they destroyed by fire.

NOTES

20:1–17. These verses provide a calculated contrast to the conclusion of Joshua (ch. 24) with its account of the great ceremony at Shechem, which had established the definitive form of the federation. On this occasion, however, another such assembly is stampeded (cf. 18:8–10), as it rises in wrathful indignation persuaded by one man telling half of the truth.

1. *all the Israelites.* Elsewhere within the Book of Judges, this expression occurs only in the Deuteronomic indictment (2:1–5). In 8:27, where Gideon has likewise used the federal militia in pursuit of private vengeance, "all Israel" prostituted themselves. These expressions occur nowhere else in the book.

2. *leaders.* Heb. *pinnōt,* "corners"; elsewhere only in I Sam 14:38 and Isa 19:13 (Syr. and Targ.). The figure may have a technical sense.

all the Israelite tribes. Probably a variant. LXX^A and Vulg. have a prefixed conjunction, an early resolution of the ambiguity.

5–7. He presents his case in the best possible light: It was either me or my concubine!

5. *the nobility.* Lit. "the lords," also used sarcastically in 9:2.

6. *deliberate and senseless.* Some early Greek manuscripts read merely "a senseless disgrace," often followed by commentators who argue that *zimmā* is a late word. See Moore, p. 425. But its insertion cannot be explained, whereas a simple haplography explains the gap: *'św (zmh w)nblh*.

9. *we will go up against it.* With LXX, where the verb was lost by haplography in MT.

10. The translation follows LXX^A, Syr.^h, which alone preserve an intact reading. MT may be understood as the result of merging variants and subsequent haplography:

"to those ⎱
          ⎰ setting forth . . ."
* "for their ⎱

LXX^A *lab-bā'īm la-'ᵃsōt   lᵉ-gib'a[t]*
*   *lᵉbō'ām la-'ᵃsōt lᵉ-gib'a[t]*
MT (. . . .)   *la-'ᵃsōt lᵉbō'ām (. . .) lᵉ-gib'a[t]*

Thus a pair of haplographies account for the unintelligible combination in MT (where even in the received text, six of seven words in sequence begin with *lamedh!*). We emend *gb'* to read "Gibeah," as usually suggested. The translation follows early Greek and Syriac manuscripts, reading *'āśū (they committed)* for MT's singular. Boling, VT 16 (1966), 294–95.

What seems to be described is a ten percent levy of eligible troops on this occasion, with the expectation that one tenth of those involved will be needed for the quartermasters corps. On one Mari expedition involving twelve thousand troops, at least one thousand were assigned the task of transporting grain. *Archives royales de Mari,* VI, 27:16, noted by Glock in "Warfare in Mari and Early Israel," p. 100. Here however the total of the army activated was much smaller.

11. *uniting.* With LXX^A, reading the participle *hōbᵉrīm* in place of the noun *hᵃbērīm,* "companions." LXX^A also has them assembling "from the cities," but this is probably contamination from vs. 14.

as one man. The phrase forms an inclusio with the first clause of vs. 8. Here at last is all Israel gathering to act as a unified body, brought together by an outrageous covenant violation.

12. *tribe.* The Heb. *šbṭy,* mispointed as plural in MT, probably preserves an archaic genitive case ending, as pointed out to me by Freedman. The versions correctly read the noun as singular.

15. *twenty-six . . . contingents . . . seven hundred.* The Masoretes seem to have thought the figures to be separate and unrelated, the seven hundred as referring to the levy from Gibeah alone. More likely the total "seven hundred" resumes and summarizes the figure "twenty-six contingents" at the outset. In vs. 35 the same device is used to report the Benjaminite casualties, and the figures are simply connected by the explicative conjunction: "twenty-five contingents (one hundred men)."

For some unexplained reason, Gibeah was not included in the counting behind vs. 15. The number of units varies in the versions ("twenty-five" in LXX^A and "twenty-three" in LXX^B).

For the approach taken here, I am indebted to Freedman (private communication), who follows up the pioneering work of G. E. Mendenhall on the "census lists" of Num 1 and 26; the lists are better described as sets of quotas for the tribal levies. Mendenhall, JBL 77 (1958), 52–66. At one time Benjamin was accountable for 35 units totaling 400 men, which the Masoretes misunderstood as calling for 35,400 men (Num 1:36–37). At another time Benjamin was responsible for 45 units totaling 600 men, treated by the Masoretes as 45,600 men (Num 26:38–41). These figures show that the expectation for a normal levy was in the neighborhood of ten men per unit. Together with the lists from which they are drawn, they also reflect the fluctuating fortunes and relative strength of the tribes at different times.

The totals in our account reflect an especially serious situation. In contrast to the twelve-tribe total of 598 contingents in Num 1 (596 in Num 26), the tribes apart from Benjamin could muster only some 400 contingents in the civil war, according to vs. 17. While a normal levy called for about ten per cent of all able-bodied men (see vs. 10), the Benjaminites on this occasion fielded some 27 men per unit, reflecting perhaps a thirty percent levy. This is entirely plausible in view of the opposition. The decline in numbers of units between the lists in Numbers and the story in Judges are proportional: 596–598 in Numbers and 400 in Judges for the rest of Israel; 35–45 in Numbers and 26 in Judges for Benjamin. It is roughly a drop of thirty percent in both cases, thus confirming the general approach taken here, as in the story of Gideon's three hundred in 7:1–8.

16. In this verse the narrator is apparently concerned to counter the tremendous odds against Benjamin: twenty-six contingents versus four hundred contingents (vs. 17). He seems to be suggesting that the reason they will be able to hold out for so long and, in fact, administer two resounding setbacks to the army of the confederation (vss. 19–25), is that the seven hundred were all supermarksmen. The famous Benjaminite, Ehud, was similarly "restricted in his right hand" (3:15). Cf. also the reference to ambidextrous Benjaminites, kinsmen of Saul, among David's heroes (I Chron 12:2).

without missing. Lit. "without sinning."

18. *the sanctuary.* Heb. *bēt-'ēl*, indistinguishable, out of context, from the place-name "Bethel" (vs. 26); cf. John Gray, *Joshua, Judges and Ruth* (London: Nelson, 1967), p. 241. The wordplay involved in these verses is often obscured by source-critical analysis which would have a compiler abruptly shift the scene of mobilization from Mizpah to Bethel without narrative preparation or redactional comment. The "sanctuary" involved in both vss. 18 and 23 is the lesser local one at Mizpah (west of Gibeah, exact location uncertain; do not confuse with Mizpah in Gilead: 11:11, 29). Only after being twice "spanked" by little Benjamin, does the Israelite militia seek its orders at Bethel.

to inquire of God. Not "Yahweh" (consistently used for narrative description in Judges, as in the response here). They were now in for a fight, and the light camaraderie was past; someone would have to go first.

Who of us shall go first. As in 1:1, neglecting to ask the prior question: "Shall we go, or not?"

Judah will go first. With LXX, where the verb dropped out of MT by haplography, *yhwdh* [*y'lh*]. This response balances the very beginning of the book. We have come full circle. Israel is going to have to make a new beginning. See ch. 21.

21. *ruined . . . on the ground.* The same idiom describes Onan's action in Gen 38:9 and means "to make ineffective." The idiom does not suggest total loss of the twenty-two companies, but enough dead and disabled in twenty-two companies to demoralize the remainder and force their retreat. What proportion of the total force had been committed to the initial engagement is not indicated.

22. *the men of Israel.* Probably a variant.

place. Heb. *māqōm* in its sanctuary sense, as in the etiology of The Weepers (2:5). That is, not convinced by one trouncing, the militia resumes alignment and waits oracular marching orders. Cf. the introductory theme of "learning by fighting" (3:1-4).

23. *the sanctuary.* With the versions, another case of homoioteleuton in Hebrew; *ysr'l* [*byt-'l*]. See vs. 18 and NOTE.

25. *eighteen more Israelite contingents.* With the results of the first battle (vs. 21), this makes a total of forty units or ten percent of the whole force (vs. 17). Even if they lost only an average of two men per company, that would amount to eighty men. A ten percent casualty rate for the whole force would be catastrophic. The figures here are entirely plausible. Yet the account is schematized; like Gideon's army against Midian (7:1-22), the Israelite army against Benjamin was weeded down to a decimated force so that victory could be attributed only to Yahweh.

26. *the whole force.* Probably a variant.

at Bethel. (Map 2, C-4.) That we should now read the place-name seems clear from the comment in vs. 28, which identifies it as the current resting place of the Ark and thus distinguishes its higher oracular value from that of the Mizpah sanctuary (where the Ark was absent).

fasted . . . peace offerings. It was not a matter of "rallying round the Ark." They "fasted" and sued for "peace" with Yahweh (like Gideon in 6:24), having learned from two defeats that the Lord of the Covenant had, in effect, declared them to be in rebellion against his rule.

28. *Phinehas ben Eleazar ben Aaron.* The name Phinehas is Egyptian and means "the Negro." The genealogy may mean only that this Phinehas, son of Eleazar, was of the Aaronite line of priests. He has been plausibly identified as Phinehas II, predecessor of Eli. See Myers, *The Interpreter's Bible,* II, 819 (following Albright). However, with so many other indicators of an early base to the narrative, and stylistic connections with ch. 1, it is more likely that the genealogy is to be taken at face value, explaining the authority of the Bethel sanctuary on this occasion. The story has been placed at the end of the

book, and the material of ch. 1 at the beginning, to serve a particular theological purpose. See Introduction, pp. 34–38.

tomorrow I will surrender them. Israel, having sued for peace, was promptly reconstituted; it was time to settle the score with Benjamin.

29–43. The account of the victory survives in two versions (vss. 29–36 and 37–43), both of which share more than a superficial resemblance to the capture of Ai (Josh 8), which is also presented as Yahweh's victory (not Israel's nor Joshua's), and where the ambush was Yahweh's strategy (Josh 8:2).

31. *and one to Gibeah.* MT continues *bsdh,* possibly the remnant of a variant which located the preliminary skirmishes "in the open country" instead of "on the main roads."

about thirty men. This figure of actual casualties on one occasion is extremely important for perspective on the levies described in vss. 8–17.

33. *Baal-tamar.* The site, somewhere near Gibeah, is unidentified and otherwise unknown.

west of Gibeah. With LXX, Syr., Vulg., reading *mim-ma'ªrab lag-gib'ā,* corrupted in MT as *mim-ma'ªrē gāba',* "from the open plain of Geba."

35. *Yahweh.* He played no explicit part in Benjamin's earlier victories.

put the Benjaminites to rout. Turning the boast of vs. 32 inside out, in an inclusio, using exactly the same wording.

twenty-five contingents (one hundred men). For this interpretation of the total figure of 25,100 see the NOTE on vs. 15 which describes the twenty-six Benjaminite contingents. Here the indication is that "twenty-five" of those contingents were engaged, leaving only one unit in reserve and that from these units "one hundred men" were lost. If the total of the force were seven hundred, a loss of fourteen percent would be extremely costly, especially if a reserve unit of perhaps fifty men saw no action at all. It was enough to break the back of the resistance.

37. *spread out.* For the military sense of *mšk,* see 4:6 and NOTE.

38. *the main ambush.* Repointing MT's enigmatic *hereb* and transposing the *athnah* to read the adjective *hā-rāb,* "most numerous." ALUOS[D], 20.

42. *the battle moved with them. . . .* MT continues with an obscure statement that seems to say: "and those who were from the cities were killing them in their midst." Something more is apparently missing.

43. *surrounded.* Heb. *kttw.* LXX read either *kttw* "crushed," or *krtw* "cut down," one of which may be a genuine variant.

pursued them vigorously . . . and completely subjugated them. The hiphil forms *hrdyphw* and *hdrykhw* are to be taken as the internal hiphil, with intensive meaning. Freedman, private communication.

from Nohah. With LXX[B], rejecting MT *m^enūḥā* "resting-place," which is syntactically isolated. Otherwise the name occurs only as the fourth "son" of Benjamin (I Chron 8:2), not mentioned, however, in the list of Gen 46:21, another striking piece of evidence that the genealogical linkage actually represents fluctuating clan and tribal affiliations.

Geba. The translator adopts this emendation, as often suggested, where MT "Gibeah" cannot be correct as the passage stands.

44–45. These verses give the breakdown on the general statistics of vs. 35—eighteen plus five plus two—anticipating the total of twenty-five in vs. 46.

45. *Rimmon Rock.* The name of the rocky refuge is either "Pomegranate Ridge" or "Roaring Rock." Modern Rammun is some four miles east of Bethel, on a limestone outcrop, protected by wadis on three sides and pocked with caves. Gold, IDB IV, 99–100. See Map 2, C-4.

picked off. Lit. "made a gleaning."

46. *prosperous men.* A redactional inclusio with 18:2.

47. *six hundred.* The bulk of the force fled and went into hiding. With an original force of seven hundred, and one hundred casualties, this puts the whole military picture in focus.

four months. Hiding out in caves, as happened repeatedly, yields from later periods a whole series of spectacular archaeological discoveries in the more desolate fringes of the hill country, ranging from the Samaria papyri of the fourth century B.C.E. to the Qumran finds of a bit later and the famous Bar Kochba letters of the early second century C.E.

48. *from each city, men.* Heb. *m'yr mtm.* Critics often strike the word for "city." Yet our passage clearly involves an implementation of the ḥerem, as is proved by the phrase *'yr mtm* in Deut 2:34 and 3:6 (cf. Job 24:12). The reading "men" (*mᵉtīm*) follows a great many manuscripts, where MT has been mispointed to read *mᵉtōm* "soundness."

found . . . implicated. A play on Heb. *nimṣā'*, which actually means "be caught (in the act)," as demonstrated by Iwry, *Textus* 5 (1966), pp. 34–43.

COMMENT

This account of the initial setbacks and final victory is often traced to a conflation of sources. It makes excellent sense in sequence to ch. 19, however: the Israelites proceed on their own initiative after asking the wrong question (vs. 18) at the wrong place (cf. 1:1–2:5). That is, this Deuteronomistic (exilic) redactor agreed with the earlier Deuteronomic Historian that Bethel was the wrong place *at the beginning* of the judges period (2:1–5). He insisted, however, that Bethel was the right place on this later occasion; and either he or an annotator explained why: on this later occasion the Ark of the Covenant was at Bethel, in the course of its regular visit to local sanctuaries, we may assume.

It appears that matters had dragged on, and had taken such a costly toll, because an ad hoc assembly had usurped Yahweh's prerogative to declare war. It is surely significant that only at Bethel, before the last battle, did they perform peace offerings, and admit defeat. But that was the beginning of the victory (as in Deut 2; see Introduction, pp. 36–37). There can scarcely be any doubt that initiation of the action against Benjamin had been irregular. The result, it appears, was a state of unprecedented chaos in the career of the twelve-tribe league.

And yet, it was clear to our redactor in exile that there was still time for God's Israel to be reunited in peace.

XXXIX. THE SHILOH FESTIVAL
(21:1–25)

The Silence of God

21 ¹ The men of Israel had taken an oath at Mizpah, "No man among us will give his daughter in marriage to Benjamin."

² When the people arrived at Bethel and sat there before God until evening, they cried aloud and wept with great lamentation. ³ They said, "Why, O Yahweh, God of Israel, has this come about in Israel, so that one tribe has today been counted out of Israel?"

⁴ And so, the next day the people busied themselves and built there an altar and presented burnt offerings and peace offerings. ⁵ The Israelites said, "Who is there of all the Israelite tribal Assembly that did not participate in the rally to Yahweh?" For the Big Oath was in effect for anyone who had not gone up to Yahweh at Mizpah: "He must be put to death."

A Military Solution?

⁶ The Israelites felt sorry for Benjamin their brothers. They said, "Today one tribe is cut off from Israel. ⁷ What shall we do for wives for those who are left? We have sworn by Yahweh not to give them any of our daughters for wives."

⁸ They said, "Which is the one among the tribes of Israel that did not go up to Yahweh at Mizpah?" And, indeed, no one had come to the camp from Jabesh-gilead, to the Assembly. ⁹ When the people were mustered, not a single one of the inhabitants of Jabesh-gilead was present!

¹⁰ So the community sent twelve contingents of their best men there and commanded them, "Go, put the inhabitants of Jabesh-gilead to the sword, including the women and youngsters. ¹¹ This is the thing you are to do: every male and every woman who has had in-

tercourse with a male you shall exterminate, but the virgins you shall keep alive." And they did so.

12 They found among the inhabitants of Jabesh-gilead four hundred young virgins who had not had intercourse with any male. And they brought them to the camp at Shiloh, which is in the land of Canaan.

Peace at Last

13 Then the whole community sent word; they spoke to the Benjaminites who were at Rimmon Rock and declared peace with them. 14 Benjamin returned then, and they gave them the women whom they had spared at Jabesh-gilead. But they had not found enough for them.

15 The people felt sorry for Benjamin, because Yahweh had made a breach in the Israelite tribes.

The Final Solution

16 The community's elders said, "What will we do for wives for the remainder, since women have been obliterated in Benjamin?" 17 They said, "How shall an inheritance remain for the Benjaminite survivors and a tribe not be wiped out from Israel? 18 We cannot give them as wives some of our own daughters." Indeed, the Israelites had taken the oath: "Cursed be he who gives a wife to Benjamin!"

19 Then they said, "Well, there is the annual festival of Yahweh at Shiloh, which is north of Bethel, east of the main road that goes up from Bethel to Shechem, and south of Lebonah."

20 So they instructed the Benjaminites, saying, "Go and lie in wait in the vineyards. 21 Watch and when the daughters of Shiloh come out to dance the dances, dash out from the vineyards and each one of you seize a wife from the daughters of Shiloh; then proceed to the land of Benjamin. 22 And when their fathers or brothers come to indict us, we will say to them: 'We did them a gracious deed. For we did not take each man's wife in battle; neither did you give in to them. Now, however, you will incur guilt!' "

23 The Benjaminites did just so; they took enough wives for their number from the dancers whom they seized by force. Then they set out to return to their own plots. They rebuilt the cities and settled down in them.

24 From there the Israelites went their separate ways at that time,

each man to his tribe and clan. They went forth from there, each to his own plot.

25 In those days there was no king in Israel; every man did what was right, as he saw it!

NOTES

21:1–5. These verses pose the problem in a preformed narrative unit (as indicated by the inclusio formed of vss. 1 and 5) ending with characteristic narrative suspense.

1. The prohibition of marriage with Benjaminites, previously unmentioned, would have been understood originally as a matter of league security, not restrictive piety. Cf. the statement of Solomon's problem in I Kings 11:1–10, and esp. Num 31. The latter tradition clearly lies in the background of this story, providing a precedent for an expedition to secure virgins.

2. *they cried aloud and wept.* As in 2:4, at the beginning of the era, only more so, "with great lamentation."

3. *Yahweh, God of Israel.* The descriptive "Yahweh" and the subjective "God" are climactically juxtaposed. The assembly is represented as really wanting to know why Benjamin was cut off. Yet they remained utterly frustrated; there came no oracular response, for Yahweh would not answer. They would have to rely on their own wits.

counted out. The root is Heb. *pqd*, which has to do with the counting of quotas for military service, as in vs. 9. The scene refers directly to the warfare in ch. 20, in which that narrator's preoccupation with numbers confirms overall comparison with Gideon's muster in 7:1–8.

4. *busied themselves.* For this sense of *škm* in the hiphil and without prepositional complement (as in 19:9), see 7:1 and NOTE. There is an inversion of narrative elements at this point. In 7:1 Gideon gets ready for battle after he has constructed a new altar for *Yahweh-šlm.* Here the Israelites are constructing a new "altar" and offering *šlm,* "sacrifices," after a terribly costly civil war.

5. Thrown back upon their own devices, the Israelites concluded that they would have to conduct one more small civil war so as to replenish the supply of wives for Benjamin.

of all the Israelite tribal Assembly. The question is awkward, lit. "of all the Assembly, from all the Israelite tribes"; perhaps contamination from the expressions in vs. 8.

the Big Oath. Heb. *haš-šᵉbū'ā hag-gᵉdōlā,* no doubt a reference to the imposition of the ḥerem at the end of ch. 20. Except for the end of Gideon's story (8:24–27), the ḥerem is clearly reflected in this book only in the framework. See NOTE on 1:17.

6–12. These verses restate the problem and report a proposed solution and its implementation.

cut off. Heb. *gd'*, used only here in the book except for Jerubbaal's nickname, "Gideon," another sign of narrative relationship with chs. 6–8.

8. *Jabesh-gilead.* (Map 2, D-3.) The narrative elicits sympathy for this city, later so friendly and faithful to Saul, and here alone the only segment of Israel not guilty of overreacting.

11. All the males and deflowered women are put under the ban. At the conclusion to the story of the civil war there is clear indication of the tragic use of that institution against the Benjaminites (20:48), for whom the Israelites now exercise compassion by issuing this condemnatory decree against a city that had failed to respond with its quota of troops. The terms of the original decree were regarded as providing a proper rationale for this new venture (vs. 5).

but the virgins . . . And they did so. These words are restored from LXX[B], after a sizable haplography in Heb. *thrymw* [*w't hbtwlwt thyw wy'św kn*] *wymṣ'w. . . .*

12. *Shiloh.* Apparently selected for the transfer of virgins because of its respectable distance from Mizpah and Bethel, where the warfare had been precipitated, as well as for its amphictyonic legitimacy. See Map 2, C-3.

which is in the land of Canaan. This specification regarding the great amphictyonic sanctuary sounds entirely unnecessary at the end of the era. However, it balances the frequent mention of Canaan and Canaanites in the introductory material (17 occurrences in 1:1–3:6). Elsewhere in the book Canaan is mentioned only in the Deborah-Baraq material, where the opposition is specifically "kings of Canaan" (5:19). The location of "Shiloh" by placing it "in the land of Canaan" might have been very helpful in the confusion of the earliest period, and it is another indicator that the material at the end of the book stems from the beginning of the era. By allowing the notice about the location to stand intact, the late redactor signals the irony of the situation. Conditions in the land, after all was said and done, had not changed very much. The redactor will quickly append a story about the collective devastation of Shiloh families (vss. 16–23a); but it will be legitimated by hard theological thinking, not by institutional precedent. If in ch. 1 Israel is tending to fall apart, here Israel is being reassembled.

13–15. The Benjaminites in hiding were finally enticed from their caves by the community's formal declaration of peace. There were, however, not enough women to go around, which was taken to mean that Yahweh had made a breach in the Israelite tribes. But that problem was not regarded as insurmountable.

16–23. One story concerned with the ancient revival of Benjamin was selected as a fitting conclusion to the book, in a period when "Judah" (see the emphasis in 1:1 and 20:18) and "Benjamin" stood for all that had recently remained of ancient Israel, that is, the late seventh or early sixth century.

16. *The community's elders.* Ultimate responsibility is here lodged with the decision makers.

17. *How . . . remain.* With LXX manuscripts, reading *'yk tš'r*, where MT has a sentence fragment, omitting the beginning of the question, perhaps from a mutilated copy.

19. The elders are represented as thinking aloud in this verse as they recall the fact of the important yearly celebration at Shiloh (I Sam 1:3), and struggle to fix its location precisely. The impression given is that it had been a long time since any of them had done what Elkanah as a good Yahwist did every year (I Sam 1:3). Cf. Exod 34:23, which posits three such feasts annually, but where the motivation is given that "I will cast out nations . . . and enlarge your borders."

21. *daughters of Shiloh*. For the plural masculine predicate before a plural feminine subject, see *Gesenius' Hebrew Grammar*, ed., E. F. Kautzsch, 2d English rev. by A. E. Cowley. From 28th German rev. ed., Leipzig, 1909. Oxford University Press, 1910. Section 145, pp. 462 ff.

22. *their fathers or brothers*. The pronouns are masculine, and probably originated in misunderstood dual forms, as in 19:24 (see NOTE).

22. *to indict us*. Heb. *lā-rīb;* the same element is variously nuanced in Gideon's baal-name (6:31–32, see NOTE) and in Jephthah's negotiations with the Ammonite king (11:25–28). Now the point is made, at the conclusion of the period, that what is needed is a clear theological solution to the problem.

We did them a gracious deed. With Burney (p. 493), repointing to read a perfect (*hannōnū*) in place of an imperative (*hannūnū*), which makes no sense after the fact and is not explicated by the statement which follows. Rather the thing has been so cleverly engineered that Benjaminite families can be put in a bad light by making their protest.

23. The rationalization was sufficient to settle matters, and on that note the book concludes. The Benjaminite fighters for Yahweh, an original constituent element of Israel, return to "their own plots," and are faced with "cities" that now needed to be "rebuilt."

24. As at the conclusion of the Abimelech and Micah stories, "Israelites" are those who learn from the outcome and go home (9:55, 18:26).

25. The final editor's summary is drawn from the earlier editions, where its elements are integral to the narrative depiction of Israel as having repudiated Yahweh's kingship in the premonarchic period (17:6; 18:1; 19:1), yet being periodically rescued thanks to God's gracious administration. Now that the institution of earthly kingship (like the nations) had come and gone, the late redactor's last words on the period are a reminder that in the early days, "every man did what was right, as he saw it" (cf. 14:1, 3; 17:6). Here, however, the statement has a positive thrust after the ingenious solution of problems in the final scenes. Added to the book in a period perhaps as late as the Babylonian exile, it meant that the time had arrived once again for every man to do what was right before Yahweh without any sacral political apparatus to get in the way.

COMMENT

Another rubric that suggests itself for this concluding chapter would be, "History: The School of the Dance!"

The incidents that unfold here poke fun at the institutional linkage of piety, which for many folk was shattered by the national disaster of 587 B.C.E.—

the destruction of Jerusalem and the dispersion of the nation's ruling classes, among whom the exilic redactor lived and worked.

Stories stemming from two distinct historical events have been conveniently brought together. One event was a punitive expedition against Jabesh-gilead for failing to join in the suppression of Benjamin. The other "event" was a most obscure abduction of desirable maidens during one of the annual amphictyonic festivals at Shiloh.

The word "event" is used advisedly. Tradition has it that Romulus resorted to a similar strategy to supply his ruffian subjects with wives. And the Messenians in Greek legend are reputed to have abducted maidens from Laconia during a festival of Artemis. The theme of the rape of maidens in comparable circumstances recurs in Greek poetry. "It is possible, however, that our Biblical story is, au fond, an etiological legend told originally to account for an ancient practice of mass-mating at seasonal festivals." (MLC, p. 445.) If so, we can only conclude that at Shiloh the venerable covenant sanctuary had reverted to older Canaanite patterns of celebration. But even the evil that men do, the reactor seems to be saying, could be providentially exploited on that occasion, thanks to the quick-witted reasoning of Israel's elders. As told in this context the stories serve the theme of Yahweh's rule beyond precedents, rule exercised so that the Benjaminites could be reconciled with their brothers, while the redactor's contemporaries could go on living hopefully and energetically, though far from the ruined Jerusalem temple.

Here the ancient elements of Israel's military organization and diplomatic stance toward surrounding nations are applied internally to the worship and work of Israel as "assembly" (Heb. *qāhāl*) or religious "community" (Heb. *'ēdā*). Note the calculated inversion of developments in the preceding chapter. There the sequence was: a show of legality first (20:12–13), followed by full-scale military action. Here the sequence is: fight first (vss. 8–12) and think later (vss. 16–22). There is a traditionary precedent for nearly everything that transpires in the chapter. The height of this comedy of correctness is reached where at last an ironclad rationale is devised for the premeditated abduction of the Shiloh virgins: "We did them a gracious deed!"

Thus concluded the last retrospective to be attached to the old Book of Judges. There remained only to pinpoint the purpose of the Yahwist constitution, uniquely suitable for folk in each new age to come together and to go alone as Yahweh's people. The book therefore ends with a quotation from an older source: "In those days there was no king in Israel; every man did what was right, as he saw it." According to Deuteronomy, Moses had presented such a pattern of decision making as entirely appropriate prior to Joshua's invasion (Deut 12:8). To the Deuteronomic redactor of Judges it had been most inappropriate on at least one occasion following the Yahwist takeover and had meant that in Micah's day Yahweh was not really being acknowledged as Israel's King (17:6). Quoted by the final (Deuteronomistic) redactor, where the preconquest conditions once again prevailed, it affirmed that there is no earthly king deserving of the kind of loyalty that Yahweh elicits still. Are those not two ways of saying the same thing?

APPENDICES

APPENDIX A

Evidence of the Kaige recension in Judges, LXX[A] and LXX[B].

1. Translation of Heb. $gām$.[1] kai: =, $kaige$: +

A	B	locus	A	B	locus
+	=	1:3		=	8:22a
+	+	1:22	=	=	8:22b
=	=	2:3			8:22c
=	+	2:10a	+	+	8:31
=	+	2:10b		+	9:19
+	+	2:17	=	+	9:49a
=	+	2:21		+	9:49b
+	+	3:22	=		10:9
	+	3:31	+	=	11:17
=	=	5:4a	=	=	17:2
+	=	5:4b	+	+	19:19a
=		6:35	=	=	19:19b
=		7:18	+	=	19:19c
		8:9	=	=	20:48

The distribution of this distinctive conjunction shows a pattern that will be reflected many times over. The influence of the Kaige, especially heavy in B, will be found throughout; but it will be much more prominent in the first half of B and the second half of A.

2. Use of the particle $henika$, ubiquitous in the Kaige recension.[2]

3:18		B
3:27	A	B
11:4		B
11:7	A	B
11:35	A	
15:14	A	
15:17	A	
16:22	A	
18:10		B

[1] Adapted from Barthélemy, *Les devanciers*, p. 35.
[2] For the isolation of the criterion, see Thackeray, *Septuagint*, p. 115.

3. Translation of *'anōkí* by *ego eimi* and verb.[3]

5:3		B
6:18	A	B
11:27	?	B
11:35		B
11:37		B

4. Elimination of *ekastos*, "each," in favor of *aner*, "a man," as uniform equivalent of Heb. *'îš* in the idiomatic sense of "each one."[4]

locus	*ekastos* (Old Greek)	*aner* (Kaige recension)
2:6	A	B
6:29		A, B
7:7		A, B
7:8		A, B
7:21	A	B
7:22		A, B
9:49	A	B
9:55		A, B
10:18		A, B
17:6		A, B
20:8		A, B
21:21		A, B
21:22		A, B
21:24a		A, B
21:24b		A, B
21:25	A*	B

* *aner ekastos*

5. Translation of Heb. *rādap*.[5]

locus	*katadokein* (Old Greek, Old Latin)	*diokein* (Kaige recension)
1:6	A	
3:28		
4:16		A, B
4:22		A, B
7:23	A	B
7:25	A, B	
8:4		B
8:5		A, B
8:12		A, B
9:40	A	B
20:43		B

3 Ibid.
4 Adapted from Barthélemy, *Les devanciers*, pp. 48–54.
5 This criterion is elaborated by Shenkel, *Chronology*, p. 113.

6. Translation of Heb. *liqrāt*.[6]

locus	*eis apantesin* (Old Greek)	*eis sunantesin* (Kaige recension)
4:18	A	B
4:22	A	B
6:35		A, B
7:24		A, B
11:31	A	B
11:34	A	
14:5	A	B
15:14	A	B
19:3	A	B
20:25	A	B
20:31	A	B

7. Translation of Heb. *mê'al*.[7]

locus	*epano* (Old Greek)	*epanothen* (Kaige recension)
1:14	A	
3:21		B
4:15		B
13:20	B	A

8. Translation of Heb. *lô' 'ābā*.[8]

locus	*boulesthai* (Old Greek and Latin)	*(e)thelein* (Kaige recension)
11:17		A (*eudokeo:* B)
19:10		A (*eudokeo:* B)
19:25		A (*eudokeo:* B)
20:13		A (*eudokeo:* B)

9. Translation of Heb. *zābaḥ*.[9]

locus	*thuein* (Old Greek)	*thuziadzein* (Kaige recension)
2:5	A	B
16:23	A, B[1]	B[2]

10. Translation of Heb. *hārā*.[10]

locus	*sullambanein* (Old Greek and Latin)	*en gastri exein/lambanein* (Kaige recension)
13:3	B	A
13:5		A, B
13:7		A, B

[6] For the criterion, see Barthélemy, *Les devanciers*, pp. 78–80.

[7] For the criterion, see Thackeray, *Septuagint*, p. 114; Barthélemy. *Les devanciers*, pp. 54–55.

[8] For the criterion, see Shenkel, *Chronology*, p. 116.

[9] Ibid., pp. 17–18.

[10] Ibid., p. 116.

11. Translation of Heb. *šōpar* by *keratine* in all occurrences: 3:27; 6:34; 7:8, 16, 18 (*bis*), 19, 20, 22, in both A and B. Old Greek regularly uses *salpigx*.[11]

12. A number of criteria based on translation equivalents are impressive in the cumulative evidence they give for the presence of Kaige influence in both A and B:

a. the translation of Heb. *ḥāraš* by Greek *kopheuein* in 16:2 and 18:19[12]

b. the translation of Heb. *śar* (*haṣ-*)*ṣābā'* by Greek (*tes*) *dunameos* in 4:2, 7[13]

c. the translation of Heb. *māhar* by Greek *taxunein* in 13:10[14]

Note, however, the translation of Heb. *ḥāsā* by Greek *siopan*[15] in the A text of 18:9, where B goes its own way (Greek *esuxadzo;* nowhere else used for *ḥāsā*).

13. Shenkel has shown that the Old Greek maintained a distinction in rendering Heb. *bᵉ-'ēnē,* "before," using the more literal *en ophthalmois* for a genitive other than deity,[16] as in all cases in Judges (14:3, 17:6, 19:24), except 8:7 in A, 14:1 in A, and 21:25 in B, which have *enopion*.

On the other hand, the same word was regularly rendered less literally when the divine name was the genitive, a distinction which was widely obliterated in the Kaige recension, as Greek *en ophthalmois* was leveled through for Heb. *bᵉ-'ēnē.* It is therefore interesting to note that the "pragmatic framework" in A and B tenaciously preserves the pre-Kaige distinction, with A reading *enantian* in every occurrence (2:11; 3:7, 12; 4:1; 6:1; 10:6; 13:1) but one (10:15), while B consistently reads *enopion*. On Shenkel's distinction, Gideon still thinks that he is speaking to a mere messenger in 6:17. The Kaige's obliteration of this distinction shows up nowhere in Judges except in 10:15; B reads *en ophthalmois*, A reads *enopion*.

With *bᵉ-'ēnē* rendered *en ophthalmois* in the Kaige recension, *enopion* became the standard Kaige equivalent for *lipnē,* whereas a variety of prepositional forms had stood in the Old Greek. The distribution of this characteristic[17] is as follows: *enopion* appears as the standard Kaige equivalent for *lipnē* in both A and B in twelve locations—4:15; 6:18; 8:28; 11:9, 11; 13:15; 16:25; 20:23, 28, 32, 42; 21:2. In A it appears again in 4:23, and in B in 9:39; 20:26, 35, 39. Other equivalents are *kata prosopon* (2:14 in A and B; 20:35 in A), *emprosthen* (3:27; 4:14; 18:21 in A and B, 4:23 in B), *apo prosopou* (9:39 in A), *enanti* (20:26 in A), and *enantion* (20:39 in A).

With *en ophthalmois* almost leveled throughout the Kaige recension as standard equivalent for *bᵉ-'ēnē,* and with *enopion* becoming standard Kaige for *lipnē,* *enanti* and its derivatives came to represent *neged*. Thus 9:27 and 20:34 read *exs enantias* in both A and B.

11 Thackeray, *Septuagint*, p. 114; Barthélemy, *Les devanciers*, pp. 60–63.
12 See Shenkel, *Chronology*, p. 114.
13 Ibid.
14 Ibid., p. 115.
15 Like Kaige. Ibid.
16 Ibid., p. 15.
17 Barthélemy, *Les devanciers*, p. 84.

In the following chart the distribution of the preceding Kaige characteristics in A and B of Judges are tabulated according to major divisions within the book:

	A	B
Introduction 1:1 – 3:6	3	7
Othniel, Ehud, Shamgar 3:7–31	3	6
Deborah 4:1 – 5:31	7	9
Gideon 6:1 – 8:35	18	21
Abimelech 9:1–57	2	8
Jephthah and "minor judges" 10:1 – 12:15	7	10
Samson 13:1 – 16:31	11	8
Micah 17:1 – 18:31	4	3
Gibeah and Shiloh 19:1 – 21:25	16	20
Totals	71	92

It is clear that neither A nor B preserves a consistent Kaige text, although that recension has clearly influenced both and is especially prominent in B. The pattern shifts significantly midway through the book. The influence of Kaige is lighter in B's Abimelech and minimal in A's, but becomes especially strong in A's Samson cycle and persists to the end of the book.

APPENDIX B

This outline of the syllable count in the Song of Deborah is strictly based upon the consonantal Hebrew text, with some corrections of the Masoretic scansion and vocalization as explained in NOTES to Sec. IX. In these counts we have omitted the anaptyctic vowel of the segholate noun and the *pathah furtive*. Unresolved diphthongs, however, are counted as two syllables, which is perhaps to err on the side of caution. Line by line Hebrew syllable count is included with translation.

Part I
vs. 2   10+10=20   To those presenting themselves
vs. 3   5+7=12
            6+6=12 } 36 The singer is in the foreground
            6+6=12
vss. 4–5   9+9=18
         4+7+8=19 } 61   Yahweh's initial victory
        5+8+11=24   in Canaan
vss. 6–7   7+7=14
          10+10=20 } 62 Deborah's achievement
            6+8=14
            6+8=14
vs. 8   8+7=15 } 33 The crisis is in the background
            9+9=18
vs. 9   9+12=21   To those presenting themselves

Part II
vss. 10–11d   9+6+6=21 } 47 The consultation
               6+4=10
               8+8=16
vss. 11e–13   11=11 } 60   Response and results
               7+8=15
             3+6+5=14
             10+10=20   } 107

Part III

vs. 14   11+12=23 } 46 Scorn for the laggards
             11+12=23   frames praises for the
                             participants
vs. 15a–c   11+7+7=25
vss. 15d–16   12=12
             11+8=19 } 43   } 114
                12=12

Part IV

vs. 17 $9+9=18$ ⎫
                          $8+7=15$ ⎬ 33   Scorn for the laggards   ⎫
vs. 18 $4+6=10$ ⎫   ⎪
                          $4+6=10$ ⎬ 20   Praise for the participants ⎪
vss. 19–20 $8+9=17$ ⎫   ⎬ 108
                          $9+7=16$ ⎬ 55   In the battle   ⎪
                         $11+11=22$ ⎭   ⎭

Part V

vss. 21–22 $6+7+6=19$ ⎫ 37   The victory
                          $9+9=18$ ⎭

Part VI

vs. 23 $10+8=18$ ⎫ 36   The cursing of Meroz
                          $9+9=18$ ⎭

Part VII

vs. 24 $8+5+8=21$ ⎫   Jael and the   ⎫
vs. 25 $4+5= 9$ ⎬ 40   death of Sisera   ⎪
                          $5+5=10$ ⎭   ⎬ 108
vs. 26 $8+9=17$ ⎫   ⎪
                        $7+5+11=23$ ⎬ 40   ⎪
vs. 27 $10+8+10=28$ ⎭

Part VIII

vs. 28 $12+9=21$ ⎫
                          $4+4= 8$ ⎬ 40   The mother's question   ⎫
                          $5+6=11$ ⎭   ⎪
vss.   29–30 $10+9=19$ ⎫   ⎪
                          $5+6=11$ ⎪   ⎬ 106
                          $7+3=10$ ⎬ 66   The wrong answer   ⎪
                          $8+7=15$ ⎪   ⎭
                          $5+6=11$ ⎭

Part IX

vs. 31 $4+7=11$ ⎫ 23   Concluding archaic couplet
                          $4+8=12$ ⎭

It is surely not accidental that parts IV and VII each have exactly 108 syllables, or that parts II and VIII miss that total by one and two syllables respectively. Regarding parts II and VIII, note the proportions between "consultation" (47 syllables) and "mother's question" (40 syllables), compared with the "response and results" (60 syllables) and the "wrong answer" (66 syllables), for a one syllable difference in totals! Note also the juxtaposition of the 37 syllable "victory" and the 36 syllable "cursing of Meroz."

INDICES

INDEX OF PLACE AND PERSONAL
NAMES IN THE TEXT

It is difficult, if not impossible, always to distinguish between personal names and place names, especially the names of the Israelite tribes. These, and all gentilic formations, are listed below as personal names.

Standard equivalents are presented here in parentheses, as throughout this volume in philological remarks, to indicate simply the consonantal text. See Transcription Equivalents.

PLACE NAMES

Abel-keramim (*'bl-krmym*) 11:33

Abel-meholah (*'bl-mhwlh*) 7:22

Abiezer (*'by'zr*) 8:2. See also Abiezrite(s) in *Personal and Other Names*

Acco (*'kw*) 1:31

Achzib (*'kzyb*) 1:31

Ahlab (*'hlb*) 1:31

Aijalon (*'ylwn*) 1:35; 12:12

Amaleq (*'mlq*) 5:14; 6:3; 7:12; 10:12. See also Amaleqite(s) in *Personal and Other Names*

Aphiq (*'pyq*) 1:31

Arad (*'rd*) 1:16

Aram (*'rm*) 10:6; 18:7 (LXX *et al.*), 28 (LXX *et al.*)

Armon-harim (Biblia Hebraica, *'rmnhrym*) 3:8, 10

Arnon (*'rnwn*) 11:13, 18 (*bis*), 22, 26

Aroer (*'r'wr*) 11:26, 33

Arumah (*'rwmh*) 9:41

Ashdod (*'šdwd*) 1:18 (LXX)

Ashqelon (*'šqlwn*) 1:18; 14:19

Baal-tamar (*b'l-tmr*) 20:33

Ban-town. See Hormah

Beer (*b'r*) 9:21

Beersheba (*b'r-šb'*) 20:1

Beth-anath (*byt-'nt*) 1:33 (*bis*)

Beth-barah (*byt-brh*) 7:24 (*bis*)

Bethel (*byt-'l*) 1:22, 23; 4:5; 20:26, 31; 21:2, 19 (*bis*)

Bethlehem (*byt lhm*) 12:8, 10; 17:7, 8, 9; 19:1, 2, 18 (*bis*)

Beth-micah (*byt-mykh*) 17:8, 12; 18:2, 3, 13, 15, 18, 22 (*bis*). See also Micah in *Personal and Other Names*

Beth-millo (*byt-ml'w*) 9:6, 20 (*bis*)

Beth-rehob (*byt-rhwb*) 18:28

Beth-shean (*byt-š'n*) 1:27

Beth-shemesh (*byt-šmš*) 1:33 (*bis*)

Beth-shittah (*byt-hšth*) 7:22

Bezeq (*bzq*) 1:4, 5 (*bis*), 6, 7

Bochim (*bkym*) 2:1, 5

Canaan (*kn'n*) 4:2, 23, 24 (*bis*); 5:19; 21:12. See also Canaanite(s) in *Personal and Other Names*

The Circle. See Gilgal

Dan's Camp (*mhnh dn*) 18:12

Deborah's Palm (*tmr dbwrh*) 4:5.

The Weepers. See Bochim

Zaanannim (*ṣ'nym*) 4:11
Zaphon (*ṣpwn*) 12:1

Zephath (*ṣpt*) 1:17
Zererah (*zrrth*) 7:22
Zorah (*ṣr'h*) 13:2, 25; 16:31; 18:2,
8, 11

PERSONAL AND OTHER NAMES

Aaron (*'hrn*) 20:28
Abdon (*'bdwn*) 12:13, 15
Abiezrite(s) (*'by-h'zry*) 6:11, 24,
34; 8:32. See also Abiezer in
Place Names
Abimelech (*'bymlk*) 8:31; 9:1, 3,
4, 6, 16, 18, 19, 20 (*bis*), 21, 22,
23a, 24, 23b, 25, 27, 28, 29
(*bis*), 31, 34, 35, 38, 39, 40, 41,
42, 44, 45, 47, 48 (*bis*), 49, 50,
52, 53, 55, 56; 10:1
Abinoam (*'byn'm*) 4:6, 12; 5:1, 12
Achsah (*'ksh*) 1:12, 13
Ahiman (*'ḥmn*) 1:10
Amaleqite(s) (*'mlq, 'mlqy*) 1:16;
3:13; 6:33; 12:15. See also
Amaleq in *Place Names*
Ammonite(s) (*bny-'mwn*) 3:13;
10:6, 7, 9, 11, 17, 18; 11:4, 5,
6, 8, 9, 12, 13, 14, 15, 27, 28, 29,
30, 31, 32, 33, 36; 12:1, 2, 3
Amorite(s) (*'mry*) 1:34, 35
("Westerners"), 36; 3:5; 6:10
("Westerners"); 10:8, 11; 11:19,
21, 22, 23
Anaq (*'nq*) 1:20
Anathite (*bn 'nt*) 3:31; 5:6. See
also Beth-anath in *Place Names*
Asher (*'šr*) 1:31; 5:17; 6:35; 7:23.
See also Asherite(s)
Asherah(s) (*'šrh, -wt*) 3:7; 6:25,
26, 28, 30
Asherite(s) (*'šry*) 1:32. See also
Asher
Astarte (*'štrwt*) 2:13; 10:6

Baal (*b'l*) 2:11, 13; 3:7; 6:25, 28,
30, 31, 32; 8:33 (*bis*); 9:4; 10:6,
10
Balaq (*blq*) 11:25
Baraq (*brq*) 4:6, 8, 9, 10, 12, 14,
15, 16, 22; 5:1, 12, 15
Bene-qedem (*bny-qdm*) 6:3, 33;
7:12, 8:10
Benjamin (*bnymyn*) 5:14; 10:9;
19:14; 20:4, 10, 12, 17, 20, 25,
35, 36, 39, 41; 21:1, 6, 14, 15,
16, 18, 21. See also Benjamin-
ite(s)
Benjaminite(s) (*bn-[h]ymyny, bny-
bnymn*) 1:21 (*bis*); 3:15; 19:16;
20:3, 13, 14, 15, 18, 21, 23, 24,
28, 30, 31, 32, 35, 36, 40, 43, 44,
46, 48; 21:13, 17, 20, 23. See
also Benjamin

Caleb (*klb*) 1:12, 13, 14, 15, 20;
3:9
Canaanite(s) (*kn'ny*) 1:1, 3, 4, 5,
9, 10, 17, 27, 29 (*bis*), 30, 32,
33; 3:1, 3, 5. See also Canaan in
Place Names
Chemosh (*kmwš*) 11:24
Cushan-rishathaim (*kwšn-rš'tym*)
3:8 (*bis*), 10 (*bis*)

Dagon (*dgwn*) 16:23
Dan (*dn*) 5:17; 18:29; 20:1. See
also Danite(s), and Dan's Camp
in *Place Names*
Danite(s) (*dny, bny-dn*) 1:34; 13:

2, 25; 18:1, 2, 11, 22, 23, 25, 26,
30 (*bis*). See also Dan
Deborah (*dbwrh*) 4:4, 9, 10, 14;
5:1, 7, 12, 15. See also Deborah's
Palm in *Place Names*
Delilah (*dlylh*) 16:4, 6, 10, 12, 13
(*bis*), 18
Dodo (*dwdw*) 10:1

Easterners. See Bene-qedem
Ebed ('*bd*) 9:26, 28, 30, 31, 35
Eglon ('*glwn*) 3:12, 14, 15, 17
(*bis*), 20
Ehud ('*hwd*) 3:15, 16, 20 (*bis*),
21, 23, 26, 30; 4:1
Ehyeh ('*hyh*) 6:16
Eleazer ('*l'zr*) 20:28
Elon ('[*y*]*lwn*) 12:11, 12
Ephraim ('*prym*) 1:29; 5:14; 8:2;
10:9; 12:4 (four times), 5, 15;
17:8; 19:1, 18. See also Ephra-
imite(s)
Ephraimite(s) (*bn-'prym, bny-*
'*prym*) 2:9; 4:5; 7:24 (*bis*); 8:1;
10:1; 12:1, 5 (*bis*), 6; 17:1; 18:
2, 13; 19:16. See also Ephraim

Gaal (*g'l*) 9:26, 28, 30, 31, 35, 36
(*bis*), 39, 41
Gazite ('*zty*) 16:2
Gera (*gr'*) 3:15
Gershom (*gršm*) 18:30
Gideon (*gd'wn*) 6:11, 13, 19, 21,
22, 24, 27, 29, 34, 36, 39; 7:1,
2, 4, 5, 7, 13, 14, 15a, 18, 19,
20, 24, 25; 8:4, 7, 11, 13, 21, 22,
23, 24, 27 (*bis*), 28, 30, 32, 33,
35. See also Jerubbaal
Gileadite (*gl'dy*) 10:3; 11:1, 40;
12:7. See also Gilead
God ('*lhym*) 2:12; 3:7, 20; 4:6,
23; 5:3, 5; 6:8, 10, 20, 26, 36,
39, 40; 7:14; 8:34; 9:23a, 46,

56, 57; 10:10; 11:21, 23, 24; 13:
5, 6 (*bis*) 7, 8, 9 (*bis*), 22; 15:
19; 16:17; 18:5, 10, 24, 31;
20:2, 18, 27; 21:2, 3. See also
Yahweh

Hamor (*ḥmwr*) 9:28
Heber (*ḥbr*) 4:11, 17 (*bis*), 21;
5:24
Hillel (*hll*) 12:13, 15
Hittite(s) (*ḥty, ḥtym*) 1:26; 3:5
Hivite(s) (*ḥwy, ḥwym*) 3:3, 5
Hobab (*ḥbb*) 1:16 (LXX); 4:11

Ibzan ('*bṣn*) 12:8, 10
Ishmaelites (*yšm'lym*) 8:24
Israel, Israelite (*ysr'l*) 1:28; 2:7,
10, 14, 20, 22; 3:1, 4, 8, 10, 12,
13, 31; 4:4, 6; 5:2, 5, 7 (*bis*), 8,
9, 11; 6:2, 3, 6, 8, 14, 15, 36, 37;
7:2; 8:27, 35; 9:22; 10:1, 2, 3,
7, 9, 16; 11:4, 5, 13, 15, 16, 17
(*bis*), 19 (*bis*), 20 (*bis*), 21
(three times), 23 (*bis*), 25, 26,
40; 12:7, 8, 11 (*bis*), 13, 14;
13:5; 14:4; 15:20; 16:31; 17:6;
18:1 (*bis*), 19, 29; 19:1, 29; 20:
2, 6 (*bis*), 10, 12, 13, 21, 29, 31,
33, 34, 35; 21:3, 5, 6, 8, 15, 17,
25
Israelite(s) (*bny/'yš ysr'l*) 1:1; 2:
4, 6, 11; 3:2, 5, 7, 8, 9 (*bis*), 12,
14, 15 (*bis*), 27; 4:1, 3 (*bis*), 5,
23, 24; 6:1, 2, 6, 7, 8; 7:8, 14,
23; 8:22, 28, 33, 34; 9:55; 10:6,
8 (*bis*), 10, 11, 15, 17; 11:27,
33; 13:1; 19:30; 20:1, 3 (*bis*),
7, 11, 14, 17, 18, 19, 20 (*bis*),
21, 22, 23, 24, 25, 26, 27, 30, 32,
33, 35, 36, 38, 39 (*bis*), 41, 42;
21:1, 5, 6, 18, 24
Issachar (*yśśkr*) 5:15 (*bis*); 10:1

INDEX OF SUBJECTS

See also the Index of Place and Personal Names in the Text.

INDEX OF BIBLICAL REFERENCES

KEY TO THE TEXT

Chapter	Verse	Section
1	1–36	I
2	1–5	I
2	6–10	II
2	11–23	III
3	1–6	IV
3	7–11	V
3	12–30	VI
3	31	VII
4	1–24	VIII
5	1–31	IX
6	1–2	X
6	3–10	XI
6	11–32	XII
6	33–35	XIII
6	36–40	XIV
7	1–22	XV
7	23–25	XVI
8	1–3	XVI
8	4–21	XVII
8	22–29	XVIII
8	30–32	XIX
8	33–35	XX
9	1–57	XX
10	1–5	XXI
10	6–16	XXII
10	17–18	XXIII
11	1–11	XXIV
11	12–28	XXV
11	29–40	XXVI
12	1–7	XXVII
12	8–15	XXVIII
13	1–20	XXIX
13	21–25	XXX
14	1–20	XXXI
15	1–8	XXXII
15	9–20	XXXIII
16	1–31	XXXIV
17	1–13	XXXV
18	1	XXXV